Patchwork Pandemic

STUDIES IN GOVERNMENT AND PUBLIC POLICY

Patchwork Pandemic

State Politics and the Fractured US Response to HIV/AIDS

Stephen Colbrook

University Press of Kansas

Published by the University Press of Kansas (Lawrence, Kansas 66045), which was organized by the Kansas Board of Regents and is operated and funded by Emporia State University, Fort Hays State University, Kansas State University, Pittsburg State University, the University of Kansas, and Wichita State University.

Library of Congress Cataloging-in-Publication Data

Names: Colbrook, Stephen, author
Title: Patchwork pandemic : American governance, state politics, and the fractured US response to HIV/AIDS / Stephen Colbrook.
Description: Lawrence: University Press of Kansas, 2026 | Series: Studies in government and public policy | Includes bibliographical references and index.
Identifiers: LCCN 2025031918 (print) | LCCN 2025031919 (ebook) ISBN 9780700641086 (cloth) ISBN 9780700641093 (paperback) ISBN 9780700641109 (ebook)
Subjects: LCSH: AIDS (Disease)—Political aspects—United States | HIV infections—Political aspects—United States | AIDS (Disease)—Political aspects—California | HIV infections—Political aspects—California | AIDS (Disease)—Political aspects—Illinois | HIV infections—Political aspects—Illinois | AIDS (Disease)—Political aspects—Texas | HIV infections—Political aspects—Texas | Medical policy—United States | BISAC: POLITICAL SCIENCE / Public Policy / Health Care | POLITICAL SCIENCE / Public Policy / Social Policy
Classification: LCC RA643.83 .C65 2026 (print) | LCC RA643.83 (ebook)
LC record available at https://lccn.loc.gov/2025031918.
LC ebook record available at https://lccn.loc.gov/2025031919.
British Library Cataloguing-in-Publication Data is available.
EU Authorised Representative Details: Easy Access System Europe
Mustamäe tee 50, 10621 Tallinn, Estonia | gpsr.requests@easproject.com

Cover art: Map: Wikimedia Commons
Virus: RAW DSIGN/Shutterstock.com

This book will be made open access within three years of publication thanks to Path to Open, a program developed in partnership between JSTOR, the American Council of Learned Societies (ACLS), University of Michigan Press, and the University of North Carolina Press to bring about equitable access and impact for the entire scholarly community, including authors, researchers, libraries, and university presses around the world. Learn more at https://about.jstor.org/path-to-open/.

For Cherish Watton-Colbrook

CONTENTS

ACKNOWLEDGMENTS

I have accumulated innumerable debts in the many years I spent researching and writing this book. During that period, I was blessed to have Jonathan Bell as my primary academic mentor and PhD supervisor, who provided unwavering support and encouragement, even amid a global pandemic. His insights about the history of sexuality, the American healthcare system, and the historian's craft were indispensable as I wrote and revised this book. Nick Witham, my secondary PhD supervisor, generously read over many chapter drafts with a close eye, always challenging me to improve the quality of my prose. I also benefitted enormously from the financial support of the Wolfson Foundation, which provided me with an unusually generous stipend that allowed me to conduct extensive research in the United States.

Many friends, colleagues, and scholars helped to shape this book by providing guidance on sources, offering feedback on chapter drafts and otherwise supporting my work. With heartfelt appreciation, I particularly thank Lizzie Evens, Emily Hull, Gareth Davies, Scott De Orio, Margot Canaday, Beatrix Hoffman, Gillian Frank, Katie Batza, Timothy Stewart-Winter, Joshua Hollands, Aaron Hiltner, Lauren Gutterman, Noah Riseman, Brooke Blower, Pamela Hagg, Nic Ramos, and Julilly Kohler-Hausmann. My two PhD examiners—Bruce Schulman and Iwan Morgan—generously provided very close readings of the entire text that improved it substantially. I also wish to acknowledge the years of support and guidance from Gary Gerstle, who introduced me to the joys of studying American history during my first year as an undergraduate.

A number of participants in the events described in this book kindly took the time to conduct oral interviews with me. For their insights into the "human" side of policy development, I wish to thank Michael Bosio, Larry Bush, Timothy Drake, Marty Keller, Donald Maison, Rand Martin, Glen Maxey, Stephen Morin, Frank Ricchiazzi, David Roberti, Kenneth Topper, and Tom Sheridan.

My parents, Richard and Katherine Colbrook, have opened many doors for me throughout my life. I cannot thank them enough for their steadfast support and unconditional love and for encouraging my academic development at every turn. My heartfelt thanks also go to my siblings, Matthew and Susanna, for their support and friendship over the years.

Cherish Watton-Colbrook, my wife, deserves the biggest thanks of all. I could not have finished this book without her ceaseless encouragement. She has read every word and full stop in this book in countless forms, improving the final product immeasurably with her suggestions. Her brilliance, love, and dedication have been a constant source of inspiration. Every aspect of my life is richer and more joyful for having you in it. This book is for you.

INTRODUCTION

When a new strain of influenza circled the globe in the fall and winter of 1918, it swept through the United States at terrifying speed, infecting at least twenty-five million Americans—roughly one-quarter of the population—over the next two years. Based on any metric, the pandemic was the country's largest mass-mortality episode of the twentieth century, killing approximately 675,000 Americans and surpassing the death toll of World War I.[1] Even as the virus struck the United States with unprecedented ferocity, however, the federal government left most public health decisions to the states, producing a disjointed and hyper-localized approach to a crisis that was national and global in scope. In the absence of a strong federal role, state governments carved out their own policy paths, adopting widely divergent strategies to stem the spread of the disease. This preventive playing field was wildly uneven. Some states were well-equipped with robust public health infrastructures; others lacked the tools to manage the disease's rampant spread.[2]

More than sixty years later, in the early 1980s, state governments were at the vanguard of the public health response to another rampant pandemic—HIV/AIDS. The disease triggered a wave of legislation from California to Utah: by 1988, the states had enacted over two hundred HIV-specific bills.[3] State and local bureaucracies bore the brunt of the work during the epidemic's early years, as federal health agencies reeled under a series of budget cuts enacted by the Ronald Reagan administration. Rebuffed at the national level, AIDS activists and policy elites turned to state legislatures to address a host of concerns stemming from the pandemic, including the high cost of drug therapies, the rampant discrimination experienced by those suspected of infection, and the housing and healthcare needs of people living with HIV.

Nearly four decades after the emergence of HIV/AIDS in the early 1980s, the novel coronavirus once again exposed the extreme fragmentation of public health authority in the United States. As the disease quickly escaped containment efforts, governors and other state leaders provided conflicting messages about social distancing, mask-wearing, vaccines, and a myriad of other issues. States like California and Washington acted swiftly to contain the spread of the virus while others, with equal determination, resolved to keep their economies open and not impose far-reaching public health restrictions. Meanwhile, the central government abdicated any responsibility for coordinating the prevention efforts of places afflicted by the disease, leaving the states to fend for themselves.[4]

Together, these three outbreaks bring into view a specific pattern of governance that has long shaped the history of American pandemics. In each case, the decentralized and fractured structure of the US public health system allowed states and cities to pursue their own set of preventative strategies independently of a centralized plan. Regional variation—both between and within states—became a hallmark of efforts to contain the spread of each new disease, exposing the dangerous lack of coordination between different tiers of the US government. Such disparities fueled vast geographic inequities in morbidity and mortality rates. This chaotic and disordered approach to epidemic disease was a byproduct of the messy distribution of governing authority within the US federal system. From the dawn of the American Republic through to the early twenty-first century, the right to regulate public health and hygiene rested primarily with the states and their municipalities. Far outpacing the central state in terms of spending and legislative activity on infectious disease control, subnational health authorities spearheaded attempts to stop the spread of contagion. Even after the federal government reduced the power of the states in a wide array of policy spheres during the middle decades of the twentieth century, the primacy of state and municipal governments in the arena of public health remained intact.

Spanning the period from the 1918 influenza pandemic through to the present day, this book argues that federalism has consistently shaped epidemic control efforts in the United States. Its central premise is that although each new pathogen occurs in a specific historical context, the same enduring features of American governance have defined epidemic control efforts throughout the last one hundred years. It begins with an overview of the intersections between US state development and pandemic preparedness in the twentieth century before zeroing in on a detailed case study of the AIDS epidemic. The emergence of a new infectious pathogen in the 1980s may have come as a surprise to the medical establishment, but it revealed striking continuities in the history of American public health, not least the enduring primacy of state and local governments in driving epidemic control efforts. Through the lens of the AIDS crisis, I show that one of the core functions of modern governance—public health—remained under the purview of the states well into the late twentieth century, qualifying any historical narrative that stresses a trend toward centralized, bureaucratized federal power. The history told in these pages is both a broad chronicle of the shifting relationship between American federalism and public health and a specific story about how these shifts shaped the US response to AIDS.

Tracing the state-level response to HIV/AIDS in the 1980s offers an ideal case study for examining the broader history of American federalism and pandemics. The crisis was one of the first major global outbreaks to unfold after the dramatic expansion of federal power during the middle decades of the twentieth century. It thus illuminates the remarkable resilience and staying power of the states in the arena of public health, providing evidence of the enduring importance of state-level governance. When the Influenza pandemic of 1918 erupted, there was nothing particularly distinctive about the states' leading role during the outbreak, which aligned closely with broader patterns of American governance at the time. In 1918, state and local governments retained almost exclusive jurisdiction over several crucial areas of governance: criminal justice, welfare, education—to name just a few. The federal government's authority was subordinate to that of states in many policy domains, not just public health.[5]

In the period between the 1918 influenza outbreak and the AIDS crisis, the central state was transformed, growing into an institution of extraordinary power and reach. The New Deal, the Cold War, and the Great Society dramatically extended the federal government's administrative apparatus and its fiscal and regulatory scope. Among the most visible manifestations of this newly assertive central state were a formidable military-industrial complex, an expanded executive branch, a vast array of new agencies and other administrative entities, a new system of mass taxation, and the rise of more interventionist economic and social policies.[6] The federal government also took dramatic steps to curtail the autonomy of the states in areas of governance such as civil rights, marriage, electoral districting, criminal justice, and education. Between the start of the influenza pandemic in 1918 and the emergence of HIV/AIDS in the early 1980s, the national government decisively supplanted the states as the premier site of power in the US federal system.[7]

With authority now centered squarely in Washington, DC, in a wide array of policy arenas, most of the responsibility for protecting the public from infectious diseases continued to fall on the states. Federalism remained a crucial factor in shaping the nation's approach to epidemic diseases, as exemplified by the early years of the HIV/AIDS crisis. State governments possessed a wide range of latent public health powers that ensured most of the critical early battles over AIDS policymaking occurred below the national level. Governors and legislatures exerted substantial control over decisions regarding coercive interventions like quarantine orders, mandatory testing, and public gathering bans, chiefly because such techniques remained under the legal purview of the states. Seen through the lens of federalism, the AIDS epidemic provides a rich case study in the vital but often underappreciated role of state-level governance in the late twentieth century. Despite the comprehensive shift in power from subnational authorities to the central government during the New Deal and Great Society eras, public health stood out as one of the few policy spheres where the states retained almost as much control at the end of the twentieth century as they had at the start.[8] In contrast to the 1918 influenza pandemic, then, the sprawling response to the AIDS crisis stands at odds with conventional narratives about twentieth-century US state development, which emphasize the growth of centralized federal power in the decades following the New Deal.

By asking why state governments played a leading role in responding to pandemics during the twentieth century, how this governing arrangement shaped the AIDS crisis, and what the history of federalism can tell us about public health governance more broadly, this book casts new light on the disjointed and multilayered nature of the US polity. Before laying out the structure of this study in more detail, a fuller discussion of the history of the AIDS epidemic and its myriad effects on the gay rights movement is necessary.

The AIDS Epidemic and the States

This book provides the first sustained study of state politics and policy in the early years of the AIDS epidemic. It lies at the crossroads where policy history and the history of sexuality converge, and it builds on several key themes in modern US historiography, particularly histories of the state, health, queer activism, and intergovernmental relations. More specifically, it argues that no conception of the US government's response to AIDS is complete without "bringing the states back in."[9] If we shift our attention away from the Reagan administration and toward the states, the scale and complexity of the government's interaction with the crisis becomes clear. Including state governments in the larger story of the AIDS epidemic exposes both the strengths and weaknesses of the country's federalist system of public health authority. While some states stepped in to fill the leadership vacuum left by the national government, others refused to do so, producing a fragmented and patchwork response to a complex public health emergency. As late as fiscal year 1989, eight states—Idaho, Iowa, Montana, North Dakota, South Dakota, Vermont, West Virginia, and Wyoming—appropriated zero funding for AIDS programs.[10] Through the 1980s, state action on the epidemic ran the gamut from the proactive approach of California, which centred on patient confidentiality and individual rights, to the coercive response of Texas, which focused on the disease's perceived threat to the heterosexual population. Between these two poles, states as diverse as Florida, Georgia, and New York enacted an array of AIDS-related legislation that ranged from extremely punitive to mildly progressive. There is no neat or easy way to characterize such a wide-ranging policy response to AIDS; rather, it was fragmented, uneven, and diffuse.

Compared with the states, the federal government's response to the AIDS crisis was halting at best in the 1980s. The epidemic unfolded amid a broader political backlash against gay rights, a surge of electoral support for the New Right, and a concerted effort by the GOP to court the Evangelical vote—all of which influenced the Reagan administration's response to the epidemic, which was scandalously slow and lackluster.[11] Meanwhile, budget cuts at the Centers for Disease Control and Prevention (CDC)—the chief federal agency responsible for controlling the spread of infectious illnesses—compromised its capacity to respond to AIDS. The agency only spent $1 million on research into the disease between June 1981 and June 1982, compared to $7 million spent on the more modest threat of Legionnaires' disease during the late 1970s.[12] Congress, meanwhile, did not enact its first AIDS-related law until 1988, seven years after the official start of the epidemic.[13]

Although scholarship on the AIDS crisis has flourished over the last decade, the resulting literature captures only a sliver of the subnational policy response to the crisis and typically overlooks the complex role played by state governments.[14] For the most part, state governments are absent from major works on the history of AIDS, and historians have yet to explain how federalism shaped the contours of early AIDS policymaking.[15] Equating the US government with the *federal* government, many historians have framed the legislative and policy response to AIDS around national political developments, leaving unexamined and unexplained the flurry of HIV-specific laws passed by the states. Much recent scholarship has focused on the various policy divisions within the Reagan administration, the conservative backlash against federal funding for prevention education, and the lack of an effective national approach to the disease. This focus on federal inaction and indifference is not so much incorrect as incomplete. As this book makes clear, the national focus of current scholarship neglects, perhaps even obscures, critical aspects of state politics and policy that shaped the initial response to AIDS. To gauge the extent of the government's response to the epidemic by looking simply at the actions of the federal executive branch and bureaucracy is to overlook where the locus of public health authority remained in the 1980s—the state and local levels.

Though state action on the epidemic was uneven and diffuse, the states enacted hundreds of HIV-specific laws and outpaced the national government on non-Medicaid-related AIDS expenditure for most of the 1980s.[16] As the crisis crystallized in the early 1980s, it presented state legislators with a string of political challenges as they confronted a disease that overwhelmingly affected stigmatized minorities—especially gay men and IV drug users. As one California bureaucrat argued, "There has never been a disease in which issues of morality, sexuality, individual and social responsibility, race, class, health and other philosophical and social issues are so intertwined."[17] On one issue after another, ranging from the politics of antibody testing to the funding of prevention education, the states acted as policy incubators during the epidemic's early years.

Below the national level, the policy response to AIDS often transcended traditional partisan divides and the ebb and flow of electoral politics. To readers versed in popular and scholarly accounts of the epidemic, this statement may come as a surprise. In national politics, the disease became a flashpoint in culture war battles between liberals and conservatives over gay rights, sexuality, and a myriad of other issues.[18] The reactionary politics of the Reagan administration, the rise of the Christian Right, and the rightward shift in electoral politics in the 1980s loom large in conventional narratives of the crisis.[19] As the evidence here shows, however, the policy response to AIDS at the state level often hinged on a variety of factors that did not map neatly onto partisan cleavages, including interest group lobbying, distinctive state political cultures, and different modes of governance like public/private partnerships and federalism. Many of the crucial legislative initiatives of the early epidemic found support from across the political spectrum, including putatively "conservative" and "liberal" policies like HIV criminalization, anonymous testing, and funding for AIDS nonprofits. A rigid focus on partisan politics and election cycles cannot account for the bipartisan origins of some of the most significant HIV/AIDS legislation.[20]

By bringing into focus the often-neglected middle tier of American governance, this book illuminates how the history of AIDS looks different when we consider the foundational role of federalism in shaping disease control efforts across American history. It joins a growing wave of historical work on the continuing importance of state governments in the late twentieth century. To understand the history of the American state during this period, these scholars contend, we must center the vital role played by nonnational governments, federalism, and intergovernmental arrangements.[21] Much has been written on the plural, decentralized nature of the American polity, the growth of state power in the twentieth century, and the evolving relationship between the federal government and non-national governments after the New Deal.[22] This study brings the history of federalism and the history of AIDS into the same frame, spotlighting how the states enjoyed considerable latitude over public health policy in the late twentieth century. It provides an example of what political scientists and legal scholars term "compensatory federalism": the development of policies at the subnational level precisely because of inactivity at the federal level.[23] The relative absence of a well-defined and coordinated federal approach to AIDS made state politics and policies particularly significant. The intention here is not to exaggerate the scale of the states' response to the epidemic, to ignore the federal government's callous indifference toward people with AIDS (PWAs), or to downplay the vital role played by grassroots AIDS activists. Rather, I demonstrate that historians of the AIDS crisis, in particular, and historians of sexuality, more broadly, must take into account the plural, multilayered character of the American state.

If historians of the AIDS crisis have neglected histories of federalism, a similar observation can be made about the treatment of epidemic disease in the scholarship on American statecraft. The literature on modern US pandemics is vast and continues to unfold in new directions, as scholars of medicine pay closer attention to the cultural politics of public health and the complex links between capitalism, racism, and infectious diseases.[24] Yet, coverage of epidemics among historians of US statecraft remains far from even. The historiography of the twentieth-century American state says comparatively little about even world-historic outbreaks like the 1918 influenza pandemic, probably because of an ingrained assumption that epidemics are peripheral, episodic events that do not influence state formation.[25] While scholarship produced over the last three decades has substantially improved our understanding of diseases such as the 1918 flu, polio, and HIV/AIDS, this work has not affected how most historians write and think about US state development.

This book aims to repair this neglect by setting forth why the history of infectious disease deserves to figure more prominently in accounts of the twentieth-century American state. Returning the state to the study of modern epidemics and bringing public health governance back into our discussion of state-building over the last century, it argues that pandemics offer a particularly revealing window into the contested boundaries of government authority in the American federal system. By the closing decades of the twentieth century, public health was one of the few policy areas where the legal constraints of federalism continued to prevent the national government from taking a leading role.

Bringing pandemics and statecraft into the same analytical frame demonstrates the degree to which the centralization of state power in the twentieth century coexisted with older, seemingly antithetical styles of governance rooted in nineteenth-century traditions of social regulation, community welfare, and local self-government. It illuminates what the political scientists Karen Orren and Stephen Skowronek have termed "intercurrence": the coexistence of multiple overlapping governing orders at any single moment in the history of American statecraft.[26] In other words, vestiges of an older political order, one that was a far cry from what scholars identify as the key features of the modern liberal state, had remarkable staying power within the sphere of public health, surviving even through the expansion of federal power during the New Deal and Great Society eras.

The enduring power of the states in the sphere of public health matters deeply. Such a legally decentralized system fueled wildly uneven responses to public health crises. During the AIDS epidemic and other outbreaks of infectious disease during the twentieth century, state governments failed to implement equitable eradication campaigns, perpetuating and even exacerbating racial, sexual, regional, and other health disparities.

Sexual Minorities and the States

A large cast of individuals and organizations influenced state-level AIDS policymaking in the 1980s: elected officials, public health experts, community nonprofit organizations, grassroots activists, legislative staffers, religious leaders, conservative women's groups, employees of government agencies, researchers and academics, and philanthropic foundations. The epidemic particularly galvanized gay rights activists to play an increasingly prominent role in state politics and policymaking. Because of the misguided belief that HIV only affected certain marginalized communities, especially gay men and IV drug users, the view that the disease was a punishment for immorality and deviant behavior quickly became widespread in the 1980s. Reflecting the animosity many Americans felt toward PWAs during the early years of the epidemic, Patrick Buchanan, the future director of communications for the Reagan administration, wrote an opinion piece for the tabloid the *New York Post* in 1983 in which he sarcastically stated, "The poor homosexuals—they have declared war upon nature, and now nature is exacting an awful retribution."[27] Gay activists responded to this renewed stigmatization and public hostility by mobilizing with growing sophistication and energy at the state level. Political struggles over antibody testing, HIV criminalization, and prevention education became a platform for gay men and lesbians to acquire power and influence in the legislative realm. Gay rights groups pursued a multifaceted strategy to shape the early state-level response to AIDS, lobbying legislators, engaging the courts, and campaigning during ballot initiatives. They proved remarkably successful at forging alliances with lawmakers from different sides of the political spectrum, projecting an image of moderation and pragmatism and orienting themselves toward the political center.

By delving into the state-level political struggles over the AIDS epidemic and foregrounding the crucial role that gay rights activists played in these disputes, this book contributes to a recent wave of scholarship on the evolving relationship between the gay rights movement and the US government. In recent years, historians have increasingly grappled with the complex and often contradictory interactions between sexual minorities and the American state in the latter decades of the twentieth century. From the early 1970s, as queer scholars have richly documented, gay activists advocated for enhanced legal protections, improved access to state bureaucracies, and a seat at the policymaking table. In cities across the United States, from

San Francisco to Houston to Chicago, politicians courted the so-called gay vote, forming new electoral coalitions that redefined the status of sexual minorities. Attending to the themes of urban liberalism, social movement organizing, and intersectional politics, a recent string of books and articles has charted the rise of gay political clout after the 1970s, tracing the emergence of gay voting blocs in urban centers, the gradual enmeshment of gay nonprofits with the state, and the intersections between AIDS, healthcare capitalism, and the welfare state.[28] Considered together, these histories demonstrate that the gay movement's orientation toward the state gradually shifted from one of confrontation and militancy to one of accommodation and assimilation. By the end of the twentieth century, many gay activists no longer saw the state as a repressive force to be kept at arm's length but rather as a potential ally in efforts to secure and protect individual rights.

The state-level response to the AIDS epidemic was a key pivot in this shift. Spurred to action by the urgency of the crisis, gay rights activists all over the country intensified their lobbying efforts in state capitals, forming an array of umbrella organizations that strengthened their influence over the legislative realm. In the 1980s and 1990s, the number of states with professional LGBTQ lobbying groups shot up.[29] Among the more prominent of these new organizations were the Lesbian and Gay Rights Lobby of Texas, the Lobby for Individual Freedom and Equality in California, and Illinois Federation for Human Rights, founded in 1982, 1986, and 1991, respectively. As the pages that follow will demonstrate, each of these organizations played a vital role in the genesis and passage of crucial AIDS legislation. With this new organizational infrastructure, activists engineered a more professional lobbying style, honing their ability to influence lawmakers across the ideological spectrum. Initially created and steered by volunteers, state LGBTQ groups underwent a rapid process of professionalization, as they hired paid lobbyists and streamlined their organizational structures. Even as the AIDS crisis decimated urban queer communities, then, it had a catalyzing effect that drew in and mobilized activists at the state level. The legislative struggles over the epidemic intertwined with debates over the political and legal status of sexual minorities.

By telling the story of the AIDS epidemic at the state, rather than the city or national, level, this book uncovers the growing political clout of the gay rights movement in legislatures across the country during the 1980s. Assumptions about the metropolitan and urban nature of queer activism have too often rendered the states marginal to the history of gay politics in the late twentieth century. The field of LGBT history cut its teeth on research about identity and community formation in urban neighborhoods like San Francisco's Castro district, New York City's Greenwich Village, and Chicago's Lakeview. A favored way of interpreting queer politics after the 1960s is to emphasize the relative success of gay rights activists at gaining political and electoral influence at the metropolitan level.[30] Casting the gay political movement as inseparable from urban liberalism, the historian Timothy Stewart-Winter has even gone as far as claiming that "gay politics until recently was urban politics."[31] Typically urban spaces like bars and nightclubs loom large in accounts of late twentieth-century gay rights politics, which are often preoccupied with how the metropolis made queer communities legible to lawmakers. Newer work is more attuned to the dynamic interplay between urban politics and rural and suburban spaces, but, on the whole, historians of the recent gay rights movement have tended to focus on national political developments or specific local case studies.[32] Discussions about state politics and policymaking have been far less frequent and more fleeting.[33] Yet, the states became key sites for the emergence of a more formalized and professionalized gay rights movement during the early years of the AIDS epidemic. The struggle for gay rights may have begun at city hall, but it quickly moved to the statehouse as well. It was in the 1980s and 1990s that the movement made its most significant early strides toward becoming an influential political constituency at the state level. Galvanized by the AIDS epidemic, gay men and lesbians moved from the margins to the center of politics in states across the country, gaining traction in some of the most crucial debates over the policy response to the disease.

The Plan of the Book

To trace the evolving relationship between American federalism and pandemics across the full arc of US history exceeds the limits of a single book. To overcome this constraint, this study adopts a distinctive structure that is intended to strike a constructive balance between breadth of coverage and depth of analysis. Chapter 1 begins the book with a synthetic overview of epidemics and American state development in the twentieth century. Readers will find in this chapter neither an exhaustive account of every disease outbreak nor prolonged discussions of individual state policies. Rather, the objective here is to chart the broad patterns of US policymaking during epidemic outbreaks and the changing balance of power between federal, state, and local levels of authority over time. In the federalist structure of government established by the Constitution, the power to protect the population from infectious diseases lay firmly with state and local governments. The legal foundation of this authority was the doctrine of police power, which endowed the states with broad latitude of action to curb property rights and personal liberties in order to protect the people's welfare. Invoking their capacious and ubiquitously felt police power, the states exercised sweeping forms of control over individual behavior to ward off epidemics. State health departments expelled suspected disease carriers from their homes against their will, enacted social distancing requirements during epidemic outbreaks, and enforced coercive and far-reaching quarantine and isolation orders. When the 1918 Influenza pandemic struck, the states wielded far-reaching powers to stem the spread of the virus, enforcing public gathering bans, shutting down nonessential businesses and schools, and implementing mask mandates. The crisis also foreshadowed the US government's approach to epidemic disease over the next one hundred years, as the federal government abdicated responsibility for coordinating the nation's response, leaving subnational authorities to fend for themselves.

In the period spanning from the New Deal to the Great Society, the American public health system evolved into an exceedingly complex patchwork of overlapping agencies and bureaucracies at the federal, state, and local levels, with power dispersed across hundreds of distinct governmental units—approximately sixteen hundred by the 1950s.[34] The states retained their primacy in this policy realm, however. Even as legal control over many key aspects of economic and social life moved from the subnational to the federal level, state governments possessed the ultimate authority to control the spread of infectious diseases within the nation's borders.

Having explained how the states remained predominant in the American public health system before the 1980s, this book then transitions into an in-depth study of the HIV/AIDS crisis. Focusing on California, Illinois, and Texas, while making comparisons to elsewhere, the next three chapters examine the uneven and fragmented state-level response to the epidemic in the 1980s. Unsurprisingly, given their political and cultural diversity, each of these states adopted a distinctive approach to the epidemic: California enacted some of the most proactive AIDS legislation in the country, Illinois implemented coercive public health strategies such as mandatory testing, and Texas virtually ignored the disease until it threatened the heterosexual population. All three captured national headlines and commanded the attention of federal-level policymakers at various points, largely because they became key battlegrounds over the major policy issues stemming from the crisis—antibody testing, quarantine, prevention education, HIV criminalization, and patient care. Examining California, Illinois, and Texas thus highlights the various paths that states followed in the early years of the AIDS epidemic.

The varying richness of archival collections in different states also shaped my selection of case studies. In California, the organizational records of gay groups in Los Angeles, Sacramento, and San Francisco revealed the concerted lobbying efforts by sexual minorities to secure the passage of HIV-specific legislation. Among the largest and best-funded in the nation, the California state archive contained reams of useful material on AIDS policymaking: speeches, pamphlets, correspondence, memoranda, newspaper clippings, and the personal papers of individual lawmakers. The paper trail left by gay activists and AIDS policymakers in Illinois was similarly voluminous. In Chicago, the Gerber/Hart Archives, a community-based LGBTQ archive, housed a wide variety of collections on the organizations and individuals involved in the state's response to the epidemic, including a very detailed set of records on the most influential statewide gay lobbying group, the Illinois Gay and Lesbian Task Force.

In comparison, many states held virtually no material on the genesis and enactment of major AIDS legislation. Archival documentation was especially scattered and fragmentary in the South. Originally, I hoped to include Florida as one of this book's case studies, as the state had one of the largest caseloads in the nation during the 1980s and implemented a range of far-reaching policies to combat the crisis. In 1988, the legislature passed the Omnibus AIDS Act, one of the most comprehensive AIDS laws passed by any state, which, among other things, furnished HIV-positive individuals with legal protections against discrimination, funneled resources into prevention education efforts, and criminalized the so-called intentional transmission of HIV. Unfortunately, the source base on the political history of this legislation proved highly constrained. No collection whatsoever existed for the Florida Task Force (FTF), the gay rights organization involved in campaigning for the law's passage.[35] Sadly, I was also unable to track down for oral interviews any of the professional lobbyists who worked for the FTF in the late 1980s. While the state archive in Tallahassee contained transcripts of committee hearings on the Omnibus AIDS Act, these sources yielded few insights into the political factors behind the law's enactment and the tactics used by gay activists to shepherd it through the legislature.[36]

With such a thin set of records to work with, it proved impossible to piece together a detailed enough picture of the legislative politics surrounding the epidemic in Florida. Elsewhere, in Alabama, Arkansas, and Mississippi, few archival sources remained to document the behind-the-scenes wrangling over significant AIDS policies.[37]

While Texas was home to significantly more primary source material on the epidemic than most Southern states, it still presented more of a research challenge than California and Illinois.[38] The papers of the Lesbian/Gay Rights Lobby—the Texas organization most heavily involved in pushing for a more proactive response to AIDS during the 1980s—were small and incomplete, providing very little material on the HIV-specific laws enacted by the legislature. To overcome this difficulty, I took full advantage of the state's major gay newspapers, especially *This Week in Texas* and the *Dallas Voice*, which contained detailed coverage of the policy debates over the epidemic in the late 1980s. I also conducted oral interviews with former gay lobbyists and analyzed hundreds of hours of audio recordings of legislative committee testimony over pending AIDS bills. Combining these sources, I was able to chart the state's response to the epidemic in almost as much detail as California and Illinois.

Beginning this book's exploration of state-level AIDS policymaking, chapter 2 examines the state of California, its long tradition of rights activism, and its uniquely robust response to the epidemic. Through a clandestine network of legislative assistants, "closeted" bureaucrats, and liberal politicians, gay activists played a vital role in shepherding proactive AIDS bills through the state legislature. At the heart of this network stood three influential gay staffers: Stan Hadden, who drafted a substantial portion of the state's early AIDS legislation; Larry Bush, a prominent legislative assistant and speechwriter; and Bruce Decker, a well-known Republican consultant and advisor to Governor George Deukmejian. California's proactive response to the epidemic drew significant impetus from the behind-the-scenes maneuvering of these gay policymakers. By the mid-1980s, Bush, Decker, and Hadden had achieved some impressive political and legislative victories, including the passage of legislation that established the country's most robust anonymous testing regime, the forging of effective alliances with powerful liberal lawmakers, and the funneling of state funding toward prevention education and biomedical research.

The whiteness of this gay policy network, however, exposed racial fault lines in California's response to AIDS. The influence of Bush, Decker, and

Hadden hinged on their ability to appear moderate, and their strategy of conforming to middle-class notions of respectability foreclosed any possibility of structural reform and marginalized members of the broader queer community, especially people of color. In the process, white gay men became a stand-in for the entire queer community, perpetuating preexisting inequities within the gay rights movement. As the state grew more ambivalent toward sexual minorities, gay identity no longer precluded integration into the policymaking process. Rather, access to the state depended on professional conformity and assimilation within a heteronormative policymaking apparatus. By the early 1990s, moreover, cutbacks to state spending generated a zero-sum approach to AIDS education, pitting older "risk groups" against racial minorities in the battle for state funding.

The third chapter moves to the state of Illinois, where the politics of AIDS did not fit neatly into the rigid binaries of right and left, red and blue, Republican and Democrat. Instead, the split between Chicago and the rest of Illinois informed the state's early response to AIDS, which was among the most coercive in country. In the Illinois legislature, gay activists confronted a powerful coalition of downstate and suburbanite lawmakers, who supported repressive AIDS legislation. Facilitating this alliance was Penny Pullen, a longtime conservative activist and state representative from the Chicago suburb of Park Ridge. Much like conservatives at the national level, Pullen framed the AIDS epidemic as a symbol of America's moral decline and blamed gay men and IV drug users for the disease's spread. Igniting contentious debate in the state legislature, she built an alliance with downstate and suburban Democrats who were responding to the growing fear among their constituents that the epidemic would cause a widespread outbreak among the heterosexual population. From this broad coalition emerged some of the most controversial AIDS legislation in the country, including a 1987 act that required antibody testing for all marriage license applicants—a population that had virtually no risk of contracting HIV. To rally support for this measure, Pullen drew on the activist network created by anti-feminist organizers in the 1970s during the battle over the Equal Rights Amendment (ERA), which would have embedded gender equality into the US Constitution. She forged especially close ties with Phyllis Schlafly, who led the conservative crusade against the ERA and turned her attention to the epidemic in the late 1980s, believing it posed an existential threat to the sanctity of the male-led heteronormative family.

Chapter 4 examines the politics of AIDS in Texas, which did the least of any hard-hit state to tackle the crisis. Of the fifty states, Texas had the fourth largest caseload in 1989 but only spent fourteen cents per capita on AIDS compared to nearly three dollars in California and New York.[39] In a state that still had a sodomy statute on the books, the mere idea of promoting safer gay sex to curb HIV was anathema to many legislators, medical professionals, and civil servants. Only in 1989 did Texas lawmakers pass their first major AIDS-related statute, but they did so only because the epidemic threatened the state's public finances rather than any commitment to providing PWAs with better care and treatment. As with previous epidemics, then, the decentralized response to HIV/AIDS produced stark healthcare disparities between the states.

While California, Illinois, and Texas adopted vastly different approaches to the AIDS epidemic, the politics of fiscal conservatism permeated debates about the disease in all three states. The onset of the AIDS crisis overlapped almost precisely with the election of Ronald Reagan as president, and this new political landscape directly shaped the rhetorical strategies used by AIDS activists and policymakers. Throughout the 1980s, the Reagan administration preached the gospel of small-government conservatism and led an assault on the social welfare policies of the New Deal order. It slashed spending on welfare programs, cut taxes, and curbed the central government's regulatory reach.[40] Against this backdrop, AIDS activists capitalized on Americans' growing animosity toward state power, portraying draconian AIDS measures as ineffective, inefficient, and an onerous financial burden. In California, Illinois, and Texas, homophobic politicians regularly called on public health officials to use the traditional tools of infectious disease control—such as quarantine, isolation, and mandatory testing—against PWAs. They proposed coercive new limits on the freedoms of people with HIV infection, arguing that protecting the public from infection should take precedence over the civil liberties of those who already had the disease.

Tapping into the rhetoric of fiscal conservatism, AIDS activists countered that this approach would place an undue financial burden on the states, many of which faced sharp budget shortfalls after the Reagan administration eviscerated federal support for subnational governments in the early 1980s. By the end of the decade, states across the country experienced a series of fiscal crises, a situation made worse by their inability to run large budget deficits over a prolonged period (unlike the federal government).[41] In this context, AIDS policymakers portrayed quarantine, mandatory testing, and other traditional public health measures as excessively interventionist and costly policies that would increase the tax burden on ordinary citizens and achieve little in the fight against the disease. Instead, they supported less draconian policies aimed at preventing the transmission of HIV through education and early treatment. In rhetoric designed to appeal to fiscal hawks, they couched their support for these measures in the language of small-state conservatism, arguing that stemming the transmission of HIV would prevent people from falling ill, losing their jobs, and relying on welfare payments. This strategy allowed AIDS policymakers to build coalitions with politicians from across the ideological spectrum and portray their policy proposals as consistent with the growing fiscal conservatism of the Reagan era.

Another persistent theme in the state-level response to AIDS was the prominence played by the "closet"—a topic almost entirely missing from the existing literature on the crisis. In California, Bush, Decker, and Hadden wielded the hidden power of the closet to ferret out homophobia within the state bureaucracy. During the early 1980s, they frequently clashed with the agency responsible for coordinating the state's response to the epidemic, the Office of AIDS, which refused to collaborate with gay policymakers or even officially meet with them. To overcome this bureaucratic obstructionism, they met regularly with a group of closeted officials to gather intelligence on the inner workings of the agency and its handling of the epidemic. Through this network, they managed to undermine the authority of the Office of AIDS and force it to engage more constructively with gay rights activists. While California reveals the unexpected ways that gay policymakers could use the closet to achieve policy victories, Illinois shows how conservative politicians could raise the specter of the closet to push for coercive AIDS measures. Both Pullen and Schlafly stoked panic and fear over the prospect of closeted husbands contracting HIV and passing it on to their unwitting wives and children. Invoking the rhetoric of child protection, they claimed that imposing strict restrictions on the civil liberties of PWAs was necessary to prevent secretly bisexual men from infecting their children, who were otherwise unlikely to come into contact with the virus. During the early years of the epidemic, then, the closet proved to be a remarkably malleable political and rhetorical device, used by gay policymakers and conservatives alike to push for very different policy agendas.[42]

Although the states were at the vanguard of the policy response to the AIDS crisis in the 1980s, the central government dramatically expanded its involvement in fighting the epidemic in the 1990s. The fifth chapter traces the genesis and passage of the Ryan White Comprehensive AIDs Resources Emergency Act (CARE Act), a landmark measure that marked a tectonic shift in the federal response to AIDS. Passed by Congress in 1990 by overwhelming bipartisan margins, the law offered grants to all fifty states for AIDS treatment and healthcare and provided direct assistance to the cities with the highest HIV caseloads. Henceforth, the federal government would assert greater responsibility for the delivery of AIDS healthcare and services, marking an important departure from the traditionally small role it played in responding to pandemics. But the CARE Act also delegated substantial authority over program design and implementation to states, cities, and local nonprofit organizations, ensuring that substantial governments continued to play an important role in AIDS policymaking during the 1990s. Furthermore, as federal lawmakers deliberated over the law, they looked to the states and their municipalities for inspiration, enacting a measure that federalized a public/private model of AIDS healthcare that originated in California.

Echoing a strategy first used by their counterparts at the state level, federal AIDS lobbyists secured bipartisan support for the CARE Act partly by claiming that it was a fiscally prudent measure. The law instructed state and local governments to distribute federal grants to AIDS nonprofits, which would then provide care to PWAs in non-hospital settings. Drawing on a series of studies published by healthcare economists in the mid-1980s, AIDS activists claimed that this model would save the federal government money in the long term by preventing PWAs from relying on expensive hospital care, an increasing proportion of which was funded by Medicaid. Such an argument appealed to Republicans and Democrats alike, who overwhelmingly supported the legislation in both chambers of Congress. As with the political struggles over AIDS at the state level in the 1980s, then, fiscal conservatism dominated the legislative debate over the CARE Act. In the end, Congress only began to take the epidemic seriously when it became clear that it threatened the country's public finances.

Chapter 6 examines the administration and enactment of the CARE Act at the state and local levels during the 1990s. By design, the law divided and shared governmental responsibility for implementation between the different levels of the US federal system, leaving state and municipal officials free to decide the range of services covered, eligibility criteria, and the precise allocation of funding. As a result, the program remained very uneven in coverage, leaving whole swaths of the American population with inadequate

AIDS health care and treatment. Only a few states, mostly located on the coasts, received enough federal money to create a robust continuum of care for PWAs whereas the majority obtained less than their fair share of grants under the law's skewed funding formulas. As the epidemic entered its second decade, regional variation remained a hallmark of the policy response to it, even as the federal government funneled an unprecedented amount of funding toward AIDS treatment and healthcare.

The conclusion ends the book with an analysis of how the American system of federalism shaped the epoch-making coronavirus pandemic. As with the AIDS crisis in the 1980s, COVID-19 was a major anchor point in the broader history of America's chaotic and disjointed approach to pandemics. Agreement on how to confront the outbreak collapsed over the spring of 2020, and the government's response quickly fractured along intergovernmental and partisan lines. In the absence of clear guidance from the White House, the states once again forged ahead with their own set of highly divergent and contradictory policies. While the initial response to COVID-19 revealed the power of subnational governments in the American public health system, the long-term legacy of the outbreak may be to undermine the authority of the states in this policy area. In response to a political backlash against the perceived overreach of health officials during the first wave of the pandemic, legislatures across the country enacted a wave of bills to restrict the powers of public health departments, raising fundamental questions about who will have the authority to tackle the next pandemic.

The colossal failure of the US government during the early months of COVID-19 speaks to the urgency of fleshing out the history of public health governance across the long sweep of American history. As the crisis starkly exposed, pandemics are not merely a function of individual microbes and pathogens; they also reflect how states and governments wield power. The emergence, severity, and duration of disease outbreaks are inseparable from a wide range of social and political factors, including broader structures and patterns of governance. Fusing synthetic analysis with in-depth archival work, the pages that follow illuminate how one of these factors—American federalism—has shaped epidemic control efforts from the early twentieth century to the AIDS crisis to the present day.

CHAPTER ONE

The Structure of American Public Health Policy Before the AIDS Epidemic

It is impossible to grasp the fragmented response to AIDS without first accounting for how the locus of public health authority remained with state and local governments across the long sweep of American history. Throughout the nineteenth and twentieth centuries, the power to implement the traditional tools of infectious disease control—such as vaccine mandates, isolation orders, and restrictions on public gatherings—rested primarily with the states. As a result, public health policymaking remained a very decentralized affair, with subnational authorities adopting divergent strategies to manage the spread of pandemic disease. While the central government has always had a role in the nation's public health infrastructure, its involvement remained modest for much of the last two hundred years, relegated to implementing quarantine orders at the country's borders and providing financial assistance and technical advice to local health departments, which retained the final say over which policies to implement. When pandemics struck, federal authorities typically lacked the political will to coordinate the nation's response, leaving states and municipalities to fend for themselves.

Through a longue durée perspective, this chapter casts a wide net over the history of infectious disease control in the nineteenth and twentieth centuries, providing an overview of the policy structures and precedents that animated the early response to AIDS. It surveys two hundred years of history to reveal the primary importance of federalism in shaping the variegated American public health system. It begins with a glance back to the nineteenth century, when the balance of power in the US polity consistently favored the states over the national government. Less encumbered by the restraining impulse of the US Constitution, states and localities had the power to restrict individual liberty and property for the sake of protecting the public's health. The policing of health and hygiene legitimated a capacious conception of the regulatory authority of the states and formed a central building block of nineteenth-century governance.

I then chart the history of pandemic preparedness and infectious disease control from the Progressive Era to the 1980s. At the dawn of the twentieth century, the tools and resources available to federal health officials were limited, and most epidemic control efforts continued to take place at the subnational level. With the coming of the New Deal, however, a series of congressional acts and policy initiatives transformed the national government's relationship to public health. The most lasting and far-reaching of these reforms was Title VI of the 1935 Social Security Act, which tripled the federal health budget and funneled a vast amount of money toward subnational health departments. Like so many other New Deal programs, Title VI relied on a complex series of intergovernmental partnerships between federal, state, and local bureaucrats. Over the coming years, it empowered states and municipalities to build more effective public health infrastructures. Slowly but steadily, federal authorities also acquired new institutional capacities to manage the spread of infectious disease. A cluster of new health agencies emerged, expanding the mandate and administrative reach of federal health officials. During its mid-century heyday, the Centers for Disease Control gradually increased the scale and scope of the national government's disease surveillance infrastructure. But even amid these changes, states and localities retained control over the administration and implementation of many federal health initiatives. Even during the New Deal and Great Society eras, when faith in the central state was at its apex, subnational governments had broad authority to shape epidemic control efforts. On the eve of the AIDS crisis, states and municipalities far outpaced the national government in terms of spending and legislative activity on infectious disease control. The American public health system continued to be characterized by bewildering institutional sprawl, weak federal institutions, and immense fragmentation and unevenness. In a political system increasingly dominated by Washington-generated mandates and policies, the national government's authority in the area of public health remained limited.

Pandemics and Police Power in the Nineteenth Century

Authority over public health was not one of the powers enumerated to the federal government by the US Constitution, falling instead under the legal purview of the states. Throughout the early national period, states and municipalities regularly invoked the legal doctrine of police power, which endowed the states with an almost limitless capacity to regulate civil society for the public good. Derived from Anglo-American common law and sanctioned by the constitution, police power was part of what legal historian William Novak has termed the "well-regulated society," "where the polity assumed control over, and became implicated in, the basic conduct of social life."[1] Equipped with discretionary and vaguely defined authority, state legislatures broadly deployed their police powers in the nineteenth century, passing thousands of laws to regulate drunkenness, gambling, corporations, migration, workplace conditions, food inspections, guns, animals, fisheries, usury, highways, lotteries, and trade.[2]

In the early years of the American republic, when outbreaks of cholera, bubonic plague, and yellow fever struck cities with regular and devastating force, this governing philosophy also endowed the states with expansive legal authority to prevent the spread of infectious disease. Public health measures adopted in the face of looming pandemics therefore became a decisive force in shaping the contours of early American governance and in defining the boundaries of the states' sovereignty. The common law maxim *salus populi suprema lex* (the health of the people is the highest law) conveyed the well-established belief that individual rights were subordinate to the states' interest in promoting the public's health and well-being. Police power jurisprudence legitimated state efforts to quarantine the sick, enforce mandatory vaccination laws, and condemn unsanitary property. The grave threat that infectious diseases posed to a rapidly urbanizing society justified coercive health measures that curtailed individual freedoms and liberties.[3]

Throughout the nineteenth and early twentieth centuries, in dozens of cases at every jurisdictional level, the courts affirmed the states' legal authority to preserve and protect the public's health. Emblematic was the US Supreme Court's decision in *Jacobson v. Massachusetts* (1905), which upheld the constitutionality of a mandatory smallpox vaccination law in Cambridge, Massachusetts.[4] Conveying the view that the states were preeminent in the realm of public health, Supreme Court Justice John Marshall Harlan argued that "the safety and the health of the people of Massachusetts are, in the first instance, for that Commonwealth to guard and protect. They are matters that do not ordinarily concern the National Government."[5] Unlike many cases of its era, *Jacobson* endured well into the twenty-first century, with state and federal courts frequently citing it during the initial months of the COVID-19 pandemic.[6]

The federal government played a distinct but limited role in the regulation and promotion of public health during the nineteenth and early twentieth centuries. As early as 1798, Congress established the national government's first public health program when it created the Marine Hospital Service (MHS) to treat merchant sailors. Although Congress initially legislated a narrow role for the MHS, centered around the operation of hospitals for mariners entering the United States, the agency's range of activities evolved over the course of the nineteenth century to include basic scientific research and interstate quarantine efforts.[7] By the 1880s and 1890s, the MHS had acquired a slew of new responsibilities, including formal control over the medical inspection of immigrants at the nation's borders and the authority to curb the interstate spread of yellow fever, smallpox, cholera, and the bubonic plague.[8]

During this same period, however, several ill-fated attempts to improve the nation's public health infrastructure fell victim to intergovernmental tensions. In 1879, following a devastating yellow fever epidemic in the South, Congress took the unprecedented step of creating a National Board of Health and empowered it with the authority to provide state and local health departments with technical expertise, collect vital statistics, and impose interstate quarantines. But, as the president of the Louisiana State Board of Health noted, many local administrators harbored deep suspicions about this perceived incursion into their domain and decried "the insolent pretensions of the National Board of Health with its odious system of espionage and intermeddling."[9] Unable to stem the growing tide of criticism against the board, Congress discontinued its funding in 1883.[10]

The curtailment of the central state's authority by intergovernmental friction would recur so frequently over the following decades as to constitute a core component of American public health. To take just one further example, in the early 1910s, a sweeping legislative proposal for a national department of health faced a chorus of objections from state officials, federal bureaucrats, and, most prominently, surgeon general Walter Wyman, who feared it would undermine the institutional autonomy of the MHS.[11] Eventually, after vigorous debate, Congress passed a far more anemic bill in

1912 that made only a few statutory changes to the MHS's research authority and renamed it the Public Health Service (PHS).[12] Four decades would pass before the establishment of the first cabinet-level position for health in 1953.[13] Even as Populists and Progressives developed an administrative state capable of addressing some of the ills of unfettered capitalism, the federal government's reach in the sphere of public health remained limited.

Progressive Era Federalism and the 1918–1919 Influenza Pandemic

The limits of the federal government's public health authority became starkly evident during the 1918–1919 Influenza pandemic. A complex interplay of viral, biological, and social factors made it one of the deadliest pandemics in world history, killing some fifty million people. With a fatality rate of just under 2.5 percent, the virus was particularly virulent and contagious during 1918, inflicting high fevers, extreme nausea, and deadly attacks of pneumonia on its victims.[14] The growth of densely populated cities in the early twentieth century also facilitated the virus' spread. From the outset, public health professionals associated the disease with crowded urban spaces such as movie theaters, parades, and religious gatherings. In many respects, the "Spanish flu" was the first modern global pandemic—the first to occur in the contexts of mass transportation, total warfare, and rapid urbanization.[15]

In recent years, scholars have developed a rich understanding of the racialized and gendered nature of the American response to the 1918 flu as well as its other cultural and social facets and effects.[16] But they have not analyzed it in relation to the history of US state development. Even monographs that focus on the American state's evolution during the First World War often mention the disease only in passing, treating it as a peripheral episode in the context of the war.[17] But the pandemic constitutes more than an aberrational event or a devastating appendix to the First World War: it foreshadowed the consequential role American federalism would play in shaping the nation's approach to modern epidemics.

Although the Influenza catastrophe was unprecedented in its size and scope, the federal government nevertheless proved unable and unwilling to coordinate the nation's response. Only in October 1918, as the second wave of the pandemic reached its crest, did Surgeon General Rupert Blue begin issuing public statements on influenza management.[18] Congress infused the

PHS with $1 million of extra funding to fight the outbreak, but this figure amounted to less than a third of what New York City alone spent on public health in 1918.[19] From the beginning, the Health Service signaled its constitutionally subordinate role to state and local governments, aiming, as Surgeon General Blue put it, "to aid and not supplant state and local health authorities in their work." Accordingly, "instructions were issued that all requests for medical, nursing, and other emergency aid in dealing with the epidemic should come to the Public Health Service only through the State Health Officers."[20] Even as the pandemic sowed death and panic, Woodrow Wilson never made a public statement about it, opting to ignore the danger it posed rather than divert attention away from the war effort.[21]

Instead, state and local authorities dominated the public health response to influenza, deploying police power, which provided states with the governing authority to order schools, bars, and theaters to close; to issue sweeping bans on nonessential public gatherings; to place restrictions on transportation; and to impose other unprecedented measures. However, given the sprawling and disjointed character of the nation's public health system, and because health experts could reach no consensus about which social-distancing measures were most effective, even basic epidemic control strategies spawned a myriad of different local approaches, leading to vast regional disparities in morbidity and mortality rates. Decisions about which specific institutions to close—and for how long—generated particular controversy. Not surprisingly, those municipalities that imposed restrictions promptly—and kept them in place until the pandemic receded from view—lost fewer lives to the disease.[22] With its advanced public health infrastructure, New York City acted quickly against the pandemic, mounting a largely effective response that led to the lowest mortality rate on the East Coast.[23] The city of Detroit, Michigan, by contrast, was among the municipalities slow to impose public gathering bans, because its health commissioner, James W. Inches, insisted that a prolonged closure of the city's businesses would cause more harm than good. When health leaders in other Michigan cities implemented a multitude of strict social-distancing measures, Inches only redoubled his resolve to keep Detroit open, lifting the city's closure order on November 6, 1918, well before the peak of the pandemic.[24] Not wanting to incite panic among the city's large population, he downplayed the disease's danger and overstated his department's ability to control it, informing the public that "if you are otherwise in good health, the chances are over 200 to one that you will get well and be alright again in a short time."[25]

Despite Inches's optimism, or perhaps precisely because of it, the pandemic struck Detroit particularly hard: of the ten largest cities in the United States in 1918, Detroit experienced the fourth-highest mortality rate from the disease (see table 1.1).

Friction between the federal government and the states, and between state governments and municipal authorities, quickly emerged as a defining feature of the American response to influenza. For example, the surgeon general issued guidelines to state and municipal health departments, advising them to close their schools.[26] But in New York, the health commissioner decided against suspending lessons, because he believed that children would fare better in the city's public education system than at home.[27] As the virus hit Chicago, Illinois, the city's health department likewise elected to improve its school inspection and hygiene programs instead of shutting down.[28] The American Red Cross—since 1900 tied to the executive branch by federal charter—also found itself subordinated to the authority of state and local health officials. "Cooperate in every way with the local Boards of Health," Elizabeth Ross, the director of the Nursing Bureau for the New England Division, informed her colleagues: "Take great pains not to force [your] opinions or services or criticize in any way their actions."[29] Meanwhile, from Illinois to Michigan to Pennsylvania, fault lines also developed between state and local public health experts. Many municipal officials questioned—and sometimes even circumvented—statewide closure orders, complaining that such blanket interventions were ill-suited to the specific problems of urban public health. In Detroit, for instance, Health Commissioner Inches openly defied the Michigan Board of Health when he lifted the city's public gathering ban.[30]

Examining the fractured response to the 1918 influenza outbreak illuminates how the history of pandemics can modify conventional understandings of US state development during the early twentieth century. The prevailing narrative is that World War I triggered an unprecedented flow of power to the central government in an array of different policy spheres. Many scholars have traced the origins of the surveillance state, the national security state, and the military-industrial complex to the expansion of federal power during the war years.[31] The demands of total warfare legitimated a vast extension of the national government's reach into the everyday lives of its citizens, fore shadowing the rise of the modern federal leviathan under the auspices of the New Deal. Through price controls, rationing, conscription, censorship, surveillance, and propaganda, the central state tightened

Table 1.1: Characteristics of the response to the 1918–1919 influenza pandemic in the ten most populous cities in the United States in 1920.

	Length of Public Health Response (Days)	*Public Health Expenditure, 1918 (Million $)*[a]	*Mandatory School Closure*	*Weekly Excess Pneumonia and Influenza Deaths (Deaths/100,000 Population)*[b]
Baltimore	43	0.3	Yes	559.3
Boston	50	0.6	Yes	710.0
Chicago	68	1.8	No	373.2
Cleveland	99	0.6	Yes	474.0
Detroit	23	0.7	Yes	637.0
Los Angeles	154	0.2	Yes	579.8
New York City	73	3.4	No	452.3
Philadelphia	51	0.8	Yes	748.4
Pittsburgh	53	0.4	Yes	806.8
St. Louis	143	0.3	Yes	358.0

[a]Public health expenditure includes expenditure on local health boards, the collection of epidemiological statistics, the treatment of communicable diseases, and food regulation. [b]Average for the weeks between September 8, 1918, and February 22, 1919. Sources: Howard Markel et al., "Nonpharmaceutical Interventions Implemented by US Cities During the 1918–1919 Influenza Pandemic," *Journal of the American Medical Association* 298, no. 6 (August 8, 2007): 644–654; United States Bureau of the Census, "Financial Statistics of Cities Having a Population Over 30,000" (US Government Printing Office, 1918); Selwyn D. Collins et al., "Mortality from Influenza and Pneumonia in 50 Large Cities of the United States, 1910–1929," *Public Health Reports (1896–1970)* 45, no. 39 (September 26, 1930): 2277–2328; "State Grip Decree: Close Up Detroit," *Detroit Free Press*, October 19, 1918; "State Closing Ban Lifted for Friday," *Detroit News*, November 7, 1918, 2.

its grip over the economy, political speech, and American society. In the process, the relationship between the state and its citizens grew closer and more complex. However, the influenza pandemic exposed the limits of the national government's influence at this critical juncture in the history of the American state. Not even the wartime spike in sentiments of self-sacrifice and social responsibility could legitimate a truly national response to pandemic disease. Even as the federal government mobilized for total warfare, protecting the people from new viruses and epidemics remained the prerogative of states and municipalities. Only in the 1930s, with the arrival of "big government" more generally during the New Deal, did the central state begin to play an influential role in responding to pandemics.

Public Health, Polio, and the New Deal Order

Despite the Progressive Era flurry of reform to governance generally, the American public health system limped into the 1920s as fragmented and disjointed as ever. The United States had no national health department, and the PHS was still a relatively small agency whose budget plateaued in the years immediately following the influenza pandemic. Throughout the 1920s, the Health Service's single biggest expenditure continued to be the operation of marine hospitals, which consumed nearly 50 percent of its budget.[32] A truly national approach to pandemic preparedness did not emerge until the 1930s when a surge of New Deal–era legislation empowered the federal government to play a more central role in the nation's public health infrastructure. Yet curiously historians have all but ignored public health in their studies of this pivotal moment in US state development.[33]

As growing numbers of Americans put faith in robust government during the 1930s and 1940s, and as communicable diseases continued to threaten the nation's economic and social well-being, a diverse chorus of voices rose in favor of the idea that the central state should assume responsibility for regulating and promoting public health. This viewpoint found adherents among state health administrators, PHS officers, and even Southern Democrats.[34] As the president of the Mississippi Board of Health mused in 1937, "A developing social consciousness is leading people generally to the conviction that community health is the concern—the paramount concern—of the state. Within the last decade this idea, more or less indefinite for a time, has crystallized into a new conception of the duties, responsibilities, and functions of government."[35]

Passage of the Social Security Act in 1935 represented the pinnacle of New Deal efforts to expand federal involvement in public health. But to the dismay of many reformers, the chief drafters of the legislation retreated from an initial proposal for national health insurance in hopes of placating the powerful American Medical Association (AMA), which opposed any perceived encroachment by the central government into physicians' professional autonomy. As part of the resulting compromise, Title VI of the Social Security Act instead authorized $8 million for a new grants-in-aid program—administered through the PHS—to assist state and local health departments.[36] For the first time, the national government would play a decisive role in developing and coordinating the nation's public health infrastructure, which opened the door for an unprecedented degree of cooperation between the PHS and state and local health authorities. During the various congressional hearings over the Social Security Act, few objected to these public health provisions.[37] State health officers were receptive to this new level of federal investment in public health, because the Great Depression had triggered a sharp decline in their political and institutional clout. Municipal health departments' per-capita expenditure plummeted by 30 percent between 1931 and 1934, and most health departments teetered on the edge of fiscal collapse.[38] In a letter to the drafters of the Social Security Act, E. L. Bishop, a Tennessee health officer, explained his support for Title VI: "We are spending huge sums for the relief of almost every agency and for the maintenance of almost all other functions of government, but we are permitting our health agencies, so painstakingly developed through the last two or three decades, to perish from a lack of support."[39]

Title VI of the Social Security Act undoubtedly took federal involvement in public health to unprecedented heights, but out of political and pragmatic necessity it did so by simultaneously enhancing the governing power of state and local authorities.[40] To be eligible for Title VI funds, states had to, among other things, increase their spending on health and sanitation programs.[41] As almost every state did so, total state appropriations for public health increased nearly sevenfold between 1935 and 1950, rising from $13 million to $85 million.[42] Given broad discretionary control over the administration of Title VI, the PHS formulated a slew of new regulations, including training standards and rules of practice for state and local health administrators to follow. The agency also created dozens of new training programs that educated over three thousand local government employees to a postgraduate level in 1937 alone. To conform with the new guidelines set by the PHS, state health officials expended a great deal of energy on professionalizing their ranks, adopting uniform personnel guidelines in 1936.[43]

Many state legislatures also used Title VI funds to professionalize and bureaucratize their health departments. New Mexico led the way in 1935, passing a statute that created ten new district health departments, each staffed with an epidemiologist, a public health nurse, and a sanitation official.[44] Prior to this legislation, New Mexico had been a public health laggard relative to other states, experiencing the country's second-highest death rate from tuberculosis during the 1920s.[45] With a steady stream of federal dollars bestowed by the Social Security Act, New Mexico's public health budget climbed nearly 200 percent between 1935 and 1946.[46] Elsewhere, in places as varied as Georgia, Kansas, Missouri, Texas, and Wisconsin, the Social Security Act facilitated new programs in maternal and child health, venereal disease control, and rural sanitation, as well as the rapid growth of a more professionalized and dedicated corps of state health officers. These multifaceted initiatives invariably dwarfed previous public health efforts in terms of resources, size, and scope, reversing the budget austerity of the early Great Depression and producing powerful new state health bureaucracies.[47]

Considering the transformative impact of Title VI, it is surprising that the Social Security Act's public health programs often warrant only passing mention at best in leading histories of the New Deal.[48] Historians have similarly overlooked the series of additional statutes that expanded the PHS's role in coordinating the nation's public health work, enacted by Congress during the decade and a half after the passage of the Social Security Act. These included the La Follette–Bulwinkle Act of 1938, which provided federal grants to states for venereal disease control programs; the Public Health Service Act of 1944, which codified and strengthened the role of the PHS; and the Hill–Burton Act of 1946, which funded federal hospital construction in underserved regions.[49] Together, these laws solidified the federal government's commitment to supporting state and local health authorities and facilitated two decades of rapid expansion for the PHS, which saw its annual budget increase nearly twentyfold between 1934 and 1950.[50]

Federal public health agencies subsequently ballooned. Emerging in 1946 from a wartime government program focused on eradicating malaria in the South, the Communicable Disease Center (CDC) quickly enhanced the federal government's role coordinating efforts to prevent the spread of contagion. In the two decades after its founding, the CDC's activities expanded beyond its initial focus on tropical diseases into areas as diverse as smallpox eradication, disease surveillance, and family planning.[51] After a brief period of inadequate funding, the agency enjoyed significant political support and resources: its budget increased at a rate of about 16 percent per year between 1953 and 1969.[52] The emergence and rapid growth of the CDC deepened the institutional and regulatory reach of the central government over state and local health departments. Already in 1950, two of the nation's largest federated public health organizations—the American Public Health Association and the Association of State and Territorial Health

Officials—acknowledged that the CDC was the nation's premier government agency for determining which communicable diseases to prioritize.[53] As the CDC expanded, it carved out a central space for itself in the nation's public health infrastructure, coordinating the responses of state and local officials to over fifty disease outbreaks in 1959 alone.[54]

However, one must be careful not to overstate the degree of change ushered in by the New Deal and subsequent developments. Federal health officials continued to face serious constraints on their authority and capacity. Traditional containment and control strategies—such as quarantine and isolation—remained largely under the legal purview of the states.[55] Meanwhile, the nation's public health infrastructure still consisted of a patchwork quilt of institutions, agencies, regulations, and laws, distributed across over sixteen hundred separate governmental units.[56] The enduring impact of federalism on Americans' health once again became clearest when confronted with large-scale disease outbreaks.

In 1957, a new pandemic strain of influenza circled the globe, arriving on US shores in the spring. Although it lacked the lethality of the Spanish flu, seldom causing pneumonia or acute respiratory distress, it still claimed an estimated two million lives worldwide. Despite important lessons learned since 1918, the 1957 flu again prompted chaotic and uncoordinated responses from the US government. The CDC did take on an authoritative role when the pandemic reached its crescendo in the fall of that year, expanding its surveillance infrastructure and coordinating the containment efforts of state and local health experts.[57] But because this particular strain was relatively mild, agency officials did not encourage the kind of strict social-distancing measures that state and local governments had used against the 1918 flu, pinning most of their hopes instead on the rapid distribution of a vaccine. Eisenhower, however, rebuffed repeated calls for a national vaccination program, insisting that the pharmaceutical industry would do enough to immunize Americans against the disease. In a memo written on October 3, 1957, a White House official noted that "vaccine manufacturers have agreed to voluntary distribution among States according to population. . . . This voluntary type of distribution system cannot be expected to be uniformly effective, but more stringent controls are not recommended at this time."[58] This near-exclusive reliance on the private sector and free enterprise hampered efforts to contain the disease. Without government coordination, the vaccine rollout was painstakingly slow, and pharmaceutical corporations manufactured most of the doses only after the pandemic had already receded.[59] Influenza continued to sweep through America unchecked by medicine or policy until the winter of 1958.

In the mid-twentieth century, polio was more of a public health priority than influenza, and its history illustrates the delicate balance of power between the states and the federal government, even during the New Deal and Cold War eras. A terrifying viral infection that frequently caused paralysis in children, polio had left an indelible imprint on American society and culture from the moment that the first cases hit Vermont in 1894. The fear and uncertainty surrounding the disease extended past World War II, when outbreaks erupted summer after summer across the United States, even as other infectious diseases receded from view due to antibiotics, immunization, and improved living standards.[60] When Dr. Jonas Salk of the University of Pittsburgh developed the first working polio vaccine in the early 1950s, parents quickly lined up to have their children immunized.[61] In 1955, just after this scientific breakthrough, Congress enacted the Poliomyelitis Vaccination Assistance Act, which created the first national immunization program. This statute allotted over $30 million for the distribution of the Salk vaccine, but each state retained the authority to determine who would receive these shots.[62] The AMA, the Eisenhower administration, and Republican members of Congress all balked at a more ambitious proposal for universal childhood vaccination, fearing, in the words, of Senator Barry Goldwater, that it was "a backdoor approach to socialized medicine."[63] The Eisenhower administration sidelined proposals for a more centralized approach to the production and distribution of the Salk vaccine, and instead left these responsibilities to the states and pharmaceutical corporations.[64]

Eisenhower's successor took a different tack. In February 1962, President John F. Kennedy announced his intention to vaccinate all American children against polio, with the help of "a nationwide vaccination program to stamp out" the disease.[65] A few months later, after some wrangling over details, Congress passed the Vaccination Assistance Act, which gave states grants to immunize their citizens against diphtheria, pertussis, tetanus, and polio.[66] The goal of this legislation, Health, Education, and Welfare Secretary Abraham Ribicoff explained, was to "provide federal leadership in assuring that [vaccines] will be so utilized as to achieve the maximum benefits and protection to the public."[67] The 1962 act moved away from simply providing federal dollars for vaccines: it expanded the CDC's role in coordinating state and local immunization efforts, it precipitated the broadscale distribution of federal educational material on childhood vaccination, and it provided nonnational health departments with technical personnel.[68] In its early years, the legislation had an impressive track record, contributing to a sharp decline in polio rates across the country.[69] By the tail end of the 1960s, the CDC was coordinating over one hundred separate state and local immunization projects that covered 90 percent of the US population.[70]

From the earliest phases of the New Deal to the late 1960s, American public health entered a new era, with three defining characteristics: a flow of federal dollars to nonnational health departments through an array of new laws and grant-in-aid programs, most notably Title VI of the Social Security Act; increased regulatory oversight of public health work by the CDC; and unprecedented levels of cooperation and collaboration between health officials across all levels of government. Yet even as the federal government assumed more decision-making power, the day-to-day work of responding to epidemics still often took place at the state and local levels. National and subnational state-building efforts were mutually constitutive: the growth of federal administrative capacity went hand in hand with the consolidation of state and local health departments. The federal government turned again and again to the private sector for assistance with its public health work, which often meant, as before, fragmented and disjointed approaches to diseases such as influenza and polio.

The Great Society, the Rights Revolution, and Reagan's New Federalism

The political ferment of the 1960s triggered a massive shift in power from the states to the central government. During the Great Society era, the Lyndon B. Johnson administration enacted legislation that expanded the responsibilities of the central government in policy areas traditionally reserved for the states—most notably, education, civil rights, and criminal justice. Simultaneously, federal policymakers attached new strings to the funds they distributed to subnational authorities, forcing the states to comply with Washington-generated directives and policies.[71] In the arena of health care policy, Johnson shepherded a raft of major legislation through Congress that expanded the role of the central government. New policy and legislative initiatives, often premised on a link between illness and low socioeconomic status, poured resources and expertise into medical care for disadvantaged communities. In the 1960s, Congress passed over fifty statutes related to health, including the landmark Medicare and Medicaid programs of 1965, two of the most significant pieces of healthcare legislation in American history.[72]

Even though medical care was at the forefront of the Johnson administration's legislative agenda, the Great Society did not undermine the leading role of the states in the sphere of public health. The social policy innovations of the 1960s raised fundamental questions about the position of preventative medicine in the nation's healthcare system. From the early twentieth century onward, the ever-shifting institutional, political, and professional boundaries between public health and medicine had shaped American health policy. Public health practitioners, concerned with the health of populations rather than individual medicine, remained institutionally and politically weaker than the medical profession. By the middle decades of the twentieth century, physicians delivered most individual medical care, severely limiting the direct-care responsibilities of public health professionals, who focused most of their energies on preventative activities.[73] The Great Society and War on Poverty sharpened the conceptual boundaries between medicine and public health. If Medicare and Medicaid were genuine policy breakthroughs that minimized the burden of medical costs for tens of millions of poor and elderly Americans, they also had some unforeseen consequences for the institutional strength of the public health profession. Both programs favored intensive hospital-based care over preventative medicine, entrenching the fee-for-service insurance model and sowing doubt that a universal healthcare system would ever be feasible.[74] In the 1960s and 1970s, federal spending on healthcare increased astronomically, and the budgetary imprint of Medicare and Medicaid ushered in a period of runaway medical inflation. During the same period, however, expenditure on public health remained comparatively small (see figure 1.1).

The healthcare reforms of the Great Society coincided with dramatic changes in the judicial branch of government. Starting in the 1960s, the US Supreme Court sharply curtailed the power of the states in areas of governance as diverse as education, voting rights, and criminal justice. In doing so, it enshrined constitutionally protected individual rights—such as equal protection, due process, and freedom of travel—that superseded the doctrine of police power.[75] Public health law, as it developed in the 1960s and 1970s, aligned with this legal transformation. A raft of court decisions at every jurisdictional level found that medical patients were entitled to equal protection and due process guarantees, including the right to a fair hearing

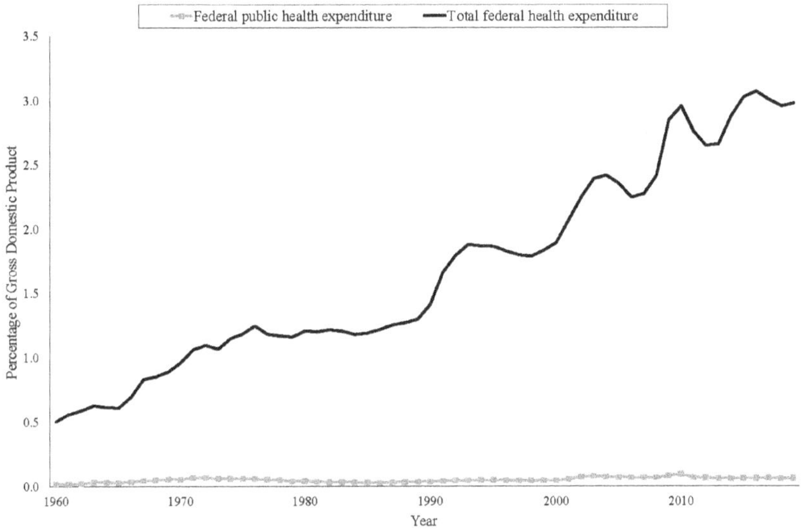

Figure 1.1: A comparison of federal public health expenditure with total federal health expenditure, 1960–2019. Public health expenditure measures government spending to organize and deliver public health services, such as epidemiological surveillance, vaccination and immunization services, disease prevention programs, and the operation of health departments and public health laboratories. Source: Centers for Medicare and Medicaid Services (CMS), National Health Expenditure Data, accessed April l, 2021, https://www.cms.hhs.gov/NationalHealthExpendData.

and to adequate notice.[76] Typical was a decision handed down by the West Virginia Supreme Court in 1980 that struck down a tuberculosis quarantine statute because it did not provide adequate due process protections.[77] While cases like this one imposed new constitutional constraints on public health authorities, they did not undermine the leading role of the states in controlling the spread of epidemic disease. Even as the rights revolution dislodged expansive notions of police power, states and localities continued to be the chief sources of quarantines, isolation orders, and other disease control measures.[78]

Indeed, the conservative political revolution of the 1980s served to reaffirm the centrality of the states in the sphere of public health. In 1981, President Ronald Reagan sailed into office espousing the conviction that the government had become too large, expensive, and obtrusive. Over the next eight years, he pushed legislation through Congress that slashed federal taxes, rolled back the regulatory power of the central government, and dismantled key components of the New Deal state.[79] However, discrepancies between rhetoric and action were a hallmark of the Reagan administration, and there was often tension between the president's call for limited government and policies that expanded the size of the central state. As he cut taxes, Reagan beefed up spending on national defense and the military-industrial complex, saddling the federal government with huge deficits that tripled over the course of his tenure.[80]

Yet in the realm of public health policy, there was less of a disconnect between the rhetoric of limited government and reality. Reagan and his advisors sought legislative and policy changes to strengthen the states' decision-making powers—a "New Federalism" to recalibrate the balance of power between the federal government and nonnational governments.[81] After six months of heated rhetoric on both sides of the aisle, Congress passed the president's showpiece enacting this philosophy, the Omnibus Budget Reconciliation Act of 1981.[82] This legislation not only cut grant-in-aid programs for state and local governments but also transformed a wide array of categorical grants (that is, grants that Congress had earmarked for specific programs) into smaller block grants over which states had more discretion. In addition, it slashed the overall appropriation for federal public health programs by 30 percent, overturned many New Deal and Great Society health regulations, and eviscerated federal support for municipal health departments.[83] Under Reagan's watch, the CDC faced sustained cutbacks, and federal expenditure on public health declined as a percentage of GDP by nearly half.[84] With federal health agencies under fire, the states began to outspend the national government three to one on public health in the 1980s and 1990s (see figure 1.2). By the start of the AIDS epidemic, then, most of the burden for stemming the spread of infectious diseases continued to fall primarily on the states and their municipalities.

* * *

The historical themes chronicled in this chapter lay the groundwork for understanding why the states were at the vanguard of the policy response to the AIDS epidemic. For centuries, states and localities remained at the leading edge of pandemic preparedness, despite the federal government's assertion of a more significant role in other aspects of American life from the 1930s onward. Each outbreak was unique, but the political ramifications

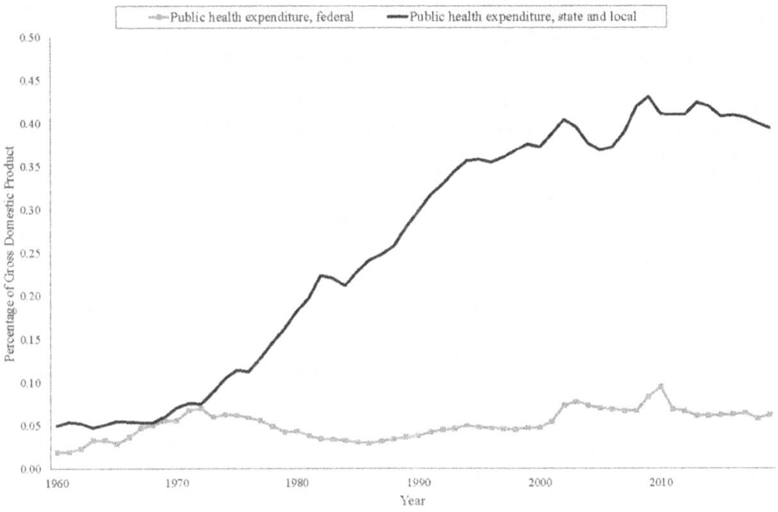

Figure 1.2: A comparison of federal public health expenditure with state and local public health expenditure, 1960–2019. Public health expenditure measures government spending to organize and deliver public health services, such as epidemiological surveillance, vaccination and immunization services, disease prevention programs, and the operation of health departments and public health laboratories. Source: Centers for Medicare and Medicaid Services (CMS), National Health Expenditure Data, accessed April l, 2021, https://www.cms.hhs.gov/NationalHealthExpendData.

were often similar because of structural factors deeply embedded in the history of US state development. Whether facing yellow fever, smallpox, or Influenza, subnational authorities assumed most of the responsibility for protecting citizens from public health threats. Wielding their police powers, states implemented sweeping measures when confronted with the spread of contagion, such as bans on public gatherings, quarantine and isolation orders, and vaccine mandates. In the 1960s and 1970s, the courts carved out a sphere of constitutionally protected individual rights that health officials could not touch. But states and localities still outspent the federal government on pandemic preparedness and retained substantial public health powers, including the authority to impose far-reaching disease control measures.

Given this history, it is unsurprising that the states played a crucial role during the early years of the AIDS crisis. The remainder of this book examines how the themes explored in this chapter—especially state and local control, intergovernmental conflict, and American federalism—shaped the policy response to the epidemic. With the Reagan administration disavowing itself of any responsibility for fighting HIV/AIDS, state governments necessarily took center stage during the first decade of the crisis, passing hundreds of laws to address the disease's spread. States such as California, Illinois, and Texas adopted widely divergent approaches to combatting the epidemic, leading to an uncoordinated, inconsistent, and chaotic response to a national health crisis. As the outbreak entered its second decade, the central government began to take more responsibility for coordinating the nation's response to AIDS. Passed in 1990, the CARE Act bucked prevailing trends in pandemic preparedness by dramatically expanding federal involvement in the fight against the disease. Yet, the states retained a great deal of influence over AIDS policymaking, as the law devolved most decisions over policy design and implementation to the subnational level. As with every other major disease outbreak in American history, state governments were major players during the initial years of the AIDS epidemic, revealing the continued importance of the much neglected "middle tier" of American governance in the late twentieth century.

CHAPTER TWO

Clandestine Networks and Closeted Bureaucrats

AIDS and the Forming of a Gay Policy Network in California

In the spring of 1981, exhausted after spending several years participating in the San Francisco gay rights movement, Stan Hadden headed for Sacramento, intent on pursuing a career as an IT consultant. A few months later, Hadden secured his first lucrative contract when David Roberti, the president of the California Senate, hired him to install a new computer system. As he worked on this contract, Hadden learned that a new and deadly disease—acquired immunodeficiency syndrome (AIDS)—was moving through San Francisco's urban gay community.[1] Horrified by reports of his old friends succumbing to this terrible illness, Hadden swiftly brought the epidemic to Roberti's attention, imploring him to introduce legislation to curb its spread. Much to Hadden's surprise, Roberti responded by offering to recruit him as a full-time legislative assistant specializing in AIDS. After a few weeks of deliberation, Hadden accepted Roberti's offer, abandoning his plans to pursue a career in IT.[2] Embracing this serendipitous opportunity, he quickly emerged as a policy expert and would craft some of California's most important AIDS-related bills. Hadden's star continued to rise throughout the mid- to late 1980s, and he soon achieved notable prominence for a legislative staffer, with the Sacramento press lionizing him as an "AIDS Tsar."[3]

By excavating the career arcs of individuals such as Hadden, this chapter traces the history of a nascent gay policy network that emerged in California at the height of the AIDS crisis. It spotlights a small but prominent group of gay men and lesbians who—like Hadden in the previous vignette—moved to Sacramento early in the epidemic, determined to build careers as legislative staffers. Personal experiences of the AIDS epidemic sharpened their sense of urgency as they lobbied state legislators for a more robust response to the crisis. Hoping to solidify their relationship with the gay movement, Democratic and Republican lawmakers alike turned to these gay activists for their personal connections and expertise, hiring them as office assistants, policy consultants, and community liaisons. Backed by a bipartisan group of politicians—including the Speaker of the assembly and the president of the Senate—gay appointees gained unprecedented influence in Sacramento during the 1980s, propelling California toward the most far-reaching government response to AIDS in the United States.[4] Legislative debates over antibody testing, biomedical research, and prevention education provided a rich opportunity for gay activists to assert their political clout, forge alliances with powerful lawmakers, and gain a seat at the policymaking table. As table 2.1 illustrates, California spent more than any other state on AIDS during the mid-1980s, including New York, the epicenter of the disease.[5] In fiscal year 1986, only Massachusetts appropriated more funds per AIDS case than California.[6] Through the 1980s, California acted as a crucible for the enactment of experimental policies, such as early intervention programs, home care services for people with AIDS (PWAs), and funding for an AIDS vaccine.[7] It is against this baseline picture that this chapter details the growing political clout of gay policymakers in Sacramento during the 1980s.

The considerable influence wielded by Hadden and his colleagues pushed California toward the country's most proactive policy response to the AIDS epidemic in the mid-1980s. An array of HIV-specific laws, all drafted by gay policymakers, solidified the state's leading role in the fight against the disease. In 1985 alone, gay policymakers wrote legislation that expanded the state's prevention education programs, restricted the insurance industry's access to blood tests, and established the country's most robust anonymous testing regime. These efforts, in turn, set off an avalanche of attacks from conservative Republicans, who favored more traditional public health strategies like quarantine and isolation. Conservative Republicans denounced California's liberal approach to the epidemic, arguing that it privileged the civil liberties of PWAs at the expense of the wider population. They couched their support for coercive AIDS measures—like quarantine and mandatory testing—in the language of public health, arguing that the disease was receiving special treatment from the legislature because of the gay movement's growing political clout. In the late 1980s, conservative lawmakers introduced a string of punitive AIDS-related bills, framing each as a "common sense" public health measure. Ultimately, though, gay

Table 2.1: State-only expenditure on AIDS in fiscal year 1986, ranked by spending per AIDS case.

State	*Spending on AIDS ($)*	*Cumulative AIDS Caseload*	*Spending per Case ($)*
Massachusetts	1,603,667	997	1608
California	16,020,000	10,544	1519
Minnesota	397,000	266	1492
Illinois	500,000	365	1370
New Hampshire	55,000	49	1122
Michigan	325,000	462	703
New Jersey	1,969,000	2,877	684
Maryland	450,000	830	542
Alabama	103,605	202	513
New York	4,500,000	12,429	362
Washington	225,000	654	344
Arizona	91,500	325	282
Missouri	83,950	361	233
Virginia	100,000	554	181
Florida	576,000	3,421	168
Oregon	40,955	266	154
North Carolina	40,000	327	122
Georgia	82,297	1,015	81
Hawaii	9,000	175	51
Texas	72,000	3,245	22
Iowa	1,000	61	16

Note: The remaining twenty-nine states are excluded because they had yet to appropriate any funding for AIDS. Figures exclude Medicaid-related expenditure.
Sources: M. J. Rowe and C. C. Ryan, "Comparing State-Only Expenditures for AIDS," *American Journal of Public Health* 78, no. 4 (April 1988): 424–429; United States AIDS Program, "United States Cases Reported to CDC," AIDS Surveillance Report, December 29, 1986, 2.

policymakers successfully defeated most of these repressive AIDS measures, partly because they secured the cooperation of moderate Democrats and Republicans. To forge a bipartisan coalition, they established the country's first statewide AIDS lobbying group, the Lobby for Individual Freedom and Equality (LIFE). Founded amid a flurry of legislative activity on AIDS, LIFE quickly emerged as an influential voice in Sacramento, winning the support of lawmakers from across the political spectrum. Under the leadership of Rand Martin, a veteran gay rights lobbyist, LIFE blocked the passage of several coercive AIDS measures, including proposals to quarantine PWAs.

Despite these initial successes, gay policymakers struggled to enact new legislation in the late 1980s. They increasingly faced opposition from Governor George Deukmejian, a strict fiscal conservative, who insisted on balanced budgets, tight spending controls, and a prudent state reserve. As the decade wore on, fiscal constraints severely limited the scope of AIDS policymaking, as California entered a period of intense budgetary pressures. At the same time, Hadden and his colleagues failed to prevent the passage of several HIV-specific criminal bills in the late 1980s. These laws, often enacted with bipartisan support, disproportionately targeted sex workers, IV drug users, and communities of color. Television and newspaper reports of "recalcitrant" AIDS carriers fueled a punitive turn in disease control, which funneled resources away from AIDS healthcare and toward the carceral state. Cognizant of the political capital yielded by "law and order" proponents, gay policymakers remained largely indifferent to the growing calls for HIV criminalization.

Finally, the history of AIDS policymaking in California casts new light on the contradictory role of the "closet" in the modern gay rights movement. While gay policymakers could rely on powerful advocates in the California legislature, the state bureaucracy often lacked the dedication needed to implement key pieces of AIDS legislation. Again and again, state health officials declined to collaborate with gay legislative assistants and dragged their feet over the distribution of funding for new AIDS programs. To push back against this recalcitrance, gay policymakers built a clandestine network of "closeted" bureaucrats, using it to ferret out homophobic-fueled obstructionism in the state civil service. In a somewhat paradoxical fashion, they privately used the closet as a tool to undermine homophobic parts of the state bureaucracy but publicly asserted that "coming out" was critical to increasing the gay movement's political clout. While institutional homophobia forced many state employees to hide their identities in the workplace, the closet provided gay legislative assistants with a weapon to fight the civil service's obstructionism. This chapter thus highlights not only the intergovernmental dynamics that shaped the initial response to AIDS but also the strategies used by gay activists to gain influence at the state level.

Gay Policymaking in Sacramento

The 1970s saw gay rights activists make their first significant inroads into state politics in California. In December 1974, George Raya, Sacramento's first full-time LGBT lobbyist, successfully pressured the legislature to repeal the state sodomy statute.[8] Four years later, activists confronted Proposition 6, the nation's first statewide referendum on gay rights, which would have banned openly gay individuals from teaching in public schools. After a bitter and fierce campaign, and after intense mobilization among gay men and lesbians, California voters overwhelmingly rejected the initiative, by a margin of nearly two to one.[9] As gay men and lesbians slowly emerged as a legitimate constituency in statewide politics, they blazed ahead with campaigns to broaden legal protections for sexual minorities, including a decades-long push to add sexual orientation to the state's antidiscrimination laws. This effort, however, failed in the 1970s, and activists were often more effective at defeating anti-gay legislation than securing new civil rights.[10]

The AIDS epidemic further spurred the movement of gay activists into statewide politics. As early as 1983, Steve Morin, a gay psychologist based in San Francisco, worked with state representative Willie Brown to secure the first state funding for AIDS. Later reflecting on the episode, Morin recalled that

> on one of my early trips to the state capital . . . I was joined by Gary Walsh, a friend and psychiatric social worker who had been diagnosed with [Kaposi's sarcoma] in December 1982. We discovered in Sacramento that the legislature knew very little about AIDS. . . . Gary would often engage the legislators, look them straight in the eye, roll up his shirtsleeve, and show a KS lesion. It was very difficult to ignore him.[11]

The legislature's response to this sustained lobbying effort was threefold: first, it appropriated nearly $3 million for AIDS research; second, it directed the state Health Department to dedicate more resources to fighting the epidemic; and finally, it established the California AIDS Advisory Committee to provide lawmakers with technical advice on the disease.[12]

As the AIDS crisis unfolded, an influential group of state lawmakers played a pivotal role in formulating a proactive policy response, often relying on their preexisting ties with the gay movement and a coterie of newly employed gay legislative staffers. Having established a close relationship with his gay constituents in the 1970s, Roberti, whose senate seat encompassed the gay urban enclave of West Hollywood, hired Hadden in 1982 to signal his commitment to tackling the disease.[13] Motivated in part by his desire to increase the gay movement's influence in Sacramento, Hadden emerged as a pivotal figure in California's response to the AIDS crisis. He was affable, forthright, and pragmatic, burnishing a well-deserved reputation as the AIDS Tsar of California.[14] By 1987, his monthly AIDS newsletter had twenty-five thousand subscribers, and his correspondence reached beyond California to activists in Texas, Illinois, and New York.[15] Exercising a significant degree of autonomy, Hadden crafted a large portion of California's early AIDS legislation, including Senate Bill 1251 (SB 1215), a 1985 act that expanded the state budget for prevention education by $11 million.[16] Passed by an overwhelming bipartisan majority in both the Assembly and Senate, SB 1215 cemented the state's leading role in the fight against AIDS: in fiscal year 1985, California accounted for nearly 50 percent of total state spending on the epidemic.[17]

Other state lawmakers also responded to the epidemic by hiring gay legislative assistants. In 1984, state representative Art Agnos, a longtime ally of the San Francisco gay community, hired Larry Bush, a nationally renowned gay journalist, as a speechwriter and political aide. As Washington, DC, correspondent for the *Advocate* in the late 1970s, Bush was the first openly gay reporter to obtain press accreditation from the White House.[18] In 1985, he cowrote Assembly Bill 403 (AB 403), a landmark measure that provided confidentiality protections for those undertaking the AIDS antibody test. The first bill of its kind, it became the model for similar legislation in Florida, Massachusetts, New York, and Wisconsin.[19]

While Democrats stood at the forefront of these efforts to hire gay legislative assistants, the emergence of California's gay policy network transcended the left-right binary of electoral politics. Although the 1980s witnessed the meteoric rise of the Religious Right and the growing strength of "pro-family" conservatives within the GOP, self-defined moderate Republicans remained open to working with gay men and lesbians. One Republican willing to collaborate with gay men and lesbians was Governor George Deukmejian. Renowned for his low-key style, Deukmejian's brand of politics emphasized management and procedure over ideology and specific policy goals.[20] His governorship, from 1982 to 1990, witnessed an unprecedented expansion of California's penal system, along with cutbacks to welfare, education, and Medicaid.[21] He was a staunch supporter of the state's nascent anti-tax movement, a prominent advocate of "law and order" politics, and an unabashed fiscal conservative.[22] Upon entering office in 1982, Deukmejian promised to pinch government spending, reduce crime, and stave off tax increases.[23] One reporter writing in August 1983 explained that "as governor, Reagan promised 'to cut, squeeze, and trim.' But he was never as successful in two terms as Deukmejian has been in half a year of a first term."[24] Deukmejian signaled, at least rhetorically, a commitment to addressing the AIDS epidemic, but discrepancies between rhetoric and action were a hallmark of his handling of the crisis.

Gay Republicans scored a surprising victory in 1983, when Deukmejian appointed Bruce Decker, an openly gay political consultant, to chair the California AIDS Advisory Committee. Coming from a renowned and respected Republican family, Decker was a natural fit for Deukmejian's brand of conservatism and had assisted the governor during his 1982 election campaign.[25] Hoping to turn the GOP into a viable front in the battle for gay rights, Decker established Concerned Americans for Individual Rights in 1984, a political organization formed of "moderate to conservative Gays and Lesbians" uneasy with the impact of "the Religious Right . . . on the Reagan Administration and the Republican Party."[26] At the group's inaugural meeting, he declared that "Gays and Lesbians are direct beneficiaries of the Reagan Administration. . . . Only under a limited and frugal government, a market economy, and a social structure based on free and voluntary association can we as Gay and Lesbian Americans fully be ourselves and realize our potential."[27] The values and objectives of Reaganite conservatism resonated with Decker, who championed fiscally conservative AIDS policies like tax credits for corporate funding of biomedical research.[28]

During his tenure as chair of the AIDS Advisory Committee, Decker emerged as one of the most controversial and prominent figures in California's gay policy network. He embodied many of the contradictions exhibited by gay republicans in the 1980s: he championed the Reagan administration but railed against the profamily politics of the Christian Right; he celebrated the diversity of gay experiences but criticized the left-leaning politics of many grassroots activists; and he aggressively supported measures that bolstered the individual rights of PWAs but balked at any hint of aggressive state intervention.[29] Decker's frequent overtures to conservative Republicans—including individuals who actively opposed the expansion of civil liberties for PWAs—invited widespread criticism from gay activists.

He made headlines in the California gay press in 1985 when he defended the Reagan administration's record on AIDS. Speaking to a gathering of activists in San Diego, he proclaimed that they "should be very proud of the federal government's role on AIDS. I know everyone in this room has been conditioned to believe otherwise."[30] Prompting audible gasps from the audience, Decker also questioned why the state should give direct aid to people with HIV infection: "There are going to be certain parts of the funding that are not going to be supplied by government. Why do we look to government to fund everything?"[31] With these words, Decker pithily summarized his belief that the principles of limited government and fiscal restraint should guide the state's response to AIDS.

While Decker quickly became a polarizing figure within activist circles, he still cultivated a close relationship with Bush and Hadden, working with them to end homophobic bias in the state bureaucracy, to amplify the gay movement's voice in statewide politics, and to strengthen the legislature's response to AIDS. Despite their very different partisan allegiances, all three quickly built alliances with one another. At the middle of this policy network stood Hadden, who organized regular bipartisan meetings between Sacramento's gay legislative assistants.[32] Throughout the 1980s, memos zipped between Decker's and Hadden's offices, as they collaborated on the issues of AIDS testing, HIV discrimination, and prevention education.[33] While they differed sharply over policy specifics and frequently clashed over the state AIDS budget, they shared a commitment to policies grounded in privacy, individual rights, and voluntary behavior change.[34] Above all, they were political pragmatists, willing to negotiate with politicians from across the ideological spectrum to enact their preferred policies.

The California Bureaucracy and the Complexity of the "Closet"

Even as the AIDS crisis ravaged California's urban queer communities, the civil service's institutional homophobia remained a critical roadblock to a more expansive response to the disease. State officials prevaricated on important legislative mandates, actively discriminated against gay employees, and opposed calls for a coordinated response to the epidemic.[35] To overcome this institutional homophobia, gay policymakers coordinated a loose network of closeted bureaucrats, regularly meeting with them to gather information on the internal workings of the bureaucracy. They reserved special ire for the California Department of Health, accusing it of botching the state's early response to the epidemic. By the mid-1980s, Hadden had successfully used this information to ferret out homophobia in several state agencies, even as his tactics remained clandestine and illicit.

In the years immediately before the advent of AIDS, gay activists fought to end institutional homophobia in the California bureaucracy. They scored a notable victory in April 1979, when Governor Jerry Brown issued Executive Order B-54–79, which declared that "the agencies, departments, boards, and commissions within the Executive Branch of state government under jurisdiction of the Governor shall not discriminate in state employment against any individual based solely upon the individual's sexual preference."[36] The responsibility for implementing the order fell on the State Personnel Board—the agency charged with handling most discrimination complaints against the civil service. On April 30, 1980—over a year after Brown issued the order—the Personnel Board hired Leroy Walker, an attorney based in Los Angeles, to liaise with local gay activists, root out homophobia in the bureaucracy's recruitment process, and educate the state civil service about the specific needs of gay employees.[37] With such a wide range of responsibilities, however, Walker quickly suffered from burnout, leaving his position after little more than a year.[38] At this point, the civil service lacked the dedication needed to implement the order, neglecting to hire a replacement for Walker because of cuts to the fiscal 1982 budget.[39] With a growing sense of desperation, a group of gay bureaucrats established Advocates for Gay and Lesbian State Employees (AGLSE), a statewide organization that sought to reform the bureaucracy's hiring practices.[40] From the outset, it struggled against an avalanche of bureaucratic inertia, failing to persuade the State Personnel Board to implement a training program on sexual-orientation-based discrimination. In an April 1982 letter, the group excoriated the agency's record, glumly observing that

> very few managers below the Central Office or Personnel levels have even heard of the executive order. A still smaller percentage of line workers in state service have heard of it. . . . In short, management does not know its responsibilities and rank and file employees do not know their rights, or how to seek redress when those rights are denied them. Under these circumstances, Executive Order B-54–79 is virtually ineffective. . . . Under the circumstances, the gay and lesbian community must question the commitment of this administration to the protection

> of gay and lesbian employees. Is state government willing to provide effective employment protections for lesbian and gay state employees, or will it merely give lip service to this issue?[41]

A subsequent letter, written in July 1982, labelled Brown's executive order a "useless formality."[42] Bearing out this conclusion, statistics collected by the State Personnel Board indicated that gay and lesbian state employees made only two discrimination-related claims between 1979 and 1984.[43]

Antagonism between gay policy elites and the state bureaucracy only escalated during the early years of the AIDS epidemic. Brown's executive order was utterly ineffective at preventing anti-gay discrimination, and instances of institutionalized homophobia persisted, as officials within the bureaucracy widely ignored discrimination complaints made by gay employees.[44] In the early 1980s, gay bureaucrats penned scores of letters to Hadden, complaining of the bureaucracy's institutional homophobia. Some letter writers protested that the state was slow to release funds to AIDS service organizations and actively discriminated against gay-run groups; others wondered why state officials declined to coordinate their efforts across different agencies.[45] Examples of obstructionism proliferated in the early 1980s. In one particularly egregious incident, officials withdrew funding from an AIDS prevention education film only after learning that a gay production company had developed it.[46]

While numerous state agencies had little appetite for working with Hadden and his colleagues, the Health Department's initial response to AIDS was perhaps the clearest manifestation of this institutional homophobia. The coterie of public health officials, bureaucrats, and medical professionals who guided the department's initial response to AIDS often lacked any previous interaction with the organized gay movement.[47] Well into the mid-1980s, state health officials only met with gay policymakers in secret and outside of normal business hours, even during important discussions over pending legislation.[48] Programs conducted through the Health Department suffered from delays, limited funding, and poor administrative oversight, prompting Hadden to note that "the department's decision-making process, lack of direction and lack of leadership make it more difficult for them to provide services."[49] Perhaps most importantly, through 1983 and 1984, several AIDS-related bills failed precisely because of opposition from the Health Department. In the spring of 1984, health officials actively fought for a reduction in funding for prevention education. Agnos and Roberti successfully staved off their efforts, but only after tense negotiations with the Deukmejian administration.[50] That same year, Senate Bill 2244, which would have mandated a coordinated response to AIDS, languished in committee after it faced opposition from state health officials.[51]

Spurred by the health department's recalcitrance, Bush and Hadden began holding secret meetings with a group of closeted state employees, who provided them with confidential information about the bureaucracy's response to AIDS.[52] By the mid-1980s, a core of twelve closeted bureaucrats regularly attended these gatherings; most were motivated by their personal experiences of the AIDS epidemic, including close ties and friendships with PWAs.[53] From 1983 to 1985, they regularly leaked information to Bush and Hadden about the bureaucracy's internal workings and stances on important AIDS legislation.[54] As Kenneth Topper, Hadden's partner and office assistant, recalled years later, "We had people planted in various state organizations, agencies, that would be in position to overhear conversations to know what they were going to try to change, or try to block, and we were able to get around them."[55] Armed with information gathered from this clandestine network, Hadden flooded the Health Department with letters of complaint, demanding greater public scrutiny over the allocation of AIDS funding. Tellingly, his correspondence reveals an intimate knowledge of the agency's internal policies and practices.[56]

Through these behind-the-scenes-machinations, Hadden eventually saw an opening to challenge the Health Department's entrenched obstructionism, filing a formal complaint with the State Personnel Board in the autumn of 1984.[57] At a subsequent hearing in Sacramento, he and his colleagues unleashed a slew of complaints against the Health Department, calling attention to its dismal record on the epidemic.[58] Though the exact details of this hearing are muddy, Topper took the agency to task for his experience of applying for a job there, pointing to discriminatory remarks made by officials during his interview. He also cited multiple anonymous examples of workplace discrimination against his closeted colleagues.[59] In its final verdict, the State Personnel Board decided in Hadden's favor and appointed an oversight committee to reform the Health Department's hiring practices. Working for two years, the committee, which included Hadden, pressed the agency to employ medical professionals over career civil servants and engage with gay men and lesbians.[60] Paradoxically, then, the

Health Department's failure to establish a constructive relationship with Hadden led to greater scrutiny of its hiring practices, exposing the agency's homophobic record.

Through the mid-1980s and after, the Department of Health continued to rack up a mixed record. Hoping to deflect any further internal scrutiny, the agency updated its hiring practices, made some meaningful overtures to gay activists, and appointed Hadden to a number of its advisory committees.[61] Less positively, state contracts administered through the Health Department continued to suffer from unnecessary delay, threatening the financial viability of many AIDS service organizations.[62] Still, Hadden and his colleagues had forged a constructive relationship with the Health Department, successfully rooting out most of its institutional homophobia. By the dawn of the 1990s, according to one gay bureaucrat, "more and more staff members are coming out to their bosses and each other."[63]

Hadden's reliance on closeted bureaucrats sheds light on the ambivalent and contradictory role of the closet within the modern gay rights movement. In the late 1960s and early 1970s, gay liberationists had proclaimed that coming out was an important marker of gay political strength; they popularized the notion that disclosing one's homosexuality was an essential element of gay politics and identity.[64] At the same time, gay rights organizations advanced a strategy that emphasized public visibility, an approach summarized by the popular mantra "Out of the Closets, Into the Streets."[65] As the AIDS crisis came into clearer focus, it inspired renewed calls for gay people to "come out of the closet," as activists sought to counterbalance the mobilization of anti-gay forces within the Christian Right. In the autumn of 1988, the National Gay Rights Advocates, a gay rights law firm, organized the first National Coming Out Day (NCOD), an event designed to illuminate the gay movement's growing political clout. Hadden played a major role in organizing NCOD during the late 1980s, coordinating efforts in Sacramento and San Francisco. In one letter promoting the event, he proclaimed that "NCOD promotes gay and lesbian visibility and urges people to 'take the next step.' . . . NCOD is a call to action, a campaign about truth, power, and liberation."[66]

Despite publicly asserting that coming out was an essential part of gay identity, Hadden depended on closeted state officials to ferret out homophobia in the California bureaucracy. Paradoxically, he wielded the closet as a weapon against the very employment practices that prevented his colleagues from publicly disclosing their homosexuality. For their part, these bureaucrats believed that concealing their identities, rather than coming out, would provide them with better opportunities to undermine government obstructionism. It is important to stress that the weaponization of the closet extended well beyond California. In Illinois, Tim Drake, the cochair of the Illinois Gay and Lesbian Task Force, formed a similar, if less well developed, network of openly gay and closeted state officials. One individual, who worked for the Illinois House of Representatives, regularly tipped Drake off whenever a lawmaker filed a repressive AIDS bill.[67] The closet, then, afforded gay policymakers with opportunities to subvert and undermine state repression, serving as an effective weapon against bureaucratic inertia and draconian AIDS measures.[68]

Antibody Testing and the California Legislature

With powerful advocates in the California Assembly and Senate, gay policymakers secured a string of impressive policy victories in the mid-1980s. Because of their preexisting ties with the gay rights movement, lawmakers from San Francisco and Los Angeles proved far more willing than state bureaucrats to work with Hadden and his colleagues. The two most powerful California state legislators—the Speaker of the Assembly and the president of the Senate (Brown and Roberti, respectively)—both had solid liberal credentials and relied heavily on gay appointees when it came to formulating policy. Although Deukmejian won the governorship in 1982 and 1986, Democrats controlled both chambers of the legislature throughout the 1980s, and gay policy elites could rely on long-established relationships with liberal, reform-minded lawmakers. It was not just Democrats who supported proactive AIDS legislation, however: moderate Republicans did so too, especially in the early and mid-1980s.

Predictably, though, a small but influential group of conservative lawmakers championed repressive legislation aimed at curbing the spread of the disease. Within the legislature, disputes raged around the question of whether the state should use traditional public health techniques, like quarantine and mandatory testing, to prevent the spread of AIDS. On the one hand, gay policymakers argued that these techniques would generate a rift between public health officials and PWAs, deterring at-risk individuals from seeking treatment or testing.[69] Public health techniques had traditionally dovetailed with and reinforced homophobia, meaning that a coercive, involuntary approach to AIDS would inhibit cooperation between gay men and the state.[70] Already skeptical of public health officials, gay men would avoid them altogether if the state embraced punitive measures against AIDS. That observation appeared in a policy report issued by Rand Martin, California's first full-time AIDS lobbyist, in 1987: "Mandatory testing would create either an adversarial relationship between physician and patient or will frighten people away from voluntary testing and counselling."[71] On the other hand, conservative lawmakers supported a draconian and moralistic response to AIDS. They justified the use of traditional public health techniques by drawing historical analogies between AIDS and other infectious diseases—most notably, bubonic plague, influenza, and tuberculosis. These illnesses, all communicable through casual contact, had historically prompted coercive containment strategies, leading some conservative Republicans to argue that AIDS should be subject to the same treatment.[72] Articulating this sentiment, William Dannemeyer, a GOP congressman from Orange County, accused his liberal counterparts of "attempting to shield male homosexuals with a venereal disease, which is communicable, from the same restrictions as any other person must sustain who harbors a communicable disease."[73]

The conflict between gay policymakers and conservative Republicans heated up after the Federal Drug Administration (FDA) licensed the first AIDS antibody test in March 1985. ELISA, as the test was called, immediately became a lightning rod of controversy: it was notoriously inaccurate, it sparked calls for mass quarantine, and it opened the way for more extensive contact tracing. The clash between gay policy elites and conservative lawmakers energized debates over antibody testing in the mid-1980s. Fundamentally, they differed over the question of whether testing should be voluntary or mandatory. Blaming gay hedonism for the outbreak of AIDS, conservatives argued that patient-initiated testing risked sacrificing public health for the sake of the privacy rights of at-risk individuals. They supported more traditional containment and control strategies over noncoercive interventions. For them, HIV ought to be treated like any other communicable disease. Summarizing the attitudes of many conservative legislators, one Republican state senator thundered that voluntary testing violated the "public right to life."[74] Gay policymakers, for their part, championed voluntary, anonymous testing, robust antidiscrimination provisions for those undertaking the test, community-based AIDS education, and strict penalties for those who thwarted the privacy rights of antibody-positive individuals.

They feared that indiscriminate use of the test would provide employers and insurers with sensitive information on thousands of at-risk individuals, regardless of their infection status, exposing them to workplace and insurance discrimination. This fear was not without merit: a 1984 survey of PWAs in San Francisco found that 66 percent had experienced some discrimination in employment, housing, or healthcare.[75] Without stringent confidentiality protections, then, the antibody test would dampen trust between gay rights activists and the medical profession and fuel more systemic employment discrimination against PWAs. Shortly before the FDA licensed ELISA, the National Gay and Lesbian Task Force issued a policy statement on antibody testing, warning that

> irrational fears about AIDS have led to blanket discrimination against gay men. . . . While not a diagnostic tool for AIDS, in the wrong hands [ELISA] could be used as a surrogate marker of homosexuality. It certainly can be used as a form of AIDS discrimination for those who chose to ignore the fact that the test's clinical value is still unknown. The blood test could make more systematic or "scientific" the screening out of gay employees; a very significant number of employers already use blood tests as a medical screening device; this would be just one more test to be administered. . . . A positive test could also become a medical justification for denial of health insurance—at a minimum making a positive test result proof of a pre-existing condition.[76]

With the passage of Assembly Bill 403 (AB 403) in February 1985, the proponents of anonymous testing secured a decisive victory in the California legislature. Drafted by Bush and pushed through the legislature by Agnos, the law furnished antibody-positive individuals with legal protections against employment discrimination and banned insurance companies from using ELISA to screen potential customers.[77] The immediate impetus behind AB 403 was the FDA's ruling in early 1985 that blood banks should test potential donors for HIV antibodies, a decision that stoked public fears about the safety of the blood supply. At first, the federal government licensed ELISA only for use in blood banks, prompting health officials to warn that at-risk individuals would donate blood in order to determine their HIV/AIDS status. During a newspaper interview that occurred less than one month before the FDA approved the test, Mervyn Silverman, San Francisco's director of health, asserted that "individuals in populations at high risk for AIDS, who have refrained from donating blood, will resume doing so in order to be tested for exposure to the . . . virus."[78] Several concurrent studies appeared to support this claim: one survey of gay men in San Francisco found that 50 percent were planning to visit a blood bank in order to obtain an antibody test; another study suggested that the figure was closer to 70 percent.[79] Because ELISA detected only 96 percent of HIV-infected blood samples, health officials warned that at-risk donors could inadvertently contaminate the blood supply.[80] "It all adds up to a frightening scenario," noted the *Bay Area Reporter*: "People who have been exposed to AIDS donate blood to get the antibody test; and 5 percent of that blood slips into the blood supply."[81] Responding to these concerns, Agnos tied the passage of AB 403 to the establishment of alternative test sites—government-run clinics that guaranteed anonymity and robust pre- and post-test counselling. As he explained in a press release, "Blood banking officials had expressed strong concern that unless such a step were taken, many individuals who believed themselves at-risk for AIDS might have turned to blood donations as a way of being tested. . . . The result would be a larger number of at-risk donors who could not be screened with fail-safe methods."[82] Anonymous testing as a policy idea thus rested on the claim that it would prevent at-risk individuals from contaminating the blood supply. Although several states enacted laws regulating the insurance industry's use of the antibody test, AB 403 was unusually extensive, providing for anonymous testing, strict penalties for those who disclosed test results to third parties, and counselling for individuals who tested positive.[83] The passage of AB 403 demonstrated the power of gay political organizing in Sacramento and the crystallization of an influential AIDS policy network.

To galvanize widespread support for anonymous testing, Bush modelled AB 403 on existing laws protecting the confidentiality of people with cancer and liaised with key interest groups to secure their backing.[84] These negotiations led to endorsements from a cluster of influential interest groups.[85] Support for AB 403 came from the San Francisco Health Department, the US Conference of Local Health Officers, and most emphatically from the Red Cross, which assisted Bush with the drafting of the bill.[86] Through February and March 1985, Agnos shepherded AB 403 through various committees, artfully courting the votes of Republican legislators by framing it as a public health measure rather than as a civil liberties bill.[87] Years later, reflecting back on the political debate over AB 403, Bush noted that "we were able to educate the legislature that the issue was not a balancing of civil rights against public health, but actions in both arenas which complemented each other to further assure a worried public."[88] Less than ten days after Agnos had introduced AB 403, it passed the Assembly with a bipartisan vote of 63–5. At this point, objections to anonymous testing were few and far between in the California legislature.[89]

The debate over AB 403 also signaled the extent to which liberal legislators and gay appointees relied on cost-centered arguments to buttress the political chances of their AIDS legislation. The 1980s heralded a new "era of limits" in California, as the nascent anti-tax movement constrained the development of the welfare state.[90] In 1982, Deukmejian leveraged his record as a staunch fiscal conservative to win election as governor. During the next eight years, he cut spending on welfare, education, and Medicaid.[91] Against this backdrop of budget squeezes and fiscal austerity, Agnos and Bush went to great lengths to portray anonymous testing as a cost-saving device. During behind-the-scenes discussions with state lawmakers, they argued that allowing insurance companies to use the antibody test would raise the number of uninsurable individuals, shifting the cost of AIDS healthcare onto the state.[92] As Bush highlighted in a lengthy memo to Agnos: "AIDS discrimination will cost California taxpayers millions of dollars."[93] Hadden also deployed cost-centered arguments in favor of AB 403. While touting the virtues of the bill to the San Diego Democratic Club, he argued that without anonymous testing, the state "would have to absorb a larger share of the cost for AIDS patient care."[94] AB 403 was thus propelled through the legislature by mounting fears of a contaminated blood supply, the lobbying efforts of Agnos and Bush, and the fiscal climate of the 1980s. Absent was any sustained discussion of the privacy concerns of people taking the test or the wider needs of those who tested positive.

While the passage of AB 403 revealed the influence of the policymaking network that Bush, Decker, and Hadden had built, it also underscored the drawbacks of their pragmatic approach to politics. To shore up bipartisan support for the bill, they emphasized the issue of the blood supply, downplayed the privacy concerns of gay men, and fashioned their arguments with an eye toward the fiscal conservatism of the 1980s. Several activists and liberal lawmakers pointed out that AB 403 appropriated $5 million for alternative test sites, more than the state had cumulatively spent on AIDS prevention education before 1985. "Why," asked one legislator on the senate floor, "has California, in a flash, been able to come up with $5,000,000 to protect 2% of the potential victims of AIDS, but had spent only $3,900,000 in 1984 for the other 98%."[95] In the end, however, Agnos and Bush had turned their intense lobbying and interest group mobilization into a significant policy achievement, one that would withstand a two-pronged attack in the late 1980s from conservative lawmakers and the insurance industry.

The Backlash Against Anonymous Testing

While AB 403 sailed through the legislature with overwhelming bipartisan support, it quickly provoked a backlash, as the issue of anonymous testing became a political hot potato. In 1986 and 1987, as fears of widespread heterosexual transmission reached their apex, antibody testing emerged as a central polarizing issue that guided political responses to the epidemic. The first sustained attack on California's liberal testing regime came in the spring and summer of 1986, when the electorate debated Proposition 64, a menacing ballot initiative that would have quarantined individuals suspected of HIV infection and enforced mandatory testing for certain "risk groups." In July 1986, Decker and Hadden were part of a group of gay activists and doctors who founded No on 64, a statewide organization that spearheaded the media campaign against the initiative.[96] Acting as the group's chief fundraiser, Decker raised over $1 million for television and radio spots, with 90 percent of donations coming from gay men and lesbians.[97] Over the summer of 1986, he encouraged prominent gay funders to divert money away from grassroots AIDS service organizations and toward the campaign against Proposition 64.[98] "It's like forming a $3 million corporation in three months," he summarized in a newspaper interview.[99] Drawing on the same cost-centered rhetoric used by Agnos and Bush to pass AB 403, No on 64 characterized the initiative as a fiscally onerous policy that was out of step with the budget tightening of the 1980s. The group's campaign literature focused less on the civil liberties of people living with HIV infection than on the financial implications of enforcing a mass quarantine. One newspaper advert produced by the organization listed various reasons to vote against Proposition 64, chief among them being that it would "cost California taxpayers billions of dollars each year, but not one dollar of these massive expenditures will bring us any closer to stopping AIDS."[100] During the debate over Proposition 64, California became a stage for national battles over anonymous testing, quarantine, and other coercive public health measures. Tom Stoddard of Lambda Legal, a nationally prominent gay rights organization, warned that "because of California's size, and because it is one of the two states most heavily affected by AIDS, the initiative will be to some degree a barometer of public opinion on the issue. . . . A bad result will haunt us all."[101] Backed by a broad coalition of medical and religious organizations—including the California Catholic Conference of Bishops, the California Medical Association, and the American Red Cross—AIDS activists defeated the initiative by a wide margin in November 1986.[102]

The struggle over Proposition 64 unfolded alongside a fierce legislative debate about California's liberal testing policy. Within the legislature, the driving force behind conservative attacks on anonymous testing was John Doolittle, a Republican state senator from Sacramento. In the summer and fall of 1986, he crafted ten AIDS-related bills, each designed to apply coercive health techniques to HIV. This legislation, among other things, would have overturned the provisions of AB 403, made it a felony for PWAs to donate blood, and enforced mandatory testing against sex offenders.[103] A controversial figure within the GOP, Doolittle nonetheless wielded tremendous influence in the state legislature. As the party's caucus chair, he was the second-ranking Republican in the Senate and the chief fundraiser for GOP senatorial candidates.[104] Reflecting on Doolittle's legislative expertise, one gay policymaker warned that "his knowledge about AIDS is hardly rivalled in the legislature and he has used that knowledge to lend credibility and reasonableness to his proposals."[105] Doolittle was also a longtime opponent of gay rights legislation in the California legislature, informing gay activists in 1986 that "if you follow politics, then you are aware that I have always strongly opposed efforts to legitimize the homosexual lifestyle."[106] Framing his legislation as a corrective to the state's "AIDS exceptionalism," Doolittle told the *Sacramento Bee* in early 1987 that "all [I] would like is for AIDS to be treated like we treat other venereal diseases, and those things are handled with great sensitivity and with confidentiality. But what we've done with AIDS is create a whole special set of procedures."[107]

Such arguments ran parallel to the claim that mandatory testing was a crucial means of preventing AIDS from "crossing over" into the heterosexual population and causing a more widespread epidemic. In 1986, the Centers for Disease Control and Prevention (CDC) reported a spike in cases caused by heterosexual transmission, leading the National Institute of Medicine to claim "that over the next five to ten years there will be substantially more cases of HIV infection in the heterosexual population and that these cases will occur predominantly among the population subgroups at risk for other sexually transmitted diseases."[108] At the same time, polling data revealed the public's growing fear of widespread heterosexual transmission. A Gallup poll conducted in November 1986 claimed that 73 percent of Americans felt that "AIDS will eventually become an epidemic for the public at large," an increase of 11 percent from fifteen months earlier.[109] In fact, the CDC's new figures were not an accurate reflection of the epidemic's changing contours—the agency had determined in December 1986 that a significant proportion of unclassified cases were because of heterosexual contact.[110] Ignoring these complexities, conservative politicians actively buttressed the public's growing fear of AIDS. For his part, Doolittle explicitly linked his AIDS legislation to the CDC's figures on heterosexual transmission, declaring on the floor of the state senate that "there should be no doubt in anyone's mind that AIDS is not a 'gay disease.' The deadly disease does not discriminate against homosexuals or heterosexuals. Although the disease was first discovered in the homosexual community, it is slowly but steadfastly becoming a plague for all Americans. In fact, the Centers for Disease Control are currently warning us that the number of heterosexual AIDS cases will double by 1991."[111]

To illustrate the perceived dangers of AIDS for the heterosexual population, Doolittle invoked the powerful symbol of the "innocent child," with one of his bills proposing to reduce mother-to-child HIV transmission by requiring mandatory testing for pregnant women. When he introduced this legislation onto the floor of the state Senate, he tapped into the "pro-family," antiabortion rhetoric of the religious right: "Frankly the right to privacy is coming in conflict with the right to life and that conflict must be resolved in favor of the greatest right, which is the right to life."[112] Doolittle's legislative proposals, then, drew significant impetus from mounting fears that AIDS was turning into a generalized epidemic, with widespread heterosexual transmission.[113]

The fiery political debates over Doolittle's repressive AIDS legislation prompted a vigorous lobbying campaign by gay policymakers, who coordinated their efforts under the auspices of one umbrella organization, the Lobby for Individual Freedom and Equality (LIFE), founded, in part, by Hadden and Topper in the spring of 1986.[114] California's first statewide AIDS lobbying firm, LIFE concentrated, in its early years, on leading the fight against draconian HIV bills in the state legislature. Central to its effectiveness, LIFE marketed itself as a nonpartisan organization and drew support from a politically diverse set of gay rights groups, including several chapters of ACT UP and the Log Cabin Republicans.[115] These groups found common cause both in their opposition to coercive AIDS legislation and in their support for enhanced legal protections for PWAs. Rand Martin, who served as LIFE's executive director between 1986 and 1990, built constructive relationships with both Democrats and Republicans, working feverishly to make anonymous testing a point of bipartisan consensus. With Martin at the helm, LIFE established close ties with several Republican lawmakers, most notably state representative Bill Filante, who sponsored several of the group's bills during the late 1980s.[116]

As AIDS cases continued to rise precipitously in the late 1980s, gay men and lesbians intensified their lobbying efforts in states across the country, founding an array of new organizations to mobilize grassroots activists and forge alliances with sympathetic lawmakers. These included the Rhode Island Alliance for Lesbian and Gay Civil Rights, the Kentucky Fairness Alliance, the New Jersey Lesbian and Gay Coalition, the Coalition for Lesbian and Gay Rights (New Mexico), the Free State Justice Campaign (Maryland), and the Empire State Pride Agenda (New York State).[117] LIFE was almost unique among these new organizations for its swift professionalization and impressive organizational capacity. Well into the 1990s, most state LGBTQ groups continued to rely entirely on volunteers, but LIFE hired its first professional lobbyist as early as 1986.[118] LIFE's membership also grew rapidly in its first years, rising from twelve member organizations in 1986 to eighty-six in 1991.[119] With access to a large constituency and audience, the group quickly built the political capital and lobbying infrastructure necessary for effective advocacy in the California legislature.

Faced with Doolittle's legislative maneuvering, LIFE ramped up its lobbying efforts in the winter and spring of 1987, coordinating a letter-writing campaign, organizing several lobby days, and courting sympathetic lawmakers. As the group sprang into action, it formed crucial ties with prominent lawmakers, including the chairman of the Assembly Health Committee, Bruce Bronzan. Working in close collaboration with LIFE, Bronzan led the fight against Doolittle's bills in the Democratic caucus. To ensure success, Bronzan and Rand Martin consulted with the infamous "Gang of Ten," a group of conservative Democrats opposed to speaker Willie Brown.[120] These negotiations yielded a favorable compromise and most of Doolittle's bills languished in committee for the rest of the legislative session. As one internal LIFE report put it, "What resulted was the passage of two innocuous Doolittle bills and the redirection of others to interim study, a graveyard for bills that legislators would prefer not voting against."[121] In the wake of this bruising defeat, Doolittle's singular obsession with mandatory testing began to alienate his supporters in the state legislature, and his AIDS-related legislation repeatedly languished in committee after 1987.[122]

A comparison with other states reveals that California was at the leading edge of implementing a liberal testing regime in the 1980s. While several states enacted laws regulating the insurance industry's use of the test, only AB 403 remained in place by the end of the 1980s, an indication of the gay movement's growing political clout in Sacramento.[123] After insurers mounted a vigorous lobbying effort in the late 1980s, some states—including New York, Florida, Massachusetts, and Wisconsin—overturned laws banning the industry from screening for HIV.[124] Other states, meanwhile, explicitly permitted insurers to test prospective customers for HIV infection. In December 1987, the Texas Insurance Board ruled that insurers could use ELISA to test current and prospective customers; the industry responded by excluding residents of several gay urban enclaves from coverage. That same year, by the lopsided margin of 58–0, the Illinois Senate passed a law providing the insurance industry with broad discretion over its use of the antibody test.[125] Bowing to pressure from the state's powerful insurance lobby, Senator William A. Marovitz—a frequent ally of the Chicago gay community—sponsored the measure, generating sharp criticism from the Illinois Gay and Lesbian Task Force (ILGTF), a statewide LGBTQ lobbying group launched in the late 1970s. According to the organization's executive director, Marovitz's sponsorship represented "a betrayal both to his gay constituency and to those of us who have worked so hard on behalf of an AIDS confidentiality act."[126] The contrasting fortunes of LIFE and the ILGTF stemmed in part from their different organizational capacities. While LIFE's influence grew rapidly as it hired paid lobbyists and forged close ties with politicians across the ideological spectrum, the ILGTF was plagued by organizational issues, relying on volunteers throughout the 1980s and only mustering a budget of $4,000 to combat repressive AIDS legislation in 1987.[127]

A close look at the politics of antibody testing highlights the significance of California's policy leadership during the early years of the AIDS crisis. In addition to enacting the country's most robust confidentiality protections for individuals taking ELISA, California was the only state that continued to ban medical insurers from using the test in the late 1980s. This policy record was the product of two interlocking factors: a burgeoning network of gay policymakers, who were willing to use clandestine strategies, and the rapid organizational growth of LIFE, one of the largest state LGBTQ groups in the country. As the next two sections will outline, however, California's policy leadership began to unravel in the late 1980s as attempts to enact further reform stalled, beset by a punitive turn in AIDS policymaking and a looming budget crisis.

HIV Criminalization and the Specter of "Recalcitrant" AIDS Carriers

For gay policymakers, the years after 1987 proved disappointing. While the provisions of AB 403 remained intact, attempts to enact further reform failed, and Hadden and his colleagues had to contend with the public's growing fear of heterosexual AIDS. By the late 1980s, not only in California but across the United States, the fight over HIV criminalization emerged as one of several vital issues—including the fear of heterosexual transmission, the specter of "recalcitrant" AIDS carriers, and a broader backlash against gay rights—fueling a punitive turn in AIDS policymaking. Media reports of intentional HIV exposure, often sensationalized, sparked calls for punitive action against recalcitrant AIDS carriers. Between 1986 and 1990, twenty-two states enacted HIV-specific criminal laws, leading one policy report to note "that the frequency with which state legislatures have acted to criminalize knowing exposure of transmission of HIV suggests that they are more willing to use criminal laws to deal with recalcitrant individuals than to rely on traditional public health measures."[128] Often framed as "victim's rights" measures, these laws expanded the state's surveillance of HIV-positive individuals and contributed to the growing rate of incarceration for sex offenders in the late twentieth century.[129] As Trevor Hoppe, René Esparza, and others have argued, HIV-specific criminal laws coincided with a broader punitive turn in US policymaking, as "law and order" proponents increasingly championed criminalization as a solution to various social problems.[130]

Rare, isolated cases of recalcitrant AIDS carriers generated outsized media attention in California, propelling the state to enforce escalated penalties for HIV-positive sex offenders. In the spring of 1987, several newspapers reported on the case of Stephanie Smith, a sex worker from Fresno, California, who continued to work after testing positive for HIV. Fresno police initially sought to charge her with attempted murder, but their prosecution fell apart "because California law requires proof of a specific intent to kill in order for the charges to be made."[131] Later that year, police in Los Angeles accused an HIV-positive gay man of attempted murder after he repeatedly tried to sell his blood to a plasma bank. However, a judge quickly dismissed the prosecution's argument on the grounds that it "failed to show the defendant intended to kill anyone."[132] Most press commentary on the case was highly sensationalized, with the editors at one newspaper declaring that "it is time for Sacramento to exercise the political will needed to prevent unstable AIDS victims from passing on a death sentence to others."[133]

These widely reported cases dovetailed with a groundswell of public concern about "intentional" HIV transmission. When polled, most Americans backed criminal sanctions against PWAs who remained sexually active. A 1986 NBC poll found that 51 percent of those surveyed supported "governmental restrictions . . . on the sexual activities of people who are known carriers of AIDS."[134] One year later, 68 percent of those polled by the *Los Angeles Times* favored the criminalization of intentional HIV transmission.[135] Meanwhile, the National Opinion Research Center's 1988 General Social Survey indicated that 63.7 percent of Americans supported mandatory identification tags for people with HIV infection.[136] Although public opinion data is frequently inaccurate, these polls sent a clear signal to state lawmakers that a substantial number of Americans backed a punitive policy response to the epidemic.

Galvanized by this mounting public hysteria, California legislators surged into action, crafting over 140 HIV-specific bills in 1988 alone.[137] That year, nearly half of all state lawmakers—ranging from liberal Democrats to conservative Republicans—drafted or sponsored an AIDS bill.[138] Reflecting on the legislative session, Rand Martin remarked that "in both houses the AIDS agenda was typified by a fervent desire to introduce and enact a variety of measures that would hopefully please the voters."[139] This legislative ferment yielded two new HIV-specific criminal laws in 1988: the first, Senate Bill 1913 (SB 1913), permitted mandatory testing of inmates in state correctional facilities; the second, Senate Bill 1007 (SB 1007), enacted stiffer penalties for HIV-positive sex workers.[140] The punitive turn heralded by this legislation had a particularly detrimental impact on sex workers: between 1988 and 2014, 95 percent of all HIV-specific criminal convictions in California targeted sex workers.[141]

LIFE lacked the political clout and influence to prevent the passage of this legislation. In a report issued at the end of the 1988/89 legislative session, Martin summarized the group's lackluster record in the area of HIV criminalization:

> The arena in which LIFE had limited success was AIDS and criminal justice. Most legislators, either with an inherent sense of strong law and order or with a concern that the voters might perceive them as weak on law and order, responded favorably to legislation that was marketed as protecting "innocent victims." Unable to stop most of these bills, LIFE. . . . succeeded only in ensuring that these bills were at least medically accurate and sensitive to due process.[142]

As they jockeyed to present themselves as tough on crime, both Democrats and Republicans advocated for a punitive response to intentional HIV transmission. Even one of LIFE's staunchest allies, Bruce Bronzan, introduced a felony bill in 1988 that would have targeted sex workers living with HIV (the governor vetoed it in favor of SB 1007). He justified his support for HIV criminalization on the grounds that he was up for reelection in the conservative city of Fresno.[143] LIFE also compromised with law and order proponents in order to protect the state's liberal testing program; the group withdrew its opposition to SB 1007 in the spring of 1988 in return for securing the defeat of two bills that would have weakened confidentiality protections for those taking the test.[144]

In California, one of the most far-reaching HIV criminalization measures was Proposition 96, a statewide ballot initiative that permitted mandatory testing of individuals who bit or spat at a police officer. These behaviors posed no risk of HIV transmission, but the electorate still adopted the initiative in November 1988, by a margin of nearly two to one.[145] Uniting an ideologically diverse groups of politicians, Proposition 96 received backing from Sherman Block, the arch-conservative sheriff of Los Angeles County; Bill Filante, a prominent moderate Republican in the state legislature; and Bruce Bronzan, the Democratic chair of the Assembly Health Committee.[146] Supporters framed the initiative as a victims' rights measure, with one campaign poster arguing that "current law perpetuates a grave injustice to victims."[147] Persistently anxious about the views of law and order proponents, gay policymakers downplayed their opposition to Proposition 96. Amid mounting public clamor for swift action against recalcitrant AIDS carriers, they deflected media attention away from the initiative, with one activist telling the *Los Angeles Times* that it was "less a statement of voter sentiment about AIDS than a statement about crime."[148] Fighting an uphill battle, gay appointees funneled less than $3,500 into the battle against Proposition 96, a sum that amounted to little more than "petty cash in most state-wide campaigns."[149] Working with such a limited budget, the official campaign against Proposition 96 struggled to gain momentum or mobilize grassroots support over the summer of 1988. It was also plagued by an abundance of logistical and financial problems. Less than seven weeks before the vote, the campaign had yet to produce any official campaign literature or seek any free publicity in the press.[150]

Although individual policymakers and activists condemned the rising tide of public hysteria over HIV criminalization in the summer of 1988, oppositional forces never congealed into a sustained or effective campaign against Proposition 96. The racial composition of California's nascent gay policy network was partly responsible for this lackluster response to the initiative. Even as the burden of the epidemic fell disproportionately on communities of color, most AIDS policymakers and lobbyists in Sacramento were white, middle-class, and male. The bedrock of LIFE's membership consisted of middle-class gay men who were politically active in the gay urban enclaves of Los Angeles and San Francisco. As late as 1990, only 2 percent of the group's delegates were African American, and only one person of color had been appointed to the California AIDS Advisory Committee.[151] Like many other state-level LGBT lobbying groups, LIFE's policy preferences reflected and reinforced racial fault lines within the gay movement. The cornerstone of the group's campaigning—voluntary, anonymous testing—met the needs of white middle-class gay men far more successfully than those of queer people of color. Well into the late 1980s, most testing sites were located in predominately white, gay urban enclaves in San Francisco and Los Angeles.[152] Even before the electorate approved Proposition 96, grassroots activists publicly chided gay policymakers for pouring all of their political resources into issues that primarily affected the white gay population. In a newspaper interview in October 1988, Priscilla Alexander, a sex-worker-rights activist, accused the "predominately white gay male community" of "let[ting] Prop. 96 go."[153] Echoing this critique, in a seething editorial, one gay newspaper wrote that "the reason why there has not been a more active outcry over Prop. 96 is because it will have a disproportionate impact on ethnic minority communities, and the traditional powers who organize campaigns on a statewide level don't perceive it to be a personal threat."[154] Tragically, this criticism proved prophetic, as HIV criminalization disproportionately targeted communities of color. Of the eight hundred people charged with HIV-specific crimes in California between 1988 and 2014, two-thirds were African American or Latino/as.[155]

As with the formation of the carceral state more broadly, HIV criminalization received support from a bipartisan group of politicians.[156] Sensational media reports convinced lawmakers from across the political spectrum that intentional HIV transmission represented a grave and growing problem. In this frenzied context, gay policymakers proved all too willing to downplay their opposition to HIV criminalization and use it as a bargaining chip in their effort to protect anonymous testing. LIFE's political scope was too narrow to transcend the narrow interests of its predominately white gay male membership. While California's approach to anonymous testing marked a triumph for gay policymakers, it came hand-in-glove with a punitive shift in disease control, one that disproportionately affected sex workers and communities of color.

The State Budget and the Shifting Landscape of AIDS Policymaking

Many of the difficulties that gay policymakers encountered in the late 1980s also stemmed from California's mounting fiscal difficulties, as exemplified by a series of acrimonious disputes over the state budget. AIDS ravaged urban gay communities just as the Reagan administration enacted huge cuts to grant-in-aid programs for the states.[157] From the start of the decade, the president set the tone of the policy agenda with the passage of the Omnibus Budget and Reconciliation Act of 1981, which reduced federal grants to state and local governments by $6.6 billion.[158] At the same time, anti-tax sentiment significantly limited California's ability to raise new revenue. Across the 1970s and 1980s, a succession of ballot initiatives slashed property tax, constrained state expenditure, and abolished the inheritance tax.[159] Together, these developments pushed budgetary issues to the fore of California politics in the late 1980s. As Rand Martin noted, in a report issued to LIFE's supporters in 1987, "AIDS is now above all a money issue."[160]

Another major stumbling block in the way of new AIDS reform was Deukmejian's increasingly ambivalent attitude toward the crisis. As a staunch fiscal conservative and political pragmatist, the governor consistently vetoed any extension of the California AIDS budget in the late 1980s, citing concern over the state's budgetary problems and ballooning deficits. While he was willing to openly negotiate with gay policymakers like Decker and Hadden, he insisted on balanced budgets, tight spending controls, and a prudent state reserve. Frustration at the governor was compounded by his habit of vetoing most new AIDS legislation: in 1988 alone, he vetoed over ten AIDS-related bills, including Assembly Bill 87 (AB 87), which would have protected PWAs from job and housing discrimination.[161] He justified this veto on the grounds that furnishing PWAs with legal protections would generate another costly and inefficient layer of bureaucracy.[162]

By the late 1980s, Bush and Hadden had to grapple with the problem of growing fiscal pressures, diverting them away from efforts to enact further reform. Their private correspondence reveals frequent clashes with the Deukmejian administration and a growing obsession with defeating draconian AIDS bills. As early as 1986, Hadden noted that he had "dropped" most work on new AIDS legislation in order to "focus on the budget."[163] One year later, in a memo circulated to Agnos, Bush suggested that "if we tried to introduce AB 403 now—with all of its safeguards against insurance and employment discrimination based on the antibody test—we could never get it passed, much less signed."[164] As the decade wore on, Bush and Hadden abandoned their efforts to pass more AIDS-related bills, focusing instead on defeating attempts to cut the state budget. In the end, Decker also lost faith in the governor and resigned from the California AIDS Advisory Committee in May 1988. The final straw was Deukmejian's decision in 1988 to endorse Proposition 102, a statewide ballot initiative that would have extended California's quarantine powers.[165]

As Deukmejian's desire to rein in government spending intensified, a particularly bruising confrontation emerged over the state budget for fiscal year 1989. Much of the debate revolved around a changing perception of AIDS healthcare, as doctors increasingly saw the disease as a more manageable condition that required years of medical treatment. By the late 1980s, the availability of new drug therapies for AIDS, such as AZT and pentamidine, provided a clinical rationale for earlier diagnosis, intervention, and treatment. As the medical historian Daniel P. Fox has noted, "Most health professionals talked about AIDS as the end stage of a chronic disease of uncertain course that could be modified by chemical therapies."[166] On June 16, 1989, the CDC issued guidelines to state governments recommending that they undertake widespread HIV testing and treat seropositive individuals with aerosolized pentamidine to prevent the onset of pneumocystis pneumonia, the largest cause of death among people with HIV infection.[167] Less than two months later, in early August, federal health officials announced that the antiviral drug AZT delayed the onset of AIDS in people with HIV infection.[168] The high cost of these new treatments meant HIV was becoming an increasingly expensive disease to manage, with significant fiscal implications for the states, which still spent more than the federal government on non-Medicaid-related AIDS healthcare. A 1989 article in *American Medical New* estimated that the CDC's recommendations alone could cost up to $2 billion to implement.[169]

In the late 1980s, the rising expense of AIDS healthcare attracted the attention of a growing cohort of lawmakers and activists across the United States, who would press the case for increased government intervention to mitigate the disease's ballooning costs. States as diverse in politics, society, and culture as California, Michigan, New Jersey, New York, and North Carolina enacted laws to provide PWAs with early intervention services.[170] In California, Assemblyman John Vasconcellos, a frequent ally of LIFE, used his influence as chair of the Assembly Ways and Means Committee to organize a series of hearings on early intervention during the spring of 1988, more than a year before the CDC's announcement that aerosolized pentamidine was an effective drug therapy for PWAs. Dozens of witnesses, including medical professionals, gay policymakers, and AIDS activists, testified in favor of an increase in state spending on early diagnostic and clinical services.[171] The hearings initially proved effective. On May 18, 1988, after two months of deliberation, Vasconcellos issued a press release urging his colleagues to include over $50 million of extra funding for AIDS in the state budget—an amount he described as "a fiscally sound and morally essential investment."[172] Seeking to build a case for more spending on early intervention, he went on to explain that "scientific data indicates that early treatment will prolong the health and productivity of an infected person."[173] When the legislature debated the 1989 state budget one month later, most of Vasconcellos's recommendations gained the backing of Democratic lawmakers in both the Assembly and Senate, but they received a much frostier reception from Republicans, who remained staunchly committed to addressing a $1 billion shortfall in the state budget.[174] Leading the charge for increased AIDS funding in the Assembly were several influential allies of LIFE: Burt Margolin, who represented parts of Los Angeles and North Hollywood; Terry Friedman, who spearheaded efforts to pass gay employment rights legislation in the late 1980s and early 1990s; and Bruce Bronzan, who chaired the Health Committee.[175] Despite the opposition of some Republican lawmakers, the legislature included a $40.5 million augmentation for AIDS programs in its proposed budget, including $10.7 million of new funding for early intervention.[176]

With limited fiscal elbow room, however, Deukmejian ignored the legislature's requests for more funding and slashed $29.5 million out of its proposed AIDS budget.[177] In addition to cutting everything from prevention education to mental health services, he vetoed nearly all funding for early intervention programs, ignoring the changing clinical context of AIDS.[178] While gay policymakers pushed for increased spending on AIDS healthcare, treatment, and prevention, the Deukmejian administration continued to prioritize biomedical research and HIV testing. In his veto message, Deukmejian asserted that the legislature's augmentations were "simply . . . inconsistent with the need to protect current, vital programs and provide for a prudent reserve for economic uncertainties."[179] Attentive to the importance of cultivating a reputation for fiscal responsibility, gay policy elites framed their opposition to these cuts in cost-saving terms, defending early intervention on the grounds that it would save the state money over the long term. In an interview with the *Bay Area Reporter*, Rand Martin opined that "[Deukmejian] slashed all the funds for HIV screening and reduced home health care. But it's more cost effective to keep people out of the hospital. . . . Taxpayers will pay for more expensive programs in the long run."[180] Vasconcellos made a similar point when he claimed in a press release that "keeping HIV infected people on available drugs means that they can lead productive lives as family and community members, workers, and taxpayers for much longer before needing other costly forms of treatment."[181] Grassroots AIDS activists also incorporated the language of fiscal conservatism into their appeals for more state funding. At a press conference organized by LIFE in early July 1988, John Mortimer, a spokesperson for AIDS Project Los Angeles, the city's largest AIDS service organization, slammed Deukmejian's cuts as "both a human tragedy and an economic tragedy for the state of California."[182] In the end, these pleas did not persuade the governor to restore funding for early intervention. Unable to leverage concessions from the Deukmejian administration, Vasconcellos and LIFE lacked the political clout to force the issue and could only boost augmentations for preexisting AIDS programs.[183]

Much to the disappointment of gay policymakers, liberal legislators, and

AIDS activists, Deukmejian continued to veto most new appropriations for early intervention during the rest of his gubernatorial term, imposing critical constraints on the state's response to the epidemic. In 1989, for example, the legislature appropriated $40 million for early intervention, but the governor cut this back to $3.5 million.[184] Despite a frenzied lobbying effort, LIFE failed to muster enough support from Republican lawmakers to override Deukmejian's vetoes.[185] As the ink was drying on the state budget, Martin issued a memo that once again invoked the rhetoric of fiscal restraint to critique Deukmejian's decimation of AIDS funding:

> For an elected official who promotes himself as fiscally conservative and prudent, George Deukmejian is remarkably irresponsible in tackling a variety of chronic health care problems, including AIDS. Not only is the state obligated to care for people with AIDS who do not have private insurance but fiscal prudence dictates that the state spend money now to prevent people from converting to AIDS or [AIDS-related complex]. . . . The only alternative is to spend even more money in the future when people with HIV become ill with AIDS.[186]

Even as LIFE established itself as an important voice in state politics, its calls for more AIDS funding failed to gain any traction with the Deukmejian administration, which remained steadfastly committed to balancing the budget.

At the tail end of the 1980s, California's burgeoning and increasingly formalized gay policy network found itself in a particularly challenging position. The bipartisan consensus that emerged around antibody testing in the mid-1980s did not extend to early intervention or expanding the state AIDS budget. While gay policymakers had played a crucial role in building support for liberal testing policies, pressing vigorously for the passage of laws to protect the civil liberties of people taking the test, their success was contingent on tapping into the language of limited government and working closely with Republican allies in the legislature. Since they never abandoned their rhetorical commitment to fiscal conservatism, there was an underlying tension between their demands for more government services and the language they used to marshal support for their policy positions. Hadden and his colleagues neglected to build support for a more sustained and interventionist approach to the AIDS epidemic that would go beyond protecting the rights of people suspected of HIV infection. After their breakthrough success with the passage of AB 403, they spent the rest of the decade protecting existing legislative gains rather than securing substantial new funding for early intervention or other HIV-related programs.

Fiscal pressures remained evident in the early 1990s, as California entered a deep recession. Saddled with large budget deficits, lawmakers cut spending on welfare, healthcare, and social services.[187] Due to a combination of budget cuts and rising caseloads, funding per person living with AIDS declined 30 percent between 1989 and 1994.[188] While early intervention came up again in debates over the budget in the 1990s, Deukmejian's successor—Governor Pete Wilson (1990–1998)—was equally reticent about funding it. As late as 1991, California's appropriation for early intervention still stood at a meager $3.5 million, $200,000 less than what the state spent on mandatory testing in correctional facilities.[189] As the prospect for further reform dried up, gay policymakers soft-pedaled their support for expansive and proactive AIDS legislation. Framing their objectives around the theme of fiscal restraint, they proposed policies that boosted individual rights but required minimal state spending, such as employment protections for PWAs. A newsletter distributed by LIFE in 1990 asserted that "we cannot continue to rely on the rhetoric of the 60's and the emphasis on protections for the individual. We are living in a time when the politics of scarcity dominates our collective consciousness. It is not time to be asking for a handout or even a hand-up. The gay and lesbian community is not immune from the problems created by economic uncertainty."[190] This basic framework of supporting legislation that required little or no budget augmentation informed LIFE's lobbying strategy for much of the 1990s. Many of the group's proposals took the form of new state regulations that did not require spending increases. In the 1989–1990 legislative session, for example, LIFE sponsored two bills on nursing home regulation but neglected to attach a budget augmentation to either.[191] Just as they gained access to the levers of state power, gay policy elites faced a rapidly shifting political landscape—and their strategies bore the imprint of a new "era of limits." Stifled by the tight fiscal climate of the late twentieth century, they failed to markedly increase the state AIDS budget, couching their own policy preferences in the language of fiscal restraint.

At the same time, mounting budgetary pressures undermined the state's leading role in responding to AIDS. As John Duran, the cochair of LIFE, proclaimed in 1990, "During the first years of the epidemic, this state took the lead in addressing the costs of AIDS. Now California is moving away from its responsibilities and letting the federal government take over."[192]

Of the ten states with the highest caseloads in 1992, California ranked eighth in terms of funding for non-Medicaid patient care.[193] As lawmakers embraced a punitive stance on a range of social issues, concerns about recalcitrant HIV carriers informed a wave of repressive AIDS legislation, funneling much-needed resources away from healthcare programs. The gay movement's political success in beating back coercive testing measures occurred at the same time that the legislature passed HIV-specific criminal laws that disproportionately targeted queer people of color and sex workers. Perhaps most critically, California's gay policy network reflected and reinforced racial inequities within the gay rights movement, a subject that I will explore in greater depth in chapter 5. The overarching consequence of both the state's fiscal woes and the punitive turn in AIDS policymaking was the eclipse of California's significant but short-lived liberal approach to the epidemic.

CHAPTER THREE

Anti-Feminism, Bisexuality, and the Protean Politics of Child Protection

The Anti-ERA Movement and the Illinois Response to AIDS

In the center of Park Ridge, Illinois, a commuter town fifteen miles northwest of Chicago, lay a pristine storefront with a giant makeshift globe in the window. At the top of the globe, staring menacingly down from the North Pole, sat a homemade red papier-mâché octopus, with its tentacles reaching into every part of the world. "Godless communist tyranny holds more than a billion people captive," read a sign in the window. "And, like an octopus, it reaches out far and wide for new victims."[1] This peculiar storefront served as the constituency office of Penny Pullen who represented Park Ridge in the Illinois House of Representatives between 1976 and 1992.[2] A lifelong member of the GOP, Pullen's political career reflected the broader trajectory of conservatism in the latter half of the twentieth century, especially the movement's gradual shift from a singular focus on anti-communism to a wider emphasis on profamily politics. Starting out as an anti-communist crusader in the 1960s, she turned her attention to an array of cultural and social issues in the 1970s and 1980s, such as gay rights, feminism, and religious freedoms. In the process, she became a major player in the nascent anti-feminist movement, championing patriarchal family values and traditional gender roles while organizing against abortion rights, gender equality, and sex education in schools.[3]

As social issues came to the fore of Pullen's politics, she emerged as one of the Illinois legislature's most vocal critics of the gay movement, portraying homosexuality as a threat to the heteronormative nuclear family. In session after session, she fought strenuously against gay rights bills in the state House of Representatives, including proposals to grant sexual minorities more access to housing and employment opportunities.[4] With the arrival of the AIDS epidemic in the 1980s, Pullen, a committed Evangelical Christian, saw the disease as yet another sign of the moral decay of American society and a divine punishment from God against homosexuality.[5] In one letter to her constituents in April 1987, she accused PWAs of "actively courting death" through their "alternative lifestyles." She then quoted St. Paul's moral condemnation of homosexuality in his letter to the Romans: "Men committed indecent acts with other men, and received in themselves the due penalty for their perversion."[6] Determined to protect the heterosexual family from the deadly scourge of AIDS, Pullen introduced among the most capacious and reactionary set of AIDS-related bills in the country during the 1987 legislative session. The measures included compulsory contact tracing for people who tested positive for HIV, enhanced quarantine powers for public health officials, and mandatory antibody testing for all prisoners, marriage license applicants, and hospital patients between the ages of thirteen and fifty-five.[7]

This chapter details the political and legislative battles over Pullen's 1987 AIDS legislation. Examining Illinois's response to the epidemic brings into sharp focus the strategies used by conservative women to shape the political direction of state AIDS policymaking. Throughout the late 1970s and early 1980s, Pullen forged a productive relationship with Phyllis Schlafly, a fellow resident of Illinois who spearheaded the national campaign against the Equal Rights Amendment (ERA), which, if ratified, would have enshrined gender equality in the US constitution. When shepherding her AIDS bills through the Illinois legislature, Pullen tapped into the activist and leadership networks built by anti-feminists during the battle over the ERA in the 1970s. Employing many of the strategies that were fundamental to the anti-ERA campaign, Eagle Forum—an anti-feminist organization founded by Schlafly in 1975—became one of the most active supporters of Pullen's HIV proposals, initiating several letter-writing campaigns to encourage state lawmakers to enact them. Pullen was successful because she drew energy and ideas from the anti-feminist movement and because her rhetoric and strategies mirrored some of the defining characteristics of Schlafly's anti-ERA activism.

The politics of child protection facilitated Pullen's push for coercive AIDS policies. In the 1970s and 1980s, conservatives often portrayed gay men as a threat to children, implying that they sought to lure them away from the sexual norms of the heteronormative family. Leaders of the Christian Right suggested that, by nature, gay men were predators who corrupted the young. The imperative to protect children from sexual minorities animated anti-gay crusades across the country. Most famously, Anita Bryant, a nationally known gospel singer, led a vitriolic campaign in 1977 to overturn an antidiscrimination ordinance in Dade County, which protected gay men and lesbians from housing and employment discrimination. As a mother, Bryant framed her opposition to the measure as her parental right to guard her children against the influence of homosexuality, declaring that she had a "Godgiven right to be jealous of the moral environment for my children."[8] In pamphlets and public statements, she made wildly inaccurate claims about the propensity of gay men to prey on the young, alleging that "homosexuals cannot reproduce—so they must recruit. And to freshen their ranks, they must recruit the youth of America."[9] The anti-ERA movement also drew on the stereotype that gay men sought to influence and pervert the young. Throughout the 1970s, Schlafly and her acolytes often fixated on the most extreme possible effects of the amendment, including the prospect that it would enable gay men and lesbians to marry and adopt children. They claimed that such outcomes would expose more children to homosexuality, undermining the stability of the normative, heterosexual family.[10]

Similarly, Pullen employed the rhetoric of child protection during her campaign for punitive AIDS legislation in the 1980s, propagating the myth that sexual minorities were a threat to the young to drum up support for her policies. But the dynamics of this child endangerment narrative changed in the context of the epidemic. While the anti-ERA movement depicted all gay men as an existential threat to the heteronormative family, Pullen concentrated on the dangers posed by bisexual men, especially those who remained in the "closet" and hid their sexuality from their female spouses. She insisted that bisexual men often contracted the disease from other men and then passed it on to their unwitting female partners and children who were otherwise unlikely to come into contact with the virus. According to this logic, bisexuality was an even graver and more insidious threat to the nuclear family than homosexuality, as it acted as a bridge connecting the epidemic among gay men to heterosexual women and children. This narrative helped to shore up bipartisan support for policies designed to protect the family from the specter of the unfaithful, bisexual husband, especially mandatory premarital antibody testing, which Pullen argued would prevent HIV-positive men from marrying and infecting their wives and children. Bisexuality, which remains chronically understudied by historians of sexuality and the AIDS crisis, featured prominently in the anti-feminist crusade for punitive AIDS policies in Illinois.[11]

While legislators from across the political spectrum proved all too willing to support Pullen's coercive AIDS legislation, there was pushback from gay rights activists, who insisted that the bills would undercut efforts to contain the virus. Few lawmakers listened to this argument, and Pullen's proposals passed the legislature by substantial margins in the spring of 1987. When the measures reached Governor James R. Thompson's desk in the autumn, he vetoed several of them on fiscal grounds, but he still signed into law Pullen's signature AIDS policy—mandatory premarital antibody testing. By invoking the rhetoric of child endangerment and portraying bisexual men as a threat to the heteronormative family, Pullen ensured that Illinois was one of only two states to require marriage license applicants to obtain an antibody test (the other was Louisiana). But her success quickly provoked a backlash. Bemoaning their apparent lack of influence in the Illinois legislature, gay men and lesbians worked hard to boost their organizational infrastructure at the state level after the 1987 session, forging alliances with powerful lawmakers, establishing political action committees, and building a statewide network of grassroots organizers. Eventually, these efforts bore fruit when a coalition of gay rights and pro-choice activists successfully unseated Pullen from the legislature in the early 1990s, marking the end of her political career. Like California, the AIDS epidemic served as a catalyst for more effective political organizing by gay men and lesbians at the state level in Illinois.

Anti-ERA Activism and the AIDS Epidemic

Passed by Congress in March 1972, the ERA emerged as a central political issue of the 1970s, pitting the women's movement against the nascent New Right. At first, ratification by the states seemed extremely likely, as one legislature after another approved the amendment over the following months. Within a year, thirty of the necessary thirty-eight states had ratified the ERA.[12] But anti-feminist activists led by Phyllis Schlafly quickly mobilized to halt the amendment's progress. An archconservative Catholic from Alton, Illinois, Schlafly painted the ERA as an attack on family values and traditional gender roles. She contended that most women wanted to stay in the home and look after their families and that the amendment would make it impossible for them to assume these roles. In her 1972 polemic "What's Wrong with 'Equal Rights' for Women?," she claimed that "women libbers view the home as a prison, and the wife and mother as a slave. . . . The women libbers don't understand that most women want to be a wife, mother and homemaker—and are happy in that role."[13] Through relentless organizing, Schlafly enlisted hundreds of thousands of women to her anti-feminist cause, drawing together Evangelicals, traditional Catholics, and Republican activists into a single conservative movement. In 1972, she established STOP ERA, which spearheaded the national campaign against the amendment through dozens of state chapters.[14]

As the political showdown over the ERA reached a fever pitch in the mid-1970s, anti-feminist activists successfully defeated it in state legislatures across the country, permanently stalling the ratification process. The legislative battle over the amendment was especially fierce in Illinois. Between 1972 and 1982, when the time limit on the ratification process ran out, Illinois lawmakers voted on the ERA every year but declined to ratify it each time.[15] Throughout this period, anti-ERA activists mounted a tireless campaign against the amendment, distributing tens of thousands of pamphlets, printing adverts in all of the state's major newspapers, and descending in droves on Springfield to lobby legislators directly. Already in 1975, the Illinois chapter of STOP ERA had coordinators in all of the state's legislative districts.[16] The anti-ERA movement was also assisted by a particular provision of the state constitution, which required a three-fifths majority in both chambers of the legislature to pass a constitutional amendment. While the ERA repeatedly received support from a simple majority of lawmakers, it never gained the votes necessary to meet the three-fifths threshold in both the House and the Senate.[17]

Elected to the Illinois House in 1976, Penny Pullen threw herself into the cause of defeating the ERA during the late 1970s, emerging as one of the legislature's most vocal and outspoken critics of the amendment. A longtime Republican activist, Pullen cut her political teeth during the 1964 presidential election when she volunteered for the youth wing of the Barry Goldwater campaign. Over the ensuing years, she participated in various neighborhood and college GOP organizations, even winning Young Republican of the Year in 1968. During her early legislative career in the late 1970s, Pullen attached herself to various anti-feminist and conservative crusades, pushing for abstinence-only sex education in schools, a dramatic cut in business regulations, and new restrictions on abortions.[18] But she became best known for her opposition to the ERA. In press conferences, newspaper adverts, and speeches on the floor of the House, Pullen attacked the amendment for violating traditional gender norms and family values.[19]

Through this activism, she became a close friend of Schlafly's and an active participant in Eagle Forum, an organization launched by Schlafly in 1975 to fight the ERA and other feminist causes. As one newspaper profile noted, Pullen was "generally considered to be the Eagle Forum's floor leader on abortion and other issues in the Illinois House."[20] The personal and organizational connections forged between Schlafly and Pullen during the ratification battle over the ERA would later prove crucial to the legislative fight over HIV/AIDS in Illinois.

In Illinois and elsewhere, most of Schlafly's arguments against the ERA relied on exaggerating its potential effects. Given that the courts would have to interpret the amendment's precise meaning, there was genuine disagreement among legal experts over its likely impact. Exploiting this uncertainty, STOP ERA emphasized the most extreme possible outcomes, casting the amendment as a threat to the economic interests of women. According to the organization, the ERA would render women more vulnerable to the vicissitudes of the market, as it would eliminate the legal obligations of husbands to act as breadwinners for their wives and provide them with financial support, forcing most married women to join the labor force. A typical pamphlet disseminated by STOP ERA argued that the "ERA will invalidate all state laws which require a husband to support his wife. ERA will impose on women the equal (50%) financial obligation to support their spouses (under criminal penalties, just like husbands)."[21] Opponents also claimed that the ERA would permit abortions on demand, conscript women into the armed forces, and force women to use mixed-gender restrooms. In a letter circulated to state lawmakers, the Alabama chapter of STOP ERA produced a long list of potential issues that the amendment may impinge on: "There is no way for anyone to say positively how the Supreme Court will apply the ERA to conscription, combat duty, alimony, child support, wife support, divorce, homosexuality, public restrooms, separate gym classes and athletic teams, single sex education, sexual crimes, and prostitution."[22]

A strain of anti-gay rhetoric ran through many of these arguments against the ERA. If critics of the amendment asserted that it would degrade heterosexual marriage and undermine the traditional family, they also claimed that gay men and lesbians would be direct beneficiaries of its ratification. As Gillian Frank, Alison Lefkovitz, and other scholars have pointed out, anti-ERA activists insisted that the amendment would embed gay rights into the US Constitution.[23] In the September 1974 edition of her monthly national newsletter, the *Phyllis Schlafly Report*, Schlafly argued that the ERA would legalize gay marriage because it would require state legislatures to "delete the 'sexist' language from state laws (e.g. man, woman, husband, wife, male, female) and replace all such words with sex-neutral language (e.g. person, spouse). Thus, a law that defines a marriage as a union of a man and a women would have to be amended to replace those words with 'person.'"[24] The persistent myth that sexual minorities were a threat to children gave force and direction to much of this homophobic rhetoric. Anti-ERA literature frequently asserted that the amendment would permit gay men and lesbians to adopt children and indoctrinate them into a life of promiscuity and sexual licentiousness. One flier circulated by ERA opponents in Florida speculated that it would expose more children to homosexuality, eventually leading to a "pervert generation" of people raised by gay men and lesbians.[25] Such incendiary rhetoric implied that the mere presence of sexual minorities in close proximity to children would damage their well-being and prevent them from developing into gender-conforming heterosexuals.

Anti-gay language and tropes permeated the campaign against the ERA in Illinois. Throughout the 1970s, anti-ERA activists in the state produced a steady stream of booklets, fliers, and newspaper adverts warning that the amendment would provide gay men and lesbians with the constitutional rights to marry and adopt children.[26] To illustrate the unforeseen consequences of the amendment's ratification, one small Illinois-based organization, ERA Opposed, distributed a pamphlet full of fictional news stories and headlines from an imaginary future in which the ERA was in force. An especially sensationalized news piece in the pamphlet told the story of two opposite-sex inmates staying in the same prison and having a child because the ERA had abolished sex segregation in all correctional facilities. Under the outlandish headline "Two in Prison for Murder Expecting," the report noted that "a female inmate serving a 30-year sentence at the Adult Correctional institutions for murdering her child, has become pregnant. Officials said she identified the father as a fellow inmate."[27] At the bottom of the pamphlet, another fictitious story implied that the ERA would allow gay men to adopt children. It referenced the activism of Jack Baker, a gay man from Minnesota who garnered national attention after he and his partner, Michael McConnell, applied for a marriage license in Hennepin County in 1970. When local officials declined their application, they fought a legal battle for the right to marry all the way to the Supreme Court, which summarily dismissed their case in a one-sentence statement.[28] Speculating about the future effects of the ERA, the pamphlet quoted Baker, stating that "same sex marriages will be legalized when the ERA is approved" and suggested that the amendment would also permit him to adopt a child.[29] Beyond the grassroots organizing of anti-feminist activists, lawmakers in the Illinois legislature actively buttressed the fear that the ERA would furnish sexual minorities with more rights. In an interview with the state chapter of the Christian Right organization Moral Majority, Betty J. Hoxsey, a Republican and conservative state representative, contended that "not only could homosexual marriages be permitted" under the ERA but "gay couples may be allowed to adopt children."[30] During the decade-long struggle over the ERA in Illinois, opponents of the amendment constantly infused their rhetoric and arguments with homophobia, raising the specter that ratification would undermine the traditional family by allowing gay men and lesbians to marry and adopt.

When the AIDS epidemic struck, anti-feminists doubled down on the supposed links between the ERA and gay rights. In 1983, Eagle Forum produced a factually misleading and sensationalistic pamphlet entitled "The ERA-Gay-AIDS Connection," which posited, in an astounding leap of logic, that the amendment would leave the heterosexual population unprotected from the spread of the disease. The pamphlet claimed that the ERA would thwart efforts to stem the spread of HIV/AIDS because it would furnish gay men and lesbians with legal protections against discrimination, preventing society from protecting "itself against a class of people who have a high rate of various contagious diseases (some fatal)." It then alleged that gay men would use these new rights to prey on the young, charging that they would be able to adopt children, become teachers, and be "active in the Boy Scouts."[31] Already in 1983, the homophobic trope that sexual minorities were a threat to children, a key strain of anti-ERA discourse, featured in Eagle Forum's writings on the AIDS crisis.

During the legislative battle over the epidemic in the Illinois legislature, Pullen used the ideas and institutional architecture created by anti-feminists during their campaign against the ERA. From an organizational standpoint, she channeled much of the activist energy from Eagle Forum's previous mobilization against the amendment into her campaign for a more punitive response to the disease. Ideologically, Pullen drew on the same rhetoric of child protection that had guided Schlafly's anti-gay activism and early writings on the AIDS epidemic, arguing that coercive disease control measures—especially mandatory premarital testing—were necessary to prevent "closeted" husbands from passing on the disease to women and children.

A strong emphasis on the danger posed by homosexuality to the nuclear family—and children in particular—linked the anti-ERA movement with the anti-feminist response to AIDS. In these ways, the debate over the ratification of the ERA in Illinois set the stage for Pullen's later attempts to pass coercive AIDS legislation.

Eagle Forum's Response to the AIDS Crisis

Nineteen eighty-seven marked a major point of inflection in the state-level response to HIV/AIDS across the country. It represented the beginning of a significant uptick in AIDS policymaking, as lawmakers across the country sought to respond to the public's growing anxiety about the disease, especially the potential for a mass outbreak of HIV among the heterosexual population. As the previous chapter indicated, the CDC reported a sharp rise in AIDS cases caused by heterosexual transmission in 1986. This increase was mainly due to changes in how the agency compiled its epidemiological data on the disease rather than the changing nature of the epidemic itself. Nonetheless, the CDC's statistics convinced media outlets, policymakers, and the American public alike that the crisis represented a dire and growing threat to the population at large. Opinion polls conducted in 1987 revealed widespread anxiety about the epidemic. That year, more than two-thirds of Americans polled by Gallup said AIDS was the most urgent health problem facing the nation.[32] Of the 601 people surveyed in another 1987 study, roughly half said it was "very likely" that HIV would cause mass death among the whole American population.[33] At the same time, media outlets set aside more print space and airtime to cover the AIDS crisis. In 1987, the television and print media ran approximately twelve thousand stories on the disease, up from five thousand the previous year.[34] This coverage often bordered on the sensationalistic, with fearmongering headlines such as "The Second Stage of the Epidemic: Heterosexuals and AIDS" and "New Warning of Threat of AIDS to Straights."[35] Galvanized into action by the public's anxiety about the epidemic, state legislatures enacted a string of HIV-specific measures in 1987. Figure 3.1 plots the number of AIDS bills introduced and enacted by all states between 1983 and 1991. It shows a dramatic increase in the number of AIDS measures passed by lawmakers in 1987 compared with previous years.[36]

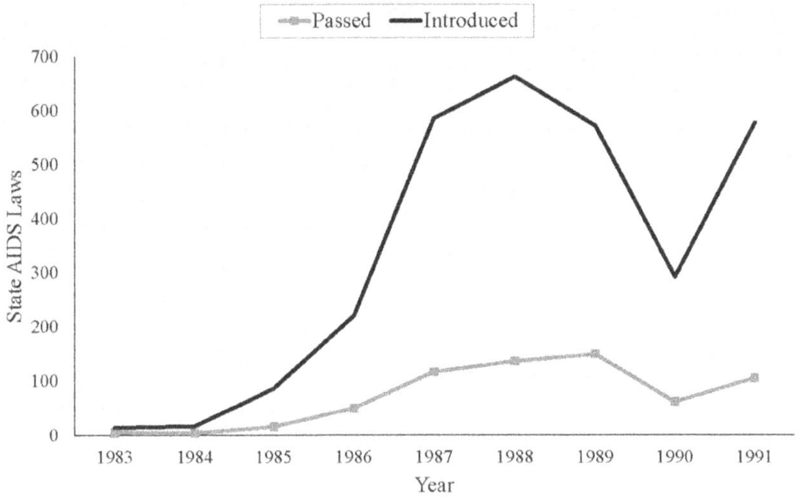

Figure 3.1: States AIDS laws introduced and enacted, 1983–1991. Sources: Intergovernmental Health Policy Project, "A Synopsis of State AIDS Laws Enacted During the 1983–1987 Legislative Sessions," NCJRS Virtual Library, accessed July 26, 2025, https://www.ojp.gov/ncjrs/virtual-library/abstracts/synopsis-state-aids-laws-enacted-during-1983-1987-legislative; Intergovernmental Health Policy Project, "A Summary of AIDS Laws from the 1988 Legislative Session," NCJRS Virtual Library, 1989, https://www.ojp.gov/ncjrs/virtual-library/abstracts/summary-aids-laws-1988-legislative-sessions; Intergovernmental Health Policy Project, "A Summary of AIDS Laws from the 1989 Legislative Session," NCJRS Virtual Library, 1990, https://www.ojp.gov/ncjrs/virtual-library/abstracts/summary-aids-laws-1989-legislative-sessions; Ingrid A. Bowleg, "A Summary of AIDS Laws from the 1990 Legislative Session," AIDS Policy Center, Intergovernmental Health Policy Project, George Washington University, 1991; Lisa Bowleg, "A Summary of AIDS Laws from the 1991 Legislative Session," AIDS Policy Center, Intergovernmental Health Policy Project, George Washington University, 1992; Mary Ellen Hombs, *AIDS Crisis in America: A Reference Handbook* (ABC-CLIO, 1992), 96; "AIDS Bill Introduced and Passed," *Intergovernmental AIDS Reports* 3, no. 5 (July 1990): 1–3.

In this climate of paranoia, Schlafly leveraged the public's growing fear of the disease to push for coercive AIDS policies at the state level. The epidemic resonated with Schlafly as a political issue because she saw HIV/AIDS as a symbol of the nation's moral decline and the erosion of traditional family values. When surgeon general C. Everett Koop, a devout evangelical Christian, released a major report on AIDS in October 1986, she emerged as one of his fiercest critics, believing he had failed to put the epidemic in its proper moral context. Despite Koop's own conservative convictions, he avoided denouncing homosexuality and sexual immorality in his report, focusing instead on practical public health strategies for fighting the epidemic, such as AIDS education in schools "from the lowest grade possible."[37] He expressed opposition to compulsory testing and argued that "quarantine has no role in the management of AIDS."[38] Koop's approach infuriated Schlafly, who slammed him for capitulating to the values of sexual liberalism and downplaying the moral aspects of the epidemic. In a widely circulated open letter to the surgeon general, she accused him of "running a massive campaign to institutionalize and validate promiscuity of both the heterosexual and homosexual varieties."[39] She even alleged that Koop's report would encourage the "teaching of safe sodomy in public schools."[40] To Schlafly, the outbreak of HIV/AIDS confirmed the narrative she had told about American society since the early 1970s, especially the dangers posed by the decline of the heteronormative family and traditional morality. She believed that the disease's true origins lay in the sexual permissiveness and sinfulness of sexual minorities. In her eyes, the obsession of many liberal policymakers and gay activists with the civil liberties of HIV-positive people ignored the fact that most people had acquired the disease through immoral behavior, which deserved to be punished.[41]

As the epidemic garnered more attention from politicians, media outlets, and ordinary Americans in 1987, Schlafly invested considerable time and energy in pushing AIDS policymaking in a more punitive direction. For Schlafly, the first responsibility of policymakers was to protect the uninfected—especially women and children—from the disease, not to safeguard the civil liberties of HIV-positive people or provide them with more effective treatment options. She was willing to trample over the rights of PWAs to reduce the perceived risks of infection for others, even if that meant supporting extremely capacious, costly, and poorly targeted policies, such as mass mandatory testing and quarantine provisions. To pressure lawmakers into adopting this approach at the state level, Schlafly published a set of policy proposals for tackling the epidemic in 1987, calling for, among other things, compulsory premarital antibody testing, the closing of all gay bathhouses, abstinence-oriented sex education, and mandatory contact tracing of all HIV-positive individuals.[42]

With Schlafly's approval, Pullen introduced a set of bills at the start of the 1987 legislative session that closely mirrored these policy suggestions. She drafted legislation to require contact tracing of HIV-positive people and their sexual partners, strengthen the quarantine powers of public health professionals, and mandate antibody testing for marriage license applicants, prisoners, and hospital patients between the ages of thirteen and fifty-five.[43] To marshal support for her policies, she relied on the organizational infrastructure anti-feminists had built in the 1970s during the struggle over the ERA. Throughout the spring of 1987, Schlafly worked to generate political enthusiasm for Pullen's AIDS measures among Eagle Forum's members in Illinois, who bombarded their representatives with phone calls and letters and descended on Springfield to provide testimony during crucial committee hearings.[44] In total, the organization generated over ten thousand letters to lawmakers in support of Pullen's legislation.[45] Ultimately, anti-ERA activism provided anti-feminists with a commanding platform for later promoting repressive HIV policies in the Illinois legislature.

Like the anti-ERA activism of the 1970s, the rhetoric of child endangerment permeated Pullen's push for coercive AIDS policies. The trope that sexual minorities were a threat to children resurfaced and once again gave force to anti-feminist organizing. But, in the face of the AIDS epidemic, the specific target of these rhetorical attacks shifted. In the minds of Pullen and Schlafly, bisexuality now posed an even more insidious threat to the sanctity of the family than homosexuality, as closeted husbands may contract HIV and unwittingly pass it on to their wives and children. In a letter disseminated to her supporters in early 1987, Pullen warned that "the AIDS virus is spreading into the heterosexual community, in part because a large percentage of homosexuals are bisexuals—many of them married—whose homosexual habits are hidden from their spouse and friends."[46] Both Pullen and Schlafly invoked the figure of the philandering bisexual man to legitimize their punitive approach to AIDS policymaking. They particularly emphasized the need for premarital antibody testing, claiming this policy would protect hapless women and children from getting infected by secretly closeted husbands. In a newsletter to her followers, Schlafly claimed that mandatory testing for marriage license applicants was "a women's rights issue" because "93 per cent of those with AIDS are men." She then asserted that "every woman should have the right to have the state ascertain that her prospective husband is just as free from the AIDS virus as from syphilis and gonorrhoea [*sic*]. Women have a right to this information so they can avoid a pregnancy that might result in an AIDS-infected baby."[47] Echoing Schlafly, Pullen called on public health officials to confront the "bisexual threat to women" by "requiring AIDS testing before issuance of marriage licenses."[48] According to Schlafly and Pullen, mandatory premarital testing was the only means of safeguarding wives and children against the specter of the unfaithful, HIV-positive husband.

By blaming bisexual men for spreading HIV to women and children, Pullen and Schlafly capitalized on the public's anxiety that bisexuality would serve as a vector of widespread infection among heterosexuals. Indeed, bisexuality figured prominently in the public's growing paranoia about the epidemic. Throughout 1987, major news outlets published a string of inflammatory stories on bisexual men infecting their female partners with HIV, fanning fears about AIDS becoming embedded into the heterosexual population. "Women today increasingly find their thoughts turning to past and present lovers, asking themselves if anyone with whom they were intimate might have a bisexual history," reported the *New York Times* in a front-page story in April 1987: "The figure of the male bisexual, cloaked in myth and his own secretiveness, has become the bogyman of the late 1980s, casting a chill on past sexual encounters and prospective ones."[49] That same month, Cox Media Service, a media conglomerate, printed a story in several of its local newspapers on the prospect of bisexuality causing a mass outbreak of HIV among heterosexuals. The report quoted several AIDS workers claiming that they "know of marriages in which wives contracted AIDS from their husbands and passed it on to their infants."[50] Meanwhile, the *Atlantic* published an article in February 1987 predicting that widespread heterosexual transmission, fueled in part by bisexuality, would constitute the next phase of the epidemic. According to the piece, "The potential role of bisexuals in heterosexual transmission of AIDS has been gravely underestimated."[51] As the Illinois legislature considered Pullen's AIDS proposals, the dominant news media warned of an impending heterosexual epidemic caused by bisexuality, fueling the demonization of bisexual men that undergirded her calls for premarital antibody testing.

In reality, these reports grossly distorted the epidemiology of the AIDS crisis. Scientific studies conducted in the late 1980s repeatedly concluded that very few women contracted HIV through sex with bisexual men. One survey of PWAs in New York City found that less than 0.4 percent of AIDS cases were likely to have been caused by bisexual men transmitting the virus to women.[52] Similarly, according to public health officials in San Francisco in 1987, only four of the city's thousands of PWAs were women who acquired the virus by having sex with a bisexual man.[53] Despite the lack of evidence that bisexuality was about to embed the epidemic into the heterosexual population, the mere prospect that bisexual husbands could infect their wives and children with HIV pushed Schlafly and Pullen to campaign for premarital antibody testing.

The Political Geography of AIDS in Illinois

As Pullen's campaign for coercive AIDS policies gathered steam in early 1987, the political geography of Illinois ensured her bills received bipartisan support in the legislature. During the second half of the twentieth century, Illinois politics was characterized by sharp regional divisions, with three geopolitical areas vying for influence: Chicago, the suburban counties surrounding the city (often referred to as the collar counties), and downstate Illinois. Politicians representing these three regions were frequently at odds on a host of issues, including gun control, LGBTQ rights, environmental regulation, and the allocation of the state budget. A particularly deep gulf loomed between Chicago and downstate Illinois. Over twenty times larger than any other city in the state, Chicago was an economic and political behemoth.[54] Its large and diverse population returned a large proportion of Democrats to the state legislature. By contrast, downstate Illinois was markedly more conservative and Republican, with an economy almost entirely centered around agriculture.[55] As a result, animosity toward Chicago often drove the region's politics. In 1981, an editorial in the *Chicago Tribune* noted that "there are legislative candidates who literally campaign on an anti-Chicago platform. The more awful things they can say about the big city, the greater their voter appeal."[56]

With the unchecked expansion of the collar counties after the Second World War, Chicago and downstate Illinois had to contend with a third regional force in state politics. The mass migration of people to suburbia weakened the political influence of Chicago in the legislature during the latter half of the twentieth century. Between 1950 and 1990, 837,000 people moved out of Chicago, with approximately two-thirds migrating to the collar counties.[57] By the 1980s, the suburbs were the largest of the three geopolitical regions in Illinois in terms of wealth, population, and political representation in the legislature.[58] Although less of a GOP stronghold than downstate Illinois, the collar counties still mostly returned Republicans to the statehouse.[59] Against the backdrop of these political, economic, and demographic fault lines, the three-way competition between Chicago, its suburbs, and downstate Illinois came to dominate the political agenda in the legislature. The state government often functioned as a political broker between these three regions, especially over the distribution of tax dollars for highways, schools, and mass transit.[60]

The AIDS epidemic further inflamed these geopolitical divides. Epidemiological data collected by the Illinois public health department revealed that Chicago accounted for the vast majority of the state's caseload. According to the agency, 73 percent of people diagnosed with AIDS in Illinois during the 1980s lived in the city, 15 percent lived in the collar counties, and only 8 percent lived in downstate Illinois.[61] The concentration of PWAs in Chicago led many suburbanites to perceive the epidemic as an urban danger that threatened to encroach into their neighborhoods and erode the suburb's status as a comfortable, secure, and tranquil place. As the historian Kyle Riismandel has noted, the predominantly white American suburb entered a "new era of endangerment" in the 1970s and 1980s, marked by pervasive cultural anxieties about suburbia's future viability as a safe space removed from the discord and crime located in the city.[62] In Illinois, the AIDS crisis buttressed this atmosphere of malaise and fear about the declining safety of the suburb. During the battle over Pullen's legislation, the press ran several articles on the gradual spread of HIV into the collar counties, undercutting the long-standing expectation that suburbia would remain free from the disease. In one front-page story, the *Daily Herald*, a newspaper distributed in Chicago's northern and western suburbs, declared that the collar counties could no longer "escape" the epidemic. "Five years ago, AIDS was a strange disease that primarily stalked San Francisco and New York, preying on homosexuals and drug abusers. It was hardly the plague of Middle America," the newspaper noted. "Now, nearly 1,100 in Illinois have fallen victim to the fatal immune system disorder and the disease no longer goes unrecognized. Every hospital in the Northwest suburbs has treated AIDS patients."[63] In February 1987, the *Northwestern Herald*, a suburban newspaper based in McHenry County, warned that "although no cases have been reported" in the area, this was likely to change soon because of "the steady spread of the disease from the gay community to the heterosexual population."[64]

As the press stoked fears of the epidemic moving from the cities to the suburbs, opinion polling showed overwhelming support for coercive AIDS policies in the collar counties. One poll conducted by the *Chicago Sun-Times* in early 1987 revealed that residents in these counties supported mandatory premarital testing by a margin of 9 to 1, compared with 4 to 1 in Chicago.[65] Under pressure from their anxious constituents, both Democrats and Republicans from the suburbs and downstate Illinois overwhelmingly backed Pullen's legislation (the only substantial opposition came from liberal Democrats in Chicago).[66] State Senator Aldo A. DeAngelis, a moderate Republican and ally of the gay rights movement, voted for all of Pullen's bills, informing the *Chicago Tribune* that his constituents from the suburb of Olympia Fields were ready to banish PWAs "to a leper island."[67] In an anonymous interview with the same newspaper, a Democratic representative from downstate Illinois confessed that they voted for Pullen's legislative package despite believing it was "wrongheaded." "I don't like the bills, but when I go home, I want to be re-elected," admitted the legislator. "If I take a stand against the bills, opponents at home can cut my throat next year."[68] The vote on Pullen's AIDS proposals thus reflected the regional divisions within Illinois state politics. Her most reliable support came from politicians in downstate Illinois and the suburbs, who were responding to their constituents' fears of the epidemic spreading out of the city.

As the debate over Pullen's bills drew to a close in the spring of 1987, the gay rights movement found itself with limited options to make its voice heard in the legislature. The Illinois Gay and Lesbian Task Force (IGLTF), a lobbying organization based in Chicago, spearheaded efforts to defeat the legislation. Although it portrayed itself as a statewide group, in reality, the ILGTF was a small organization with a narrow membership base, overwhelmingly concentrated in Chicago.[69] In the late 1980s, only two members of its eleven-person board of directors hailed from outside the city.[70] Anchored in cultural and political milieu of Chicago's gay movement, the IGLTF made few inroads with politicians from the suburbs or downstate Illinois. For most of the debate over Pullen's bills in 1987, Democratic state senators William Maravitz and Clark Netsch, who both represented neighborhoods in Chicago with large gay populations, were the only lawmakers who spoke against the measures on behalf of the gay rights movement.[71] With the IGLTF struggling to obtain the support of politicians outside of Chicago, the legislature passed Pullen's AIDS measures by staggering margins in

June 1987. Although Pullen was a staunchly conservative Republican, her legislation drew considerable support from Democrats representing suburban and downstate districts. In the House, forty-three out of sixty-seven Democrats voted for her premarital testing bill, as did twenty-seven out of thirty-one Democratic state senators.[72]

With lawmakers across the ideological spectrum supporting Pullen's AIDS bills in the legislature, the IGLTF turned its attention to the executive branch, launching a last-ditch effort to convince Governor James R. Thompson, a moderate Republican and fiscal conservative, to veto the legislation.[73] To persuade Thompson to strike down the measures, the group organized a petition drive, orchestrated a mass letter-writing campaign, and successfully arranged for a direct meeting with him.[74] It also worked with gay newspapers in Chicago to publicize its efforts and urge as many gay men and lesbians as possible to participate. According to the group's own estimates, over four thousand people sent letters to Thompson asking him to veto Pullen's measures.[75] Throughout this campaign, the IGLTF sought to appeal to the governor's fiscal conservatism by emphasizing the financial burden of implementing mass antibody testing and other coercive AIDS policies. In one flier, it encouraged those writing letters to Thompson to highlight the "inefficiency" of "mandatory testing" and cite an estimate that testing all prisoners would cost the state over $60 million.[76] For his part, the governor complained that lawmakers had not adequately considered the financial implications of Pullen's measures. "While the legislators passed what they heralded as the toughest anti-AIDS package in the nation, they didn't give me a dime to do anything with it," he stressed at a press conference in July 1987: "In other words, they appropriated no money for mandatory contact testing beyond the current budget of the Department of Public Health. They appropriated no funds to make this enforceable as far as I can see."[77]

After spending the summer deliberating over whether to sign Pullen's legislation, Thompson vetoed most of it in September 1987, but he did so mostly because of the cost implications of mass testing rather than any concern about the civil liberties of PWAs. He struck down proposals to test all prisoners and hospital patients between the ages of thirteen and fifty-five, as well as a bill that would have subjected PWAs to mandatory contact tracing and quarantine, arguing in each case that the measures would be too expensive.[78] After being inundated with letters from members of Eagle Forum over the summer, he still signed Pullen's premarital testing bill into law, proclaiming that "we have a responsibility to protect the most unwitting victims of this dreadful virus, the children, and we have an obligation to protect our healthy children."[79] Pullen's and Schlafly's skillful use of the rhetoric of child protection, combined with the paranoia caused by the epidemic in the suburbs, convinced the legislature and the governor to support Eagle Forum's signature AIDS policy.

Thompson's decision to approve this measure set Illinois apart from most other states. While thirty-five statehouses considered some form of premarital AIDS testing bill in the late 1980s, only Illinois and Louisiana enacted legislation requiring all marriage license applicants to obtain an antibody test.[80] In both states, the policy quickly proved ineffective and counterproductive. Only one month after it came into effect, the Louisiana Medical Society complained that the state's premarital testing statute had left physicians in a "cloud of confusion over forms, procedures, and patient confidentiality."[81] At the urging of medical professionals, legislators repealed the law in July 1988, less than a year after its initial passage.[82] In Illinois, compulsory premarital testing prompted a sharp increase in the number of couples travelling to neighboring states to get married, as they hoped to avoid paying the $35 fee for an antibody test.[83] Because individuals planning to marry were at low risk of contracting HIV, the measure did little to stem the disease's spread, identifying only twenty-three HIV-positive people in 1988.[84] That year, marriage license applicants spent $5.6 million on antibody tests in Illinois—significantly more than the state's $3.5 million annual budget for HIV/AIDS programs.[85] As it threw up these problems, the statute became the subject of scorn in the national press. "The Illinois Legislature and Gov. James Thompson have set an inglorious example of what not do about AIDS," proclaimed a scathing editorial in the *New York Times* in February 1988.[86] In the summer of 1989, after it had been on the books for less than two years, legislators repealed the statute without much controversy.[87] All told, Illinois's experiment with premarital antibody testing proved to be a costly distraction from more effective methods for preventing the spread of HIV.

Although only two states enacted Schlafly's flagship policy of premarital antibody testing, anti-ERA and conservative women's organizations across the country mobilized to influence the state-level response to AIDS. In Alabama, the state chapter of Eagle Forum joined a coalition of conservative groups clamoring for abstinence-only AIDS education in schools. When the state board of education announced plans to develop a curriculum for AIDS education in early 1987, the organization insisted that the syllabus should denounce all forms of sexual activity outside of heterosexual monogamy, downplay the effectiveness of contraceptive products, and uphold chastity before marriage as an absolute moral good. In early October, the board published a preliminary draft of its curriculum, which instructed teachers to discuss various topics deemed off-limits by Eagle Forum, such as safer sex and condom use. The proposed syllabus also contained no moral condemnation of either homosexuality or sex outside of marriage. Immediately, Eagle Forum became a major voice of resistance to the board of education's draft curriculum. It inundated state officials with letters condemning the teaching of safe sex, sent witnesses to testify before public hearings on the syllabus, and invited Schlafly to Alabama to campaign for abstinence-only education.[88] Under pressure from Eagle Forum and other conservative groups, the state board of education made a set of sweeping changes to its AIDS curriculum in early 1988. The final version of the syllabus placed much greater emphasis on abstinence, blamed homosexuality for causing the epidemic, and included factually misleading statements about safe sex, such as the claim that "the failure rate of condoms in preventing the spread of the AIDS virus is as high as 30 to 50 per cent."[89] Elsewhere, in places such as Kentucky, Nevada, and Utah, Eagle Forum pushed for abstinence-based AIDS education during the late 1980s and early 1990s, often joining forces with other conservative and anti-feminist groups.[90] Thanks in part to Eagle Forum's activism, conservatives quickly racked up a string of victories in this policy area. According to one survey, thirty-three states required AIDS education in schools by 1989, with 85 percent of programs emphasizing abstinence and only 9 percent teaching safe sex.[91]

The effects of Pullen's AIDS policymaking also reverberated far beyond Illinois. After the 1987 session of the Illinois legislature, Pullen briefly gained a degree of influence over national AIDS politics. At the behest of Schlafly and Gary Bauer, a socially conservative policy advisor in the White House, Reagan appointed her to the presidential commission on AIDS in July 1987, which held dozens of highly publicized public hearings on the epidemic over the next year.[92] Even more significantly, Pullen played a major role in precipitating the wave of HIV criminalization bills that swept through the states in the late 1980s.[93] Throughout her legislative career, she had a close relationship with the American Legislative Exchange Council (ALEC), a conservative clearinghouse for state-level legislation, having been a member of the organization since first entering the Illinois House of Representatives in 1976.[94] In 1989, ALEC, which had a history of supporting homophobic legislation, convened a working group on the epidemic, bringing together representatives of the business community and conservative lawmakers. On the heels of her work for the presidential commission on AIDS, Pullen provided this working group with testimony on her experience of AIDS policymaking. She encouraged ALEC to support a set of punitive measures, including a model bill for criminalizing the "intentional" transmission of HIV (she had sponsored similar legislation in the Illinois House during the 1989 session).[95] After hearing Pullen's testimony, the working group adopted her model statute in its final 161-page report. As the historical sociologist Trevor Hoppe has noted, over the next few years, seven state legislatures considered twenty-two separate HIV criminalization bills with a similar structure to this model statute, often lifting language from it verbatim.[96] Through her work with ALEC, Pullen thus achieved an astonishing level of influence over AIDS policymaking for a single state legislator, inspiring a string of coercive AIDS proposals in statehouses across the country.

The AIDS Epidemic and the Rise of a Gay Lobbying Infrastructure in Illinois

The 1987 legislative session strengthened the conviction of many gay rights activists in Illinois that the movement needed to boost its influence over state politics to block the enactment of more coercive AIDS proposals. To this end, Ron Sable, a gay physician and veteran activist from Chicago, established IMPACT in 1987, a political action committee (PAC) devoted to increasing the government's responsiveness to the needs of sexual minorities.[97] The organization's expressed purpose was to "raise money to support, financially and otherwise, organizations, campaigns, and candidates for federal, state, local, and party office supportive of lesbian and gay rights and progressive causes."[98] In its early years, IMPACT achieved a number of quick, decisive victories. Within five years of its founding, the organization had distributed over $80,000 to state and local candidates who were friendly with the gay movement.[99] As well as supporting politicians committed to gay rights, IMPACT mobilized to increase the electoral clout of sexual minorities. When the 1988 election loomed, it coordinated a major voter-registration drive among gay men and lesbians in Chicago. The organization joined forces with several prominent gay rights and feminist groups to get out the vote in gay neighborhoods, including Planned Parenthood, the National Abortion Rights Action League, the National Organization for Women, and the Lesbian and Gay Progressive Democratic Organization.[100] By the early October deadline for registering to vote, this campaign had added 17,225 people to the electoral rolls, far more than IMPACT's initial target of ten thousand.[101]

In addition to holding voter registration drives and donating to the campaigns of gay-friendly politicians, IMPACT provided the IGLTF with an influx of money to enhance its lobbying efforts in the legislature. For much of the early and mid-1980s, the IGLTF was a tiny organization that relied on volunteers rather than paid lobbyists and operated on a shoestring budget. But several major donations from IMPACT allowed the organization to evolve into a more formidable political force and establish a more permanent and professional lobbying presence in Springfield. Thanks to IMPACT's financial support, the group employed a full-time paid lobbyist for the first time in 1988. "This is an important step for us," noted the group's cochair, Grant Thornley: "When an organization retains a professional lobbyist, it gains added credibility and legitimacy in the eyes of the General Assembly."[102] As well as hiring a lobbyist to influence the policy process in Springfield, the IGLTF dramatically expanded its organizational structure by opening chapters in cities across the state, including Springfield, Rockford, and Urbana.[103] For the first time, the organization developed a membership base beyond Chicago, allowing it to forge a number of alliances with politicians outside of the city. This restructuring meant the IGLTF could tap into a genuinely statewide network of rank-and-file gay rights activists who received regular "action alerts" from the group asking them to bombard their lawmakers with mail and phone calls about specific pieces of legislation.[104]

As the IGLTF became more sophisticated in its lobbying techniques, it racked up some significant political victories in the early 1990s, mobilizing successfully during several major legislative battles to stem the tide of coercive AIDS policies. During the 1990 session, Pullen introduced another package of AIDS bills aimed at subjecting HIV-positive people to punitive disease control measures. Unlike in 1987, the IGLTF successfully lobbied lawmakers to defeat all of her proposals, except for House Bill 3998 (HB 3998), which permitted physicians to notify spouses of positive HIV test results. Behind the scenes, gay lobbyists worked with their allies in the House and Senate Ways and Means Committee to stall the rest of

Pullen's legislation in committee and prevent it from reaching the floor of the legislature.[105] The following year, Pullen drafted three more AIDS bills, including one proposal that would have mandated HIV testing for people convicted of child sexual abuse. The IGLTF responded by mounting a sustained lobbying blitz against the legislation. Across the winter and spring of 1991, the organization issued directives to its members across the state, calling on them to write to their lawmakers and demand they vote against Pullen's measures. It also placed editorials in major gay newspapers asking gay men and lesbians to flock to Springfield and lobby their legislators directly. Through this campaign, the IGLTF ensured that all three of Pullen's AIDS bills died in committee.[106]

Eventually, gay activists used their growing influence in Illinois state politics to unseat Pullen from the legislature. With the 1992 election on the horizon, IMPACT donated funds to her Republican primary challenger, Rosemary Mulligan, who was prolife and sympathetic to gay rights. Pullen responded by launching an aggressively homophobic campaign against Mulligan.[107] In one particularly vicious mailout to voters, she focused exclusively on attacking Mulligan's gay allies. "What really motivates these militants to go after my political scalp is my leadership in trying to protect the uninfected public from the deadly scourge of AIDS," declared Pullen: "They seem to be frightened of legitimate public health efforts to stop the spread of the AIDS virus, so they see me as their enemy because of my fight to stem the tide of this tragic epidemic. Their tactics—constant references to me in their newspapers, carrying my larger-than-life photo on posters in their parades, plastering my picture all over their lampposts in their neighborhoods—are intended, I am sure, to intimidate me."[108] After receiving donations from IMPACT and several prolife groups, Mulligan defeated Pullen in the Republican primary with 9 percent more of the vote.[109] In a clear indication of the gay movement's growing ability to shape electoral outcomes in Illinois politics, activists successfully removed Pullen, the architect of the nation's most coercive AIDS legislation, from the state House of Representatives.

Despite IMPACT's remarkable growth and early political successes, it quickly garnered a reputation for being a predominantly white organization. Middle-class, white, gender-conforming gay men formed a majority of the organization's supporters and board members.[110] An evaluation of IMPACT's voter registration drive in 1988 reported that "where we fell down on the job was primarily in securing representatives from the Black community and representatives from the Hispanic community."[111] Although the group often spoke as if it represented the entire LGBTQ community, most of its funding came from a $125 a plate annual fundraising dinner, which was largely attended by affluent middle-class gay men and lesbians.[112] Because of its limited racial diversity, IMPACT estranged many people of color, who often reported feeling unwelcome at its events. Ahead of the organization's annual women's fundraising brunch in 1993, an unidentified group of queer women of color produced a poster critiquing IMPACT for its failure to reach out to minority communities.[113] Of the twenty-three officials and candidates who attended the brunch, only one—state senator Alice Palmer—was African American.[114] As in the case of California, the AIDS epidemic prompted a flurry of political activity among sexual minorities at the state level in Illinois, but this activism reflected the interests of white gay men more effectively than other groups of queer people.

* * *

The legislative politics of AIDS in Illinois vividly showcases how the anti-feminist movement of the 1970s influenced the policy response to the epidemic in the 1980s. During the heated debates over the ERA that flared in the 1970s, Eagle Forum blossomed into a formidable political force in Illinois backed by thousands of conservative women across the state. Tapping into this activist network, Pullen succeeded in mobilizing grassroots support for coercive AIDS policies and pressuring lawmakers across the ideological spectrum to support premarital AIDS antibody testing. Equating homosexuality with child endangerment—a theme that also suffused anti-ERA activism in the 1970s—she portrayed HIV-positive gay men as a threat to children and the stability of the nuclear family. The specter of closeted husbands passing on the disease to their families rendered the epidemic an insidious threat to the sanctity of traditional, heterosexual marriage. As gay activists rallied to counter Pullen's legislative victories, they obtained a previously inaccessible level of influence in Illinois state politics, beating back many punitive AIDS bills in the early 1990s. The epidemic prompted a groundswell of political activity among sexual minorities as affluent, gender-conforming gay men and lesbians built a more robust lobbying infrastructure in Springfield and poured more resources into defeating homophobic politicians. By the mid-1990s, the gay movement had emerged as an influential constituency in Illinois politics.

CHAPTER FOUR

An Unequal Epidemic

Sodomy, State Legislative Capacity, and the Texan Response to AIDS

On April 30, 1989, thousands of gay men and lesbians from across Texas gathered in Austin to denounce the state government's discrimination against sexual minorities and call for more legislative action on the AIDS epidemic. Shortly after noon, they marched for two miles through the city's streets to the steps of the Capitol Building, where they congregated for the afternoon. In the ensuing hours, protestors chanted demands for more AIDS funding and held a candlelight vigil for the four thousand Texans who had succumbed to the disease since the epidemic began. With an estimated thirty thousand participants, the march was the largest gay political protest ever assembled in the history of Texas.[1] The following day, a smaller group of activists streamed through the corridors of the Capitol Building to meet with lawmakers individually and lobby for the Omnibus AIDS Bill, a comprehensive reform package that promised to boost expenditure on prevention education and HIV healthcare. Armed with a set of talking points distributed by Glen Maxey, a gay rights lobbyist, they touted the fiscal benefits of the legislation, arguing that it would stave off future costs by preventing the transmission of an expensive disease.[2] Over the next month, gay activists and lobbyists continued to orchestrate both large-scale political protests and behind-the-scenes lobbying to push for the passage of the Omnibus AIDS Bill, which gradually made its way through both chambers of the legislature.[3] After weeks of political wrangling and compromise, lawmakers finally passed the bill on the last day of the legislative session.[4]

The passage of the Omnibus AIDS Act capped off a yearslong struggle to enact major AIDS legislation in the statehouse. For most of the 1980s, the Texas legislature virtually ignored the epidemic even though the state had the fourth largest caseload in the country, behind only California, Florida, and New York. While sexual minorities lobbied hard for more investment in prevention education and AIDS healthcare, their efforts were met with stiff resistance from conservative legislators who successfully exploited AIDS hysteria and rampant homophobia to stall the legislative response to the crisis. By the time gay men and lesbians converged on Austin in April 1989, Texas spent a fraction of what other hard-hit states did on the epidemic. It ranked last in spending on HIV/AIDS out of the ten states with the highest caseloads, allocating a mere $289 per case, five times less than Pennsylvania, which was the second stingiest state (see table 4.1).

This chapter examines the Texas legislature's feeble response to the AIDS crisis in the 1980s and early 1990s. It offers a striking contrast to the previous case studies of California and Illinois, where legislators took a more proactive stance against the disease, even if they disagreed over whether to prioritize coercive measures such as quarantine and mandatory testing or more progressive interventions like prevention education. While the political differences between the California and Illinois legislatures were stark, both served as policy incubators during the initial phase of the epidemic, enacting legislation that other states sought to emulate.[5] In Texas, however, conservative sexual politics and the legislature's weak institutional capacity constrained the ability of lawmakers to act. Between 1983 and 1987, California and Illinois implemented thirty-five and fifteen AIDS-related laws, respectively, while Texas enacted only two.[6]

The structure of the legislative process in Texas diverged sharply from other states with high case rates. By the start of the AIDS epidemic, many legislatures were professionalized institutions with expert staff, annual sessions, and full-time lawmakers. Throughout the 1960s and 1970s, states like California, New York, and Illinois all implemented major reforms to augment their legislative capacities.[7] By contrast, the Texas legislature remained an amateurish body that met only once every two years, impeding the ability of lawmakers to respond quickly and efficiently to the AIDS crisis. Because legislators convened so infrequently, they had far fewer opportunities to influence the policy response to the epidemic. Faced with a tight window of opportunity for legislative action, AIDS activists and lobbyists rushed at the end of each session to pass laws before time ran out, forcing them to make significant compromises with conservative lawmakers. The story of AIDS in Texas reveals that the varying policymaking capacities of the states—especially the amount of time legislatures spent in session—shaped the unequal response to the epidemic.

The criminalization of same-sex sexual conduct constituted another

Table 4.1: State-only expenditure on AIDS in fiscal year 1989, ranked by spending per AIDS case. The table shows the ten states with the highest cumulative AIDS caseloads.

State	*Spending on AIDS ($)*	*Cumulative AIDS Caseload*	*Spending per Case ($)*
Massachusetts	14,754,308	2,502	5,897
California	76,877,000	23,265	3,304
Maryland	5,148,751	2,150	2,395
New York	52,844,926	26,126	2,023
Florida	17,765,244	9,975	1,781
New Jersey	13,012,804	7,918	1,643
Illinois	5,636,261	3,449	1,634
Georgia	4,840,215	3,051	1,586
Pennsylvania	4,645,000	3,249	1,430
Texas	2,336,572	8,092	289
Average	19,786,108	8,978	2,198

Note: Figures exclude Medicaid-related expenditures. Sources: Mona Rowe and Rita Keintz, "National Survey of State Spending for AIDS," *Intergovernmental AIDS Reports* 2, no. 3 (September-October 1989), 6–7; Centers for Disease Control and Prevention, "HIV/AIDS Surveillance Report," CDC, January 1990, https://www.cdc.gov/hiv/pdf/library/reports/surveillance/cdc-hiv-surveillance-report-1989-vol-2.pdf.

obstacle to legislative action on AIDS. Until the Supreme Court struck it down in 2003, the Texas sodomy statute outlawed oral and anal intercourse between people of the same sex, attaching the stigma of criminality to sexual minorities and rendering them second-class citizens. In the realm of legislative politics, the criminalization of gay men—who accounted for roughly 80 percent of the state's caseload in the 1980s—dictated the terms of the debate over the AIDS epidemic.[8] By categorizing the majority of PWAs as criminals, the sodomy law served as a rationale for ignoring the disease. Throughout the 1980s, conservative legislators invoked the statute to constrain the nature and extent of AIDS reform, depicting PWAs as serial lawbreakers underserving of state support.[9]

As cases of HIV mounted in the mid-1980s, the Lesbian/Gay Rights Lobby (LGRL), the state's only LGBT lobbying organization, led calls for more legislative action on the epidemic. In the face of obstructionism from conservative lawmakers and deep-seated homophobia in the Texas legislature, the LGRL initially struggled to rally support for its proposals. After years of racking up only piecemeal victories, the organization eventually embraced the language of fiscal conservatism to push for AIDS legislation, claiming that prevention education and other interventions were financially sensible because they would stem the spread of a costly disease. This change of strategy paid off, paving the way for the passage of the Omnibus AIDS Act in 1989. During deliberations over the legislation, conservative lawmakers used their enormous influence in the legislature to exact substantial concessions, including amendments that criminalized the "intentional" transmission of HIV. The result was a piece of legislation that bore the imprint of gay lobbyists and conservative legislators alike. Even after the passage of the Omnibus AIDS Act, Texas spent considerably less on the disease than most other large states. With its weak policymaking capacity and climate of rampant homophobia, the Texas legislature remained ill-equipped to tackle a rapidly evolving epidemic that disproportionately affected sexual minorities.

The Structure of Legislative Politics in Texas

In the middle of the twentieth century, state legislatures were administratively weak institutions that trailed well behind Congress when it came to legislative pay, staffing resources, and session lengths. Most legislatures met only every other year, paid lawmakers a paltry salary, and employed few staff members to assist in writing legislation and researching policy.[10] By the 1960s and 1970s, a nationwide movement had emerged among politicians and academics to professionalize legislatures and turn them into more effective governing bodies. At the vanguard of this push for legislative reform was Jesse Unruh, who served as Speaker of the California Assembly between 1961 and 1969. During his tenure, he improved legislative pay, campaigned for a successful ballot initiative that removed restrictions on the number of days lawmakers could meet, and provided each member of his chamber with funds for a district office, secretary, and administrative aide.[11] Although Unruh was particularly zealous in his campaign for a more professional legislature, the impetus for reform was not limited to California. In the 1960s and 1970s, scores of commissions and studies converged on the same set of recommendations for streamlining the legislative process, including increased lawmaker pay, more frequent sessions, improved physical facilities, and the establishment of a permanent corps of expert staff.[12] Many states heeded these calls for more professional and competent lawmaking and implemented sweeping changes to remedy the shortcomings of their legislatures. Influenced by the various commissions and studies on legislative reform, states increased the average compensation for lawmakers by roughly 223 percent between 1960 and 1970.[13]

The scale of these reforms differed markedly from one state to another, leading to disparities in the ability of lawmakers to govern effectively. Some states, such as California and New York, treated legislative seats as full-time professional positions, adopting year-round sessions and providing their legislators with ample resources, including generous salaries and large teams of staffers. Others, including Utah, Texas, and Wyoming, upheld the ideal of the "citizen legislature," meaning lawmakers served only part time and combined their policymaking work with other vocations.[14] As a result, the length of legislative sessions—a key metric for measuring legislative professionalism—varied dramatically across the country. While California and Massachusetts had sessions that stretched over most of the calendar year, some legislatures, like those in Montana, Nevada, North Dakota, and Texas, met only once every two years.[15] Legislative pay also ranged wildly across the states. In the 1988–1989 biennium, the most generous state, New York, offered lawmakers $57,500 in annual compensation while the least generous, New Hampshire, paid legislators only $102.[16]

While the most professionalized legislatures were typically in large, populous states like California and New York, the situation was very different in Texas, which lagged significantly behind its peers in its legislative capacity. Well into the late twentieth century, lawmakers remained underpaid amateurs who often had to find other jobs to make ends meet.[17] Under the Texas constitution, legislators convened for less than five months every two years and exercised few duties during the rest of their terms. In a typical session, they hurriedly scrambled to enact laws before time ran out, leaving little time for serious deliberation.[18] "Many bills are passed by the legislature after consideration lasting one minute," the prominent journalist Molly Ivins observed sardonically in 1975: "During the traditional end-of-the-session logjam, this bill-a-minute pace is sometimes sustained for four or five days."[19] In 1973, the Citizens Conference on State Legislatures, a nonprofit dedicated to advancing the cause of legislative reform, produced a damning report that summed up the institutional weaknesses of the Texas

Table 4.2: Average annual compensation for state legislators and frequency of state legislative sessions in 1989.

State	*Annual Compensation for State Legislators ($)*	*Frequency of State Legislative Sessions*
California	40,816	Annual
Florida	25,134	Annual
Georgia	12,884	Annual
Illinois	35,661	Annual
Maryland	25,000	Annual
Massachusetts	49,550	Annual
New Jersey	35,000	Annual
New York	57,500	Annual
Pennsylvania	47,000	Annual
Texas	10,185	Biennial
Average	33,873	—

Note: The table shows figures for the ten states with the largest cumulative number of AIDS cases. The figures for legislative compensation include salaries and estimated expenses. Sources: David L. Sollars, "Institutional Rules and State Legislator Compensation: Success for the Reform Movement?," Legislative Studies Quarterly 19, no. 4 (November 1994): 509; Centers for Disease Control and Prevention, "HIV/AIDS Surveillance Report," January 1990, https://www.cdc.gov/hiv/pdf/library/reports/surveillance/cdc-hiv-surveillance-report-1989-vol-2.pdf.

legislature: "Burdened by restrictions from another century, the Legislature has been unable fully to rise to the challenges of the present age. Instead of a strong legislature performing its intended tasks of representation, problem resolution and oversight of state administration, the present Legislature is a weakened body constrained by limited biennial sessions, by its inability to review vetoed bills after adjournment or to call itself into special sessions."[20] When the AIDS epidemic struck, Texan legislators possessed significantly fewer resources than their colleagues in other hard-hit states. Of the ten states with the largest caseloads in the 1980s, Texas was the only one to maintain biennial sessions. It also ranked at the bottom in terms of legislative pay, awarding each lawmaker $10,185 in 1989 compared with $40,816 and $35,661 in California and Illinois, respectively (see table 4.2).

These characteristics of the Texas legislature—low policymaking capacity, biennial sessions, and the hasty production of laws—shaped the state's response to the epidemic. Because legislators only met for five months every two years, gay activists and lobbyists scrambled in the final hours of each session to overcome the logjam of bills and pass AIDS legislation, even if that meant making substantial concessions or accepting flawed proposals. By turning legislative seats into part-time jobs, the Texas constitution spawned a frenzied and amateurish environment in the legislature, with lawmakers often lacking the time and expertise to delve into the substantive details of new AIDS policies. At times, gay lobbyists used the frantic dash at the end of each session to their advantage, introducing last-minute amendments to AIDS legislation that their opponents had no time to read. On the whole, however, the limited amount of time Texan lawmakers spent in session served as a roadblock to effective AIDS policymaking and generated a hurried and careless approach to legislating.

AIDS and the Texas Sodomy Statute

In addition to its low policymaking capacity, the Texas legislature was a deeply conservative political body, especially on matters related to sexuality. By the beginning of the AIDS epidemic, the Texas political landscape had entered a period of protracted partisan realignment that gradually moved the state from Democratic control to Republican dominance. Foreshadowing the state's eventual transformation into a GOP stronghold, Ronald Reagan carried Texas by the overwhelming margins of 55 and 64 percent in the 1980 and 1984 presidential elections, respectively. Throughout the 1980s, the Democratic Party retained majorities in both the state Senate and House of Representatives, but the GOP slowly made inroads into state politics.[21] Even as Democrats and Republicans vied for control of the state's levers of power, however, homophobia permeated both sides of the political aisle in the legislature. Except for a few liberal politicians representing gay enclaves in Austin, Dallas, and Houston, most lawmakers were not friendly with the gay movement.[22]

One of the most visible manifestations of the Texas legislature's homophobia was the existence of a state sodomy statute, which provided legal justification for discrimination against sexual minorities. During the 1960s and 1970s, statehouses enacted a wave of bills to update their penal codes, often overturning their sodomy laws in the process. By 1981, twenty-four states had decriminalized gay sex, including California and Illinois.[23] In

Texas, however, a sodomy statute remained on the books for most of the 1980s and 1990s, despite repeated efforts by gay men and lesbians to overturn it through litigation and the legislative process. Originating in the mid-nineteenth century, the Texas sodomy law was an extremely broad and capacious law for most of its history. It criminalized oral and anal sex not only between members of the same sex but also between heterosexual couples. That changed in 1973 when the Texas legislature enacted a new penal code, which singled out gay men and lesbians for unequal treatment. While the new law legalized anal and oral intercourse between heterosexual couples, it contained a provision—Section 21.06—that made it illegal to engage in these activities with members of the same sex. For the first time in Texan history, the sodomy law specifically targeted gay men and lesbians, transforming them into a separate class of citizens with fewer rights than heterosexual individuals.[24]

By branding all gay men criminals, Section 21.06 loomed large over the state's initial response to the AIDS crisis. Early in the epidemic, conservative lawmakers and activists used the outbreak of HIV to defend the sodomy statute, arguing that criminalizing gay sex represented an effective public health strategy in light of the disease's disproportionate impact on sexual minorities. After a federal district court briefly struck down Section 21.06 in 1982, conservative doctors and attorneys in Dallas founded two organizations—Dallas Doctors Against AIDS (DDAA) and Alert Citizens of Texas (ACT)—to campaign for its reinstatement.[25] Both groups suggested a causal link between the legalization of gay sex and the spread of HIV/AIDS. "Homosexuality is extremely dangerous from a public health standpoint," proclaimed H. Clem Mueller, a member of ACT and vice president of the DDAA, in a widely distributed letter: "Strong, enforceable laws are our only protection from an explosion of sex clubs, glory holes, bathhouses, and the incurable diseases that are incubated in their steamy dark rooms."[26] Over the next couple of years, both organizations mounted a relentless drive to reinstate the sodomy statute, often exploiting the fear and misinformation associated with the AIDS epidemic to argue that criminalizing gay sex was necessary to protect the public's health.[27]

During the 1983 legislative session, the DDAA's and ACT's campaign dominated the legislature's early deliberations over the AIDS epidemic. With the support of both organizations, Republican representative Bill Ceverha, one of the legislature's most homophobic lawmakers, introduced House Bill 2138 (HB 2138) in April.[28] Even more draconian than Section

21.06, the bill proposed to reinstate the state sodomy statute and upgrade the penalty for violating it from a misdemeanor to a felony.[29] When the House Criminal Jurisprudence Committee convened a hearing on HB 2138 on April 19, supporters of the bill argued that the state government had a compelling interest to recriminalize gay sex because of the AIDS epidemic. At the start of proceedings, Ceverha informed those assembled in the committee room that the legislation aimed to protect the public from sexually transmitted infections.[30] In the testimony that followed, proponents of HB 2138 emphasized the supposed link between the legalization of gay sex and the spread of HIV. The first person to testify was psychologist Dr. Paul Cameron, an anti-gay crusader who produced a string of misleading and pseudoscientific pamphlets on the supposed dangers of homosexuality in the late 1970s and 1980s.[31] As the AIDS epidemic mounted, he proposed extreme measures to mitigate the disease's spread, including the use of concentration camps for "sexually active homosexuals."[32] During his testimony, Cameron informed the committee that HB 2138 would protect the public from the "health-risks attendant" to gay sex. To increase the shock value of his remarks, he cited several outlandish statistics, such as the claim that 22 percent of gay men incorporated fecal matter into their sexual encounters.[33] Shortly after Cameron finished speaking, Mueller appeared before the committee to argue that HB 2138 would mitigate the spread of AIDS and prevent the disease from affecting heterosexuals. He told lawmakers that "there's increasing evidence that [AIDS] is a danger to the population in general, and we might consider that in our mind when we are referring to laws regulating homosexual activities."[34] In the end, HB 2138 proved too extreme for even the Texas legislature, and it died in committee at the end of the 1983 session.[35] Though defeated, the bill signaled the growing interplay between debates over the AIDS epidemic and the state sodomy statute.[36]

Two years later, after a period of legal wrangling, the federal Fifth Circuit Court of Appeals reinstated Section 21.06 by a 9–7 vote.[37] For the rest of the 1980s, the criminalization of gay sex undermined the state's response to the epidemic. In expert testimony submitted to the Texas Court of Appeals in 1990, Ron J. Anderson, who served as chair of the Texas Board of Health between 1983 and 1987, recounted the harmful effects of the sodomy statute on efforts to contain the disease. He told the court that outlawing gay sex had discouraged many people at risk of HIV from getting tested and seeking treatment: "People are less likely to come forward for testing when the results of the test may be used in a manner that results in criminal prosecution, discrimination or personal or financial injury." Acknowledging that he personally opposed gay and lesbian equality, he nonetheless testified that the sodomy law had impeded "public health efforts to accomplish early screening, earlier treatment, and, most importantly, prevention of transmission."[38] At the same time, Section 21.06 hampered the operations of grassroots AIDS service organizations, many of which grew out of the gay movement. William Waybourn, a veteran gay activist and president of the Dallas Gay Alliance (DGA) in the late 1980s, recalled that the statute dissuaded private foundations from providing grants to local AIDS nonprofits. In 1985, the DGA founded the AIDS Resource Center (ARC), which gradually expanded into one of the city's largest HIV service providers.[39] In its early years, the ARC struggled to secure support from private foundations, which often cited the sodomy statute when rejecting funding bids from the organization, arguing that affiliating with a gay group represented too much of a representational risk.[40] For all these reasons, the sodomy statute hindered the public health response to AIDS in Texas. By prohibiting certain sexual activities only when performed by gay men and lesbians, it justified discrimination against HIV-positive people, damaged the relationship between health officials and sexual minorities, and prevented vital funds from going to AIDS service organizations.

Two other states with large AIDS caseloads—Florida and Georgia—also had sodomy statutes on the books in the 1980s. Unlike in Texas, however, neither state criminalized certain sexual activities only when performed by members of the same sex. Instead, the Florida and Georgia sodomy laws theoretically applied to everyone, outlawing all anal intercourse between heterosexual and same-sex couples.[41] In both states, the sodomy statute also did not intrude as much into political debates over the epidemic. When the Supreme Court upheld Georgia's sodomy law in 1986, the state declined to use the AIDS crisis in its defence of the statute.[42] In Florida, the legislature enacted a sweeping AIDS law in 1988, which criminalized "intentional" transmission of HIV, pumped money into local AIDS service organizations, and provided HIV-positive people with legal protections against discrimination. During committee hearings and floor debates over this legislation, not a single lawmaker cited the state sodomy statute.[43] Moreover, the epidemiology of the disease in Florida differed sharply from Texas, as gay men accounted for a much smaller percentage of cases. In this context, it was much harder for conservative lawmakers to pin the blame for the epidemic solely on sexual minorities and use the criminalization of gay sex to mobilize support for a more draconian approach to the disease.[44] To a much greater extent than in other high-incidence states, then, the Texas sodomy statute shaped the legislative politics of AIDS.

Gay Rights Lobbying and the Texan AIDS Epidemic

For most of the mid-1980s, the Texas legislature all but ignored the AIDS epidemic. During the 1985 legislative session, lawmakers introduced only one AIDS-related bill: House Bill 1102 (HB 1102), which proposed to ban blood banks from purchasing blood from individuals with certain communicable diseases, including HIV/AIDS. Referred to the House Public Health Committee in early March, HB 1102 received no public hearings and failed to make it to the floor of the legislature.[45]

Gay rights activists, troubled by the Texas legislature's lack of action on the epidemic, responded by ramping up their lobbying efforts in Austin. In December 1986, the Lesbian/Gay Rights Lobby of Texas (LGRL), the state's only gay organization focused solely on legislative politics, intensified its push for AIDS reform by hiring Glen Maxey as its first full-time executive director.[46] Established in 1981, the LGRL received donations from gay groups across the state, pooling their resources to craft a coherent lobbying agenda in Austin. Its member organizations included the Austin Lesbian/Gay Political Caucus, the Dallas Gay Alliance, the Houston Gay/Lesbian Political Caucus, Lesbian/Gay Democrats of Texas, the Tarrant County Gay Alliance, and the Lubbock Lesbian/Gay Alliance.[47] The hiring of Maxey proved to be a significant milestone in the LGRL's organizational development. Before then, the group typically employed freelance lobbyists for the duration of a single legislative session, leaving no time or resources for crafting policies when the legislature was adjourned. With Maxey's hiring, the organization finally had a permanent presence in Austin all year round, including when lawmakers were out of session.[48] A former legislative staffer, Maxey proved to be a skilled political operator. Despite the legislature's unbridled homophobia, he managed to forge alliances with several prominent politicians, most notably state senator Craig Washington, whose district in Houston included the gay neighborhood of Montrose.[49] In the late 1980s, Washington sponsored numerous HIV-specific bills drafted by Maxey, including the Omnibus AIDS Act. Besides Washington, the LGRL could count on several other senators from Dallas and Houston for support but had fewer allies in the House, which contained a larger share of conservative and homophobic lawmakers.[50]

As the 1987 legislative session opened, Maxey prepared to lobby for a range of AIDS-related proposals, including discrimination protections for PWAs, more expenditure on prevention education, and a ban on mandatory antibody testing.[51] In the hostile and homophobic climate of the Texas legislature, conservative lawmakers successfully blocked most of these measures in committee. Despite these setbacks, Maxey still succeeded in persuading lawmakers to enact two AIDS-related laws in 1987. The first, Senate Bill 1405 (SB 1405), protected the confidentiality of people taking the antibody test when donating blood.[52] The second, House Bill 1829 (HB 1829), revised and updated the state's fifty-year-old Communicable Diseases Act, which provided public health officials with broad and capacious powers to control the spread of contagion. Perhaps the most significant part of HB 1829 was that it gave people with infectious diseases substantial due process protections against quarantine and isolation orders, including the right to a hearing to contest their case. Rooted in the legal doctrine of police power, which permitted state governments to violate individual liberties to protect the common good, the old Communicable Diseases Act had contained virtually no due process procedures, allowing health officials to exercise almost total discretion over the use of quarantine.[53]

Before the passage of HB 1829, gay rights activists had worried that public health professionals might use these discretionary powers against PWAs. This fear almost came to fruition in late 1985, when Robert Bernstein, the Texas health commissioner, advanced a proposal to add AIDS to the state's list of diseases subject to quarantine. Under this plan, local officials could isolate any person with AIDS involuntarily if they were deemed a threat to the public's health.[54] Bernstein put forth this proposal after a flurry of high-profile media accounts of PWAs allegedly continuing to have sex without disclosing their infection status. In perhaps the most infamous case, newspapers across the nation reported on Fabian Bridges, a Black man with AIDS from Houston who struggled with homelessness and poverty after his diagnosis. Over the summer and fall of 1985, media accounts insinuated, without conclusive evidence, that Bridges was engaging in sex work with other men without first communicating his infection status.[55] Rattled by these reports, James Haughton, the Houston city health director, publicly called for AIDS to be a quarantinable disease, pushing Bernstein to announce his plan to give local officials the power to isolate PWAs.[56] While

Bernstein eventually withdrew his proposal after a backlash from civil libertarians, AIDS workers, and medical professionals, many gay activists were deeply disturbed that the state health department would even consider such a draconian policy, prompting Maxey to prioritize reforming the Communicable Diseases Act during the 1987 legislative session.[57]

As HB 1829 made its way through the legislature, conservative members of the House attempted to saddle the legislation with several draconian provisions. During a bitter floor debate over the bill in late May 1987, Democratic state representative Jim McWilliams, a fervid opponent of gay rights and the AIDS movement, submitted a string of punitive amendments, including proposals for premarital antibody testing and mandatory reporting of test results to spouses.[58] With few allies in the House, Maxey decided to accept these changes temporarily and then try and remove them when the law came before the Senate. On May 29, three days before the end of the session, the House approved a draconian version of the bill that included most of McWilliams's proposals. When the Senate began its deliberations over HB 1829 the next day, Maxey worked with Senator Chet Brooks, a supporter of the LGRL, to rewrite key sections of the law, adding new due process protections for people with communicable diseases and removing most of McWilliams's punitive amendments.[59] Brooks then took advantage of the usual logjam of bills at the end of the session to ensure the passage of HB 1829. With time running out to enact new laws, he introduced the revised legislation before the Senate, hoping busy lawmakers would pass it without reading the changes made by Maxey. This gamble paid off. On the penultimate day of the session, the Senate enacted the bill unanimously after a short debate that never mentioned the AIDS epidemic or Maxey's revisions.[60]

Soon afterward, the House enacted Maxey's revised legislation by the wide margin of 108–37.[61] In private discussions with lawmakers in the House, Maxey used antigay rhetoric to persuade them to pass the new version of HB 1829. Evoking the case of Fabian Bridges, he falsely claimed that the bill would make it easier to quarantine people with HIV infection, telling legislators that "the only way you're gonna get somebody, some queer guy, some faggot off the street, transmitting AIDS in your district, is if this bill is in place. . . . So, get the faggots off the street, help us pass this bill."[62] Paradoxically, Maxey relied on the same homophobic language that had hobbled the state's response to AIDS, using the stigma and fear associated with the epidemic to deceive lawmakers into believing HB 1829 would promote a more punitive approach to disease control. Determined to use any tactics necessary to make some headway on AIDS policy, he depicted gay men as vectors of disease, drawing on well-worn stereotypes that conflated homosexuality with danger, illness, and "deviance."[63] Pressed for time at the end of the session, legislators in the House failed to notice Maxey's bluff, probably because they had not read the contents of the bill in full.[64] Like so many other AIDS-related laws passed by the states in the mid-1980s, the gay movement achieved a qualified victory with the enactment of HB 1829. While Maxey successfully reformed the Communicable Diseases Act and staved off attempts by conservative lawmakers to introduce draconian amendments, he reinforced prevalent stereotypes about gay men and PWAs to secure the votes of legislators in the House.

In the end, the 1987 legislative session yielded only modest gains for the LGRL and the AIDS movement. Compared to laws enacted in other high-incidence states in the mid-1980s, both HB 1829 and SB 1405 were piecemeal bills that were out of step with the scale of the crisis. Funding remained scarce for prevention education, antibody testing, and AIDS patient care. In 1988, Texas spent only $1.5 million on the epidemic, less than thirteen cents per capita.[65] By contrast, Florida appropriated over $12 million for a range of HIV/AIDS programs, including the creation of a new AIDS ward at Jackson Memorial Hospital in Dade County, where roughly 46 percent of the state's cases had been reported.[66] Meanwhile, New Jersey spent over $8 million on tackling the epidemic, five times more than Texas, despite both states having near-identical case rates.[67] Although gay activists had become better organized in Austin, Texas still lagged significantly behind other large, hard-hit states in its response to the AIDS crisis.

The Genesis and Enactment of the Omnibus AIDS Act

In the 1987 legislative session, Texan lawmakers rejected most attempts to enact significant AIDS legislation. Yet two years later, with cases of the disease soaring, they reversed course and passed a major HIV-specific law that funnelled millions of dollars into the fight against the epidemic. This sudden change of heart stemmed from the looming fiscal burden of the AIDS crisis. During the late 1980s, Texas entered a period of intense budgetary problems, as the state faced a slump in oil prices, a real estate recession, and a slowdown in the economy.[68] As the economy began to falter, AIDS lobbyists shifted tactics, portraying prevention education and AIDS healthcare as financially sensible solutions to an expensive and rapidly escalating epidemic. A strain of rhetoric arose among gay activists, medical workers, and sympathetic lawmakers that the disease would become an enormous tax burden in the long term if the legislature did not intervene to slow its spread.

This argument coalesced during a series of public hearings on the epidemic between the 1987 and 1989 legislative sessions. In May 1987, Lieutenant Governor William B. Hobby announced plans to appoint a task force to study the issue of AIDS and report back in time for the next session. After receiving suggestions on whom to nominate over the summer, Hobby announced the final composition of the commission in October. The nineteen-member task force included lawmakers, medical professionals, and representatives from the business community but no PWAs.[69] Despite this disappointment, AIDS activists secured a significant victory when Hobby selected Reverend Chris Steele, who had previously worked with him on other projects, to lead the commission. An Episcopal priest from Houston, Steele proved sympathetic to the concerns of sexual minorities and PWAs and forged close ties with Maxey and other AIDS activists.[70] During her tenure as chairperson of the commission, she faced the unenviable task of steering a diverse group of members toward a consensus on AIDS policy. Attuned to the political realities of the epidemic, Steele knew that simply emphasizing the social and medical needs of PWAs would not work in the climate of AIDS hysteria and homophobia that pervaded Texas state politics. Early in the commission's work, she decided to play to the political popularity of fiscal conservatism and focus on the economic benefits of progressive AIDS policies like prevention education and early intervention.[71]

Over the next thirteen months, the task force convened eight public hearings across the state to solicit testimony from PWAs, medical workers, and HIV service providers.[72] During these gatherings, witness after witness emphasized the threat AIDS posed to the state's public finances. When the commission met in San Antonio on March 16, 1988, Susan Weddington, a Republican attorney, testified that "every citizen in Texas, including our corporate citizens, is a victim of AIDS as regards to economic impact. . . . We must have compassion for the healthy individuals who will be the major cost bearers of this health crisis."[73] Adding to this chorus of concern about the fiscal burden of AIDS was the notion that discrimination against PWAs was forcing them to leave their jobs and rely on welfare. At a public hearing in Austin, Dara Gray, the executive director of the Texas Human Rights Foundation, an LGBT legal advocacy organization, informed the commission that "as employers continue to force people out of work and insurance companies are allowed to deny insurance, [people with HIV infection] have no choice but to become public wards. The eventual cost to the state is inestimable."[74] In addition to holding public hearings, the task force commissioned several studies to analyze the problem of AIDS in Texas.[75] Among the most important was an analysis of the lost earnings caused by people dying prematurely from HIV/AIDS. Conducted by a team of researchers at the University of Texas School of Public Health, the study calculated that "state and local tax revenue lost due to premature deaths from AIDS will be between $110 million and $170 million in 1988."[76] Consistent with Steele's aim to recast the epidemic as an economic question, the belief that AIDS was becoming a drain on public finances suffused the commission's deliberations in 1988.

In January 1989, the task force issued its final set of recommendations. Throughout its seven-chapter, 160-page final report, the commission was adamant that prevention education, patient care, and discrimination protections for PWAs all represented financially sensible policies.[77] In a chapter on the legal aspects of the epidemic, the report emphasized the costs associated with discrimination against PWAs: "The stigma that so often accompanies an HIV-related diagnosis directly effects the earning power and economic productivity of Texans with HIV. . . . Ultimately, discrimination results in increased economic burden and loss of revenue for local taxpayers."[78] With a set of sweeping and far-reaching recommendations, the task force's final report finally met the pleas of those who demanded a more proactive response to the epidemic. Written chiefly by Steele, it urged lawmakers to increase expenditure on prevention education and patient care, furnish HIV-positive people with legal protections, expand the availability of experimental drug therapies, and funnel more resources toward AIDS service organizations.[79]

When the legislature went back in session at the start of 1989, Senators Craig Washington and Chet Brooks, in consultation with Maxey, introduced the Omnibus AIDS Bill, which incorporated most of the task force's recommendations.[80] Echoing the language of the commission's final report, supporters of the measure emphasized its fiscal benefits. When the Senate Committee on Health and Human Affairs decided to hold a series of public hearings on the bill in late March, several AIDS service organizations sent witnesses to testify, seizing the opportunity to warn lawmakers of the economic costs of failing to address the epidemic.[81] Thomas Bruner, the executive director of the Community Outreach Centre in Fort Worth, one of the area's largest AIDS nonprofits, registered his support for the Omnibus AIDS Bill by calling it "efficient and cost effective." He insisted that funding AIDS service organizations would save the state money by reducing the reliance of PWAs on welfare programs. To prove his point, he noted that his group ran a successful food pantry service for HIV-positive people, which "reduced their dependence on the county welfare food stamp program."[82] As the hearings proceeded, public health officials also framed their support for the bill in economic terms. King Hillier, the director of government relations for the Harris County Hospital District, told the committee that the epidemic would cost the county $100 million in patient care by 1992 if the legislature failed to act.[83]

After these hearings, Maxey worked tirelessly to ramp up the LGRL's lobbying efforts. At his instigation, gay men and lesbians across the state flooded lawmakers' offices with letters urging them to enact the bill.[84] Maxey also served on the steering committee for the gay movement's mass protest in Austin on April 30, 1989, which brought thirty thousand gay men and lesbians to the steps of the state Capitol Building (as described at the start of this chapter). The day after, Maxey organized a "lobby day" for the protestors, encouraging them to meet personally with their legislators to demand a swift passage of the Omnibus AIDS Bill. In a flyer for the event, he told participants to "emphasize the cost effectiveness of community-based treatments and education programs. Point out the tremendous financial savings to the state to provide PWAs the drugs which will keep them out of costly acute care hospitalization."[85] At the same time, Maxey collaborated in secret with the Austin chapter of the direct-action group ACT/UP, which staged regular demonstrations outside and inside the Capitol Building in April and May. After urging the group to be as provocative as possible, he used its rallies as leverage during personal conversations with lawmakers, informing them that enacting AIDS legislation was the only way to prevent future disruptions.[86] By skillfully managing the state's dense network of gay rights and AIDS organizations, the LGRL deployed a multipronged campaign to garner support for the AIDS Omnibus Bill, which included direct lobbying, mass mailouts, and civil disobedience. Thanks to this lobbying blitz and the support of Craig Washington, the Senate passed the Omnibus AIDS Bill by a voice vote with no significant amendments on May 15.[87]

The real battle over the Omnibus AIDS Bill occurred in the House, where conservative lawmakers used their committee positions to ram through a much more draconian version of the law. Republican Representative Brad Wright and Democratic Representative Billy Clemons, both fervid opponents of gay rights, led a counteroffensive against the task force's recommendations. Wright and Clemons served as chair and vice chair, respectively, of the House Public Health Committee, which held jurisdiction over HIV-related legislation. During the committee's hearings over the Omnibus AIDS Bill in late April and early May, they solicited testimony from a group of conservative medical professionals who used Section 21.06 to argue that the legislature should focus more attention on punishing PWAs than funding prevention education.[88] "I think we should stop people from practicing sodomy and stop people from using drugs in Texas," Dr. Robert Eltman, a cardiovascular surgeon from Houston, told the committee: "[AIDS] is a law enforcement problem."[89] Another witness, Dr. Steven F. Holtze, warned lawmakers that prevention education would be "a boon for homosexual organizations who have promoted homosexual activities throughout the state." Near the end of his testimony, Holtze argued that PWAs were to blame for contracting the disease because they had violated the law:

> They need to be punished and their lifestyle needs to be condemned, not promoted, not pandered to, not sanctioned publicly. We need to maintain strictly our anti-sodomy law in the state of Texas. We need not give these guys special privileges and special rights and minority status. We need to say what you're doing is wrong. It violates criminal statutes. You've got to stop it or you're going to die. If you die, it's your fault. It's not my fault as a Physician. It's not your fault as a legislator that they die. It's their fault.[90]

Steeped in homophobic rhetoric, the committee's hearings framed the AIDS epidemic as a law enforcement rather than a public health issue, weaponizing Section 21.06 to undermine the case for prevention education and antidiscrimination provisions for PWAs.

After holding these hearings, Wright and Clemons persuaded the other members of the Public Health Committee to approve a significantly modified version of the Omnibus AIDS Bill. The new measure removed legal protections for PWAs, mandated that all state-funded education materials must mention that homosexuality was illegal, and instructed the Texas health department to focus its prevention efforts on young people and heterosexuals rather than gay men and IV drug users.[91] Furious at the changes made to the original legislation, Steele told the *Houston Chronicle* that "many of the bill's provisions would fuel rather than dampen the wildfire of the AIDS epidemic in Texas."[92] In an interview with the same newspaper, Maxey noted that "it was fairly obvious that the Public Health Committee was hellbent to make [AIDS] into a criminal issue and not a public health issue. The sections that the Public Health Committee put in [the bill] are probably some of the most outrageous and illogical responses to AIDS that have come out of any state legislature."[93] Despite these objections, the full House unanimously approved Wright's and Clemons' bill on May 23.[94]

Since the House and Senate versions of the Omnibus Act differed substantially, both bodies entered into arduous conference negotiations to reconcile the two bills. The joint committee appointed for these deliberations contained several conservative members of the House, who leveraged their influence to ensure that the final version of the law included numerous draconian and homophobic elements. Among other concessions, they successfully watered down the Senate's proposals for protecting PWAs from employment discrimination, which had been a crucial recommendation of the Legislative Task Force on AIDS. The bill that came out of these conference negotiations was not as extreme as the version passed in the House, but it still contained several homophobic provisions. It criminalized the "intentional" transmission of HIV and stipulated that all prevention education in schools must inform students that homosexuality was not a socially acceptable lifestyle.[95]

Once the conference negotiations had concluded, the Omnibus AIDS Act squeaked through the legislature on the last day of the session. It passed the House with only twenty-two minutes to spare, forcing Maxey to sprint across the Capitol Building with the bill in hand to the Senate chamber, where lawmakers hurriedly approved it with a voice vote.[96] Although Maxey worried about the impact of the law's many draconian provisions, he accepted them because of the constraints imposed by the biennial session. Given that the legislature only met every other year, he was determined to pass *any* bill that boosted investment in AIDS programs rather than wait another two years, even if that meant compromising with conservative and homophobic lawmakers in the House.[97] He defended this decision in a lobby report to the supporters of the LGRL: "Anyone who cries that the Omnibus AIDS Bill is bad or dangerous is absolutely correct. But what was the alternative? No bill? Sorry, but we weren't given that option at 11:45 pm on the last night of the session."[98] Because the legislature met so infrequently, Maxey accepted the idea that some reform was better than none, regardless of the concessions he had to make.

After the passage of the Omnibus AIDS Act, gay activists had to contend with obstructionist bureaucrats in the state government who used the sodomy statute to stall the smooth implementation of the law. The Texas health department, the agency tasked with administering the legislation, initially struggled to interpret a last-minute and vaguely worded clause that banned AIDS service organizations from receiving state funds if they supported breaking the law.[99] Lacking guidance from legislators about the exact meaning of this provision, health officials requested that the state attorney general, Jim Mattox, weigh in and provide an opinion. In the meantime, the department issued a preliminary set of guidelines to AIDS nonprofits, warning them that any group affiliated with the gay movement would initially not receive funding. Effectively labelling all sexual minorities criminals, the agency explained that gay organizations automatically supported violating the law because of the state sodomy statute. The guidelines even banned groups from receiving grants if they lobbied for the repeal of Section 21.06 or allowed volunteers and staff members to wear pink triangles, a symbol of LGBT identity, on their lapels.[100] Outraged by this blatant act of discrimination, Maxey described the health department's actions in the gay press as "the most direct attack on the lesbian/gay community ever proposed by any agency of the state of Texas."[101] After several weeks of these guidelines being in force, Mattox issued his much-awaited opinion on the Omnibus AIDS Act's funding provisions in January 1990. In a seven-page statement, he argued that the health department had no mandate from the state legislature to deny grants to gay organizations and ordered the agency to rescind its preliminary guidelines.[102] He also noted that the guidelines raised serious constitutional concerns, as they potentially violated "freedom of association, freedom of speech, and freedom to petition the government."[103] While this decision compelled the health department to restore funding to gay organizations, the agency's initial set of guidelines had already delayed the distribution of funding to several AIDS nonprofits, including the AIDS Resource Center, one of the largest HIV service providers in Dallas.[104]

Notwithstanding the health department's obstructionism, the Omnibus AIDS Act poured a significant amount of money and resources into the AIDS service industry in Texas. Funded at $18 million for the 1990–1991 biennium, the law increased the state's AIDS budget by roughly sixfold.[105] In 1990 alone, the health department used this money to provide grants to twenty-five AIDS service organizations for prevention education and patient care, a sizeable increase from the mere six contracts it offered for these activities during the previous year.[106] Despite this influx of funding, Texas still spent a relatively small amount on the epidemic when measured against other states. In 1992, it had the fourth highest caseload of any state in the nation but ranked thirty-second on spending per case.[107] That year, California outspent Texas on HIV/AIDS programs by more than threefold despite experiencing its deepest economic slowdown since the Great Depression because of defense cuts after the end of the Cold War.[108]

As Texas continued to underinvest in HIV/AIDS programs during the early 1990s, gay lobbyists found themselves on the defensive, hamstrung by organizational problems and AIDS hysteria in the state legislature. In the 1991 session, the LGRL invested most of its energy into defeating a trio of coercive bills introduced by conservative members of the House, which would have criminalized people suspected of exposing police officers and firefighters to HIV, enforced mandatory testing for health care workers, and repealed most of the provisions of the Omnibus AIDS Act. The group successfully worked behind the scenes to defeat all three measures but failed to get any of its own legislation out of committee.[109] When the legislature met again in 1993, the LGRL pared back its lobbying efforts as it confronted a major budget shortfall, which forced the organization to reduce its staff size and temporarily stop sending mail updates to its supporters.[110] With a diminished presence in Austin, gay lobbyists failed to secure any increase in the state's AIDS budget, even though caseloads were skyrocketing.[111] Confronted with inadequate budgetary and personnel resources, the LGRL carved out what few piecemeal gains it could in the early 1990s, which usually amounted to defeating discriminatory bills introduced by conservative lawmakers.

* * *

As the case of Texas illustrates, an important but often overlooked aspect of the early AIDS epidemic was the unequal response of the states. On issue after issue, ranging from the funding of prevention education to discrimination protections for PWAs, regional variation became a hallmark of efforts to contain the spread of the virus. Whereas some states were at the forefront of formulating AIDS policies during the 1980s, others failed to take the disease seriously. For much of the decade, California led the way in confronting the epidemic, passing one reform after another and sinking tens of millions of dollars into prevention education, antibody testing, and patient care. At the other end of the spectrum lay Texas, where lawmakers enacted only a handful of HIV-specific laws and spent a tiny amount on the crisis. For much of the 1980s, the Texas sodomy statute served as a persistent barrier to legislative action on the epidemic as conservative activists and legislators used it to portray HIV-positive people as criminals who had contracted the disease through illegal activities. In this climate of intense homophobia, lawmakers were deliberately unresponsive to the needs of PWAs until they believed the crisis threatened the state's public finances, at which point they finally enacted the Omnibus AIDS Act. Even then, Texas trailed behind most other large states in its response to the epidemic well into the 1990s.

CHAPTER FIVE

A New Federal Role Is Born

The Genesis and Enactment of the Ryan White CARE Act

The year 1990 marked a major turning point in the federal government's response to the AIDS epidemic. After years of lobbying from activists, state-level lawmakers, and public health officials, Congress enacted the Ryan White CARE Act, a landmark bill that provided direct relief to all fifty states and the cities hardest hit by the crisis. Backed by a broad and diverse coalition of interest groups, it sailed through Congress in the spring of 1990 with overwhelming bipartisan support. Over the next few years, it funneled billions of dollars to state and city governments for the provision of AIDS healthcare, contributing to a portentous increase in federal spending on the epidemic. While the states had spearheaded the policy response to AIDS in the 1980s, often acting independently of each other and without much guidance from federal policymakers, the passage of the CARE Act signaled that the national government would take a more active interest in the epidemic during the 1990s. During its initial five-year funding cycle, the law provided the states with over $2.8 billion of funding for AIDS patient care.[1] In 1990, the total federal budget for AIDS-related programs was $3.1 billion; by 2000, it had climbed to more than $12.2 billion, a nearly four-fold increase.[2]

The passage of the CARE Act was a watershed moment in the relationship between federalism and AIDS policymaking, transforming the national government's involvement in the fight against the disease. However, it did not spell the end of the states' critical role in the policy response to the epidemic. The legislation prompted a massive infusion of federal dollars into AIDS patient care, but it left state and local authorities with substantial discretion over which entities would receive this funding and what specific programs they would pursue. Under the CARE Act, grants were allocated to state governments for AIDS care with limited federal oversight and relatively few conditions attached, decentralizing control over the law's implementation to the subnational level. In the 1990s, state-by-state variation remained a hallmark of AIDS policymaking and continued to reflect distinct political conditions, legal arrangements, and administrative capacities. The result was vast regional disparities in the quality of services offered to PWAs. The CARE Act combined a massive expansion of federal spending on the AIDS epidemic with the devolution of policy implementation and planning to the state and local levels. As the epidemic entered its second decade, the federal government set the agenda for the nation's political and policy response to a much greater extent than in the past, but states and municipalities retained primary responsibility in implementing key policies on the ground.

This chapter explores the politics surrounding the enactment of the CARE Act. When drafting the law, AIDS lobbyists and their congressional allies on Capitol Hill turned to the state and local levels for inspiration. They modelled the CARE Act on a system of AIDS healthcare that was first developed by activists and public health officials in San Francisco, one that emphasized outpatient care, outsourcing to nonprofit and voluntary organizations, and a robust series of partnerships between AIDS service organizations and the state. The perceived cost-effectiveness of this model shaped the congressional response to AIDS in the early 1990s. Proponents of the CARE Act gained widespread support by arguing that it would prioritize outpatient care, preventing PWAs from relying on overstretched public hospitals. As Senator Pete Wilson (R–CA), a cosponsor of the bill, told Congress on March 6, 1990: "[The CARE Act] recognizes the need to shift our orientation from inpatient care to coordinated, integrated networks of community-based care, guiding HIV infected individuals along a continuum of the most appropriate and cost-effective services."[3] The structure of the CARE Act owed a great deal to San Francisco's network of government-nonprofit partnerships, as the drafters of the legislation sought to encourage other urban areas to develop equally robust systems of outpatient care in the community. To study the legislative history of the CARE Act, then, is to see the complex intergovernmental dynamics that shaped federal AIDS policymaking in the 1990s, when influence flowed from the local to the national level—and back again. In short, the law's antecedents extended back to the flurry of AIDS-related measures enacted by city and state governments during the 1980s.

Several vital factors converged in 1990 to compel Congress to enact the CARE Act: an increasingly professionalized AIDS lobbying network in Washington, DC, the growing salience of the fiscal case for funding AIDS service organizations, and the perception that the disease no longer just affected stigmatized minorities. Most importantly, the escalating costs of the epidemic in the late 1980s placed a severe strain on the medical infrastructures of hard-hit cities, pushing many public hospitals to the brink of financial insolvency. Pressure mounted on Congress to take decisive action against the epidemic as the disease created a generalized crisis in emergency rooms and hospitals that jeopardized the healthcare of people without HIV. Acting as the provider of last resort for PWAs denied health insurance, public hospitals lacked the financial and operational capacity to deal with an expanding AIDS caseload, especially after a series of cutbacks to municipal budgets and federal aid in the early 1980s. Deploying a strategy first used by activists at the state and local levels, supporters of the CARE Act portrayed it as a fiscally prudent measure that would ameliorate this burgeoning crisis by providing nonprofit groups with funds for AIDS care in outpatient settings, easing the pressure on public hospitals. Wary of antagonizing conservative members of Congress, proponents of the law were careful to frame it as a financially sensible response to a healthcare emergency that threatened to overwhelm hard-hit cities rather than as a measure that would benefit the stigmatized populations associated with AIDS.

Although recent years have witnessed a steady stream of important scholarship on federal AIDS policymaking, the legislative origins of the CARE Act remain understudied by historians. From existing accounts of the epidemic, we know a great deal about the response of the Reagan administration and the executive branch to the crisis and the various disputes within the White House over the efficacy of prevention education and mass testing.[4] But far less thoroughly examined are the policy details of major pieces of AIDS legislation enacted by Congress. Overshadowed by the failures of the Reagan administration, the CARE Act remains on the margins of much of the historiography on AIDS politics at the national level.[5] This lacuna is unfortunate, as much of the impetus for federal action on AIDS came from congressional Democrats like Senator Edward Kennedy (D–MA), Representative Henry Waxman (D–CA), and Congresswoman Nancy Pelosi (D–CA), all of whom maintained strong ties with gay rights activists. Across the late 1980s and early 1990s, Congress enacted a string of AIDS-related laws that expanded funding for AIDS healthcare and services, mandated increased spending on biomedical research, and furnished PWAs with discrimination protections.[6] Of these, the CARE Act was the most ambitious and extensive, quickly emerging as the federal government's largest domestic HIV-specific program.[7]

This chapter begins by examining the development of the San Francisco model of care at the start of the AIDS crisis, shedding light on how the nonprofit sector became so thoroughly entwined with the city's response to the epidemic. It then traces the growing popularity of government–nonprofit partnerships among AIDS activists, policymakers, and public health officials across the country in the mid-1980s. Outsourcing services to the voluntary sector became a politically expedient way of addressing the AIDS epidemic because of the perception that San Francisco had successfully contained the extraordinary costs of the disease. Meanwhile, state funding transformed many AIDS service organizations in terms of their budget, size, and ethos. After exploring the history of the San Francisco model at the state and local levels in the 1980s, attention is then turned to the early congressional response to AIDS, which was slow and fumbling at best and counterproductive at worst. In response, AIDS activists built a robust lobbying network in Washington, DC, and forged a series of alliances with powerful Democratic politicians, most notably Senator Edward Kennedy, who would play a vital role in shepherding major pieces of AIDS legislation through Congress in the late 1980s. An in-depth and extended discussion of the legislative history of the CARE Act then follows. The drafters of the law drew inspiration from the San Francisco system of care, arguing that government–nonprofit partnerships offered a solution to two policy problems emanating from the epidemic: the tremendous cost of HIV/AIDS treatment and the growing strain that people with HIV infection placed on public hospitals. To overcome the stalling tactics of a small group of conservative members of the Senate, AIDS lobbyists built a broad and diverse coalition of interest groups and reached out to politicians from across the political aisle to garner their backing. As with the most important pieces of AIDS legislation enacted at the state level in the 1980s, the CARE Act found support from across the political spectrum.

Governing Through Grantmaking: The San Francisco Model of Care

San Francisco played a pivotal role in making privatization, devolution, and outsourcing central to the federal response to AIDS. Beginning in 1982, the city developed an innovative model of HIV healthcare, centered on a well-developed network of public–private partnerships between the municipal government and voluntary organizations. In the epidemic's early years, San Francisco's response was unique in its scope and capaciousness, made possible by strong ties between LGBTQ activists and a sympathetic municipal government. During the 1960s and 1970s, gay men and lesbians had made important strides toward becoming a legitimate political constituency in the city, forging alliances with prominent politicians, establishing a range of powerful advocacy organizations, and electing openly gay local officials. As a direct result of this political advocacy, the gay movement had preexisting connections with the San Francisco public health department, which responded swiftly to calls to respond to AIDS in the early 1980s.[8] The key policy instrument used by the city to confront the epidemic was the large-scale funding of voluntary organizations through government grants. Elected officials and public health officers sought to prevent PWAs from relying on expensive hospital visits by subsidizing the provision of palliative, home-based care by nonprofit entities in the community. Grants from the municipal government allowed a wide variety of voluntary organizations to expand rapidly in the early 1980s. Foremost among these was the San Francisco AIDS Foundation (SFAF), which a group of gay activists and doctors founded in 1982. The organization grew swiftly in its early years, benefiting from the substantial influx of city funds into the fight against the epidemic. By 1985, only three years after its founding, the SFAF had an operating budget of $2 million, half of which came from contracts with the city government.[9]

The decision to work through and with nonprofits to deliver outpatient AIDS healthcare was very much in keeping with broader trends in the history of urban governance. As scholars such as Claire Dunning and Lestor M. Salomon have pointed out, the public funding of nonprofit and voluntary organizations became a central tenet of US politics and policy in the latter decades of the twentieth century. While the boundaries between the public and private have always been fluid and porous in the history of American statecraft, the idea of working through nonprofit entities and providing grants to alleviate urban problems gained greater currency during the 1960s and after. The Great Society heralded the large-scale expansion of state support for the nonprofit sector, with the national government channeling billions of dollars in revenue to voluntary organizations. Federal authorities created a wide variety of funding pots for local nonprofits, distributing grants for welfare provision, anti-poverty programs, and healthcare initiatives.[10] Propelled by this new level of government investment, the number of nonprofit entities per capita doubled between 1970 and 1990.[11] At the same time, municipalities outsourced more and more services to the voluntary sector in nearly every social policy arena, ranging from education to economic development, healthcare to housing, and neighborhood planning to social services. By the early 1980s, cities across the country were home to an increasing number of nonprofit entities, which had become a dominant force in urban governance through a series of partnerships with federal and municipal authorities.[12] In San Francisco, a robust network of gay and healthcare nonprofits sprung up in the years before the onset of the AIDS epidemic, and many of these organizations established partnerships with the municipal government.[13] By the early 1980s, the voluntary sector had become so ubiquitous in the city that government funds constituted on average 40 percent of the total revenue of nonprofit healthcare providers (exclusive of hospitals).[14]

The San Francisco model of care was one manifestation of this large-scale expansion of government–nonprofit partnerships in the latter decades of the twentieth century. The city embraced the idea of channeling public dollars through private entities to address the complex policy issues stemming from the epidemic. In this system, the distinction between nonprofit groups and public governance was blurred, and the relationship between the AIDS service industry and the state was one of mutual dependence: voluntary organizations needed the government for funding, and the government needed voluntary organizations to provide outpatient services to PWAs in the community. As Mervyn Silverman, the director of the city's public health department in the early 1980s, reflected, the San Francisco model was born out of the conviction that "government cannot do everything. Rather than expect the community alone to plan, initiate, and implement all AIDS programs, however, we began, in San Francisco, with the idea of a cooperative and collaborative arrangement—in essence, a partnership—between government and community groups."[15] Funding from the city government facilitated the emergence and survival of AIDS nonprofits, positioning them as agents of the state, not just products of the social organizing of the gay movement. As table 5.1 illustrates, many of San Francisco's largest AIDS service groups drew most of their revenue from contracts with the city government in 1984. The growing presence of voluntary organizations in urban governance fundamentally shaped the form and direction of AIDS policymaking in the 1980s and 1990s, as San Francisco's system of nonprofit–government partnerships gradually became the gold standard

Table 5.1 Different revenue sources for the San Francisco AIDS Foundation, the Shanti Project, and Hospice of San Francisco in fiscal year 1984.

Percentage of Total Revenue by Source	*San Francisco AIDS Foundation*	*Shanti Project*	*Hospice of San Francisco*
City of San Francisco	59	60	68
State of California	7	—	8
Federal Grants	5	—	—
Medicare	—	—	1
Private Donations	29	40	13
Private Insurance	—	—	8
Patient Fees	—	—	2

Note: The table illustrates the strong interdependence between AIDS service organizations and the state in San Francisco in the mid-1980s. These groups were three of the largest AIDS nonprofits operating in the city. Source: Peter S. Arno, "The Nonprofit Sector's Response to the AIDS Epidemic: Community-Based Services in San Francisco," *American Journal of Public Health* 76, no. 11 (November 1986): 1325–1330.

for other localities and states to emulate, although they often struggled to replicate the city's relative success.

Fiscal Prudence and the Political Expediency of the San Francisco Model

With its emphasis on voluntarism, public–private partnerships, and non-profit organizing, the San Francisco model of care quickly attracted the attention of politicians and officials outside of the Bay Area. Cities across the country saw the establishment of nonprofits groups to formalize the provision of services to PWAs in the early 1980s. The most prominent organizations included the Gay Men's Health Crisis (GMHC) in New York City, the AIDS Project Los Angeles (APLA), AIDS Atlanta, and the AIDS Resource Center in Dallas.[16] At first, these groups often relied exclusively on volunteer labor and private fundraising, but they quickly forged alliances with municipal governments to provide a range of outpatient services to people with HIV infection. Already in 1984, a nationwide survey conducted by the United States Conference of Mayors found that 60 percent of local health departments had contracted out services to AIDS service organizations.[17]

In an era marked by budget cuts, welfare state retrenchment, and privatization, AIDS policymakers invoked the rhetoric of limited government to marshal support for the San Francisco model, arguing that outsourcing HIV services to nongovernment organizations would prove cost-effective. They asserted that harnessing private sector donations and volunteerism would relieve some of the financial pressures on cities with high caseloads. To activists, policymakers, and public health officials, the lessons of San Francisco's early response to AIDS was clear: cities must embrace public–private partnerships with AIDS service organizations to prevent the epidemic from becoming a fiscal burden on public hospitals. When making a case for funding outpatient care before a hearing of local health officials in 1985, the APLA argued that the organization "is an extremely economical way to serve persons with AIDS as many services are provided by volunteers and coordinated by staff. Only last year volunteer psychologists contributed the equivalent of $100,000 worth of services."[18] This rhetoric was not limited to activists; economists and social scientists also highlighted and praised the cost-effectiveness of the San Francisco model. Publishing in prominent venues such as the *American Journal of Public Health* and the *Journal of the American Medical Association*, these scholars argued that San Francisco's innovative approach to delivering outpatient care had led to fewer PWAs relying on hospital stays.[19] One high-profile study published in 1986 calculated that the lifetime hospital costs of PWAs in the city was $27,571, more than five times lower than the CDC's estimate of the national average.[20] For many observers, this research indicated, in the words of one healthcare policymaker, that San Francisco had achieved "more compassionate care for less money."[21] This study was then quoted prominently in major news outlets such as the *Chicago Tribune*, the *San Francisco Chronicle*, and the *New York Times*, popularizing the idea that the city's approach to the epidemic was uniquely cost-efficient.[22]

Later, in the 1990s, health economists would question the veracity of this claim, pointing to errors in the CDC's initial estimates of the cost of AIDS, which significantly exaggerated how long PWAs stayed in the hospital across their lifetimes.[23] Accurate figures on the annual price of AIDS treatment remained elusive in the mid-1980s, and estimates ranged from a low of $26,811 to a high of $147,000.[24] The epidemic's smaller fiscal burden in San Francisco also reflected the city's unique epidemiology, not just the cost-effectiveness of outpatient care. Compared with urban areas in the Northeast, especially New York City, a much smaller number of

HIV-positive people in San Francisco were IV drug users who typically had more preexisting conditions when first infected and required more intensive care, often in a hospital setting.[25]

Regardless of their precision, statistics on the cost-effectiveness of the San Francisco model of care had a significant impact on the direction of AIDS policymaking. The notion that the city had successfully contained the costs of the epidemic through its network of government–nonprofit partnerships gained currency in many circles in the mid-1980s, emerging as a cornerstone of AIDS policy at the federal and state levels. Legislatures across the country enacted bills that provided AIDS service organizations with funds for outpatient care. In 1986, Florida became one of the first states to appropriate money explicitly for nonhospital care when it passed a law that directed $4.2 million toward the South Florida AIDS Network (SFAN), a consortium of AIDS service organizations in Miami that aimed to prevent PWAs from relying on Jackson Memorial Hospital, the city's largest public hospital. Over the next four years, the legislature funneled over $10 million toward SFAN, which also received funding from private philanthropic foundations and the federal government.[26] To sell the program in a report to funders in 1986, the founders of SFAN emphasized the long-term financial benefits of funding outpatient care, quoting various studies that demonstrated the smaller cost of the epidemic in San Francisco.[27] Legislatures in several other states—California, New Jersey, and Michigan, among others—enacted laws that funded care in outpatient settings.[28] Even Texas, where the response to AIDS had been notoriously slow in the early 1980s, set aside $3 million for the delivery of nonhospital care in community settings as part of the 1989 Omnibus AIDS Act.[29] By the end of the 1980s, fourteen states had passed legislation that provided nonprofit organizations with funding for AIDS healthcare.[30]

Government–nonprofit partnerships also became a guiding tenet of national AIDS policymaking in the mid-1980s. The Reagan administration's flagship budgetary initiative, the Omnibus Budget Reconciliation Act of 1981, contained a provision that allowed states to obtain waivers to pay for home health care for the elderly and disabled with Medicaid funds.[31] In 1986, Congress revised the legislation to permit state governments to furnish PWAs with community-based care via Medicaid, providing there was no increase to the overall cost of treatment.[32] A committee report accompanying this amendment pointed to the San Francisco model of care as a source of inspiration: "It is the committee's expectation that the implementation of this waiver will encourage other jurisdictions to develop community-based services comparable to those in San Francisco. . . . The San Francisco experience shows that new community services reduce rather than expand the cost per case for AIDS patients."[33] By 1990, nine states had obtained waivers to reimburse care for PWAs in community settings as an alternative to inpatient hospital care, using Medicaid funds to outsource a wide range of services to nonprofit entities, including case management, attendant care, and hospice services.[34]

Inspired by the San Francisco model, philanthropic foundations and the federal government also began to provide grants to hard-hit cities for outpatient care in the mid-1980s. The Robert Wood Johnson (RWJ) Foundation—the nation's largest private funder focused solely on health—launched the AIDS Health Services Program in 1986, which provided eleven localities with $17.2 million of initial funding to coordinate the provision of nonhospital care to PWAs.[35] Key figures involved in San Francisco's initial response to AIDS played a pivotal role in the development of the initiative, including Mervyn Silverman, who served as the director of the city's public health department between 1977 and 1985. He met directly with members of the RWJ's board to persuade them to fund the program in 1986 and oversaw the foundation's AIDS operations for the next four years.[36] Silverman's deputy at the RWJ, Cliff Morrison, had taken the lead in establishing a pioneering AIDS ward at San Francisco General Hospital in the early 1980s.[37] Together, Silverman and Morrison modelled the AIDS Health Service Program on San Francisco's system of nonprofit–government partnerships, employing the same cost-effective language used to justify the city's approach to the epidemic in the early 1980s.[38] A press release announcing the program noted that it planned to "help bring needed medical and supportive services to AIDS patients; demonstrate that care can be provided to them more humanely and at a reduced cost; and help relieve the burden that caring for AIDS patients has placed on many urban hospitals in the absence of alternative, community-based services." Citing a study on the low cost of the epidemic in San Francisco, the press release went on to argue that "what is needed in big cities with large AIDS and ARC populations is a coordinated system of out-of-hospital care for these patients."[39] Similar concerns about the need for more outpatient services inspired federal policymakers to commit new resources to AIDS nonprofits. In late 1986, the Health Resources and Services Administration (HRSA) established a grantmaking initiative that, in both purpose and structure, mirrored the RWJ's AIDS

Health Services Program.[40] Over the next three years, the agency, working in close consultation with the RWJ, channeled $50 million to twenty-five metropolitan areas for the purpose of developing more comprehensive systems of nonhospital care in community settings.[41] The HRSA stipulated that grant recipients could only use the funding to contract out services to nonprofit entities and explicitly forbade them from using any of it to compensate acute care in hospitals.[42]

With major grants from philanthropic foundations, the HRSA, and municipal and state governments, many AIDS service organizations grew rapidly in the late 1980s. In cities that received funding from the RWJ, the operating budget of AIDS nonprofits increased by an average of 215 percent between 1988 and 1990.[43] Several of the nation's most prominent AIDS nonprofits evolved from volunteer-run groups, reliant almost exclusively on resources raised from individual donations, to large, professional agencies that received most of their revenue from the federal government and major donors. Many of these groups became financially reliant on the state and philanthropic foundations for survival, creating new relationships of dependency between the AIDS service industry and those willing to fund its programs.[44] As table 5.2 shows, in 1987, major private and state grants accounted for a substantial proportion of the budgets of the largest AIDS service organizations in Atlanta, Dallas, Los Angeles, New York, and San Francisco—five cities that received funding from the HRSA and RWJ.

At the same moment that an influx of grants from the private sector and the federal government enabled the expansion of AIDS nonprofits in the late 1980s, many of these groups came under strain because of the mounting costs of the epidemic and a rising caseload. For all the financial and political investment in the San Francisco model, it quickly became apparent that existing funding streams alone were insufficient to address the complex needs of PWAs. The Robert Wood Johnson Foundation and the HRSA envisioned their investments in AIDS healthcare to be short-term demonstration projects that would provide evidence of the cost-effectiveness of outsourcing outpatient care to nonprofits.[45] Building a more robust and permanent AIDS safety net would require resources at a far larger scale, which the federal government was only willing to supply with the passage of the CARE Act. At a time of declining municipal revenue in the 1980s, most cities simply lacked the resources to fund AIDS service organizations at the level required to prevent PWAs from relying on expensive visits to the hospital.

Table 5.2 The proportion of revenue that came from major state and philanthropic grants in fiscal year 1987 in five AIDS service organizations.

AIDS Service Organization	*Total Revenue in Fiscal Year 1987 ($)*	*Percentage of Total Revenue from State and Philanthropic Grants*
AIDS Atlanta	354,000	55
AIDS Resource Center (Dallas)	350,000	30
Gay Men's Health Crisis (New York)	4,950,000	37
AIDS Project Los Angeles	6,190,000	33
San Francisco AIDS Foundation	3,370,000	43

Note: The table illustrates the growing entanglement between the state and the AIDS service industry in the late 1980s. The AIDS service organizations were the largest in Atlanta, Dallas, Los Angeles, New York City, and San Francisco—five cities with large caseloads. Sources: AIDS Atlanta, "First Quarter Report of 1987," James F. (Jim) Martin Papers, Richard B. Russell Library for Political Research and Studies, University of Georgia Libraries, Athens, (hereafter JMP), series VI. Disability and Health Advocacy, 1977–2008, box 1, folder 8. "AIDS Resource Center Request for Donations," December 24, 1987, LJMC, box 1, folder 7; Gay Men's Health Crisis, "1987–1986 Annual Report," GMHC, accessed March 7, 2022, https://www.gmhc.org/wp-content/uploads/2020/10/annual-report_1988.pdf; Peter D. McDermott, "New Budget for AIDS Project Los Angeles," *Issues: An AIDS Forum* 1, no. 2 (Fall 1987): 8; San Francisco AIDS Foundation, "1987 Annual Report," NGLTF, box 129, folder 14.

Nowhere were these dynamics more vividly on display than in New York City, where public health officials struggled to adapt the San Francisco model and apply it to a very different political and epidemiological context. The healthcare system in San Francisco possessed several features that meant the city was better suited for developing a robust network of outpatient services. San Francisco had a compact geography, with most public healthcare located in one hospital—San Francisco General Hospital (SFGH)—allowing health officials to coordinate services centrally and across a relatively small urban space. Approximately half of the city's PWAs received their acute care treatment at SFGH in the mid-1980s.[46] By contrast, New York's AIDS services were harder to coordinate because they were scattered across a much larger urban area. Each of the city's eleven public hospitals had a substantial AIDS caseload, and PWAs occupied one-third of their beds on average by 1987.[47] The magnitude and epidemiology of the epidemic were also considerably different in New York: total AIDS spending in the city was approximately $190 million in 1988 compared with $25 million in San Francisco. While the overwhelming majority of people with HIV infection in San Francisco were initially gay men, a substantial portion of New York's caseload was made up of IV drug users, many of whom already had complex healthcare needs before they contracted the disease and required longer hospitals stays.[48] As one report issued by the New York City Health Department in July 1987 summarized,

> AIDS services in New York City are delivered in the context of a much more complex set of hospitals and agencies, and on a much larger scale than in San Francisco. While both cities provide similar AIDS-related services, the New York City service delivery system is more geographically scattered, much larger, and more diverse. It is also confronted with a population of PWAs, many of whom suffer the combined impact of drug addiction, poverty, and HIV infection.[49]

Because of these differences between the two cities, New York City struggled to emulate San Francisco's initial success in developing a system of outpatient services. By the end of the 1980s, AIDS nonprofits in New York found themselves stretched thin and unable to keep up with the shifting demands of the epidemic. In 1990, the GMHC, the city's largest AIDS service organization, began limiting the number of new clients it took on due to budget constraints.[50]

New York's failure to build a continuum of outpatient care for PWAs was not an anomaly, as many major cities with large caseloads struggled to adopt the kind of comprehensive system of service delivery that evolved in San Francisco in the 1980s. In Dallas, the infusion of federal and private money into the AIDS service industry significantly improved the quality of care available to HIV-positive people, but the city confronted persistent administrative and bureaucratic problems as it attempted to emulate the San Francisco model. Funding levels in Dallas for HIV care had been minuscule during the early years of the epidemic, and gay rights activists and public health officials struggled to build an adequate network of services for people with HIV infection. When the RWJ furnished the city with a major grant in 1986, most AIDS nonprofits had no prior relationship with the municipal government, and virtually no bureaucratic infrastructure existed to distribute the new funding to these organizations, forcing local activists and officials to build it from scratch.[51] To administer the grant, a loose coalition of social service professionals, government officials, and community groups established the AIDS Arms Network (AAN). Tasked with coordinating and planning Dallas's broader response to AIDS, the AAN positioned itself as an umbrella organization, applying for and receiving money from national funding competitions and redistributing it to local nonprofits for the delivery of outpatient care.[52] Almost immediately, administrative chaos reigned at the ANN, which struggled to build up the capacity needed to manage grants on the scale required by the RWJ. Stories of bureaucratic delays in the allocation of funding regularly leaked to the local press, and reviews by government regulators and private auditors found damning flaws in the organization's structure and administration.[53] An independent audit issued in October 1991 called the AAN's long-term financial viability into question after discovering that it had over $180,000 of debt.[54] Around the same time, it came to light that the AAN had diverted over $170,000 of federal funding away from local AIDS service organizations to pay for its own administrative costs, forcing several groups to lay off staff and suspend crucial programs.[55] Without San Francisco's robust AIDS care infrastructure, Dallas had to play catch up when it received private and federal funding, impeding the city's attempts to develop a centralized system of outpatient services.

The San Francisco model of care embedded public–private partnerships and the voluntary sector into the local, state, and federal responses to AIDS in the 1980s. The public funding of outpatient care in community settings became a constant fixture of AIDS policymaking and a principal tool for addressing the enormous costs of the epidemic. The AIDS service industry subsequently ballooned, evolving into a highly professionalized set of nonprofit organizations with close funding ties to the state. Even as the popularity of the San Francisco model grew, however, many places struggled to replicate the city's relative success in addressing the epidemic, and the level of funding provided by grant-makers like the HRSA and the RWJ remained inadequate. As many cities teetered on the edge of fiscal ruin during the late 1980s because of AIDS, Congress finally put the full financial weight of the federal government behind this system of partnerships between AIDS service organizations and the state by enacting the CARE Act.

The Early Congressional Response to AIDS

Before the passage of the CARE Act, the response of Congress to HIV/AIDS had been halting at best and counterproductive at worst. In the early 1980s, congressional support for AIDS-related programs and funding was not forthcoming. Only a small group of lawmakers from California and New York took the epidemic seriously, primarily because they hired gay legislative assistants who brought it to their attention. At the urging of his gay staffer Timothy Westmoreland, Los Angeles Representative Henry Waxman (D–CA) used his platform as chair of the powerful Subcommittee on Health and the Environment to introduce a series of budgetary amendments that gradually increased federal spending on HIV/AIDS in the mid-1980s. However, this funding remained ad hoc and insufficient to address the complex policy issues stemming from the epidemic, as most of it went toward biomedical research rather than patient care for PWAs.[56] Meanwhile, a group of conservative politicians sought to derail any attempt to confront the crisis in Congress. The most prominent attacks on the AIDS movement came from Senator Jesse Helms (R–NC), who openly and flagrantly fueled dominant disease narratives that framed the epidemic as a punishment for deviant behavior. Most notoriously, he denounced federal spending on AIDS prevention education on the floor of the Senate in 1987, brandishing a copy of a sexually explicit pamphlet produced by the GMHC that received support from the CDC. By a wide margin, the Senate responded by passing the so-called Helms amendment, which prohibited the use of federal dollars on education material that condoned homosexuality or IV drug use.[57]

As efforts in Congress to address the epidemic stalled in the mid-1980s, AIDS activists and policymakers responded by building a more extensive and viable national lobbying network. An array of new Washington-based organizations emerged during the early years of the epidemic. By far the most significant was the AIDS Action Council (AAC), a body that gradually increased its influence over legislators in the mid-1980s and played an instrumental role in the passage of the CARE Act. Founded in 1984, the organization aimed to marshal the resources and political connections of AIDS nonprofits across the country into a coherent lobbying strategy in Washington, DC. Representing the interests of hundreds of grassroots organizations, the AAC quickly became a leading voice in national policy discussions about the epidemic, notching up several critical legislative victories in the late 1980s and early 1990s.[58] At the same time, many of the largest AIDS service organizations, including the SFAF, the GMHC, and the APLA, began to focus more attention on the formulation of public policy at the federal level. In the mid-1980s, they hired full-time lobbyists, established internal policy departments, and provided the AAC with substantial financial support.[59]

Together, these groups developed a two-pronged strategy to make the issue of AIDS more politically palatable to lawmakers. First, as they extended their political outreach, AIDS activists and lobbyists deliberately downplayed the epidemic's disproportionate impact on stigmatized minorities such as gay men and IV drug users and emphasized its threat to all Americans. Encapsulating this strategy, one of the founders of the AAC recalled that the organization "deliberately decided not to position itself as a gay organization. I think it helped to establish the fact that this disease was not just a gay disease."[60] Second, and in a related development, AIDS advocates drew together a wide variety of interest groups—not just AIDS services organizations—into a collective lobbying effort on Capitol Hill. To mobilize a broad and diverse coalition in favor of more federal action on the epidemic, the AAC founded the umbrella group National Organizations Responding to AIDS (NORA) in 1987. NORA brought together one hundred and forty influential organizations whose work had been affected by the epidemic, including the American Medical Association, the American Public Health Association, and the American Red Cross.[61] By design, most of these groups had no affiliation with the gay rights movement, reflecting efforts to decouple the epidemic from its association with homosexuality.[62] Explaining the impetus behind NORA, one of its founders told *Time* magazine that "the coalition provides an opportunity for groups to have more influence than their size would dictate. When you have 40 to 60 groups saying the same thing, that's a very compelling statement."[63] Through quarterly reports, memos, and regular meetings, NORA kept its members up to date about crucial developments on Capitol Hill and orchestrated coordinated lobbying campaigns when lawmakers considered crucial pieces of legislation.[64]

In addition to building a more robust lobbying infrastructure in Washington, DC, the AIDS movement forged a series of alliances with sympathetic lawmakers in Congress. Leading the congressional fight for more investment in AIDS were liberal lawmakers with significant connections with the gay rights movement. Most notably, the AAC and NORA built relationships with San Francisco Congresswoman Nancy Pelosi, Los Angeles Representative Waxman, and Senator Edward Kennedy, who hired two staffers to work on the epidemic in the late 1980s and held eight hearings on the disease between 1987 and 1990.[65] The emergence of Kennedy as an ally of the AIDS movement would prove especially important, as he would go on to play a crucial role in shepherding the CARE Act through Congress in 1990.

Even as AIDS lobbyists built a more formidable presence on Capitol Hill, Congress waited until 1988—seven years after the official start of the epidemic—to pass its first major AIDS-related law, the Health Omnibus Programs Extension (HOPE) Act. The legislation, sponsored by Kennedy in the Senate and Waxman in the House, appropriated new funds for prevention education and drug therapies, established grants for the training of healthcare personnel, and boosted the CDC's AIDS budget. A product of compromise, the final version of the law was significantly weaker than Kennedy's and Waxman's original proposal, which had included provisions to guarantee the confidentiality of individuals who undertook the antibody test. Conservative members of Congress had engaged in a concerted effort to push back against this element of the bill, with Helms threatening to filibuster the entire legislation, as well as several other unrelated health measures, if lawmakers did not remove it. Proponents of the law acquiesced, deleting any mention of confidentiality from the final text of the law.[66] Congressional procedures—especially the filibuster—allowed conservative lawmakers to set the terms of the debate over the bill and wield outsized influence over the direction of federal AIDS policymaking. As Senator Lowell Weicker (R–CT) complained, "I'm not happy with the package, because I don't like Jesse Helms setting AIDS policy for this country."[67]

Interest Group Lobbying, the "Degaying" of AIDS, and the Passage of the CARE Act

While the intensity of these disputes over the 1988 HOPE Act did not bode well for future reform efforts, over the subsequent two years, support for more federal funding of AIDS increased markedly due to two interconnected factors: the rising costs of the epidemic and the disease's growing strain on public hospitals. The expanding number of people with HIV infection, the longer life expectancies of these individuals, and the increasing availability of expensive drug therapies such as AZT and aerosolized pentamidine meant that the cost of HIV/AIDS rose sharply in the late 1980s, imposing significant financial stresses on state and municipal governments.[68] As early as 1987, the President's Commission on AIDS predicted that the medical expenses of the epidemic would grow exponentially over the following years, rising from $380 million in 1985 to $8.1 billion in 1991, an increase of over twenty-fold.[69] Because the insurance industry had taken aggressive steps to remove PWAs from their rolls in the mid-1980s, the public sector bore the brunt of this sudden increase in the cost of HIV/AIDS treatment.[70] By 1989, public hospitals were the provider group most likely to treat PWAs, with 5 percent of the nation's urban hospitals treating over 50 percent of people with HIV infection.[71] With few cities having the funds to finance outpatient care adequately, hospital emergency rooms increasingly acted as a safety net for people with HIV infection who had nowhere else to go.[72] Adding to the turmoil, most public hospitals had already suffered from years of shrinking funding due to cutbacks in municipal budgets and federal aid in the early 1980s.[73] In New York City, authorities eliminated eighteen hundred hospital beds between 1980 and 1985.[74]

As they became the providers of last resort for people with HIV infection, most public hospitals lacked the fiscal capacity to absorb the mounting costs and clinical demands of the epidemic, pushing the healthcare systems of many cities to the brink of collapse. The situation was acutely felt in New York City, where emergency rooms overflowed with economically vulnerable PWAs in the late 1980s, putting intense pressure on the city's already overburdened public hospitals. At New York's largest public hospital, Bellevue, people with HIV-related illnesses occupied an astonishing 27 percent of beds in 1989.[75] This hospital gridlock, together with the escalating costs of the epidemic, meant that AIDS threatened to overwhelm the city's entire healthcare infrastructure. Other cities faced similar crises, albeit on a slightly smaller scale.[76] In testimony before a congressional hearing in early 1990, the mayor of Dallas detailed the epidemic's devastating impact on the city's only public hospital, Parkland Memorial:

> Approximately 60 per cent of Dallas county's 2,300 persons with AIDS are treated at Parkland Memorial Hospital's AIDS outpatient clinic, and the majority are indigent. On any single day, 20 to 30 AIDS patients are hospitalized there for acute infections. Parkland is the county's only public hospital, and like most public hospitals, the burden of caring for AIDS patients rests with it. The hospital is at capacity, and the ever-increasing caseload is a difficult budgetary strain.[77]

By the end of the 1980s, the epidemic had driven the healthcare systems of many cities to a crisis point. According to one estimate, PWAs accounted for 28 percent of the costs and 36 percent of the financial losses of public hospitals in 1988.[78] Growing public concern over the crisis in emergency rooms made the issue of healthcare for PWAs impossible to avoid. The disease's disastrous impact on hospitals peppered public discourse and news reporting in the late 1980s, featuring in editorials and articles in major newspapers such as the *Washington Post,* the *Atlanta Constitution,* and the *Dallas Morning News.*[79] As the *New York Times* reported on its front page in February 1989, "Hospitals are increasingly filled with AIDS patients who could receive less expensive and more humane treatment through other kinds of institutions, like nursing homes, hospices and home care services."[80] Around the same time, Kennedy held a series of subcommittee field hearings that revealed the diverse and growing support for more federal action on AIDS healthcare. Beginning in New York City before moving to Los Angeles; Maplewood, Missouri; and Sparta, Georgia, the hearings brought together a wide array of witnesses who insisted that the epidemic was pushing the healthcare systems of hard-hit cities over the edge. Representatives of state and local governments, AIDS activists, members of Congress, public health officials, and medical associations all warned that swift federal intervention was necessary to prevent the total collapse of medical infrastructures in cities across the country.[81]

As pressure mounted on Congress to confront the impending disaster in public hospitals, Kennedy's staff drafted the CARE Act in late 1989 and early 1990, with close assistance from lobbyists at the AAC, NORA, the SFAF, and the GMHC.[82] The supporters of the law framed it as a fiscally prudent way of dealing with both the escalating costs of the epidemic and the burgeoning crisis in emergency rooms. As a report that accompanied the bill's introduction in the Senate summarized, the CARE Act was "intended as an emergency bail-out to those urban health care systems that are already overloaded by AIDS cases and whose continued functioning is imperiled by the [epidemic]. . . . Special corrective action is needed in these localities to avert a further deterioration of critical health service delivery to all segments of the resident population—both HIV infected individuals and others."[83] The chief drafters of the CARE Act viewed the San Francisco model of care favorably and explicitly modelled the law on its system of public–private partnerships between AIDS service organizations and municipal governments. Additionally, they contacted each of the grantees that received funding from the Robert Johnson foundation in the late 1980s to collect data on the planning and coordination of AIDS care at the state and local levels.[84] With its specific intent to federalize the San Francisco model and implement it nationally, the CARE Act foregrounded the role of nonprofits in providing services to PWAs in outpatient settings. The law instructed eligible cities and states to form planning councils responsible for distributing federal grants to local AIDS service organizations. These nonprofit groups would then serve as the provider of last resort for uninsured people with HIV infection, relieving the pressure on public hospitals.[85]

The perceived cost-effectiveness of this approach figured prominently in early conversations about the law, repeating many of the arguments made in favor of the San Francisco model in the 1980s. Under the CARE Act, PWAs without health insurance would receive preventative care in outpatient settings; as a result, fewer would rely on expensive visits to the emergency room. In a letter he circulated to members of the Senate Committee on Labor and Human Resources in February 1990, Kennedy outlined the essential contours of the fiscal case for the CARE Act: "Given the number of AIDS cases that this nation is likely to confront in the decade to come, we must invest in community-based care alternatives—or be prepared to pay an astronomical bill for the inappropriate utilization of acute-care hospital beds and emergency rooms."[86] The law's proponents made this point repeatedly. Typical was a letter distributed by NORA to members of the Senate in early March 1990, which claimed that the CARE Act "represented an investment now against a much larger price tag in the future if planning, coordination, and early interventions are not implemented."[87] By relying on cost-centerd analysis, supporters of the CARE Act stressed the primacy of outpatient care in alleviating the mounting costs of the epidemic and venerated the nonprofit sector as the most efficient means of delivering such care. Within this arrangement, the role of the state was not to deliver services directly but to broker partnerships with local voluntary organizations and support these entities through technical assistance and financial support. Like San Francisco's initial response to the epidemic in the early 1980s, the CARE Act was built on the premise that outsourcing care to the voluntary sector was the best means of reducing the astronomical cost of the AIDS epidemic. Rather than investing in the public institution most at stress because of the crisis—the public hospital—the law channeled funding through to nonprofit entities, pushing responsibility for the actual delivery of AIDS patient care back onto the private sector.[88]

The architects of the CARE Act also made devolution and state and local control cornerstones of the legislation. Rather than providing money to AIDS groups directly, the law gave states and localities the final say over which organizations would receive grants, reflecting a broader set of changes to the funding channels that transferred federal resources to nonprofit entities in the late twentieth century. Historians such as Claire

Dunning and Tracy Neumann have shown that national urban policymaking in the 1970s and 1980s granted state and city governments greater control over the distribution of federal funds to voluntary organizations. As the perceived failures of the Great Society fueled growing skepticism about the national government's ability to confront municipal problems, the Carter and Reagan administrations shifted responsibility for urban development downward to the state and city levels. At the same time, mayors, state legislatures, and governors clamored for more local autonomy in the administration of incoming federal funds. While federal grant dollars had often gone directly to community nonprofits during the 1960s, they increasingly passed through the hands of state and municipal governments in the 1970s and 1980s, giving subnational officials greater decision-making authority over the allocation of funding.[89] Like his predecessor Richard Nixon, Reagan proposed a New Federalism that altered the way the national government allocated grants to states and localities. Rather than earmarking funds for specific purposes, as had often happened during the Great Society, the Reagan administration favored transferring money to subnational governments with few strings attached and limited federal oversight. This change in funding mechanism reconcentrated authority in the offices of state and local officials, although it was coupled with a series of budget cuts that drastically reduced overall funding levels.[90]

The CARE Act encapsulated this broader shift toward greater state and local government involvement in the distribution of federal grants. Public–private partnerships are a constant theme in the history of American statecraft, but the forms these collaborations take are always evolving, and the CARE Act was enacted during a period when the US government increasingly worked through the nonprofit sector and delegated funding decisions to subnational officials. Under the law, each eligible city and state set their own financial and medical eligibility criteria for outpatient care and had the final say over which AIDS service organizations received federal grants and which programs they pursued.[91] Eager for an infusion of federal dollars with few conditions attached, state and local leaders lobbied hard for this component of the CARE Act, touting the benefits of giving subnational authorities the flexibility to spend grants in accordance with local preferences. Operating through professional organizations such as the National Conference of State Legislatures, the National Governors Associations, and the National Association of Counties, they testified before key congressional committees and wrote letters to members of Congress in support of the law's emphasis on local control. In one typical letter, Gerry Hinton, the chair of the National Conference of State Legislatures, praised the CARE Act for preserving "state and local authority to determine which activities are most beneficial for their jurisdictions when utilizing these funds."[92] The legislation's decentralized structure was also appealing to Republican members of Congress who typically placed a greater premium on granting subnational authorities flexibility and authority over federal grants. During committee hearings and the congressional debate over the CARE Act, one GOP legislator after another mentioned the themes of state and local control. Senator Alan Simpson's (R–WY), a cosponsor of the law, remarked that the CARE Act "clearly recognizes that flexibility is so important and it allows local health agencies to plan how best to meet the demand of AIDS patient care in their own communities."[93] Echoing these remarks on the floor of the House, Representative J. Roy Rowland (R–GA) argued the legislation must allow the states "to be flexible in dealing with this AIDS epidemic."[94] The CARE Act's devolution of authority to the state and local levels was thus crucial to securing the support of state leaders and Republican members of Congress.

To ensure the CARE Act received bipartisan support, Kennedy also enlisted the conservative Senator Orrin Hatch (R–UT) as a cosponsor. In language geared to appeal to his fellow Republicans, Hatch, a frequent ally and unlikely friend of Kennedy's, emphasized the themes of local control and fiscal prudence when announcing his support for the law: "We propose to give states both the funds and the flexibility to design an effective local response. . . . In responding to this totally unanticipated health emergency, we must continue to search for innovative and cost-effective programs for delivering essential support services. What works in New York City will be different from what's needed in Utah."[95] Hatch promised to rally support for the bill among Republicans and convince his colleagues to ignore any stalling tactics from conservatives like Helms.[96] Both Kennedy and Hatch unveiled the CARE Act at a carefully staged press conference in early March 1990. Flanking the two senators were several prominent municipal mayors, including David Dinkins of New York City, Art Agnos of San Francisco, and Richard Berkeley of Kansas City; a bipartisan group of federal politicians, such as Senators Alan Cranston (D–CA), Alfonse M. D'Amato (R–NY), and Paul Simon (D–IL); and prominent members of the AIDS movement, most notably the actress Elizabeth Taylor.[97] It was a symbolic display of the growing bipartisan support for more federal action on AIDS and indicated the clout that political heavyweights like Kennedy and Hatch brought to the issue.

As the bill wound its way through Congress, the AIDS advocacy network in Washington, DC, kicked into high gear, engaging in a cohesive and sustained lobbying effort on Capitol Hill. The day after Kennedy's and Hatch's press conference, Tom Sheridan, the policy director of NORA, issued an "action alert" to the organization's network of one hundred and forty members, urging them to organize phone and mail campaigns and meet directly with members of Congress to build support for the legislation.[98] Over the next few weeks, letters poured into congressional offices from groups affiliated with NORA, including the American Medical Association, the American Hospital Association, and the National Association of Public Hospitals.[99] Over the spring, these organizations provided testimony before crucial hearings and released a steady stream of press releases in favor of the legislation.[100] Coinciding with NORA's lobbying on Capitol Hill, the SFAF orchestrated a nationwide letter-writing campaign among over four hundred AIDS service organizations to generate a groundswell of grassroots support for the CARE Act. Using a pack of promotional literature and sample letters distributed by the SFAF, local activists wrote to the press, state elected officials, and members of Congress on crucial committees.[101] This indirect lobbying campaign aimed to complement the behind-the-scenes maneuvering of NORA in Washington by assuring lawmakers of the broad-based local support for the legislation.

These lobbying efforts proved effective at mobilizing a broad and powerful coalition of interest groups behind the passage of the CARE Act. Across the ideological spectrum, a wide array of organizations—representing the interests of public health experts, employers' associations, religious groups, state and local elected officials, and the medical profession—endorsed the legislation.[102] Even business interests and local chambers of commerce lined up in support of the bill, citing its cost-effective approach to tackling the AIDS crisis.[103] In a letter to Senator Daniel Patrick Moynihan in early May 1990, the New York Chamber of Commerce and Industry enthusiastically endorsed the CARE Act, arguing that without an infusion of federal dollars to alleviate the crisis in emergency rooms, the epidemic would undermine the business prospects of the city by reducing "quality of life."[104] No business leader played a more prominent role in the fight for the CARE Act than Robert D. Haas, the chief executive officer of Levi Strauss International (a member of NORA).[105] Having served on both San Francisco's task force on AIDS and the SFAF's board of directors during the late 1980s, he organized a series of meetings with business associations and individual CEOs to urge them to put their weight behind the passage of the CARE Act. In correspondence with legislators, his colleagues, and the White House, he consistently touted the fiscal benefits of the CARE Act's system of public-private partnerships.[106] The clearest articulation of this argument came in a letter he wrote in support of the law to President George H. W. Bush in early May 1990:

> I bring a business perspective to my work on this issue—I want our country to use precious health care resources efficiently and to maximum benefit. One of the real advantages of CARE is that it would help services which conserve our health care dollars. Right now, financing of AIDS care is creating disincentives for efficient use of resources. Outpatient care, support services, and housing opportunities have all proven to be cost effective because they diminish the time patients must stay in the hospital. In San Francisco, our network of outpatient support services has allowed us to keep the total cost of AIDS care far below that of many other cities. But without additional funding for these cost saving services, we won't be able to keep up with the epidemic.[107]

With such sustained pressure from interest group lobbying, Congress moved quickly to enact the CARE Act, which garnered strong bipartisan support on Capitol Hill. Endorsed by Republicans and Democrats in both chambers of the legislature, the bill went through Congress in four months.[108] During the debate over the bill, lawmakers articulated many of the same arguments that Kennedy and AIDS lobbyists used in favor of the legislation, citing the situation in public hospitals and the cost-effectiveness of outpatient care as primary reasons to enact it. Of the one hundred and seventy statements made about the CARE Act in the House and Senate, nearly half mentioned the healthcare crisis in hard-hit cities and states as a rationale for passing it. By comparison, only seven legislators in both chambers argued that the law was necessary to contain the spread of AIDS.[109] On May 15, 1990, Senator George Mitchell (D–ME) opened the floor debate in the Senate by raising the specter that AIDS now threatened people without HIV: "The AIDS epidemic has placed an enormous strain on [the] health care system in the nation's largest cities. . . . These cities need the help of the federal government if they are to help continue to provide health care to all of their citizens who rely on those hospitals that now are at a breaking point because of the AIDS crisis."[110] This emphasis on the generalized healthcare crisis in cities and states enabled lawmakers to detach their support for the bill from the stigmatized minorities affected by the disease. Only fourteen out of one hundred and seventy speeches about the legislation on the House and Senate floors mentioned gay men, even though they still accounted for a majority of people with HIV infection.[111]

The debate over the CARE Act was quick compared with previous AIDS legislation. Things moved particularly swiftly in the House, with consideration of the bill beginning in early May and lawmakers passing it one month later. In the course of the House floor debate, the most consequential amendment came from Representative William Dannemeyer (R–CA), an arch-conservative who had endorsed efforts to quarantine PWAs in California in the 1980s. Adopted by a wide margin, his amendment instructed all states, as a condition of receiving funding, to have a statute on the books criminalizing the "intentional" transmission of HIV.[112] While AIDS lobbyists bristled at the idea of mandating HIV criminalization, they opted not to fight Dannemeyer's proposal after receiving legal advice that it would not compel states to enact new laws. Because the amendment's language was sufficiently vague, the argument went, preexisting manslaughter statutes already covered its requirements.[113] Bearing out this analysis, numerous states—Maine, Massachusetts, New Mexico, Oregon, and Vermont, among others—received CARE Act funding in the 1990s without passing specific HIV criminalization laws.[114] Although Dannemeyer made a great show of demanding a more punitive approach to PWAs on the floor of the House, his amendment had a limited practical impact on the trajectory of AIDS policymaking at the state level.

Sponsors of the CARE Act successfully fended off several other punitive amendments drafted by Dannemeyer, including proposals to require name reporting of individuals who tested positive for AIDS antibodies, mandatory testing in prisons, and routine testing of all hospital patients.[115] After a relatively short debate, the House passed the law on June 13, 1990, by a voice vote, reflecting the depth of bipartisan support for more federal action on AIDS.[116] Despite the rejection of most of his amendments, even Dannemeyer voted in favor of the CARE Act, describing it as "an admirable bill."[117]

The bill faced a more uphill battle in the Senate. Led by the firebrand Helms, a small group of conservative senators threatened to filibuster the legislation and prevent it from going to a vote. Helms attacked the CARE Act with heated, homophobia-fueled rhetoric, declaring on the floor of the Senate that "there is not a case of AIDS on record that cannot be traced back in its origins to sodomy."[118] He derided his colleagues for falling prey to a concerted lobbying push by the "homosexual community" to elevate "AIDS into a political issue totally out of proportion to its medical impact on the people of this country."[119] To prevent a potential filibuster from Helms, the proponents of the CARE Act needed to persuade sixty senators to end debate over the bill and bring it to a vote. All over the spring, Kennedy's and Hatch's staff worked closely with AIDS lobbying groups to identify potential allies and secure their backing. NORA and the SFAF targeted specific senators and urged local AIDS service organizations to inundate them with letters, telephone calls, and personal meetings.[120]

To reach out to politicians from across the ideological spectrum and circumvent the stigma and homophobia associated with AIDS, this lobbying campaign focused on the so-called innocent victims of the disease, especially children and hemophiliacs. Seeking to get ahead of Helms's threat to filibuster the CARE Act, Kennedy and Hatch dedicated the bill to the memory of Ryan White, a young white hemophiliac from Kokomo, Indiana, who contracted the disease through contaminated blood products and was barred from attending school in 1985 because of the disease.[121] In the second half of the 1980s, White's long legal battle to return to school thrust him into the national spotlight, transforming him into one of the most high-profile PWAs in the country. Achieving an unlikely level of fame, he appeared on the covers of national magazines, gave frequent interviews to talk show hosts, and was befriended by a plethora of movie and music stars. The national discourse around Ryan White challenged the notion that AIDS only affected gay men and IV drug users. But it also frequently designated him as an "innocent victim" of the disease, drawing a contrast, whether implicitly or explicitly, with groups who were supposedly "guilty" for fueling the disease's spread.[122] In a particularly overt articulation of this contrast between White's "innocence" and the "guilt" of other populations affected by AIDS, one woman wrote to the Indianapolis *Star* shortly after Ryan White's death in April 1990, expressing hope that "homosexuals and drug needle users who are responsible for 94 percent of all AIDS cases will accept the responsibility for the terrible grief they bring the innocent victims of their acts—such as Ryan White and his family."[123]

Ryan White's status as an innocent victim of the disease, who had acquired the illness through "no fault of his own," as some news outlets put it, distanced the CARE Act from the marginalized populations often equated with the epidemic.[124] When the law reached the floor of the Senate, both

Kennedy and Hatch were careful not to frame it as a bill that would benefit IV drug users and gay men. Reinforcing the binary between innocent and guilty PWAs, Hatch rhetorically asked his colleagues, "What are we going to do? Are we going to let these children die because of their mothers are IV drug users? . . . Are we going to ignore a hemophiliac with six children, a wonderful family man who because he needed blood transfusions, accidentally contracted AIDS, and not do what we can do to alleviate that suffering?"[125] Mere days after Ryan White's death from AIDS-related illnesses on April 8, 1990, Kennedy and Hatch enlisted the assistance of his mother, Jeanne White, to overcome Helms's stalling tactics. Arriving in Washington, DC, for several days in mid-April, she distributed a message to every Senator urging the bill's swift passage and met directly with dozens of lawmakers to persuade them to cosponsor it.[126]

In the end, Helms overplayed his hand and badly misjudged the level of support for the CARE Act in the Senate. On May 15, 1990, after several weeks of delay, the law's proponents mustered an astonishing ninety-five votes for ending debate over the bill and bringing it to a vote, far above the three-fifths needed. Only two Senators—Steve Symms (R–ID) and Gordon J. Humphrey (R–NH), both conservative Republicans—joined Helms's effort to filibuster the legislation.[127] For the first time, AIDS lobbyists and their congressional allies had successfully resisted Helms's attempts to obstruct or weaken a major AIDS bill through parliamentary procedure.

After the proponents of the CARE Act successfully overcame the threat of a filibuster, the law encountered little further opposition in the Senate, which passed it 95–4 on May 16, 1990.[128] This wide margin reflected the diverse coalition mobilized in favor of the legislation from across the political spectrum. With the passage of the bill in the House and the Senate, attention turned to the White House, where the final version of the CARE Act went for President George H. W. Bush's signature in early August.[129] Over the previous few months, the administration had spoken out against the CARE Act, expressing concern that it was too expensive and provided the AIDS epidemic with "special treatment" compared with other diseases like cancer and heart disease. In an official statement, the White House argued that "the bill's narrow disease-specific approach sets a dangerous precedent, inviting treatment of other diseases through similar ad-hoc arrangements."[130] In a remarkable testament to the sustained bipartisan support for funding AIDS healthcare, Democrats and Republicans alike rejected the administration's calls over the spring and summer to alter the bill and reduce its price tag.

Aware that its supporters had the votes in Congress to override a potential veto, Bush reluctantly signed the CARE Act into law on August 18, 1990, in a private ceremony on Air Force One.[131]

* * *

After years of legislative battles over the epidemic in Congress, the fact that the CARE Act was such a comprehensive reform package reflected the growing strength of the AIDS movement in Washington, DC. The legislation was possible because of the emergence of a powerful national lobbying network fronted by organizations like NORA, the AAC, and the SFAF. These groups drew inspiration from the San Francisco model of care, building a federal AIDS safety net that reflected the city's emphasis on outpatient care, voluntarism, and public–private partnerships. Shifting responsibility for the delivery of AIDS care to the nonprofit sector was politically expedient because of its perceived cost-effectiveness. Politicians, activists, and interest groups from across the ideological spectrum couched their support for the CARE Act in the language of fiscal prudence. To make the issue of AIDS politically palatable to such a broad coalition, AIDS lobbyists also downplayed the devastating impact of the epidemic on gay men and focused most of their attention on perceived innocent victims of the disease, especially children. This strategy of "degaying" the epidemic came at a significant cost. It bolstered the binary between guilty and innocent people with HIV that had structured understandings about the disease since the early 1980s, reinforcing existing stigmas around populations disproportionately affected by AIDS—especially men who have sex with men and IV drug users.

In the 1990s, the CARE Act dramatically expanded the national government's involvement in the fight against AIDS, funneling hundreds of millions of federal dollars toward nonprofit entities for patient care. Far from marking the end of the states' role in shaping AIDS policymaking, though, the law granted subnational governments vast discretion over the allocation of these grants. Influenced by broader trends in the distribution patterns of federal money to nonprofits, the architects of the CARE Act pushed the responsibility for allocating funds downward to the state and local levels. The next chapter turns to the implementation of the CARE Act in the 1990s, when federalism—and the regional healthcare inequalities it engenders—remained at the heart of AIDS policymaking.

CHAPTER SIX

Public Health Divided

Devolution, Geographic Inequities, and the Mixed Legacy of the CARE Act

The passage of the CARE Act in 1990 altered the trajectory of AIDS policymaking in the United States, inaugurating a new era of growing federal involvement in the public health battle against the disease. Funded at $220 million in 1991, the law more than tripled the government's spending on outpatient HIV care overnight.[1] Over the next few years, the program's budget expanded at an exponential rate, rising to over $2 billion in 2004, at which point it accounted for approximately 15 percent of all federal domestic AIDS expenditure.[2] By almost any measure, the CARE Act dramatically improved the quality and range of healthcare services available to HIV-positive people. In 1995, over three hundred thousand people with HIV infection received care under the program, and an estimated seventy-five thousand gained access to vital, life-saving drug treatments. That same year, states and cities furnished over three thousand different nonprofits with CARE Act grants for the provision of outpatient services in community settings.[3]

Nonetheless, it is important not to exaggerate the expansion of federal involvement in AIDS policymaking during the 1990s. Even as the national government funneled an unprecedented amount of money into fighting the crisis, states and localities ultimately shaped the implementation, programmatic details, and long-term fate of national AIDS policies. This chapter uses the CARE Act as a lens to examine the enduring influence of federalism on AIDS policymaking in the second and third decades of the epidemic. Instead of digging deeply into the experience of one state, it identifies common themes across all fifty states and offers detailed case studies of three localities—Dallas, Houston, and the District of Columbia. Each of these places typified a different aspect of the CARE Act's implementation: the importance of local political conditions and idiosyncrasies

(Dallas), the weakness of federal enforcement mechanisms (Houston), and the persistence of racial segregation in the AIDS service industry (the District of Columbia).[4]

By transferring federal grants to states and cities rather than nonprofits directly, the CARE Act ensured that subnational leaders would insert themselves into the allocation process. State and local governments implemented the law in ways that reflected regional differences in the demographics of the disease, the strength of the gay rights movement, the influence of AIDS service organizations, and a host of other locally variant factors. In the relatively conservative southern setting of Dallas, Republican elites wrestled control of the grantmaking process from sexual minorities and HIV-positive people, mirroring the draconian Texan response to the epidemic in the 1980s. On the East and West Coasts, in places such as Boston, New York, and San Francisco, the gay rights and AIDS movements played a much more prominent role in the distribution of federal grants. Of equal importance, federal administrators proved reluctant to penalize states and localities for noncompliance with the CARE Act's various funding mandates, accentuating regional differences in the legislation's implementation. In a testament to the law's weak enforcement mechanisms, local political elites in Houston ignored or flouted several directives from the national government, with very few consequences.

While the CARE Act could boast of multiple accomplishments by the middle of the 1990s, it also magnified many of the spatial and regional disparities in the availability of HIV care and services. The law epitomized the importance of place—states, counties, cities, and neighborhoods—in determining who had access to healthcare. At the neighborhood and city levels, the AIDS service industry reflected and reinforced the inequities of urban segregation, with the largest, most-established organizations operating in predominantly white areas. With their highly trained staff, large bureaucratic infrastructures, and years of experience managing government contracts, these white-dominated nonprofits were well-placed to secure CARE Act funding. Conversely, many grassroots minority groups were at an earlier stage of organizational development and lacked the administrative capacity and experience to make competitive grant applications. In this way, the CARE Act benefited resource-rich AIDS service organizations and disadvantaged those in minority neighborhoods. Nowhere was the inequitable distribution of CARE Act funding more extreme than in Washington, DC, where the bulk of grants went to nonprofits located outside of majority-Black areas, even though African Americans constituted at least 70 percent of new AIDS cases in the district during the early 1990s.[5]

At the state level, the CARE Act fueled vast geographic healthcare disparities between different regions. Drafted by AIDS lobbyists and lawmakers from California, Massachusetts, and New York, the law transferred a disproportionate amount of funding to these coastal areas, deepening already yawning regional variation in the availability of HIV services. Galvanized by these discrepancies, legislators, policymakers, and health officials in underfunded states contested the CARE Act's funding structure and lobbied members of Congress for a more equitable distribution of federal dollars. Their advocacy efforts set the stage for a series of conflicts between lobbyists representing the early epicenters of the disease, who defended the legislation's original design, and AIDS activists from Midwestern and Southern states, who argued that the law skewed funding to large, coastal urban areas. These tensions burst into view when the CARE Act came up for reauthorization in 1995 and 1996. As the law wended its way through Congress, disputes raged between AIDS activists over whether its funding formulas needed a fundamental redesign. While activists from underfunded states scored a notable victory when they convinced lawmakers to support some of their proposals in 1996, regional discrepancies remained a hallmark of the CARE Act. At the turn of the millennium, HIV reached catastrophic proportions in the South, placing enormous strain on the region's already beleaguered public health infrastructure. But the CARE Act's funding formulas underestimated the scope of this proliferating epidemic, with devastating and far-reaching consequences for HIV-positive people living in Southern states.

While the CARE Act stimulated a growing federal presence in the fight against the epidemic, it evolved in a way that bolstered, rather than reduced, the importance of federalism to AIDS policymaking. States and localities developed vastly different programs for PWAs under the banner of the same federal law, breeding regional inequities in the availability, quality, and scope of AIDS healthcare. As a result, the fragmentation and fracture that characterized the policy response to the epidemic in the 1980s largely persisted in the two decades that followed.

Federalism and the Ryan White CARE Act

Following the passage of the CARE Act in 1990, attention immediately turned to the law's implementation at the subnational level. The legislation compromised four major program titles, and states and localities had substantial discretion over the first two, which were by far the most prominent and well-funded. Title I directed funds to the metropolitan areas hardest hit by the crisis while Title II provided all fifty states with grants to improve the delivery of outpatient services and care for HIV-positive people. Together, these two titles received $175 million in 1991—just under 80 percent of the funds appropriated for the act.[6] The other programs of the legislation included direct grants for nonprofit entities to deliver early intervention services (Title III) and the provision of family-centered care for children, infants, and women living with HIV infection (Title IV).

In the early years of the CARE Act, interstate variation developed in nearly every aspect of the program, from eligibility criteria to service provision. Under Title II, the states had the final authority to determine who was eligible for assistance. Some established stringent medical and income requirements, while others allowed most people with HIV infection to use the program. In Idaho and Montana, HIV-positive individuals had to have a CD4 cell count below five hundred to access outpatient care funded by the law. Colorado was even stricter, requiring a count below three hundred. By contrast, California, New York, Nevada, and Washington did not place medical limits on CARE Act programs and even allowed family members of HIV-positive individuals to access certain services.[7] At the same time, seventeen states established income eligibility limits for CARE Act recipients, even though the original legislation did not require them to do so. In 1994, these income ceilings ranged widely, from $7,360 per year in Delaware to $29,440 per year in Idaho.[8]

Each state also covered a different menu of services under the CARE Act. Colorado directed most of its Title II funding toward case management for HIV-positive people to ensure they received the most cost-effective care. The same was true in Massachusetts, Michigan, and West Virginia.[9] Other states funded a much more diverse assortment of programs, most notably California, which used Title II grants to finance services ranging from dental therapy and substance abuse treatment to housing assistance and day and respite care.[10] While most CARE Act funding went toward furnishing AIDS service organizations with grants for outpatient care, some states spent more on reimbursing drug treatments for impoverished PWAs.[11] Most strikingly, Tennessee used 99 percent of its Title II grants to subsidize life-saving drug therapies. Thirteen other states—Alabama, Idaho, Indiana, Kansas, Kentucky, Nebraska, Nevada, New Hampshire, Oregon, Rhode

Island, South Dakota, Utah, and Vermont—spent most of their funding on pharmaceuticals.[12] At the state level, then, there was endless variation in the types of healthcare subsidized by the CARE Act, and the federal government left most decision-making power over funding decisions vested in the hands of subnational authorities. Whether or not economically vulnerable HIV-positive people could access dental care, housing assistance, and drug therapies depended heavily on the state in which they lived.

Representational Politics and the Implementation of the CARE Act in Texas

Nowhere were the complex local realities of the CARE Act more vividly on display than in Texas. The state epitomized the importance of local politics and discretion to the program, as its two largest cities—Dallas and Houston—adopted a distinctive approach to allocating federal dollars that reflected local power dynamics. The political landscape of the AIDS epidemic in Dallas and Houston differed substantially from the major metropoles on the coasts. In both cities, gay men and lesbians had made notable inroads into local politics during the 1970s and 1980s, establishing active and visible political organizations and providing vital electoral support to several prominent politicians. The Montrose neighborhood in Houston and the Oak Lawn neighborhood in Dallas also emerged as flourishing centers of local gay life.[13] Compared with places like San Francisco, Los Angeles, and New York City, though, gay men and lesbians did not wield the same level of political clout in Dallas and Houston, where sexual politics was typically more conservative.[14] When the AIDS epidemic began to take a devastating toll on the gay communities in Montrose and Oak Lawn in the 1980s, local elected officials were slow to respond relative to the other major urban epicenters of the disease. Of the ten cities with the highest caseloads in 1988, Houston and Dallas ranked eighth and tenth, respectively, in spending on AIDS-related programs per case.[15] With the passage of the CARE Act, both cities received Title I grants, but conservative political elites exerted significant influence over the distribution process, preventing people with HIV infection and gay men from having much of a say over where federal money went.

No city illustrated the importance of local discretion to the CARE Act's implementation better than Dallas. Under the provisions of Title I, the highest-ranking local elected official in each eligible metropolitan area was responsible for appointing an HIV planning council to establish funding priorities, allocate grants to AIDS service organizations, and develop a comprehensive plan for the most efficient delivery of services. Because CARE Act money went to the county rather than the city government in Dallas, the chief elected official was county judge Lee F. Jackson, a conservative member of the area's Republican establishment who had served in the Texas House of Representatives between 1976 and 1986.[16] Most local AIDS and gay rights activists greeted Jackson's leadership with skepticism, if not outright scorn. Suspicions lingered as a result of his refusal to accept the endorsement of the bipartisan Lesbian/Gay Political Coalition of Dallas, one of the city's largest gay rights organizations, during his reelection campaign for the Texas legislature in 1984.[17] During his first bid for county judge three years later, Jackson further alienated the local gay community when his campaign literature critiqued his Democratic opponent, Kathryn Cain, for endorsing more spending on AIDS prevention education. One widely distributed brochure accused Cain of running "a campaign designed to attract special-interest votes" because she supported "additional funding for educational programs about how to avoid the transmission of AIDS and other venereal diseases, a critical need in the gay community."[18]

These fears over Jackson's leadership proved well-founded, as he pushed the city's implementation of the CARE Act in a conservative direction during the early 1990s. He made only half-hearted attempts to solicit the input of the local gay rights movement, even though gay men made up approximately 80 percent of Dallas's caseload.[19] In December 1990, he appointed a twenty-four-member planning council to distribute the city's first $1.3 million of CARE Act grants. The commission included business leaders, healthcare professionals, high-ranking county officials, and local and state politicians—but only two representatives from the local gay community and one person with HIV infection.[20] When appointing people to the council, Jackson sought to ferret out the kind of progressive AIDS activism that challenged existing political and economic power structures, opting instead to appoint people who were prominent members of Dallas' leadership class and shared his conservative and Republican values. Under his plan, people with HIV infection were identified primarily as passive clients and consumers, with the role of distributing funding reserved for local political elites.[21]

The near absence of HIV-positive people and gay men from the Dallas planning council soon became a lightning rod of controversy. A cadre of local AIDS workers, gay rights activists, and public health professionals argued that fighting the epidemic effectively required listening to voices of PWAs and sexual minorities. Jackson's decision to appoint former state representative Bill Ceverha to the commission quickly became the focal point of their criticisms. In the 1980s, Ceverha had been one of the Texas legislature's most vocal opponents of gay rights legislation. He frequently exploited the outbreak of AIDS to link homosexuality with disease and deviancy, arguing on one occasion that gay men represented "a serious threat to the public health."[22] Most notoriously, as outlined in chapter 4, Ceverha introduced a bill in the Texas legislature in 1983 that would have reinstated the state's sodomy statute after a federal district court briefly struck it down. The measure proposed to upgrade the criminal penalty for violating the statute from a misdemeanor to a felony and prohibit gay men and lesbians from working as police officers, teachers, food processors, and healthcare workers. Even for the Texas legislature, the bill proved too extreme and stalled in committee after being roundly condemned during hearings.[23] Upon his appointment to the Dallas HIV planning council in December 1990, Ceverha made no attempt to backpedal or soften his homophobic views, telling the *Dallas Morning News* that he remained "an ardently anti-homosexual activist."[24]

Jackson's recruitment of Ceverha soon aroused the ire of local AIDS and gay rights activists, who expressed disgust at the appointment of such a virulently homophobic figure. In a letter to Jackson in early 1991, Bruce Monroe, the president of the Dallas Gay Alliance, one of the city's most prominent gay rights organizations, described Ceverha's appointment as "an insult to the thousands of HIV-infected people who are expected to come down with AIDS in the next few years." He concluded the letter by stressing that "our concern is that Mr. Ceverha will use this council as a public forum to continue his hatred and bigotry against the gay and lesbian community."[25] That same month, an editorial in *This Week in Texas*, one of the state's most prominent gay periodicals, voiced similar concerns over Ceverha's nomination: "As a legislator, Ceverha routinely opposed gay antidiscrimination legislation, and he has gone on record as saying that too much money has been spent on AIDS already. Community leaders fear he will use the council simply as a forum to express his bigotry and to obstruct AIDS spending."[26] Despite the vitriol and attention that Ceverha's appointment received, Jackson rebuffed pleas for a more representative HIV planning council, and Dallas's initial allocation of CARE Act dollars in 1991 reflected his reluctance to work with gay rights activists. The city's two largest gay-run AIDS service organizations—the AIDS Resource Center and Oak Lawn Community Services—received only $25,000 of the $1.3 million federal grant, even though $80,000 remained unallocated.[27] Over the next few years, the CARE Act provoked a series of acrimonious debates over the proper allocation of federal grants in Dallas. Disputes raged on the planning council between local AIDS activists and Republican politicians over who should plan the city's response to the epidemic.[28]

While HIV-positive people and AIDS activists held little sway over the CARE Act's enactment in Dallas, they exerted significantly more influence in the coastal epicenters of the epidemic, where the AIDS movement typically had more political clout. In New York City, representatives of AIDS service organizations played a pivotal role in implementing the law. At the outset, the regional planning council drew its membership primarily from grassroots nonprofits, including representatives from organizations such as the Latino Leadership Commission on AIDS, the AIDS Center of Queens County, the Hispanic AIDS Forum, the Staten Island AIDS Task Force, and Asian and Pacific Islanders Concerned about AIDS.[29] In short order, a slew of HIV-positive people also joined the commission. From 1992 to 1997, Ronald Johnson, a Black HIV-positive veteran of the AIDS movement, chaired the council and served as the citywide coordinator of HIV services.[30] Elsewhere, in places such as Boston, San Diego, and San Francisco, AIDS nonprofit leaders and representatives of the local gay community assumed leadership positions within Title I planning councils. In all these cities, the highest-ranking elected official had prior connections with the AIDS service industry and proved sympathetic to calls for significant community participation in the CARE Act's enactment.[31] Because of the law's decentralized design, the influence of HIV-positive people and sexual minorities over funding decisions varied dramatically by region, based on the differing strength of the AIDS and gay rights movements and the personal prejudices of whoever happened to be an area's chief elected official.

Eventually, the lack of representation on the Dallas HIV planning council came into conflict with directives from the Health Resources and Services Administration (HRSA), the federal agency tasked with administering the CARE Act. The original legislation contained a provision instructing Title I areas to involve HIV-positive people in the planning and implementation of the program, but it said nothing about the degree of control they should have. With such a vague policy mandate, the HRSA initially adopted a relatively relaxed attitude to its enforcement and frequently turned a blind eye to areas that appointed very few people with HIV infection to their planning councils.[32] As the 1990s wore on, however, federal administrators eventually began to crack down on these places. A study commissioned by the HRSA in 1994 indicated that involving HIV-positive individuals in funding decisions led to the more effective allocation of CARE Act dollars. In response to these findings, the agency issued a memo to all Title I areas on October 3, 1994, stipulating that 25 percent of individuals on regional planning councils must be HIV positive.[33] The HRSA went a step further during the debate over the reauthorization of the CARE Act in 1995 and 1996. During committee testimony over the legislation, it recommended an amendment that would force localities to ensure that the membership of planning councils reflected the local demographics of the disease.[34] After this provision became law, the HRSA promulgated a new set of guidelines that made the involvement of certain groups in funding decisions—including women, racial minorities, and HIV-positive people—a prerequisite for receiving Title I dollars. Failure to comply with these rules, the agency warned, would lead to reduced funding.[35]

These new requirements had a mixed impact on the makeup and representativeness of the Dallas planning council. To conform with the HRSA's directives, Jackson appointed significantly more HIV-positive people to the commission after 1996. By 1999, approximately 30 percent of the council's members were HIV positive, an increase of two-fold from five years previously.[36] However, the HRSA's new guidelines contained no mention of improving representation based on sexual orientation, an omission that allowed Jackson to continue to nominate a relatively small number of gay men to the commission, even though they still accounted for the majority of Dallas's new cases between 1995 and 1997.[37] Rather than soliciting the input of gay service users, he assigned Republican officials and activists to crucial leadership positions within the council, appointing GOP member Lucy Polter as its chair in February 1997.[38] Even as the HRSA provided greater federal oversight of Title I planning councils, then, local elected officials retained some discretion over the makeup of these bodies, which had the final authority over funding decisions. Furthermore, the HRSA's requirements for community participation applied only to Title I areas and not to the states, leaving state leaders and officials with substantially more control over the use of CARE Act grants.[39]

Houston was also the site of a particularly fierce contest over the representation of HIV-positive people and gay men on its Title I planning council.

Like Dallas, CARE Act dollars flowed to the county rather than the city level in Houston. As a result, county judge Jon Lindsay, another stalwart conservative and Republican, was the highest-ranking local elected official and responsible for appointing members to the planning council. At first, Lindsay outsourced administrative responsibility for implementing the program to the Greater Houston AIDS Alliance (GHAA), an umbrella organization that coordinated the activities of local voluntary organizations involved in prevention education and patient care.[40] Founded in 1988 by Lindsay and a group of healthcare professionals, the GHAA brought together a broad range of groups with connections both to Houston's political and business elite and the local AIDS movement. Lindsay handpicked a sizeable portion of the organization's twenty-five-person board of directors, which he filled with medical, religious, and business leaders, including representatives from the Greater Houston Chamber of Commerce, the Harris County Medical Society, and a plethora of local businesses and churches.[41] As a concession to service providers and people with HIV infection, the GHAA's founding documents also permitted local AIDS nonprofits to appoint several people to the board. An array of prominent advocacy groups—including Planned Parenthood, the Montrose Counselling Center, and the Montrose Clinic (the city's oldest gay health center)—nominated representatives.[42] These individuals shaped the GHAA into a reliable advocate for PWAs and the local gay community. In July 1991, they successfully pushed the organization to amend its bylaws to include guarantees that gay men and HIV-positive people would receive adequate representation on its board.[43]

The AIDS movement's growing influence within the GHAA touched off an acrimonious power struggle over Houston's CARE Act grant. In the early 1990s, activists increasingly outvoted and outmaneuvered Lindsay's appointees on the board of directors, pushing the organization to endorse policies that he actively opposed, such as a comprehensive plan for HIV prevention education in local schools in December 1991. Over the fierce objections of Lindsay, the board passed a resolution supporting the distribution of condoms to adolescents as part of the program.[44] Having lost control of the GHAA, Lindsay sought to reassert his authority over the CARE Act's administration by centralizing the program within the county court. In July 1992, he unilaterally stripped the organization of its power to distribute federal funds and removed its staff members from the Houston planning council. In a scathing letter to the board of directors, he accused the GHAA's more outspoken members of pursuing "a hidden agenda which seems to be total control of the organization, no matter what the cost."[45] To tighten his grip over the CARE Act's implementation, he took direct control over the program's administration and appointed a new council with membership skewed toward business elites and medical professionals over AIDS workers and HIV-positive people. He refused to reappoint several prominent and distinguished people with HIV infection to the commission, including Steven Bradley and Maurice Jones, who both served on the GHAA's board.[46]

As Lindsay consolidated his control over the Houston planning council and pushed back against the activist bent of the GHAA, his actions provoked a fierce backlash from local AIDS workers. In late 1992 and early 1993, they entered into protracted legal proceedings with the county court, staged regular demonstrations, and petitioned the federal government to intervene.[47] On September 28, 1992, over thirty AIDS activists blocked traffic during rush hour in southeast Houston to protest Lindsay's decision to seize the medical files of PWAs from the GHAA, holding banners that read "Big Brother (Judge Jon) Lindsay is Watching You" and "Our Lives, Our Files, We Want Them Back."[48] Similar demonstrations erupted throughout the summer and fall, with direct action groups such as Queer Nation and ACT-UP/Gulf Coast objecting to Jackson's leadership style and his violation of the privacy rights of PWAs.[49] Meanwhile, a group of local activists pressed the federal government to censure the county court for unilaterally seizing control of the CARE Act's administration from the GHAA. In January 1993, they flew to Washington, DC, to lodge a complaint with the HRSA and deliver a report to the agency alleging discrimination by Lindsay against HIV-positive people. They claimed that toothless federal oversight had given local political elites too much discretion over the CARE Act's design:

> While the law necessarily leaves the majority of the administration of Title I funds to the local political subdivisions, the law does not specify the role of the HRSA. Noticeably absent from the legislation is the mention of recourse available to a Ryan White City if there are problems in the administration and oversight of funds . . . HRSA does have the ability to withhold funds under the proper circumstances. Yet it has become evident in the Houston case that the HRSA is reluctant to investigate due to the vagueness of the law. HRSA must be given a clearly defined role in the process which will allow to operate expeditiously . . . in the case of alleged mismanagement.[50]

After receiving this complaint, the HRSA sent a task force to investigate the Houston planning council in March 1993. Over two days, federal officers convened meetings with former members of the GHAA and representatives from the county court to try and resolve the conflict over the city's CARE Act program. With accusations of homophobia and HIV discrimination filling the air—mainly due to Lindsay's refusal to reappoint HIV-positive people to the planning council—negotiations between both sides quickly broke down.[51] Two weeks after the HRSA's site visit, Eric Goosby, the agency's director of HIV services, issued Lindsay's office with a scathing report documenting the breakdown of trust between the judge and local AIDS workers. Goosby was especially troubled by the marginalization of HIV-positive people and service providers in Houston's grantmaking process. "There is a general perception that [Lindsay's office] exercises control of all programmatic, fiduciary, and management decisions," he wrote in his report: "Members of the community expressed feeling that their input or that of service providers is neither invited nor accepted." He concluded by recommending a series of "drastic interventions" to remedy the situation, including a redrafting of the planning council's bylaws and a restructuring of its organizational design.[52] In a written response, Lindsay's chief of staff, Ron Dear, accused the agency of bias toward the "dissenters" within the GHAA. Openly defying the HRSA's instructions, he refused to commit to any of Goosby's suggestions for reforming the planning council's design or structure.[53]

On the ground level, the HRSA's investigation had very little discernable impact. Over the next few months, Lindsay's office jealously guarded its autonomy, skirmishing regularly with the agency over its findings and fending off calls for greater community participation in the Houston planning council. The HRSA continued to press the county court to reform its allocation process but stopped short of bringing pressure to bear by threatening to cut off or reduce funding, revealing the limits of federal oversight in the opening phase of the CARE Act's implementation.[54] During a follow-up site visit in April 1994, two federal field officers discovered that Lindsay's office continued to possess near-total control over appointments to the local HIV planning council and the allocation of federal grants. As they wrote in their report back to the HRSA, "There exists the perception that individuals whose views are not consistent with that of [Lindsay's] risk the possibility" of having their membership of the commission revoked.[55] Over time, the planning council would become more diverse, especially after the 1996 CARE Act reauthorization codified more requirements for community participation, but the HRSA refused to force the issue in 1993 and 1994.[56]

Houston was not the only place where local officials ignored or flouted directives from the HRSA. In the early days of the CARE Act, the national government possessed relatively modest means for ensuring states and localities adhered to the law's various complex mandates. The HRSA's only enforcement tool was the threat of withdrawing or cutting grants, but federal administrators proved reluctant to suspend funding when confronted with noncompliant states and cities, as doing so would withhold potentially life-saving funds from impoverished PWAs. Without other mechanisms of control, the agency often struggled to force subnational governments to comply with the CARE Act's funding requirements.[57] The result was considerable divergence between the letter of the law and actual practice at the state and local levels. The original legislation contained a "maintenance of effort" provision specifying that states must continue to finance outpatient care at the same level annually to receive federal funding. But the HRSA waited until 1997 to provide the states with uniform guidance on this requirement. Before then, each state used a different methodology to compile HIV expenditure data, causing significant discrepancies and inconsistencies.[58] Another condition mandated that subnational governments could only use CARE Act grants as a "payer of last resort" after exhausting all other funding options, but some states flouted this requirement. An audit of Connecticut's administration of Title II funds by the Office of Inspector General in 1996 discovered that the state had spent over $1.5 million of federal grants on various AIDS programs when other funds were available.[59]

All told, the strings attached to CARE Act funding were interpreted loosely or even ignored by many states and cities in the early 1990s. The law's toothless enforcement mechanisms, coupled with the HRSA's reluctance to take corrective actions against recalcitrant states and localities, ensured that local political conditions shaped the program's implementation, even in areas where the federal government tried to impose broad national standards. Enormous variations emerged from this devolved policy structure, reflecting regional differences in the political clout of the gay rights and AIDS movements. In Dallas and Houston, local conservative elites wrested control of the law's implementation whereas in many coastal urban metropoles HIV-positive people and gay men played a much more central role in the distribution of CARE Act grants. Even after the ostensible expansion of federal authority in the 1990s, no single, coherent national AIDS policy existed.

Residential Segregation, Race, and the CARE Act

As the CARE Act financed a patchwork of different organizations, services, and programs, it amplified deeply entrenched racial inequities within the AIDS service industry. From the beginning of the epidemic, issues of race, representation, and urban segregation figured prominently in debates over the distribution of public and private AIDS funding. In hyper-segregated cities such as Atlanta, Chicago, and Washington, DC, the first organizations to fight the AIDS epidemic grew out of predominantly white gay communities. Because of their lack of diversity, these groups often struggled to reach out to people of color and provide them with culturally sensitive prevention education, healthcare, and other services. The location of most AIDS nonprofits in white gay urban enclaves—many of which were segregated and perceived as exclusionary spaces by communities of color—rendered them less accessible to Latinos and African Americans. The cumulative result was an AIDS service industry riven by urban segregation, racial discrimination, and intense geographic barriers to care.[60] Far from alleviating these inequities, the CARE Act exacerbated them. To varying degrees, HIV planning councils funneled a large portion of their initial grant money toward larger, more established AIDS service organizations, many of which were located in neighborhoods with reputations for being specifically white spaces. Even as the epidemic took a disproportionate toll on communities of color, the geographic centering of AIDS services in predominantly white areas made it harder for racial minorities to access programs funded by the CARE Act.

Few places illustrated the racial tensions over the CARE Act's implementation better than Washington, DC, where battles over the distribution of federal AIDS dollars pitted the local white gay community against Black AIDS activists. When the epidemic erupted in the city in the early 1980s, the first nonprofits to respond geared their services primarily toward white gay men. The most prominent early AIDS service organization in Washington was the Whitman-Walker Clinic, a gay and lesbian health community center founded in the 1970s. Bolstered by its close funding ties with the District of Columbia government, the clinic quickly evolved into the dominant source of HIV services in the Washington area.[61] However, its initial efforts to fight the epidemic reflected and reinforced racial divisions within the local gay community. Black gay men and lesbians often reported feeling marginalized within Whitman-Walker, which hired relatively few minority staff members during its early years. The clinic conducted much of its initial AIDS educational outreach through bars, clubs, and other social institutions with predominantly white patrons—businesses that often actively discriminated against Black gay men.[62] James "Juicy" Coleman, a prominent AIDS activist and founder of one of the nation's first Black gay social clubs at Howard University, recalled that many within the local Black gay community dubbed the clinic "White Man Walker" because of its lack of diversity.[63]

As the number of AIDS cases among African Americans skyrocketed in the mid-1980s, pressure mounted on Whitman-Walker to improve its minority outreach efforts. Starting in 1983, the organization began to conduct a small number of HIV education forums in bars and businesses patronized by African American gay men, working closely with the DC Coalition of Black Gays, Washington's oldest Black LGBT political organization, to deliver the workshops.[64] Critics of the clinic saw these outreach efforts as inadequate. In February 1986, Jim Mercer, a prominent Black gay activist, told the city's leading gay newspaper, the *Washington Blade*, that Whitman-Walker lacked the "commitment" and "knowhow" to provide high-quality services to minority communities. He felt that the organization needed to change its "complexion" to yield more effective prevention education for Black gay men.[65] In the same article, Clif Roberson, the president of the DC Coalition of Black Gays, acknowledged that many within the Black gay community still viewed the clinic as "a white institution."[66]

Despite its failure to reach out adequately to minority communities, Whitman-Walker held a near-monopoly on major city AIDS grants in the 1980s and early 1990s. Between 1983 and 1993, the District government funneled $8 million to the organization, often without opening grants up to competitive bids from other organizations.[67] After the passage of the CARE Act, approximately 20 percent of the city's initial Title I allocation went to Whitman-Walker, cementing the clinic's dominant position within the local AIDS service industry.[68] As the district's principal recipient of city and federal grants, the organization developed close partnerships with government agencies, imbuing it with a degree of public authority. According to an external audit conducted in 1993, staff at Whitman-Walker had privileged access to officials at the DC Department of Health and Human Services and often received grants without proper oversight, bidding processes, or monitoring.[69]

With the passage of the CARE Act, Washington's AIDS service industry experienced a major injection of federal money. The city was eligible for both Title I and II funding and received over $16 million a year in Ryan White grants by 1996.[70] Unlike Dallas and Houston, AIDS workers in Washington did not have to contend with local political elites over the control of CARE Act dollars. The DC Title I planning council developed several mechanisms to ensure community participation in funding decisions. It hosted regular public meetings to solicit input from PWAs and adopted bylaws stipulating that its membership must reflect the local demographics of the disease.[71] Meanwhile, the DC Care Consortium, an umbrella organization of local AIDS groups, assumed full administrative responsibility for Title II. Rather than delivering services directly, the agency distributed federal money to local nonprofits and monitored how they spent this funding. By the end of 1993, the consortium already boasted a membership of over sixty organizations, including Whitman-Walker, the DC Coalition of Black Gays, and IMPACT-DC, which provided care and other services to minority PWAs.[72]

Despite the diverse range of organizations involved in the allocation of CARE Act dollars, Whitman-Walker retained its status as the city's dominant provider of HIV services in the early 1990s, prompting AIDS activists of color to mobilize to steer more funding and resources into minority neighborhoods. In August 1993, a dozen Black and Latino advocacy groups formed a new umbrella organization, the Sankofa Community Coalition of HIV/AIDS Services, to compete for federal and city contracts. Participating organizations included Us Helping Us, a Black-led AIDS nonprofit; URBAN Inc, which provided technical assistance and consultancy services to minority AIDS service organizations; and the DC Coalition of Black Gays.[73] Whitman-Walker's cozy relationship with the district government became the first target of their efforts. At a press conference on August 24, 1993, members of the Sankofa Coalition announced their intention to compete for a city contract that had previously gone to Whitman-Walker without a competitive bidding process. At stake was over $2 million of AIDS funding, which amounted to approximately 15 percent of the clinic's annual budget.[74] The responsibility for writing Sankofa's proposal fell on Alonzo Fair, the president of URBAN Inc. and a former grant manager for Whitman-Walker, who left the organization in 1992 after concluding that it was not doing enough to reach people of color.[75]

To bolster the case for more AIDS funding in minority neighborhoods, Fair and URBAN Inc. conducted a study in the fall of 1993 on DC's use of CARE Act money during the first three years of the program. The research offered stark evidence that the availability of AIDS care in majority-Black neighborhoods lagged significantly behind other parts of the city. Like so much else in the nation's capital, the Anacostia River was the central dividing line that determined who had access to AIDS healthcare. The river marked a geographic and racial boundary between the predominantly Black, economically vulnerable areas of the city to the east and the more affluent, mixed neighborhoods to the west.[76] Although African Americans constituted over 70 percent of new HIV cases in Washington during the early 1990s, URBAN Inc.'s study revealed that a mere 10 percent of CARE Act grants had gone to nonprofits located in Wards 7 and 8, the two districts east of the Anacostia. According to the group's findings, no organization in this part of the city had received any funding for mental health, drug assistance, or dental services.[77] Armed with this evidence, Fair attempted to rally support for Sankofa at public hearings on AIDS funding throughout late 1993 and early 1994. Citing URBAN Inc.'s glaring statistics on the CARE Act, he repeatedly implored the regional planning council and other funding bodies to stop privileging organizations west of the Anacostia and funnel more money into nonprofits rooted in disenfranchised communities.[78]

As the fight for control over the city's AIDS funding heated up, many white gay activists criticized URBAN Inc.'s characterization of the CARE Act's implementation. They insisted that Whitman-Walker and other AIDS service organizations had taken significant steps to improve their outreach to communities of color. At one particularly tense public hearing in November 1993, Richard J. Rosendall, a prominent supporter of Whitman-Walker, heaped scorn on Fair and accused URBAN Inc. of "fragmenting our community into a collection of warring interest groups."[79] Although few went as far as Rosendall, other white gay activists rallied to Whitman-Walker's defense, pointing out that the clinic had diversified its staff and board over the last few years, opened a new health center east of the Anacostia in 1992, and broadened its outreach efforts to ensure a stronger patient base in predominantly African American neighborhoods.[80] Such arguments rang hollow with members of Sankofa, who noted that the lion's share of Washington's AIDS grants continued to go to organizations on the west side of the river. Rather than seeking remedies to this situation within Whitman-Walker, an organization that many still identified with the white gay community, they argued that grants dollars coming into

Black communities should go to Black-controlled institutions, insisting that these groups were better equipped to address the unique needs of Black HIV-positive people.[81] Speaking to the Associated Press in November 1993, Fair accused Whitman-Walker of adopting a "slave/master kind of attitude" in its attempts to dominate the AIDS service industry in Washington, DC, and monopolize the distribution of AIDS funding in majority-Black neighborhoods.[82]

Even as the Sankofa Coalition brought together an array of minority-led nonprofits, Black AIDS activists did not unanimously support the organization. Many raised questions about the role of the Abundant Life Clinic in the coalition's bid for the city contract. Led by Dr. Abdul Alim Muhammad, the minister of health for the Nation of Islam (NOI), the clinic would be responsible for delivering all medical care under the grant.[83] Famous for being the spokesperson for Kemron, an alternative HIV drug therapy, Muhammad promoted several AIDS conspiracy theories in the 1980s, including the claim that the US government had manufactured the virus as a genocidal weapon to "depopulate" Africa. He also periodically pinned the blame for the epidemic on sexual minorities. In one particularly homophobic article in *Final Call*, the NOI's newspaper, he described AIDS as part of the "Judgement of the wicked by Almighty God" and argued that "AIDS victims and carriers should be quarantined and isolated from the general population."[84] After the formation of Sankofa, accusations swirled in the press that Muhammad had discriminated against gay PWAs, pushed his religious doctrines onto people using Abundant Life, and encouraged his patients to stop taking FDA-approved medications and switch to Kemron, which a clinical trial had recently proven to be utterly ineffective.[85] Alexander Robinson, the president of the DC Care Consortium, an umbrella organization of AIDS service providers, spoke for many when he told the *Washington Post* that he did not trust Muhammad "to act in the best interest of gay and lesbian people."[86] Despite Muhammad's deep-seated homophobia, many Black gay men still supported Sankofa's bid for the city contract, arguing that the coalition would provide more culturally sensitive care than Whitman-Walker. The DC Coalition of Black Gays—one of the city's most visible Black gay organizations—backed Sankofa throughout the fall and winter of 1993.[87] It was a testament to their degree of alienation from Whitman-Walker that some Black gay activists were willing to support a notoriously homophobic figure like Muhammad over the clinic.

The city's allocation procedure required Sankofa and Whitman-Walker to submit extensive applications detailing their administrative capacity, previous experience, and ability to leverage volunteers. Not surprisingly, this application process benefited a well-resourced agency like Whitman-Walker with experience managing large-scale grants. After months of complicated and heated negotiations over the city contract, the district government awarded it to Whitman-Walker in June 1994, citing the clinic's superior organizational capacity and larger volunteer base.[88] Omitted from the city's funding announcement was any mention of Abundant Life's involvement with Sankofa, but health officials likely sought to avoid awarding a large grant to such a controversial organization.

For the rest of the 1990s and into the early 2000s, Whitman-Walker continued to expand its operations, winning large government contracts, developing a slate of new programs, and growing its client base.[89] The clinic remained the largest provider of HIV services in the city, serving over seven thousand PWAs in 2004 alone.[90] As Whitman-Walker grew, the district government and regional planning council continued to underfund organizations on the east side of the Anacostia. Between 2004 and 2009, only 5 percent of Washington's CARE Act grants went to nonprofits located in Wards 7 and 8, even though one in four district residents with HIV lived in this area of the city.[91] These neighborhoods were structurally disadvantaged in funding competitions because of disparities in the number, density, and capacity of local AIDS service organizations. In 2007, there were 3.9 AIDS nonprofits per one thousand people living with HIV on the west side of the Anacostia, but only 1.9 on the east side.[92] These figures indicated that fewer groups in African American neighborhoods were eligible for CARE Act grants, as the law stipulated that funds could only go to registered nonprofit entities. Two years later, the *Washington Post* surveyed the district's AIDS service industry and reported that organizations in Black-majority areas were, on aggregate, smaller and more financially precarious than their counterparts in other parts of the city. With fewer financial and human resources, groups east of the river lacked the administrative capacity and highly trained staff to compete with older AIDS service organizations in funding competitions, which required complex and time-consuming application procedures.[93] Structural limitations with the nonprofits representing predominantly Black areas meant these neighborhoods continued to receive a disproportionately small share of CARE Act grants.

Although extreme, the racial funding disparities of Washington, DC, were not unique in the 1990s and early 2000s. By privileging resource-rich organizations, HIV planning councils around the country often ignored the places and people in greatest need of more funding. Evaluations of the CARE Act conducted in the early 1990s found that minority-led AIDS nonprofits were smaller and less well-funded than the more prominent groups established at the start of the epidemic, placing them at a competitive disadvantage in funding competitions. Older service providers were generally more adept at navigating through the complex technical details required to make grant applications under the law.[94] One study of Latinx AIDS groups in Boston and San Diego discovered that many lacked the "necessary infrastructure to compete for [CARE Act] funding."[95] The legislation compounded these discrepancies by stipulating that AIDS service organizations could not use federal grants to support infrastructural development or capacity-building.[96]

In Chicago, another city known for its entrenched segregation, the local HIV planning council directed relatively few resources toward predominantly African American areas on the city's South and West Sides. Figure 6.1 overlays demographic data from the 2000 census with the location of AIDS service organizations that received CARE Act funding in 1996. It shows that Black neighborhoods did not contain nearly as dense a concentration of government-backed AIDS nonprofits as areas in the north of the city. According to the census, Black Americans constituted at least 90 percent of the population in 294 of Chicago's 866 census tracts.[97] Of these, only nine contained AIDS service organizations that received funding from the CARE Act. Much more investment poured into Chicago's North Side, which was home to a vast array of well-resourced, high-capacity AIDS service organizations, many of which grew out of the white gay urban enclaves dotted around this part of the city.[98] Throughout the 1990s and early 2000s, more African Americans than whites contracted HIV in Chicago, but the location of most AIDS care in predominantly white neighborhoods on the North Side made it much harder for Black HIV-positive people to access CARE Act programs.[99] The unavailability of services within a reasonable distance of where they lived meant Black PWAs often had to travel significant distances to receive appropriate healthcare. One survey reported that two-thirds of Black PWAs required transportation to access CARE Act services in Chicago compared with 44 percent of white PWAs.[100]

Despite the influx of federal funding that the CARE Act provided, racial segregation remained deeply entrenched within the AIDS service industry during the 1990s. As dollars flowed from the federal government to cities

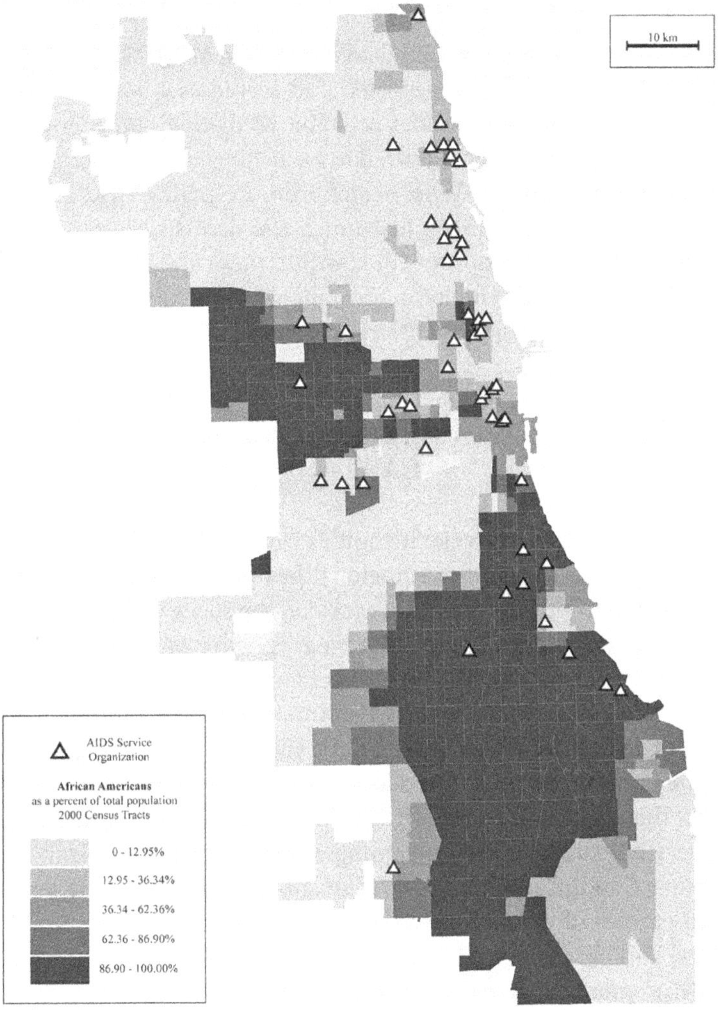

Figure 6.1: Relationship of AIDS Service Organizations to Black Neighborhoods in the city of Chicago during the 1990s. The AIDS Service Organizations mapped are those that received CARE Act funding in fiscal year 1996. The map highlights the lack of AIDS service organizations in predominantly Black neighborhoods on the West and South Sides of the city. Sources: "Care Fair: Share the Care," February 29, 1996, Tracy Baim Editorial Files, Windy City Box N (Alexander Street); Test Positive Aware Network, "Chicago Area HIV/AIDS Services Directory," institutional database, 1996. Data prepared by Social Explorer, accessed May 2022.

to grassroots nonprofits, the spatial concentration of AIDS care in primarily white gay neighborhoods persisted and served as a barrier to battling the epidemic within communities of color. Mediating outpatient services through grassroots nonprofits proved to be a wildly uneven mechanism for distributing healthcare to PWAs: neighborhoods lacking large and powerful AIDS service organizations had much less access to resources. Given the strong presence of people of color within these underserved neighborhoods, the CARE Act's emphasis on nonprofit–government partnerships exacerbated racial inequities in the provision of HIV healthcare.

Regional Disparities and the First Reauthorization of the CARE Act

In addition to amplifying racial inequities within the AIDS movement, the CARE Act generated significant regional healthcare disparities. From the beginning, the federal government provided the states with differing levels of support under the program, creating geographic variation in access to vital services and resources. The two original epicenters of the disease—California and New York—received substantially more funding from the CARE Act than most states in the South and Midwest (see figure 6.2). In 1995, the program provided the states with an average of $2,964 per AIDS case, but this average concealed significant discrepancies. On one end of the spectrum, numerous states—including Alabama, Arkansas, Idaho, Iowa, Oklahoma, South Carolina, and Wisconsin—had total funding levels less than 50 percent of the national average. On the other extreme, California and New York State received $3,096 and $3,572 per case, respectively. Even after the program expanded in the early 1990s to include more cities, both states were receiving approximately half of all CARE Act funds in 1995.[101] These funding disparities meant that the quality of care available to people with HIV infection varied tremendously. Whereas cities like San Francisco and Los Angeles used CARE Act money to fund a wide array of services for PWAs, including housing, legal advocacy, alternative therapies, mental health services, and counselling, smaller cities and rural states often struggled to provide them with even basic primary care and case management.[102]

These glaring regional discrepancies stemmed from the CARE Act's inequitable funding formula. The law disbursed money to states and localities on the basis of cumulative AIDS caseloads, with Title I and Title II

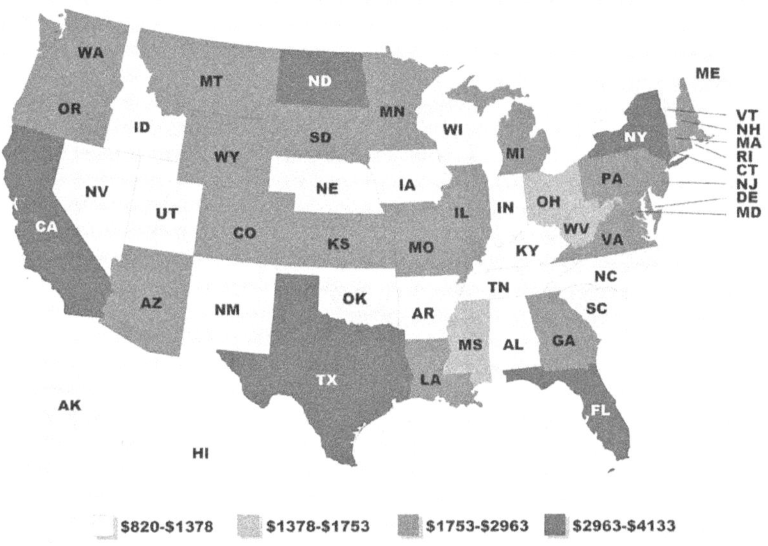

Figure 6.2: Funding from Titles I and II of the CARE Act per AIDS case in fiscal year 1995. This map reveals the differing levels of assistance states received from the federal government under the program. These figures have been adjusted to take into account the varying costs of AIDS healthcare in different states. Source: Government Accountability Office, "Revising Ryan White Funding Formulas" (GAO, 1996), 4.

appropriations calculated separately. Under this formula, PWAs in large cities were counted twice—once for Title I grants and again for statewide allocations. This double counting meant that states with Title I cities received considerably more funding, paving the way for significant geographic inequities.[103] According to one analysis, states with at least one metropolitan area eligible for Title I obtained, on average, three times more money per case than those with none.[104] In the South and Midwest in the early 1990s, only Illinois, Georgia, Texas, and Florida contained Title I cities, most of which were clustered on the East and West Coasts.[105] Framed as a form of disaster relief for cities overburdened by AIDS, the CARE Act provided the original coastal epicenters of the disease with substantially more money than other regions in its initial funding cycle, creating new forms of geographic inequality in the fight against the epidemic.

These regional disparities set the stage for a series of acrimonious struggles over the CARE Act's reauthorization in 1995 and 1996. The central conflict was between, on the one hand, state leaders and activists from underfunded regions, who sought dramatic changes to the structure of the CARE Act, and, on the other, lobbyists representing the interests of Title I cities, who favored refining the law with relatively minor amendments. In a classic example of "policy feedback," the CARE Act spawned the emergence of new lobbying organizations and interest groups, which successfully pushed for higher appropriations in the early 1990s but repeatedly clashed over which aspects of the program to prioritize.[106] Among the most prominent groups were Cities Advocating Emergency AIDS Relief (CAEAR), which represented Title I cities; the National Alliance of State and Territorial AIDS Directors, which concerned itself primarily with Title II; and the AIDS Policy Center for Children Youth and Families, which lobbied on behalf of organizations funded by Title IV.[107] In April 1994, these groups were joined by a new organization—the Campaign for Fairness (CFF)—which sought to overhaul the CARE Act's funding formulas and make them more equitable. The organization's statement of purpose called on policymakers to modify the legislation to "achieve equitable funding based on the number of people living with AIDS to ensure access to a comparable level of care and support services throughout America."[108] Led by Doug Nelson, a prominent activist from Milwaukee, Wisconsin, the CFF coordinated the lobbying efforts of nearly one hundred and fifty AIDS nonprofits from forty-eight different states.[109] Nelson founded the organization after learning that Milwaukee, which was not one of the cities initially funded by the law, was receiving approximately $1,000 annually per AIDS case in CARE Act grants compared with $6,000 in San Francisco.[110] Under Nelson's leadership, the CFF proved particularly adept at garnering the support of AIDS activists from underfunded and rural states, with groups such as the Wyoming AIDS Project, the Maine AIDS Alliance, and the Vermont AIDS Council lining up in support of the organization.[111]

The priorities of Title I cities could not have been more different. Whereas the CFF proposed a completely new system for allocating CARE Act grants, many AIDS activists in the original epicenters of the disease balked at such a proposal, fearing that it would disrupt existing programs and threaten the future of the legislation. In a widely distributed letter, Pat Christen, the executive director of the SFAF, argued that overhauling the law's funding formula amounted to "robbing Peter to pay Paul . . . in the name of equity."[112] Tom Sheridan, who played a central role in the passage of the original law in 1990, spearheaded the lobbying efforts of Title I cities during the reauthorization debate. In the early 1990s, he had left the AAC and NORA to establish a new lobbying firm—the Sheridan Group—hoping to capitalize on his personal connections with key congressional staffers. CAEAR, the umbrella organization representing Title I cities, retained Sheridan as its lobbyist in 1992, and he remained in this role for the rest of the 1990s.[113] Throughout the spring of 1994, Sheridan adopted aggressive lobbying tactics to try and block the CFF's proposals, even contacting some of the organization's key funders to try and persuade them to withdraw their support.[114]

As these debates over the reauthorization of the CARE Act heated up in the fall of 1994, they were interrupted by dramatic political developments in Washington, DC. Dubbed the "Republican Revolution," the 1994 midterm elections radically shifted the policy terrain on Capitol Hill, much to the benefit of the CFF. Led by Newt Gingrich of Georgia, the GOP seized unified control of Congress for the first time since 1952, gaining eight seats in the Senate and fifty-two in the House.[115] Although the new Republican majorities in Congress touted staunchly conservative policies such as welfare reform, tax cuts, and a balanced budget, bipartisan support for the CARE Act remained firm, undoubtedly because most representatives wanted the federal government to continue to channel much-needed AIDS funds to their districts.[116] The Republican Revolution still had significant implications for the reauthorization debate. Both Kennedy and Waxman, who had shepherded the original CARE Act through Congress and represented states that had received disproportionately large amounts of funding, lost their positions as committee chairs. After 1994, Senator Nancy Kassebaum (R–KS) replaced Kennedy as the chair of the influential Senate Labor Committee.[117] Since her home state of Kansas stood to gain more funding under the CFF's proposal for equitable AIDS funding, Kassebaum emerged as the organization's most powerful ally on Capitol Hill. Her staff met regularly with Nelson in late 1994 and early 1995 to plot a strategy to ensure the CARE Act's reauthorization.[118] Meanwhile, Sheridan, who had long-standing relationships with Kennedy and Waxman, found his influence on Capitol Hill quickly wane after the Republican Revolution. Kassebaum's staff refused to meet with him during the private discussions over the CARE Act's reauthorization in early 1995, essentially shutting him out from crucial decisions over the law's future.[119]

In late March 1995, Kassebaum introduced a new version of the CARE Act that included some crucial amendments to the original law. The mark of the CFF's influence on the legislation was plain to see. Consistent with her desire to provide states with equitable funding, Kassebaum's bill adopted many of the organization's recommendations, including new formulas that would give states without Title I cities more money. In an attempt to ward off any potential opposition from lawmakers representing Title I cities, the legislation also contained a "hold harmless" provision under which no area could lose more than 7.5 percent of its allocations over the next five years.[120] While politicians and AIDS lobbyists from California, New York City, and Massachusetts drafted the original CARE Act in 1990, the two key players during the law's reauthorization five years later—Kassebaum and Nelson—hailed from Kansas and Wisconsin, two states that had a relatively small number of PWAs in the 1980s but now experienced rapidly growing caseloads. "This is really about a shift in the balance of power," argued Robert Tracy, the public policy director for the Minnesota AIDS Project, an organization affiliated with the CFF: "A few communities are no longer going to define what our national AIDS policy is going to be. Minnesota, Wisconsin, Ohio, and Iowa are no longer going to be fly-over states when it comes to a federal AIDS policy."[121] In the battle over the law's reauthorization, Kassebaum's support was key to ensuring that the CFF's ideas won out.

Though some of its provisions were hotly debated, Kassebaum's bill passed by overwhelming margins in both chambers of Congress. The Senate enacted its version of the legislation in late June 1995 on a 97–3 vote, while the House passed its bill unanimously in mid-September. Conference negotiations were arduous, but President Bill Clinton eventually signed the legislation into law on May 20, 1996, with Kassebaum's amendments to the CARE Act's original funding formulas intact.[122]

AIDS in the South and the Persistence of Geographic Inequities

The apparent victory of the CFF did not mean that the inequities embedded in the CARE Act disappeared. While the 1996 amendments reduced the disparities between different places in the allocation of federal grants, funding discrepancies continued to take their toll on the quality of services offered to HIV-positive people in states with fewer Title I cities. The "hold harmless" clause of the 1996 amendments ensured that places like San Francisco and New York City still received a disproportionate amount of money.[123] In 2000, the Government Accountability Office (GAO) reported that the formulas used to distribute CARE Act grants continued to be flawed, leading to significant discrepancies between the states in funding per AIDS case. According to the GAO, California and New York received approximately $5,200 per AIDS case under the program in 2000 whereas states with no Title I cities received on average 40 percent less.[124] A stubborn gap in funding levels between the original epicenters of the epidemic and other states persisted.

In the twenty-first century, the burden of HIV increasingly fell on Southern states, but the CARE Act failed to reflect the disease's evolving epidemiology. The South became the new epicenter of the epidemic in the early 2000s, accounting for the greatest proportion of new HIV diagnoses and AIDS cases in the nation. Ominously, the number of deaths attributable to HIV/AIDS began to fall or level off in most parts of the United States but continued to climb precipitously in Southern states.[125] Several structural gaps and weaknesses in the South's threadbare public health infrastructure—including low levels of investment in disease prevention and sexual health education, lower overall health outcomes, entrenched poverty, and higher rates of uninsurance—enabled HIV to spread like wildfire.[126] As figure 6.3 shows, health index scores for Southern states were dramatically lower than the national average in 2006, impairing the region's ability to stop the spread of the virus. Eight of the ten states with the lowest overall health outcomes were located in the South, and nearly two in five residents in the region were medically disenfranchised.[127]

Despite the skewed impact of HIV/AIDS on the South, the CARE Act's funding structure continued to privilege large, coastal urban areas. By one count, the South accounted for 46 percent of new AIDS cases in 2005 but received only 34 percent of CARE Act grants.[128] Once again, the law's byzantine funding formulas were responsible for these discrepancies. Under the CARE Act, only metropolitan areas with populations greater than five hundred thousand could receive Title I grants; the South contained far fewer cities that met this threshold compared with other regions. Smaller cities such as Jackson, Mississippi; Columbia, South Carolina; and Baton Rouge, Louisiana, experienced rapidly expanding caseloads but remained ineligible for Title I funds in the early 2000s.[129]

These regional disparities intersected with and amplified racial

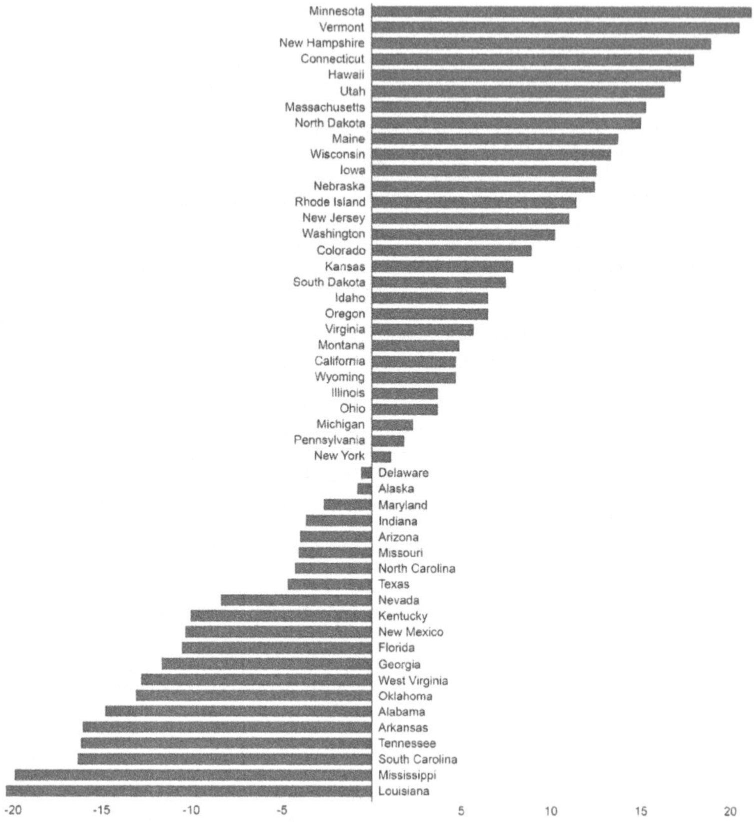

Figure 6.3: Health index scores for the states in 2006. This figure illustrates that there were vast healthcare disparities between the states, with the majority of Southern states ranking below the national average in health outcomes, hampering the region's ability to confront HIV/AIDS. The index takes into account the quality of public health programs, overall health outcomes, health behaviors, access to clinical care, and environmental health indicators. A score of zero is equal to the national average. Source: United Health Foundation, "America's Health Rankings: A Call to Action for People and Their Communities," Wayback Machine, 2006, https://web.archive.org/web/20061223121107/http://www.unitedhealthfoundation.org/ahr2006/media2006/shrmediakit/2006ahr.pdf.

inequities. From the very first cases, HIV/AIDS had a distinctive epidemiology in the South relative to other parts of the country. While the epidemic disproportionately affected communities of color in every region, this disparity was particularly stark in the South, where HIV spread aggressively among African Americans.[130] By the early 2000s, Black Americans accounted for more than 50 percent of new HIV infections in the South, though they constituted less than 20 percent of the total population.[131] In 2006, seven of the ten states reporting the highest rate of new AIDS diagnoses among African Americans were in the South (Louisiana, Mississippi, Georgia, South Carolina, Alabama, North Carolina, and Tennessee).[132] As infections among Black Americans in the South skyrocketed in the early twenty-first century, the CARE Act's funding structure ensured that the region had fewer resources to respond to this public health catastrophe.

New drug therapies for HIV/AIDS served to exacerbate rather than remedy these inequities. From the mid-1990s onward, the introduction of a new class of antiviral drugs—protease inhibitors—revolutionized treatment for the disease and dramatically cut mortality rates for people with HIV infection. In a very short time frame, HIV went from being a lethal virus to a chronic, manageable condition, at least for those who could access the new drugs. With the advent of protease inhibitors, one component of the CARE Act—the AIDS Drug Assistance Program (ADAP)—grew in importance. Originating in 1987 and incorporated into the CARE Act in 1990, the ADAP used a combination of state and federal funding to furnish uninsured and low-income HIV-positive people with access to medications. The effectiveness of protease inhibitors prompted lawmakers to increase appropriations for the program and make it a separate line item under the law in 1996. In 1997, Congress boosted the budget of the CARE Act by $258 million, and approximately 65 percent of this increase went toward the ADAP.[133] By the early 2000s, annual appropriations for the program consistently sat above $600 million, and it had evolved into the most important mechanism for providing medically indigent and impoverished PWAs with access to life-saving protease inhibitors.[134]

Like other aspects of the CARE Act, the ADAP delegated core decisions about program design and implementation to state governments, allowing them to determine which prescription drugs were covered by the policy. The result was a patchwork system that fueled geographic inequities. According to a report by the GAO, in 2004, the number of drugs included in ADAP's formularies ranged from a low of twenty in Colorado to a high of one thousand in Massachusetts, New Hampshire, and New Jersey.[135] These figures were highly significant because the more drugs a state covered, the more likely it was that people with HIV infection could switch regimens if they developed resistance to particular therapies.[136] Compounding these disparities were differing eligibility standards, copayment requirements, and caps on program enrolment in each state. In 2004, income ceilings for ADAP recipients ranged widely, from $11,638 in North Carolina to $51,764 in Massachusetts, with considerable variation in between.[137]

Southern states were especially ungenerous when determining eligibility standards for their ADAP programs and were more likely to implement waiting lists, copayment requirements, and other restrictions. With ramshackle public health infrastructures and fewer federal resources, most state health departments in the South imposed stricter requirements on ADAP recipients relative to other parts of the country. In the South, the average income ceiling on ADAP benefits was $25,370 while in the Northeast it was $36,523.[138] These discrepancies rendered impoverished HIV-positive people in the South vulnerable to gaps in the region's ADAP policies. In Alabama, the state health department imposed significant cost-containment strategies on its cash-strapped ADAP program in the early twenty-first century, including a waiting list for new applicants. By 2004, over four hundred and forty people with HIV infection were on the waiting list—the second largest number of any state in the country, behind only North Carolina—leading one health official to inform the legislature that "we think the problem in HIV and AIDS is now at crisis level."[139] In Texas in the early 2000s, barriers to accessing ADAP included a five dollar copayment for each prescription, a small number of drugs covered, and significant delays in receiving treatment.[140] As successful antiviral therapies became available, then, the South trailed behind other regions in providing access to them. Coverage gaps were particularly severe for African Americans, who had more difficulty accessing protease inhibitors than whites and were more likely to rely on inconsistent and underfunded ADAP programs rather than private insurance.[141]

These devastating geographic inequities and funding discrepancies did not go uncontested. When the CARE Act came up for reauthorization again in 2005 and 2006, a group of Southern AIDS activists, public health officials, and members of Congress pushed hard for further changes to the law's funding structure. Spearheading this campaign was the Southern AIDS

Coalition (SAC), which brought together some of the region's most influential AIDS workers into a single advocacy organization. Founded in 2001, the SAC contended that the federal government's distribution of AIDS dollars had consistently underestimated the needs of the South, allowing the virus to wreak havoc on the region's frayed public health infrastructure. In one of its first published documents, the organization excoriated federal funding formulas for fueling "inequity" in the "southern region of the country," arguing that "every individual living with HIV/AIDS in the United States deserves equal access to care and treatment."[142] During the reauthorization debate in 2005 and 2006, the SAC called on Congress to reform the CARE Act "to ensure parity of federal funding across the U.S."[143] It successfully attracted a large number of influential Southern lawmakers to its cause, most prominently Senators Jeff Sessions (R–AL) and Richard Burr (R–NC), who pushed hard on the floor of the Senate for a more equitable distribution of federal AIDS dollars.[144] As the CARE Act wended its way through Congress, civil rights groups—including local branches of the National Association for the Advancement of Colored People, the New Black Leadership Coalition, and the National Minority Health Month Foundation (NMHMF)—also endorsed the SAC's proposals, pointing to the urgent need to address the proliferating epidemic among Black Americans in the South.[145] In an op-ed in May 2006, Dr. Gary A. Puckrein, the executive director of the NMHMF, an organization concerned with racial health inequities, explained the necessity of making the CARE Act more flexible to the shifting epidemiology of the disease:

> The CARE Act was written in 1990 to respond to a problem largely confined to the biggest cities, when no effective treatments for HIV yet existed. Today, much has changed. Vital, life-saving treatments are available, but not always accessible. And HIV/AIDS has moved beyond the large cities into outer regions, especially rural minority communities in the South. . . . Consider that under the Ryan White CARE Act, funding for HIV programs for women of color continues to be primarily centered in big states like California, Texas and New York City. Places that big also have more state and local funding resources to supplement Ryan White resources. But the federal program leaves gaps in care and treatment efforts elsewhere. Increasingly, HIV/AIDS has shifted to new regions with an increase in new infections among minorities across the

> South in states like Tennessee, North Carolina, Alabama and Georgia. The money is not following them fast enough, and unless we fix Ryan White, it won't be able to.[146]

Thanks in large part to the coalition-building efforts of the SAC, the reauthorization of the CARE Act in 2006 redesigned the law's funding mechanisms to make them more responsive to the epidemic in the South. A revised formula reduced the population threshold for Title I eligibility from five hundred thousand people to fifty thousand, ensuring more Southern cities received grants.[147] The legislation also mandated new minimum requirements for ADAP programs, instructing the secretary of health and human services to establish and maintain a list of core medications to be covered by all states.[148] Though these changes meant the CARE Act better met the needs of HIV-positive people in Southern states, the epidemic continued to spread aggressively through the region after 2006. The South's chronically underfunded public health infrastructure remained insufficiently equipped to contain the virus. With the arrival of the Great Recession in 2008, many Southern states teetered on the edge of fiscal collapse and responded by scaling back their HIV/AIDS programs, imperiling any advances made since the 2006 CARE Act reauthorization. Cash-strapped states narrowed income eligibility requirements for ADAP, removed more expensive medications from their formularies, and restricted coverage to only the sickest people with HIV infection.[149] Most drastically, the North Carolina legislature enacted a bill in 2009 that slashed $3 million from the state's ADAP budget, forcing the program to stop taking new applicants.[150] By 2011, over nine thousand people living with HIV infection in the country were on ADAP waiting lists, the majority of whom resided in Southern states.[151] Even after the 2006 CARE Act reauthorization, then, AIDS care and prevention in the South continued to suffer from severe limitations, exacerbating the disproportionate impact of the epidemic on African Americans.[152]

Across its first two decades, the CARE Act achieved much, albeit at the cost of fueling regional inequities in the quality of HIV services. The law pumped federal dollars into the provision and management of HIV/AIDS healthcare for medically underserved and impoverished populations, emerging as the nation's most important and well-funded domestic AIDS program. But these benefits were not felt evenly across the country. Lawmakers framed the original 1990 legislation as a form of "disaster assistance" for large cities hard hit by the epidemic, providing more funding to the original epicenters of the disease—especially San Francisco and New York City. As the epidemic increasingly moved beyond these urban areas in the 1990s and early 2000s, the CARE Act's funding formulas failed to reflect the shifting epidemiology and geography of the disease. An amended distribution methodology in 1996 made federal grants more accessible to states with fewer large metropolitan areas. Even then, the CARE Act's funding structure skewed toward coastal areas with large caseloads and underestimated the severity of the epidemic in the South, the new epicenter of HIV/AIDS in the twenty-first century.

CONCLUSION

If the Ryan White CARE Act significantly expanded the federal government's role in the response to the AIDS epidemic, the law remains largely an aberration in the history of American federalism and public health. For the most part, during the early years of the twenty-first century, the states and their localities continued to be the locus of action and authority in the US public health system. The federalist structure that defined the US government's response to infectious diseases in the twentieth century—especially the 1918 Influenza pandemic and the early AIDS crisis—remained largely intact well into the twenty-first century.

There were moments when politicians coalesced around the idea that more federal intervention was necessary to combat infectious diseases, but these instances were invariably episodic and short-lived. In the weeks following the 9/11 terrorist attacks, the threat of bioterrorism sparked widespread calls for more government spending on public health. Throughout October and November 2001, anthrax-laced letters began arriving at the addresses of several prominent media figures and politicians, rousing fears that someone might deliberately introduce a communicable disease into the population. Public health experts detected anthrax in the offices of several major news organizations, at least thirty-five US Postal Service distribution centers, and the mailrooms of dozens of federal agencies. Five people died from breathing in the bacteria, and seventeen more developed serious complications.[1] In the months that followed, fears of a biological attack dominated opinion polls and criticism of the ramshackle state of the American public health system permeated the national conversation on healthcare policy. In a November 2001 Gallup poll, respondents were more concerned about bioterrorism than any other health-related issue, including cancer, heart disease, HIV/AIDS, rising insurance costs, and alcohol and drug abuse.[2]

Congress and the George W. Bush administration responded to these mounting concerns about bioterrorism with a flurry of legislation. With only one nay vote in the Senate, lawmakers passed the USA PATRIOT Act just a month after 9/11. Although the legislation's principal focus was to enhance federal intelligence-gathering and law enforcement capabilities, it also committed the central government to invest more in public health and boost emergency preparation for pandemics.[3] Within a year, Congress also enacted the 2002 Public Health Security and Bioterrorism Preparedness and Response Act, which established several new biodefence and disease surveillance programs and directed the CDC to channel more federal revenue toward state and local health departments.[4] Concerns about the nation's susceptibility to bioterrorism and infectious diseases reached a crescendo four years later with the passage of the 2006 Pandemic and All-Hazards Preparedness Act. Hailed as a "major milestone" by some public health experts, the legislation contained dozens of provisions to bolster and better coordinate the nation's pandemic preparedness infrastructure, ranging from a reorganization of the federal health administration to new training programs for epidemiologists.[5]

However, once the initial shock over the events of late 2001 faded into memory, politicians and the public gradually lost interest in pandemic preparedness. After a brief period of expansion following 9/11, federal expenditure on public health quickly plateaued. Between 2001 and 2003, federal spending on public health in inflation-adjusted terms grew by 52 percent, but it then declined by 4 percent between 2003 and 2005.[6] Furthermore, a large proportion of this new funding went into protecting against bioterrorism, siphoning resources away from other public health activities. In the early 2000s, federal spending on core public health functions—like traditional infectious disease control and HIV/AIDS prevention—stagnated or even declined. Between 2001 and 2006, CDC funding for counterterrorism programs jumped from $157 million to $1 billion, a 637 percent increase. Over the same period, the agency's expenditure on chronic diseases barely budged, moving from $824 million to $845 million. The concurrent decline in the CDC's spending on domestic HIV/AIDS programs—from $915 million in 2001 to $720 million in 2006—signaled the federal government's erratic commitment to public health in the early 2000s.[7]

In the 2010s, the central government's capacity to stem the spread of infectious diseases remained feeble. President Barack Obama's signature legislative achievement, the 2010 Affordable Care Act, earmarked federal funds for several new public health initiatives, but appropriations for these programs were meagre in the 2010s.[8] Meanwhile, the power and influence of the CDC remained anemic relative to its purpose and goals. Between 2010 and 2019, the CDC's budget fell by 10 percent in real terms, hampering its ability to implement rapid and well-coordinated responses to new epidemics.[9]

In the absence of meaningful federal leadership on public health, jurisdiction over disease prevention came under the purview of over 2,800 state and local health departments, which shouldered a much larger share of the financial burden for pandemic preparedness than the national government.[10] According to one estimate, subnational health agencies accounted for 82 percent of total government spending on public health in 2005.[11] In short, despite the importance of the Ryan White CARE Act in defining the US government's response to the AIDS epidemic, the 1990s did not represent a watershed in the history of American federalism and public health. During the opening decades of the twenty-first century, the locus of public health authority in the US continued to be state and local governments.

Nothing illustrates this more than the US government's reaction to COVID-19. In an echo of the early response to the AIDS crisis, the central government left most of the critical policy decisions about the pandemic to subnational authorities. On issue after issue, ranging from the procurement of medical supplies to the timing of lockdowns, regional variation became a hallmark of efforts to contain the spread of the virus. During the first wave of COVID-19, the Donald Trump White House endorsed a policy of leaving states and municipalities to fend for themselves. In a letter to Senator Minority Leader Charles E. Schumer (D–NY) in early April 2020, the president bluntly declared that "the federal government is merely a back-up for state governments."[12] The Trump administration shunned a national strategy for the procurement of personal protective equipment, refused to coordinate testing strategies, undercut the public health advice of state and local officials, and critiqued Democratic governors for implementing strict stay-at-home orders.[13] Meanwhile, the CDC, hollowed out by years of budget cuts, became a byword for bureaucratic incompetence, ensnarling itself in controversy after distributing faulty testing kits to the states in January and February 2020.[14]

As the federal government abdicated any responsibility for tackling the pandemic, many states, counties, and cities marshalled long-dormant police powers to implement far-reaching and sometimes coercive mitigation measures. The jurisdictional sprawl of the American public health system ensured that the response to COVID-19 varied significantly by state and region. On the one hand, states with Democratic governors, like California, Hawaii, and New York, typically favored strict restrictions on social gatherings, prolonged shutdowns of the economy, and mask mandates. Amid ominous warnings that the virus would overload hospital systems if left unchecked, California governor Gavin Newsom ordered the nation's first statewide stay-at-home order on March 19, 2020. Wielding the state's police powers to an almost unprecedented degree, the directive shut down most nonessential businesses, enacted a sweeping ban on public gatherings, and instructed people to remain home unless they were involved in the day-to-day operation of critical government infrastructure.[15] Over the next few days, every other state with a Democratic governor followed suit, rolling out stay-at-home orders that imposed far-reaching restrictions on individual liberties and nonessential movement.[16] On the other hand, Republican-controlled states were much slower to impose stringent public health measures during the critical early phase of the pandemic.[17] The GOP controlled the governor's office in all seven states that did not impose any statewide stay-at-home orders in March and April 2020.[18]

The parallel between the disjointed approach to COVID-19 and the sprawling response to the AIDS epidemic points to a remarkable degree of continuity in the history of American federalism and public health. Across the twentieth and early twenty-first centuries, the states and their localities remained preeminent in shaping infectious disease control efforts. Of course, there were moments when the federal government took a more proactive role in the nation's public health system—such as during the New Deal era and the 1990s with the passage of the Ryan White CARE Act—but these moments invariably proved fleeting. Moreover, the federal government relied heavily on subnational authorities to implement key pieces of public health legislation like Title VI of the 1935 Social Security Act and the CARE Act, often strengthening the capacity of state and local health departments in the process.

Bringing the history of pandemics and American state development into the same frame, as this book has done, qualifies any narrative that emphasizes the growing centralization of government power in the United States during the twentieth and early twenty-first centuries. Even after the New Deal, two world wars, the Great Society, and the Cold War channeled unprecedented levels of power toward Washington, DC, the right to regulate public health and hygiene—one of the foundational and legitimating functions of modern government systems—continued to rest primarily with the states and their municipalities. Unlike many other policy areas, subnational governments remained at the leading edge of controlling the spread of infectious diseases across the twentieth century. Historians of the AIDS crisis must take heed of this fragmented, decentralized approach to public health to fully understand the multifaceted, often contradictory US government response to the epidemic. Focusing solely on the federal government and a few localities, as many historians of AIDS have done, misses the crucial site where public health authority resides—the states.

Ultimately, the patchwork and fragmentary nature of the American public health system severely weakened the nation's ability to respond to pandemics by engendering chaos, exacerbating healthcare inequalities, and producing opportunities for state inaction and counterproductive measures. Federalism deepened geographic healthcare disparities by vesting control over disease prevention with state and local authorities—many of which lacked the capacity and willingness to invest in pandemic preparedness. During the AIDS epidemic, a PWA's ability to access high-quality public health services depended to a great extent on where they happened to live. While California led the way in the early years of the epidemic due to the mobilization of its well-organized gay rights movement, the federalist structure of the American public health system allowed states with a more repressive stance on gay rights or weak legislatures to ignore the disease. With a sodomy stature still on the books and a woefully amateurish approach to lawmaking, the Texas legislature did virtually nothing to stem the disease's spread until 1989, despite the state's large caseload. Federalism also extended the number of venues where policymakers could experiment with authoritarian and counterproductive approaches to the epidemic. Most notably, in Illinois, a conservative group of anti-feminists shaped the state's initial response to the AIDS epidemic, pushing for policies like premarital antibody testing that were wholly ineffective in containing the spread of the disease.

In the twenty-first century, the fractured approach to disease control continued to have disastrous consequences for public health. Although most public health spending occurred at the subnational level, expenditure on public health varied widely between the states, intensifying healthcare inequalities. According to one estimate, annual per capita spending on public health ranged from a low of three dollars and twenty-eight cents in Nevada to a high of $154.99 in Hawaii in 2011.[19] With the arrival of COVID-19, the fragmented and contradictory nature of the initial state response contributed directly to the severity of the outbreak. Indeed, numerous studies have shown that the states with the weakest containment measures, such as Florida, North Dakota, and Texas, had significantly higher death tolls.[20]

The collision of the American public health system with the AIDS epidemic revealed the severe drawbacks of relying on state and local governments to respond to national and global health emergencies. During the crisis, states responded in a highly irregular and haphazard fashion as they filled the policy vacuum left by the federal government. This chaotic approach heightened regional healthcare inequalities and opened the door for some states to implement counterproductive and repressive policies. Across the long sweep of the twentieth and early twenty-first centuries, the patchwork system of American public health governance meant the states and their localities were thrust onto the front line of responding to pandemics, but they often proved incapable of implementing policies that were truly capable of stemming the spread of infectious diseases.

NOTES

Introduction

1. Both these statistics are taken from Nancy K. Bristow, *American Pandemic: The Lost Worlds of the 1918 Influenza Epidemic* (Oxford University Press, 2012), 3–4.

2. For a sample of the different community responses to the 1918 influenza pandemic, see the collection of essays produced by the *Influenza Encyclopedia: The American Influenza Epidemic of 1918–1919: A Digital Encyclopedia*, University of Michigan Center for the History of Medicine and Michigan Publishing, University of Michigan Library, accessed July 1, 2025, https://www.influenzaarchive.org/cities/index.html.

3. Intergovernmental Health Policy Project, "A Synopsis of State AIDS Laws Enacted During the 1983–1987 Legislative Sessions," 1988, National Gay and Lesbian Taskforce Records, Division of Rare and Manuscript Collections, Cornell University Library, Ithaca, New York (hereafter NGLTF), box 131, folder 29.

4. For a sample of the vast literature on the state-level response to COVID-19, see Donald F. Kettl, "States Divided: The Implications of American Federalism for COVID-19," *Public Administration Review* 80, no. 4 (July–August 2020): 595–602; Nicole Huberfield et al., "Federalism Complicates the Response to the COVID-19 Health and Economic Crisis: What Can Be Done?" *Journal of Health Politics, Policy and Law* 45, no. 6 (December 2020): 951–965.

5. For some of the most important scholarship on the durability of the states' power in the nineteenth and early twentieth centuries, see William J. Novak, *The People's Welfare: Law and Regulation in Nineteenth-Century America* (University of North Carolina Press, 1996); Gary Gerstle, *Liberty and Coercion: The Paradox of American Government from the Founding to the Present* (Princeton University Press, 2015), 17–54; Noam Maggor, *Brahmin Capitalism: Frontiers of Wealth and Populism in America's First Gilded Age* (Harvard University Press, 2017); Jessica Wang, *Mad Dogs and Other New Yorkers: Rabies, Medicine, and Society in an American Metropolis, 1840–1920* (John Hopkins University Press, 2019); Kate Masur, "State Sovereignty and Migration Before Reconstruction," *Journal of the Civil War Era* 9, no. 4 (December 2019): 588–611; R. M. Bates, "Government by Improvisation? Towards a New History of the Nineteenth-Century American State," *Journal of Policy History* 33, no. 3 (July 2021): 287–316. On the resilience of the states' authority at the beginning of the twentieth century, see Gary Gerstle, "The Resilient Power of the States Across the Long Nineteenth Century," in *The Unsustainable American State*, ed. Lawrence R. Jacobs and Desmond S. King (Oxford University Press,

2009), 61–87. Both the Civil War and the First World Wars proved to be fleeting moments of federal hegemony. See Gary Gerstle, "A State Both Strong and Weak," *American Historical Review* 115, no. 3 (June 2010): 779–785; Kimberley S. Johnson, *Governing the American State: Congress and the New Federalism, 1877–1929* (Princeton University Press, 2006), 3–5.

6. For versions of this centralization narrative, see Gerstle, *Liberty and Coercion,* 185–310; Karen M. Tani, *States of Dependency: Welfare, Rights, and American Governance, 1935–1972* (Cambridge University Press, 2016), 16–19; James T. Sparrow, *Warfare State: World War II Americans and the Age of Big Government* (Oxford University Press, 2011); Anne M. Kornhauser, *Debating the American State: Liberal Anxieties and the New Leviathan, 1930–1970* (University of Pennsylvania Press, 2015). For a recent account of American state development that dates the rise of an interventionist, proactive central government to the post–Civil War era rather than the New Deal, see William J. Novak, *New Democracy: The Creation of the Modern American State* (Harvard University Press, 2022). For an earlier work that makes a similar argument about the origins of the modern American state before the New Deal, see Johnson, *Governing the American State.*

7. On the federal government's chipping away of the states' authority, especially during the 1960s, see Gerstle, *Liberty and Coercion*, 275–310.

8. For examples of other areas of governance where the states continued to play a leading role, see Sara Mayeux and Karen Tani, "Federalism Anew," *American Journal of Legal History* 56, no. 1 (March 2016): 128–138.

9. The phrase "bringing the states back in" was coined by Gary Gerstle in his agenda-setting work on the history of the American state. It is a play on the earlier phrase "bringing the state back in," popularized by a pathbreaking 1985 edited collection by Peter B. Evans, Dietrich Rueschemeyer, and Theda Skocpol. Gerstle, *Liberty and Coercion*, 56; Peter B. Evans, Dietrich Rueschemeyer, and Theda Skocpol, eds., *Bringing the State Back In* (Cambridge University Press, 1985).

10. Intergovernmental Health Policy Project, "A Comparative Review of State-Only Expenditures for AIDS–Major Trends, Fiscal Years 1983–1988," 1987, NGLTF, box 190, folder 10.

11. For more on the federal government's response to AIDS, see Randy Shilts, *And the Band Played On: Politics, People, and the AIDS Epidemic* (St. Martin's Griffin, 1987); Patricia D. Siplon, *AIDS and the Policy Struggle in the United States* (Georgetown University Press, 2002); Anthony Petro, *After the Wrath of God: AIDS, Sexuality, and American Religion* (Oxford University Press, 2015), 53–90; Jennifer Brier, *Infectious Ideas: U.S. Political Responses to the AIDS Crisis* (University of North Carolina Press, 2009), 78–121.

12. Mary Ziegler, *Beyond Abortion:* Roe v. Wade *and the Battle for Privacy* (Harvard University Press, 2018), 69.

13. Irvin Molotsky, "Congress Passes Compromise AIDS Bill," *New York Times*, October 14, 1988, A12.

14. By contrast, a rich and voluminous body of work exists on the early history of AIDS activism and its intersections with, among other things, gay liberation, radical politics, and the "long civil rights movement." To take just a few representative examples: Jennifer Brier has used the epidemic as a lens to examine the cracks and fissures within the so-called Reagan revolution; Emily Hobson has illuminated how anti-war organiz-

ing and the Central American solidarity movement shaped early AIDS activism; Dan Royles has spotlighted how the grassroots response to the epidemic fits into the longer history of the Black health movement; and Tamar Carroll has traced the connections between direct-action groups such as the AIDS Coalition to Unleash Power (ACT UP) and multiracial feminist organizing. Brier, *Infectious Ideas*; Emily K. Hobson, *Lavender and Red: Liberation and Solidarity in the Gay and Lesbian Left* (University of California Press, 2016); Dan Royles, *To Make the Wounded Whole: The African American Struggle Against HIV/AIDS* (University of North Carolina Press, 2020); Tamar W. Carroll, *Mobilizing New York: AIDS, Antipoverty, and Feminist Activism* (University of North Carolina Press, 2015). Other historians, meanwhile, have explored how the search for the first infected case of AIDS, popularly known as "patient zero," dovetailed with and reinforced homophobic responses to the disease. Richard McKay and Phil Tiemeyer have shown that the vilifying of the Canadian flight attendant Gaëtan Dugas as patient zero buttressed "blame-the-victim" narratives and fueled efforts to enact punitive legislation against PWAs. Richard A. McKay, *Patient Zero and the Making of the AIDS Epidemic* (University of Chicago Press, 2017); Phil Tiemeyer, *Plane Queer: Labor, Sexuality, and AIDS in the History of Male Flight Attendants* (University of California Press, 2013). Another constellation of historians has focused on the cultural production of Black gay artists—such as David Frechette, Essex Hemphill, and Assotto Saint—who confronted AIDS in the 1980s. Darius Bost, *Evidence of Being: The Black Gay Cultural Renaissance and the Politics of Violence* (University of Chicago Press, 2018); Dagmawi Woubshet, *The Calendar of Loss: Race Sexuality and Mourning in the Early Era of AIDS* (John Hopkins University Press, 2015); Martin Duberman, *Hold Tight Gently: Michael Callen, Essex Hemphill, and the Battlefield of AIDS* (New Press, 2014).

15. Important exceptions to this tendency include Stephen Inrig, *North Carolina and the Problem of AIDS: Advocacy, Politics, and Race in the South* (University of North Carolina Press, 2011); Ronald Bayer, *Private Acts, Social Consequences: AIDS and the Politics of Public Health* (Free Press, 1988). These works provide individual case studies of state-level responses to the AIDS epidemic but do not situate the crisis within the broader history of federalism and pandemic politics.

16. Intergovernmental Health Policy Project, "Summary of AIDS Laws from the 1987 Legislative Sessions," 1988, NGLTF, box 131, folder 31; Intergovernmental Health Policy Project, "National Survey of State Spending for AIDS," 1989, the Bush Administration and the AIDS Crisis: White House Staff and Office files, OA/ID 06961-018, Gale Archives of Sexuality and Gender.

17. Stan Hadden to David Roberti, December 4, 1987, Series 1 Communications 1983–1991, Stanley Hadden Papers, 1997–33, the Gay, Lesbian, Bisexual, Transgender Historical Society (hereafter SHP), box 2, folder 1.

18. On the history of the AIDS epidemic and the culture wars, see Andrew Hartman, *A War for the Soul of America: A History of the Culture Wars* (University of Chicago Press, 2015), 155–161.

19. Histories of AIDS activism and popular documentaries alike emphasize a series of political clashes between the conservative White House and radical direct-action AIDS groups in the 1980s. See especially Deborah B. Gould, *Moving Politics: Emotions and ACT UP's Fight Against AIDS* (University of Chicago Press, 2009); Benita Roth, *The Life*

and Death of ACT UP/LA: Anti-AIDS Activism in Los Angeles from the 1980s to the 2000s (Cambridge University Press, 2017); Sarah Schulman, *Let the Record Show: A Political History of ACT UP New York, 1987–1993* (Farrar, Straus & Giroux, 2021). For critiques of this tendency to center dramatic battles between activists and the federal government at the expense of other aspects of the epidemic, see Stephen Vider, *The Queerness of Home: Gender, Sexuality, and the Politics of Domesticity After World War II* (University of Chicago Press, 2021), 179–213; Katie Batza, "Tactical Deployments of Respectability: Religion, Race, and Rights in the United States Heartland Early-AIDS Response," in *Resist, Organize, Build: Feminist and Queer Activism in Britain and the United States During the Long 1980s*, ed. Sarah Crook and Charlie Jeffries (State University of New York Press, 2022), 229–253.

20. By focusing on the bipartisan origins of state-level AIDS legislation, this book joins a burgeoning body of literature that emphasizes political developments that cuts across partisan divisions. Rejecting a narrow focus on the "red-blue divide" of election cycles, this scholarship underlines the deeper forms of consensus in US politics that do not map cleanly onto the partisan cleavages of Republican and Democrat, conservative and liberal, right and left. For examples of historical work in this vein, see Sarah Coleman, *The Walls Within: The Politics of Immigration in Modern America* (Princeton University Press, 2021); Michael Brenes, *For Might and Right: Cold War Defense Spending and the Remaking of American Democracy* (University of Massachusetts Press, 2020); Sarah Milov, *The Cigarette: A Political History* (Harvard University Press, 2019); Brent Cebul, Lily Geismer, and Mason B. Williams, "Beyond Red and Blue: Crisis and Continuity in Twentieth-Century U.S. Political History," in *Shaped by the State: Toward a New Political History of the Twentieth Century* (University of Chicago Press, 2019), 3–23; Matthew Lassiter, "Political History Beyond the Red-Blue Divide," *Journal of American History* 98, no. 3 (December 2011): 760–764.

21. Thomas J. Sugrue, "All Politics Is Local: The Persistence of Localism in Twentieth-Century America," in *The Democratic Experiment: New Directions in American Political History*, ed. Meg Jacobs, William J. Novak, and Julian E. Zelizer (Princeton University Press, 2003), 301–326; Nicholas Dagen Bloom, *How States Shaped Postwar America: State Government and Urban Power* (University of Chicago Press, 2019); Brent Cebul, "Developmental State: The Politics of Business, Poverty, and Economic Empowerment from the New Deal to the New Democrats" (PhD diss., University of Virginia, 2014); Gerstle, *Liberty and Coercion*; Tani, *States of Dependency.*

22. For the history of state governing capacity in the twentieth century, see Jon C. Teaford, *The Rise of the States: Evolution of American State Government* (John Hopkins University Press, 2003). On the New Deal's role in amplifying the power of state-level policy elites, see Mason B. Williams, *City of Ambition: FDR, La Guardia, and the Making of Modern New York* (W. W. Norton, 2013); Brent Cebul and Mason B. Williams, "'Really and Truly a Partnership': The New Deal's Associational State and the Making of Postwar American Politics," in *Shaped by the State*, 96–122. On the messy distribution of government authority in the US polity and the decentralized, multilayered nature of the American state, see William J. Novak, "The Myth of the 'Weak' American State," *American Historical Review* 113, no. 3 (June 2018): 752–772.

23. Martha Derthick, "Compensatory Federalism," in *Greenhouse Governance: Ad-*

dressing Climate Change in America, ed. Barry G. Rabe (Brookings Institution Press, 2010), 58–72.

24. The literature on nineteenth- and early twentieth-century epidemics is particularly extensive. See, for example, Michael Willrich, *Pox: An American History* (Penguin Press, 2011); Rana A. Hogarth, *Medicalizing Blackness: Making Racial Differences in the Atlantic World, 1780–1840* (University of North Carolina Press, 2017); and Kathryn Olivarius, "Immunity, Capital, and Power in Antebellum New Orleans," *American Historical Review* 124, no. 2 (April 2019): 425–455.

25. Little or no reference, for example, is made to the 1918 influenza pandemic in canonical works such as Brian Balogh, *The Associational State: American Governance in the Twentieth Century* (University of Pennsylvania Press, 2015); Christopher Capozolla, *Uncle Sam Wants You: World War I and the Making of the Modern American Citizen* (Oxford University Press, 2010); Elisabeth S. Clemens, *The People's Lobby: Organizational Innovation and the Rise of Interest Group Politics in the United States, 1890–1925* (University of Chicago Press, 1997); Jefferson Cowie, *The Great Exception: The New Deal and the Limits of American Politics* (Princeton University Press, 2017); Gerstle, *Liberty and Coercion*; Jacob S. Hacker, *The Divided Welfare State: The Battle over Public and Private Social Benefits in the United States* (Cambridge University Press, 2002); Ellis W. Hawley, *The Great War and the Search for a Modern Order: A History of the American People and Their Institutions, 1917–1933* (St. Martin's Press, 1979); and Stephen Skowronek, *Building a New American State: The Expansion of National Administrative Capacities, 1877–1920* (Cambridge University Press, 1982). A number of agenda-setting edited collections on the history of the American state also contain no chapters on twentieth-century epidemics. For instance, see James T. Sparrow, William J. Novak, and Stephen W. Sawyer, eds., *Boundaries of the State in U.S. History* (University of Chicago Press, 2015); Cebul, Geismer, and Williams, *Shaped by the State*; and Gary Gerstle, Nelson Lichtenstein, and Alice O'Connor, eds., *Beyond the New Deal Order: U.S. Politics from the Great Depression to the Great Recession* (University of Pennsylvania Press, 2019).

26. Karen Orren and Stephen Skowronek, *The Search for American Political Development* (Cambridge University Press, 2004), 16–17.

27. Patrick J. Buchanan, "AIDS Disease: It's Nature Striking Back," *New York Post*, May 24, 1983, 31.

28. Much of this scholarship builds on and interrogates Margot Canaday's agenda-setting book *The Straight State*, which traces the coconstitutive rise of the modern bureaucratic state and the hetero/homo binary. Analyzing three federal policy areas—the military, immigration, and welfare—she argues that the state grew more precise in its policing of homosexuality over the course of the twentieth century. Margot Canaday, *The Straight State: Sexuality and Citizenship in Twentieth-Century America* (Princeton University Press, 2009). On the impact of the AIDS epidemic on the federal policing of sexuality, see Jonathan Bell, "Rethinking the 'Straight State': Welfare Politics, Health Care, and Public Policy in the Shadow of AIDS," *Journal of American History* 104, no. 4 (March 2018): 931–952. On the rise of gay political power in the closing decades of the twentieth century, see Timothy Stewart-Winter, *Queer Clout: Chicago and the Rise of Gay Politics* (University of Pennsylvania Press, 2016); Clayton Howard, *The Closet and the Cul-de-Sac: The Politics of Sexual Privacy in Northern California* (University of

Pennsylvania Press, 2019); Jonathan Bell, ed., *Beyond the Politics of the Closet: Gay Rights and the American State Since the 1970s* (University of Pennsylvania Press, 2020); Jonathan Bell, "Between Private and Public: AIDS, Health Care Capitalism, and the Politics of Respectability in 80s America," *Journal of American Studies* 54, no. 1 (February 2020): 159–183. For work on the growing entanglements between gay nonprofits and the states in the 1970s and 1980s, see Myrl Beam, *Gay, Inc: The Nonprofitization of Queer Politics* (University of Minnesota Press, 2018); Katie Batza, *Before AIDS: Gay Health Politics in the 1970s* (University of Pennsylvania Press, 2018); Lauren Jae Gutterman, "'Caring for Our Own': The Founding of Senior Action in a Gay Environment, 1977–1985," *Radical History Review* 139 (January 2021): 178–199.

29. "Federation of Statewide GLBT Organizations: 1997 Year End Report. 1996–1997," NGLTF, box 135, folder 2.

30. Scholars have generally approached the late twentieth-century gay movement through the rubric of urban and metropolitan history. For examples of this methodological tendency, see Josh Sides, *Erotic City: Sexual Revolutions and the Making of Modern San Francisco* (Oxford University Press, 2011); Christina B. Hanhardt, *Safe Space: Gay Neighborhood History and the Politics of Violence* (Duke University Press, 2013); Julio Capó, *Welcome to Fairyland: Queer Miami Before 1940* (University of North Carolina Press, 2017); Stewart-Winter, *Queer Clout*; Howard, *The Closet and the Cul-de-Sac.* This focus on cities derives partly from an earlier model of LGBT community history that emphasizes the forces of urbanization and industrialization in the formation of modern sexual identities. See Elizabeth Lapovsky Kennedy and Madeline D. Davis, *Boots of Leather, Slippers of Gold: The History of a Lesbian Community* (Routledge, 1993); George Chauncey, *Gay New York: Gender, Urban Culture, and the Making of the Gay Male World, 1890–1940* (Basic Books, 1994); Marc Stein, *City of Sisterly and Brotherly Loves: Lesbian and Gay Philadelphia, 1945–1972* (University of Minnesota Press, 2000); Nan Alamilla Boyd, *Wide-Open Town: A Queer History of San Francisco to 1965* (University of California Press, 2003). On the theoretical shortcomings of focusing exclusively on cities as sites of gay identity formation, see Jack Halberstam, *In a Queer Time and Place: Transgender Bodies, Subcultural Lives* (New York University Press, 2005); Kath Weston, "Get Thee to a Big City: Sexual Imaginary and the Great Gay Migration," *GLQ: A Journal of Lesbian and Gay Studies* 2, no. 33 (1995): 253–277. It is important to note that other scholars have analyzed national developments in LGBTQ politics during the late twentieth century. See Claire Bond Potter, "Paths to Political Citizenship: Gay Rights, Feminism, and the Carter Presidency," *Journal of Policy History* 24, no. 1 (2012): 95–114; William B. Turner, "Lesbian/Gay Rights and Immigration Policy: Lobbying to End the Medical Model," *Journal of Policy History* 7, no. 2 (1995): 208–225; Jonathan Bell, "Making Sexual Citizens: LGBT Politics, Health Care, and the State in the 1970s," in Bell, ed., *Beyond the Politics of the Closet*, 58–80. The few studies that do consider state LGBTQ politics in a sustained way include Rachel Guberman, "'No Discrimination & No Special Rights': Gay Rights, Family Values, and the Politics of Moderation in the 1992 Election," in *Beyond the Politics of the Closet*, 165–186; Amy Wright, *Gay Rights at the Ballot Box* (University of Minnesota Press, 2012); Jonathan Bell, *California Crucible: The Forging of Modern American Liberalism* (University of Pennsylvania Press, 2012).

31. Stewart-Winter, *Queer Clout*, 11.

32. For work that explores the role of suburban spaces in the formation of sexual identities, see Howard, *The Closet and the Cul-de-Sac*; Tim Retzloff, "Suburb, City, and the Changing Bounds of Lesbian and Gay Life in Metropolitan Detroit, 1945–1985" (PhD diss., Yale University, 2014). On the history of rural areas and sexuality, see John Howard, *Men Like That: A Southern Queer History* (University of Chicago Press, 2001); Colin R. Johnson, *Just Queer Folks: Gender and Sexuality in Rural America* (University of Minnesota Press, 2013).

33. Consider the relative absence of state governments in much of the most prominent scholarship on the history of the late twentieth-century gay rights movement. Timothy Stewart-Winter mentions the Illinois legislature about ten times in his study of Chicago; Clayton Howard references the California legislature a similar number of times in his work on the Bay Area; and Christina Hanhardt focuses overwhelmingly on local and national political developments in her discussions of hate crimes legislation, glossing over the states. Stewart-Winter, *Queer Clout*, 41, 43–46, 121–29, 198, 200–201, 232; Howard, *The Closet and the Cul-de-Sac*, 67, 74, 111, 179–181, 216, 249–252, 291; Hanhardt, *Safe Space*, 155–184. The field of the history of sexuality more broadly has begun to focus more attention on the states as crucial sites for the regulation of intimate behavior. As Margot Canaday, Nancy F. Scott, and Robert O. Self noted in the introduction to a recent edited collection, the states led the way in regulating intimate life during the nineteenth and early twentieth centuries, enacting hundreds of laws that governed the sexual behavior of citizens. Margot Canaday, Nancy F. Scott, and Robert O. Self, "Introduction," in *Intimate States: Gender, Sexuality, and Governance in Modern U.S. History*, ed. Margot Canaday, Nancy F. Scott, and Robert O. Self (University of Chicago Press, 2021), 1–18.

34. This figure includes forty-eight state health departments and 1,577 municipal public health institutions. E. R. Coffey, "Public Health Expands Its Facilities Under Title VI—Federal Social Security Act," *American Journal of Public Health and the Nation's Health* 31, no. 4 (April 1941): 302.

35. Robert Craig Waters, "Florida's Omnibus AIDS Act of 1988," *Florida State University Law Review* 16, no. 3 (Fall 1988): 441–529. While providing a comprehensive overview of the Florida Omnibus AIDS Act, this article focuses primarily on the legal principles behind the legislation and its interactions with existing court precedents on HIV discrimination. It contains only a small amount of material on the lobbying tactics adopted by the Florida Task Force.

36. Senate Commerce Committee, Tape 1, 1988 Florida Legislature, Regular Session, May 26, 1988, Florida State Archive, Tallahassee, Florida (hereafter FSA); Senate Appropriations Committee, Tape 1, 1988 Florida Legislature, Regular Session, May 27, 1988, FSA; Audio Recording of Senate Floor Debate, Tape 1, 1988 Florida Legislature, Regular Session, May 31, 1988, FSA; Audio Recording of Senate Floor Debate, Tape 1, 1988 Florida Legislature, Regular Session, June 6, 1988, FSA; Audio Recording of House Floor Debate, Tape 1, 1988 Florida Legislature, Regular Session, May 11, 1988, FSA; Audio Recording of House Floor Debate, Tape 1, 1988 Florida Legislature, Regular Session, June 3, 1988, FSA.

37. I was unable to locate any archival collections devoted to the state-level response to AIDS in Arkansas or Mississippi.

38. Another Southern state with an amble source base on the legislative response

to AIDS is Georgia. The special collections at Emory University and the University of Georgia contain a rich trove of archival sources on the gay rights movement and the epidemic, including material on the lobbying strategies adopted by gay activists at the state level. Ultimately, I picked Texas over Georgia as a case study because it stood out among the states for having a large caseload but doing virtually nothing to combat the disease for most of the 1980s.

39. Bruce Lambert, "In Texas, AIDS Struggle Is Also Matter of Money," *New York Times*, January 5, 1990, A18.

40. For more on the Reagan administration and fiscal conservatism, see Benjamin C. Waterhouse, *Lobbying America: The Politics of Business from Nixon to NAFTA* (Princeton University Press, 2013), 201–228; Gary Gerstle, *The Rise and Fall of the Neoliberal Order: America and the World in the Free Market Era* (Oxford University Press, 2022), 121–128. This ideological quest to shrink the size of the federal government ran squarely against the Reagan administration's deficit spending. A staunch anti-communist and Cold War Warrior, Reagan was determined to spare no expense in confronting the Soviet Union, boosting military spending by 34 percent during his first term. To the chagrin of many fiscal conservatives, the federal budget deficit subsequently ballooned, tripling in nominal terms between 1980 and 1988. Despite the incongruence between Reagan's rhetoric and policies, the language of fiscal restraint and small government still dominated the era's politics. Gerstle, *The Rise and Fall of the Neoliberal Order*, 129.

41. On the fiscal problems faced by state governments in the 1980s, see James M. Poterba, "State Responses to Fiscal Crises: The Effects of Budgetary Institutions and Politics," *Journal of Political Economy* 102, no. 4 (August 1994): 799–821.

42. Scholars have paid remarkably little attention to the role of "closeted" individuals within the gay movement, focusing instead on activists' own campaign for visibility—captured by the slogan "Out of the Closets, Into the Streets." For a critique of the scholarly tendency to focus on the politics of gay visibility, see Stephen Vider, "'The Ultimate Extension of Gay Community': Communal Living and Gay Liberation in the 1970s," *Gender & History* 27, no. 3 (November 2015): 865–881. In recent years, an interdisciplinary group of scholars have explored how the "closet" can afford LGBT people with unexpected social and cultural opportunities. Few studies, however, examine how the closet can function as a tool to subvert and reconfigure state repression. For a summary of the most recent scholarship on the closet, see Scott De Orio, "The Closet," in *Global Encyclopedia of Gay, Lesbian, Bisexual, Transgender, and Queer History*, ed. Howard Chiang (Gale, 2019), 372–379.

Chapter 1: The Structure of American Public Health Policy Before the AIDS Epidemic

1. William J. Novak, *The People's Welfare: Law and Regulation in Nineteenth-Century America* (University of North Carolina Press, 1996), 14, 191–234.

2. Gary Gerstle, *Liberty and Coercion: The Paradox of American Government from the Founding to the Present* (Princeton University Press, 2015), 55–86; Jessica Wang, "Dogs and the Making of the American State: Voluntary Association, State Power, and the Politics of Animal Control in New York City, 1850–1920," *Journal of American His-*

tory 98, no. 4 (March 2012): 998–1024; Kate Masur, "State Sovereignty and Migration Before Reconstruction," *Journal of the Civil War Era* 9, no. 4 (December 2019): 588–611.

3. For more on the intersections between police power and public health, see Barbara Gutmann Rosenkrantz, *Public Health and the State: Changing Views in Massachusetts, 1842–1936* (Harvard University Press, 1972); Lawrence O. Gostin and Lindsay F. Wiley, *Public Health Law: Power, Duty, Restraint*, 3rd ed. (University of California Press, 2016); Novak, *The People's Welfare*, 191–234.

4. James Colgrove and Ronald Bayer, "Manifold Restraints: Liberty, Public Health, and the Legacy of *Jacobson v Massachusetts*," *American Journal of Public Health* 95, no. 4 (April 2005): 571–576. It is important to stress that *Jacobson* did recognize some limits to the states' public health authority. While offering a full defense of the police power, Justice Harlan argued that courts should intervene if it was used in a way that was "arbitrary and oppressive in particular cases." *Jacobson v. Massachusetts*, 197 U.S. 11, 19 (1905). On the Janus-faced nature of *Jacobson*, see John Fabian Witt, *American Contagions: Epidemics and the Law from Smallpox to COVID-19* (Yale University Press, 2020), 57–59.

5. Quoted in Gostin, *Public Health Law*, 121.

6. Wendy E. Parmet, "Rediscovering *Jacobson* in the Era of COVID-19," *Boston University Law Review Online*, no. 100 (2020): 118–133, here 118–119; Wendy E. Parmet, "The COVID Cases: A Preliminary Assessment of Judicial Review of Public Health Powers During a Partisan and Polarized Pandemic," *San Diego Law Review*, no. 57 (2020): 999–1048.

7. Gautham Rao, "The Early American State 'In Action': The Federal Marine Hospitals, 1789–1860," in *Boundaries of the State in U.S. History*, ed. James T. Sparrow, William J. Novak, and Stephen W. Sawyer (University of Chicago Press, 2015), 21–56.

8. Daniel Sledge, *Health Divided: Public Health and Individual Medicine in the Making of the Modern American State* (University of Kansas Press, 2017), 16.

9. Joseph Jones, *Medical and Surgical Memoirs: Containing Investigations on the Geographical Distribution, Causes, Nature, Relations and Treatment of Various Diseases 1855–1890* (New Orleans, 1890), 299.

10. Margaret Warner, "Local Control Versus National Interest: The Debate over Southern Public Health, 1878–1884," *Journal of Southern History* 50, no. 3 (August 1984): 407–428; Margaret Humphreys, *Yellow Fever and the South* (John Hopkins University Press, 1992), 60–76; Jerrold M. Michael, "The National Board of Health: 1879–1883," *Public Health Reports* 126, no. 1 (January-February 2011): 123–129.

11. Manfred Waserman, "The Quest for a National Health Department in the Progressive Era," *Bulletin of the History of Medicine* 49, no. 3 (Fall 1975): 353–380.

12. Sledge, *Health Divided*, 41.

13. Martin Halliwell, *American Health Crisis: One Hundred Years of Panic, Planning, and Politics* (University of California Press, 2021), 4.

14. Jeffery K. Taubenberger and David M. Morens, "1918 Influenza: The Mother of All Pandemics," *Emerging Infectious Diseases* 12, no. 1 (January 2006): 15–22.

15. On the role of globalization in shaping the 1918–1919 influenza pandemic, see Nancy Tomes, "'Destroyer and Teacher': Managing the Masses During the 1918–1919 Influenza Pandemic," supplement, *Public Health Reports* 125, no. 3 (April 2010), 48–62; Siddharth Chandra, Julia Christensen, and Shimon Likhtman, "Connectivity and Sea-

sonality: The 1918 Influenza and COVID-19 Pandemics in Global Perspective," *Journal of Global History* 15, no. 3 (November 2020): 408–420.

16. For example, see Nancy K. Bristow, "'You Can't Do Anything for Influenza': Doctors, Nurses and the Power of Gender during the Influenza Epidemic in the United States," in *The Spanish Influenza Pandemic of 1918–19: New Perspectives*, ed. Howard Phillips and David Killingray (Routledge, 2003), 58–70; Julia F. Irwin, "An Epidemic Without Enmity: Explaining the Missing Ethnic Tensions in New Haven's 1918 Influenza Epidemic," *Urban History Review* 36, no. 2 (Spring 2008): 5–17; and Christopher McKnight Nichols et al., "Reconsidering the 1918–19 Influenza Pandemic in the Age of COVID-19," *Journal of the Gilded Age and Progressive Era* 19, no. 4 (October 2020): 642–672.

17. Christopher Capozolla, *Uncle Sam Wants You: World War I and the Making of the Modern American Citizen* (Oxford University Press, 2010), 51–52; Ellis W. Hawley, *The Great War and the Search for a Modern Order: A History of the American People and Their Institutions, 1917–1933* (Waveland Press, 1979), 29.

18. Halliwell, *American Health Crisis*, 151.

19. United States Bureau of the Census, *Financial Statistics of Cities Having a Population of Over 30,000* (Government Printing Office, 1918), 187; "Brief Outline of Activities of the Public Health Service in Combating the Influenza Epidemic: 1918–1919," Records of the Public Health Service, RG 90, National Archives and Records Administration, College Park, Maryland (hereafter NARA), box 145, file 1622.

20. Rupert Blue, "Epidemic Influenza and the U.S. Public Health Service," *Modern Hospital* 11 (December 1918): 425–426.

21. On the failure of presidential leadership during the 1918 flu, see John M. Barry, *The Great Influenza: The Story of the Deadliest Plague in History* (Viking Press, 2005), 299–313.

22. Recent work in the field of historical epidemiology has found that quick implementation of social-distancing measures reduced transmission of influenza by up to 50 percent in the fall of 1918. See Howard Markel et al., "Nonpharmaceutical Interventions Implemented by US Cities During the 1918–1919 Influenza Pandemic," *Journal of the American Medical Association* 298, no. 6 (August 8, 2007): 644–654.

23. Francesco Aimone, "The 1918 Influenza Epidemic in New York City: A Review of the Public Health Response," supplement, *Public Health Reports* 125, no. 3 (April 2010): 71–79.

24. "State Closing Ban Lifted for Friday," *Detroit News*, November 7, 1918, 10.

25. James W. Inches, "Spanish Influenza," *Detroit Free Press*, October 10, 1918, 8.

26. Blue, "Epidemic Influenza and the U.S. Public Health Service," 425.

27. "Copeland Satisfied by Influenza Tour," *New York Times*, October 30, 1918, 10.

28. Alexandra Minna Stern et al., "'Better Off in School': School Medical Inspection as a Public Health Strategy During the 1918–1919 Influenza Pandemic in the United States," supplement, *Public Health Reports* 125, no. 3 (April 2010): 68.

29. Quoted in Bristow, *American Pandemic: The Lost Worlds of the 1918 Influenza Epidemic* (Oxford University Press, 2012), 105.

30. "'Ban Off,' Says Inches; 'No Sir,' Avers Sleeper," *Detroit Free Press*, November 5,

1918, 1, 3. For other examples of intergovernmental tension between state and city health officials, see Tomes, "Destroyer and Teacher," 53–54.

31. Paul A. C. Koistinen, *Planning War, Pursuing Peace: The Political Economy of American Warfare, 1920–1939* (University of Kansas Press, 1998); William H. Thomas Jr., *Unsafe for Democracy: World War I and the U.S. Justice Department's Covert Campaign to Suppress Dissent* (University of Wisconsin Press, 2008); Capozzola, *Uncle Sam Wants You*. See also Stephen R. Ortiz's reflections in Christopher Capozolla et al., "Interchange: World War I," *Journal of American History* 102, no. 2 (September 2015): 496–497.

32. *Economic Security Act: Hearings*, 74th Cong., 1st Sess., at 312 (1935). In 1921, Congress did pass the Sheppard-Towner Act, one of the national government's first sweeping public health laws, which provided states with grants to establish infant welfare and prenatal health programs. This legislation did provide a significant boon to non-national health institutions, but the federal government's authority in the sphere of public health remained feeble and disjointed. In a 1926 report, the National Health Council, a consortium of voluntary medical organizations established in 1920, found that over forty federal agencies and five thousand civil servants had some responsibility for public health, with no clear oversight from the PHS. James A. Tobey, *The National Government and Public Health* (John Hopkins University Press, 1926), 380–386. For background on the political and legislative history of the Sheppard-Towner Act, see Molly Ladd-Taylor, "Federal Help for Mothers: The Rise and Fall of the Sheppard-Towner Act in the 1920s," in *Gendered Domains: Rethinking Public and Private in Women's History: Essays from the Seventh Berkshire Conference on the History of Women*, ed. Dorothy O. Helly and Susan Reverby (Cornell University Press, 1992), 217–227.

33. The one health history detail political historians do take note of is President Truman's failure to implement a universal health insurance program. For points of entry into this vast literature, see Colin Gordon, "Why No National Health Insurance in the U.S.? The Limits of Social Provision in War and Peace, 1941–1948," *Journal of Policy History* 9, no. 3 (July 1997): 277–310; Monte M. Poen, *Harry S. Truman Versus the Medical Lobby: The Genesis of Medicare* (University of Missouri Press, 1979).

34. On the support of Southern Democrats for increased federal involvement in public health, see Daniel Sledge, "War, Tropical Disease, and the Emergence of National Public Health Capacity in the United States," *Studies in American Political Development* 26, no. 2 (October 2012): 125–162.

35. Felix J. Underwood, "New Trends in Public Health," *Mississippi Doctor* 15, no. 4 (September 1937), 37.

36. Sledge, *Health Divided*, 96–123; Alan Derickson, *Health Security for All: Dreams of Universal Health Care in America* (John Hopkins University Press, 2005), 65–78.

37. Writing in the 1960s, Edwin Witte—one of the chief architects of the Social Security Act—recalled that Title VI was "throughout the congressional consideration of this measure a source of strength for the bill. . . . [State health officials] gave very strong testimony regarding the need for additional public health work." Edwin E. Witte, *The Development of the Social Security Act: A Memorandum on the History of the Committee on Economic Security and Drafting and Legislative History of the Social Security Act* (University of Wisconsin Press, 1962), 171, 173.

38. *Economic Security Act*, 185.

39. Quoted in *Economic Security Act*, 185–186.

40. On New Dealers' approach to intergovernmental partnerships between local, state, and federal officials, see Karen M. Tani, *States of Dependency: Welfare, Rights, and American Governance, 1935–1972* (Cambridge University Press, 2016); Brent Cebul and Mason B. Williams, "'Really and Truly a Partnership': The New Deal's Associational State and the Making of Postwar American Politics," in *Shaped by the State: Toward a New Political History of the Twentieth Century*, ed. Brent Cebul, Lily Geismer, and Mason B. Williams (University of Chicago Press, 2019), 96–122; and Mason B. Williams, *City of Ambition: FDR, La Guardia, and the Making of Modern New York* (W. W. Norton, 2013).

41. Public Health Service, *Ten Years of Federal Grants-in-Aid for Public Health, 1936–1946* (Superintendent of Documents, 1948), 7; Harriet S. Pfister, *Kansas State Board of Health* (Governmental Research Center, University of Kansas, 1955), 65.

42. Valerie A. Earle, "Post-1935 Developments in Southern State Public Health Programs," *American Journal of Public Health* 41, no. 11 (November 1951): 1404.

43. C. E. Waller, "Progress Under the Operation of Title VI of the Social Security Act," *American Journal of Public Health* 28, no. 11 (November 1938): 1299–1301.

44. Myrtle Greenfield, *A History of Public Health in New Mexico* (University of New Mexico Press, 1962), 33–34.

45. United States Bureau of the Census, *Vital Statistics Rates in the United States, 1900–1940* (Government Printing Office, 1943), 402–432.

46. Public Health Service, *Ten Years of Federal Grants-in-Aid for Public Health*, 7.

47. A full account of the Social Security's impact on state public health departments has yet to be written, but a few state-level histories analyze the topic briefly. See Pfister, *Kansas State Board of Health*, 65–75; Thomas Franklin Abercrombie, *A History of Public Health in Georgia, 1733–1950* (N.p., 1950), 137; and John Duffy, *The Sanitarians: A History of American Public Health* (University of Illinois Press, 1992), 259–260.

48. David Kennedy's *Freedom from Fear* devotes two sentences to Title VI; Ira Katznelson's *Fear Itself* does not refer to public health; and Colin Gordon's *Dead on Arrival* mentions Title VI only once. David M. Kennedy, *Freedom from Fear: The American People in Depression and War, 1929–1945* (Oxford University Press, 1999), 263–264; Ira Katznelson, *Fear Itself: The New Deal and the Origins of Our Time* (W. W. Norton, 2013); Colin Gordon, *Dead on Arrival: The Politics of Health Care in Twentieth-Century America* (Princeton University Press, 2013), 17.

49. On the Hill-Burton Act, see Beatrix Hoffman, *Health Care for Some: Rights and Rationing in the United States Since 1930* (University of Chicago Press, 2012), 63–89. On the La Follette–Bulwinkle Act, see Allan M. Brandt, *No Magic Bullet: A Social History of Venereal Disease in the United States Since 1880* (Oxford University Press, 1985), 122–160. Surprisingly few works have analyzed the history of the 1944 Public Health Services Act, but for a brief overview, see Lynne Page Snyder, "Passage and Significance of the 1944 Public Health Service Act," *Public Health Reports* 109, no. 6 (November-December 1994): 721–724.

50. *The Budget of the United States Government for the Fiscal Year Ending June 30, 1935* (US Government Printing Office, 1934), A61; *The Budget of the United States Gov-*

ernment for the Fiscal Year Ending June 30, 1951 (US Government Printing Office, 1950), A47.

51. Elizabeth W. Etheridge, *Sentinel for Health: A History of the Centers for Disease Control* (University of California Press, 1992), 1–48.

52. Dale Van Atta, *With Honor: Melvin Laird in War, Peace, and Politics* (University of Wisconsin Press, 2008), 90.

53. S. B. Thacker and D. J. Sencer, "Centers for Disease Control," in *International Encyclopedia of Public Health*, ed. Kristian Heggenhougen (Academic Press, 2008), 550.

54. *The Budget of the United States Government for the Fiscal Year Ending June 30, 1961* (Government Printing Office, 1960), 586.

55. Wendy E. Parmet, "AIDS and Quarantine: The Revival of an Archaic Doctrine," *Hofstra Law Review* 14, no. 1 (Fall 1985): 53–90.

56. This figure includes forty-eight state health departments and 1,577 municipal public health institutions. E. R. Coffey, "Public Health Expands Its Facilities Under Title VI—Federal Social Security Act," *American Journal of Public Health and the Nation's Health* 31, no. 4 (April 1941): 302.

57. D. A. Henderson et al., "Public Health and Medical Responses to the 1957–58 Influenza Pandemic," *Biosecurity and Bioterrorism: Biodefense Strategy, Practice, and Science* 7, no. 3 (September 2009): 266–267.

58. "Special Staff Note," October 3, 1957, Toner Notes October, DDE Diary Series, Dwight D. Eisenhower Papers as President, box 27, Dwight D. Eisenhower Presidential Library, Abilene, Kansas (hereafter DEPL).

59. J. Donald Millar and June Osborne, "Precursors of the Scientific Decision-Making Process Leading to the 1976 National Immunization Campaign," in *History, Science, and Politics: Influenza in America, 1918–1976*, ed. June Osborne (Prodist, 1977), 22–23.

60. There is now a rich literature on the cultural and social aspects of polio in the postwar years. For points of entry, see David M. Oshinsky, *Polio: An American Story* (Oxford University Press, 2005); and Heather Green Wooten, *The Polio Years in Texas: Battling a Terrifying Unknown* (Texas A&M University Press, 2009).

61. On the development of the Salk vaccine, see Jane Smith, *Patenting the Sun: Polio and the Salk Vaccine* (William Morrow, 1991).

62. On the legislative wrangling over the Poliomyelitis Vaccination Assistance Act of 1955, see Elena Conis, *Vaccine Nation: America's Changing Relationship with Immunization* (University of Chicago Press, 2015), 21–23.

63. *Poliomyelitis Vaccine: Hearings*, 84th Cong., 1st Sess., at 46 (1955).

64. Patrick M. Vivier, "National Policies for Childhood Immunization in the United States: An Historical Perspective' (PhD diss., Johns Hopkins University, 1996), 40.

65. John F. Kennedy, "Special Message to the Congress on National Health Needs, February 27, 1962," in *Public Papers of the Presidents of the United States: John F. Kennedy* (Office of the Federal Register, 1963), 168.

66. On the political impetus behind the Vaccination Assistance Act, see Conis, *Vaccine Nation*, 19–38.

67. *Intensive Immunization Programs: Hearings*, 87th Cong., 2nd Sess., at 1 (1962).

68. James Colgrove, *State of Immunity: The Politics of Vaccination in Twentieth-Century*

America (University of California Press, 2006), 144–147; Vivier, "National Policies for Childhood Immunization in the United States," 66–105.

69. Vivier, 95.

70. F. Robert Freckleton, "Progress and Horizons in Immunization," in *Proceedings from the Fifth Annual Immunization Conference*, San Diego, California, March 12–14, 1968, 2–6. Both presidents Jimmy Carter and Bill Clinton built on Kennedy's vaccine law by strengthening federal involvement in the area of mass immunization. The Clinton administration's vaccination initiative, enacted in 1993, was especially capacious, transforming vaccines into a government entitlement for certain groups of children. Elena Conis, "Measles and the Modern History of Vaccination," *Public Health Reports* 134, no. 2 (March/April 2019): 118–125.

71. Gerstle, *Liberty and Coercion*, 275–310.

72. James Colgrove, *Epidemic City: The Politics of Public Health in New York* (Russell Sage Foundation, 2011), 19.

73. On the philosophical and professional boundaries between physicians and public health practitioners, see James Colgrove, "Reform and Its Discontents: Public Health in New York City During the Great Society," *Journal of Policy History* 19, no. 1 (January 2007): 3–28; Paul Starr, *The Social Transformation of American Medicine* (Basic Books, 1982), 180–197; Daniel M. Fox, "The Politics of Public Health in New York City: Contrasting Styles Since 1920," in *Hives of Sickness: Public Health and Epidemics in New York City*, ed. David Rosner (Rutgers University Press, 1995).

74. Paul Starr, "The Health Care Legacy of the Great Society," in *LBJ's Neglected Legacy: How Lyndon B. Johnson Reshaped Domestic Policy and Government*, ed. Robert H. Wilson, Norman J. Glickman, and Laurence E. Lynn (University of Texas Press, 2015), 235–258.

75. Gerstle, "The Resilient Power of the States across the Long Nineteenth Century."

76. Ronald Bayer and Laurence Dupuis, "Tuberculosis, Public Health, and Civil Liberties," *Annual Review of Public Health* 16 (1995): 307–326; Trevor Hoppe, *Punishing Disease: HIV and the Criminalization of Sickness* (University of California Press, 2018), 27; Ronald Bayer, "Ethics and Infectious Disease Control: STDs, HIV, TB," in *Ethics and Public Health: Model Curriculum*, ed. Bruce Jennings, Jeffery Kahn, Anna Mastroianni, and Lisa S. Parker (Health Resources and Services Administration, 2003), 133–146.

77. Colgrove, *Epidemic City*, 207.

78. Witt, *American Contagions*, 80.

79. Gerstle, *Liberty and Coercion*, 318–319.

80. On the growth of the national security state during the Reagan years, see Julian E. Zelizer, *The Politics of National Security—From World War II to the War on Terrorism* (Basic Books, 2009), 300–332.

81. On the ideology of New Federalism, see Timothy Conlan, *From New Federalism to Devolution: Twenty-Five Years of Intergovernmental Reform* (Brookings Institution Press, 1998).

82. John F. Cogan, *The High Cost of Good Intentions: A History of U.S. Federal Entitlement Programs* (Stanford University Press, 2017), 295–305.

83. William Shonick, *Government and Health Services: Government's Role in the Development of U.S. Health Services, 1930–1980* (Oxford University Press, 1995), 110–111.

84. Statistic derived from National Health Expenditure Data, Centers for Medi-

care and Medicaid Services (CMS), accessed October 12, 2021, www.cms.hhs.gov/NationalHealthExpendData.

Chapter 2: Clandestine Networks and Closeted Bureaucrats

1. For media portrayals of the AIDS epidemic, see Paula A. Treichler, *How to Have Theory in an Epidemic: Cultural Chronicles of AIDS* (Duke University Press, 1999), especially chapter 2.

2. The details of this story were outlined to me in oral interviews with David Roberti and Kenneth Topper—Stan Hadden's partner and office assistant in the 1980s. Before moving to Sacramento, Hadden worked as a pilot in the US Air Force and as an associate editor for the gay newspaper *Mom Guess What*. Kenneth Topper, phone interview with the author, November 12, 2018; David Roberti, interview with the author, Los Angeles, December 12, 2018.

3. Dell Richards, "Living and Working Together," *Mom Guess What*, October 1988, 9.

4. With a few notable exceptions, historians have overlooked the statewide response to AIDS in California, focusing instead on activist efforts in San Francisco and Los Angeles. To date, narratives of California's early response to the epidemic have invariably spotlighted how San Francisco adopted one of the most extensive AIDS programs in the country, outspending other hard-hit cities like New York. For more on the San Francisco "model of care," see Brier, *Infectious Ideas: U.S. Political Responses to the AIDS Crisis* (University of North Carolina Press, 2009), chapter 2; Andrea Milne, "'A Caring Disease': Nursing and Patient Advocacy on the United States' First AIDS Ward, 1983–1995" (PhD diss., University of California, Irvine, 2017). For the response of Los Angeles to AIDS, see Lilian Faderman and Stuart Timmons, *Gay L.A. A History of Sexual Outlaws, Power Politics, and Lipstick Lesbians* (University of California Press, 2009), 301–322; Nic John Ramos, "Poor Influences and Criminal Locations: Los Angeles's Skid Row, Multicultural Identities, and Normal Homosexuality," *American Quarterly* 71, no. 2 (June 2019): 541–567. For a rare discussion of the California legislature's approach to AIDS, see Ronald Bayer, *Private Acts, Social Consequences: AIDS and the Politics of Public Health* (Free Press, 1988), chapters 4–7.

5. Intergovernmental Health Policy Project, "Comparative Review of State-Only Expenditures for AIDS–Major Trends, Fiscal Years 1983–1988" (George Washington University, 1987), National Gay and Lesbian Taskforce Records, Division of Rare and Manuscript Collections, Cornell University Library, Ithaca, New York (hereafter NGLTF), box 190, folder 10.

6. Early in the epidemic, the state of Massachusetts focused most of its energies on biomedical research and protecting the blood supply, allocating, unlike California, only minimal funding for patient care and prevention education. See Nancy Weiland Carpenter, "AIDS Initiatives in Massachusetts: Building a Continuum of Care," *New England Journal of Public Policy* 1 (1988): 429–439.

7. For example, in 1986, the California legislature enacted Assembly Bill 2404 (AB 2404), which appropriated $4 million for research into a HIV/AIDS vaccine. The passage of AB 2404 made California the first state to allocate funds for the development of a vaccine. "'Duke' Vetos, Signs Some Bills," *Update*, October 8, 1986, A8.

8. Jonathan Bell, *California Crucible: The Forging of Modern American Liberalism* (University of Pennsylvania Press, 2012), 262.

9. For more on the history of Proposition 6, see Clayton Howard, *The Closet and the Cul-De-Sac: The Politics of Sexual Privacy in Northern California* (University of Pennsylvania Press, 2019), 285–289; Sara Smith-Silverman, "'Gay Teachers Fight Back!': Rank-and-File Gay and Lesbian Teachers' Activism against the Briggs Initiative, 1977–1978," *Journal of the History of Sexuality* 29, no. 1 (January 2020): 107–129.

10. Gay men and lesbians only received legal protection from employment discrimination in 1992. For more on the history of gay employment rights activism, see Katherine Turk, "'Our Militancy Is in Our Openness': Gay Employment Rights Activism in California and the Question of Sexual Orientation in Sex Equality Law," *Law and History Review* 31, no. 2 (May 2013): 423–469.

11. Stephen Morin, "AIDS: Public Policy and Mental Health Issues," in *What To Do About AIDS: Physicians and Mental Health Professionals Discuss the Issues*, ed. Leon McKusick (University of California Press, 1986), 192.

12. Morin, "AIDS: Public Policy and Mental Health Issues."

13. David Roberti, interview with the author, Los Angeles, December 12, 2018.

14. Dell Richards, "Living and Working Together," *Mom Guess What*, October 1988, 9; Michael Bosia, phone interview with the author, December 22, 2018.

15. Stan Hadden to David Wilson, July 1, 1987, Stanley Hadden Papers, 1997–33, the Gay, Lesbian, Bisexual, Transgender Historical Society (hereafter SHP), box 2, folder 1.

16. "Senate Bill No. 1251 Background," n.d., Art Agnos Papers, San Francisco History Center, San Francisco Public Library (hereafter AAP), box 13, folder 20.

17. M. J. Rowe and C. C. Ryan, "Comparing State-Only Expenditures for AIDS," *American Journal of Public Health* 78, no. 4 (April 1988): 424–429; Amy Bayer, "California Leads in Allocating State Funds for AIDS Programs," *San Francisco Chronicle*, August 31, 1989, 8.

18. Larry Bush, interview with the author, San Francisco, December 17, 2018.

19. Art Agnos to Arlo Smith, June 14, 1985, AAP, box 13, folder 15.

20. Richard Zeiger, "Duke's Landslide," *California Journal*, December 1986, 579–581; Dan Walters, "Unspectacular Governance," *Sacramento Bee*, February 19, 1986, 16; William Endicott, "Deukmejian's Legislative Style Viewed as 'Stubborn,'" *Los Angeles Times*, August 18, 1983, 46.

21. For the broad changes to California's political economy in this period, including the unprecedented expansion of the state's penal system, see Ruth Wilson Gilmore, *Golden Gulag: Prisons, Surplus, Crisis, and Opposition in Globalizing California* (University of California Press, 2007).

22. Daniel J. B. Mitchell, "From Jerry-Rigged to Petered Out: Lessons from the Deukmejian Era for Contemporary California State Budgeting," in *California Policy Options 2008*, ed. Daniel J. B. Mitchell (UCLA School of Public Affairs, 2008), 39–76.

23. Mitchell, "From Jerry-Rigged to Petered Out."

24. William Endicott, "Deukmejian's Big Advantage Was Surprise," *Los Angeles Times*, August 7, 1983, 22.

25. Kenneth Topper, phone interview with the author, November 12, 2018.

26. Concerned American for Individual Rights, "1984 Year End Report," December

15, 1984, Concerned Americans for Individual Rights records, ONE National Gay and Lesbian Archives, Los Angeles (hereafter CAIR), box 1, folder 1.

27. Bruce Decker, "Why Gays and Lesbians Should Re-Elect Ronald Reagan," n.d., CAIR, box 1, folder 1.

28. Decker proved willing to work with members of the fringe right while lobbying for research tax credits. In 1990, for example, he solicited the support of Representative William Dannemeyer, a virulently homophobic conservative from Orange County. Letter, Bruce Decker to William Dannemeyer, May 30, 1989, Newton R. Russell Papers, LP457:780, California State Archives, Office of the Secretary of State, Sacramento, California.

29. "Critics Rebut Decker's Defense," *San Diego Gayzette*, August 22, 1985, 1. For more on the political organizing of gay Republicans in the late twentieth century, see Clayton Howard, "Gay and Conservative: An Early History of the Log Cabin Republicans," In *Beyond the Politics of the Closet: Gay Rights and the American State Since the 1970s*, ed. Jonathan Bell (University of Pennsylvania Press, 2020).

30. "Critics Rebut Decker's Defense," *San Diego Gayzette*, August 22, 1985, 1.

31. "Critics Rebut Decker's Defense."

32. Kenneth Topper, phone interview with the author, November 12, 2018.

33. Memorandum from Bruce Decker to Stan Hadden, September 27, 1985, SHP, box 2, folder 12; Memorandum by Stan Hadden to Bruce Decker, December 19, 1986, SHP, box 2, folder 6.

34. Although this chapter concentrates on the careers of Bush, Decker, and Hadden, other LGBT people transitioned into policymaking roles during the 1980s. In 1986, State Representative Willie Brown hired Brandy Moore, a veteran gay rights activist, to serve as a community liaison with the gay movement. Moore would later become the only person of color appointed to the California AIDS Advisory Council. Two Republican state lawmakers—Bill Filante and Milton Marks—both employed gay legislative assistants in the mid-1980s. I focus on Bush, Decker, and Hadden because their work focused exclusively on AIDS and they left substantial archival traces. Brandy Moore, "Curriculum Vitae," National Task Force on AIDS Prevention, MSS 94-59, UCSF Library and Center for Knowledge Management, Archives and Special Collections, University of California, San Francisco, box 4, folder 14; Michael Bosia, phone interview with the author, December 22, 2018. Unfortunately, few archival sources make reference to Moore, who tragically succumbed to AIDS-related disease in the early 1990s. Even Willie Brown's papers, held at San Francisco State University, gloss over Moore's contributions. Willie L. Brown Jr. Papers, San Francisco State University, J. Paul Leonard Library, Special Collections and Archives.

35. "AIDS Office under Fire for Funding Delays," in unknown newspaper, undated clipping, SHP, box 5, folder 55.

36. Executive Order B-54-79, SHP, box 5, folder 17.

37. "Gov. Brown's Executive Order Put into Action," *Bay Area Reporter*, August 28, 1980, 10.

38. Kenneth Topper, phone interview with the author, November 12, 2018.

39. Pat Burke, "Ellis, Campbell Kill Funds to Enforce Gay Civil Rights," *Update*, June 12, 1981, 1.

40. Memorandum by California State Personnel Board to All State Agencies, April 30, 1980, Phyllis Lyon and Del Martin papers, GLBT Historical Society, San Francisco (hereafter PLDM), box 75, folder 19.

41. Boyce Hinman to Alice A. Lytle, April 12, 1982, PLDM, box 75, folder 19. As late as 1984, AGLSE raised concerns that the Department of Corrections had no written policy related to gay and lesbian employees. Letter, Daniel J. McCarthy to Boyce R. Hinman, August 17, 1984, SHP, box 5, folder 16. For an example of a legal case concerning the bureaucracy's homophobia, see *Hinman v. Department of Personnel Admin*, Civ. No. 23749 (C.A. Calif 1985).

42. Phyllis Lyon to Alice A. Lytle, June 3, 1982, PLDM, box 75, folder 19.

43. George Deukmejian, untitled press release, March 13, 1984, AAP, box 13, folder 10. The reluctance of state bureaucrats to collaborate with gay activists was just one example of broader patterns of employment discrimination during the 1980s. With the emergence of AIDS, gay men in a range of professions lost their jobs because of the misplaced fear that the disease could be transmitted through casual contact. On AIDS-related employment discrimination, see Margot Canaday, *Queer Career: Sexuality and Work in Modern America* (Princeton University Press, 2023), 187–226.

44. Stan Hadden to David Roberti, February 11, 1987, SHP, box 2, folder 1.

45. Kenneth Topper, phone interview with the author, November 12, 2018.

46. Letter, Stan Hadden to Dr. O'Connor, April 29, 1986, SHP, box 2, folder 6.

47. Kenneth Topper, phone interview with the author, November 12, 2018.

48. Steve Morin, phone interview with the author, October 19, 2018.

49. Stan Hadden to David Roberti, February 5, 1986, SHP, box 2, folder 6.

50. Memorandum from Stan Hadden to David Roberti, May 8, 1985, SHP, box 3, folder 22; Kenneth Topper, phone interview with author, December 18, 2018. For more on the Health Department's obstructionist stance on the state AIDS budget, see Memorandum by Stan Hadden to David Roberti, May 13, 1985, SHP, box 5, folder 47.

51. Morin, "AIDS: Public Policy and Mental Health Issues," 193.

52. Excavating the careers of these closeted bureaucrats proved difficult. They left few archival records, engaged in illicit and illegal activity, and did not agree to conduct oral interviews. For much of this chapter, I rely on the oral testimony of their "out" colleagues, an approach that risks filtering their experiences through the assumptions of the gay rights movement. However, the essential fact—the existence of a clandestine network of gay policymakers—was corroborated by several interviewees and the contents of Hadden's correspondence. For a newspaper report of this clandestine network, see "Fighting for LIFE," *Advocate*, March 15, 1988, 12–13.

53. Kenneth Topper, phone interview with author, December 18, 2018.

54. Topper, phone interview with author.

55. Topper, phone interview with author.

56. For an example, see Stan Hadden to David Roberti, February 5, 1986, SHP, box 2, folder 6.

57. Topper, phone interview with author.

58. Topper, phone interview with author.

59. Topper, phone interview with author. Unfortunately, the personnel files within

the Stan Hadden papers are restricted, so I have relied on oral testimony to recover the details of this hearing.

60. Topper, phone interview with author.

61. Material Review Committee to AIDS Community Education Contractors, December 18, 1985, SHP, box 11, folder 33. The Health Department also collaborated with Hadden over California's application for a Home and Community-Based Waiver for Medicaid eligible PWAs. Department of Health to Stan Hadden, September 11, 1987, SHP, box 11, folder 40.

62. Jean Merle, "Grant Process for AIDS Hurting Agencies," *Los Angeles Times*, April 18, 1988, A8.

63. Karen Ocamb, "Coming Out Holds Hollywood's Future," *Update*, June 19, 1991, A15.

64. George Chauncey, *Why Marriage? The History Shaping Today's Debate over Gay Equality* (Basic Books, 2004), 23–31.

65. Stephen Vider, "'The Ultimate Extension of Gay Community': Communal Living and Gay Liberation in the 1970s," *Gender & History* 27, no. 3 (November 2015): 867.

66. Stan Hadden to Tim Grieve, June 29, 1990, SHP, box 1, folder 3.

67. Timothy Drake, phone interview with the author, August 25, 2019.

68. From the late 1980s, gay policymakers in California no longer relied on either clandestine tactics or closeted bureaucrats. Rather, Hadden, and Decker formed a constructive relationship with the Health Department, one that involved open cooperation on the issues of AIDS testing and HIV discrimination. In the 1990s, an unprecedented number of openly gay men and lesbians entered state employment, partly because Pete Wilson, who succeeded Deukmejian as governor in 1990, established close ties with gay Republican groups. As a candidate, Wilson openly courted the endorsement of the Log Cabin Republicans and proceeded to appoint several of its members to positions within the state bureaucracy. Keith Clark, "Wilson Appoints Log Cabin Member to DMV Post," *Bravo! Newsmagazine*, February 20, 1992, 8.

69. "LIFE Fact Sheet for SB 2788," n.d., Bill Wuzzy Spaulding Papers, ONE National Gay and Lesbian Archives, University of South California Libraries, Los Angeles (hereafter BWSP), box 2, folder 31.

70. From the late nineteenth century, doctors had pathologized homosexuality, equating it with "sickness," "psychopathy," and "deviancy." See Katie Batza, "Sickness and Wellness," in *Routledge History of Queer America*, ed. Don Romesberg (Routledge, 2018), 287–299.

71. Rand Martin, "Bill to Drive Disease Underground Gains," May 16, 1988, BSWP, box 2, folder 29.

72. For more on the historical analogies between AIDS and other infectious diseases, see Peter Baldwin, *Disease and Democracy: The Industrialized World Faces AIDS* (University of California Press, 2007), 125–128.

73. William E. Danneyemer, untitled press release, July 23, 1988, SHP, box 6, folder 29.

74. Scott Reeves, "AIDS Bills Focusing on Testing," *Arizona Republic*, August 30, 1987, 97.

75. San Francisco Human Rights Commission, "AIDS Discrimination Reporting Project," 1985, PLDM, box 74, folder 5.

76. National Gay Task Force and Lambda Legal Defense and Education Fund, "Statement on AIDS Confidentiality," background paper, July 26, 1985 AAP, box 11, folder 15.

77. California Community Care Facilities Act, Calif. A.B. 403, Reg. Sess. (1985); Larry Bush, oral interview with the author, San Francisco, December 17, 2018.

78. Quoted in Brian Jones, "AIDS Test May Imperil Blood," *Bay Area Reporter*, February 7, 1985, 4.

79. Jones, "AIDS Test May Imperil Blood."

80. Lauren B. Leveton et al., *HIV and the Blood Supply: An Analysis of Crisis Decisionmaking* (National Academies Press, 1995), 78.

81. Jones, "AIDS Test May Imperil Blood."

82. Art Agnos, "Agnos Introduces Blood Safety Bill," press release, January 25, 1985, AAP, box 11, folder 15.

83. When the FDA licensed ELISA in early 1985, state governments clustered around two distinct policy approaches. One group of states responded by applying traditional public health techniques to individuals who tested positive despite the vocal opposition of gay activists, liberal lawmakers, and public health officials. Another handful of states enacted laws that guaranteed anonymous, patient-initiated testing. "The AIDS Viral Antibody Test," *AIDS Policy and Law*, February 1987, 28–29.

84. Larry Bush, oral interview with the author, San Francisco, December 17, 2018.

85. Bush, oral interview with the author.

86. Art Agnos to Margaret M. Heckler, March 28, 1985, AAP, box 13, folder 15.

87. After the passage of AB 403, Agnos even received a letter of congratulations from Orrin Hatch, the Republican senator from Utah. Letter, Orrin Hatch to Art Agnos, April 19, 1985, AAP, box 13, folder 15.

88. Bush, oral interview with the author.

89. Jerry Gillam, "Assembly Floor Action," *Los Angeles Times*, March 29, 1985, 51; "Assembly Tries Calming Blood Donors, Users," *San Francisco Examiner*, February 15, 1985, 25.

90. Bell, *California Crucible*, 269–280.

91. Zeiger, "Duke's Landslide."

92. Bush, oral interview with the author.

93. Memorandum from Larry Bush to Art Agnos, "AIDS Discrimination Issues," n.d., AAP, box 13, folder 24.

94. "Activists Clash on the Antibody Test," *San Diego Gayzette*, May 17, 1985, 1.

95. "Milton Marks Keynote Speech on AIDS," November 9, 1985, Milton Marks AIDS Files, San Francisco History Center, San Francisco Public Library (hereafter MMAF), box 1, folder 2.

96. A detailed analysis of the campaign against Proposition 64 is beyond the scope of this chapter, which focuses more on the politics of antibody testing in the state legislature. The initiative has also received extensive attention from scholars of the AIDS crisis. See Emily Hobson, *Lavender and Red: Liberation and Solidarity in the Gay and Lesbian Left* (University of California Press, 2016), 163–165; Faderman and Timmons, *Gay L.A.*, 308–309.

97. "No on 64 Campaign Report," November 30, 1986, AAP, box 13, folder 29; No on 64, "Major Themes for Campaign Speakers," n.d., AAP, box 13, folder 29.

98. Stephen E. Wright, "AIDS Groups Lose Cash to No on 64," *San Jose Mercury News*, September 13, 1986, A1.

99. Wright, "AIDS Groups Lose Cash to No on 64."

100. "Vote No on Prop 64," *Hastings Law News*, October 14, 1986, 11.

101. Quoted in Amy Wright, *Gay Rights at the Ballot Box* (University of Minnesota Press, 2012), 43.

102. "No on 64 Campaign Report."

103. "Senate Bill 1000 Report (1986–1987)," John Doolittle Papers, LP401:86, California State Archives, Office of the Secretary of State, Sacramento, California (hereafter JDP).

104. Rand Martin, "Grappling with AIDS Policy: A 1987 Debriefing," n.d., SHP, box 7, folder 30.

105. Martin, "Grappling with AIDS Policy."

106. John Doolittle, "An Open Letter from Senator John Doolittle to California's Gay Community," May 4, 1987, BSWP, box 2, folder 34.

107. Jeff Raimndo, "Doolittle: Gay Lobby at Work," *Sacramento Bee*, March 11, 1987, 8.

108. Quoted in Paula A. Treichler, *How to Have Theory in an Epidemic: Cultural Chronicles of AIDS* (Duke University Press, 1999), 56.

109. Eleanor Singer et al., "The Polls—A Report: AIDS," *Public Opinion Quarterly* 51, no. 4 (Winter 1987): 587.

110. Treichler, *How to Have Theory in an Epidemic*, 55.

111. Doolittle, "Senate Bill 1001 Senate Floor Statement," JDP, LP401:87.

112. Doolittle, LP401:85.

113. For more on how the rhetoric of child protection mobilized the Religious Right, see Gillian Frank, "'The Civil Rights of Parents': Race and Conservative Politics in Anita Bryant's Campaign Against Gay Rights in 1970s Florida," *Journal of the History of Sexuality* 22, no. 1 (January 2013): 126–160.

114. The League for Individual Freedom and Equality, "Preliminary Development Plan," January 21, 1992, BSWP, box 3, folder 16.

115. LIFE Executive Meeting minutes, December 1991, BSWP, box 4, folder 9.

116. Rand Martin, "LIFE 1987 Year End Report," n.d., BSWP, box 2, folder 34.

117. John D'Emilio, "The State of Statewide Organizing: A Partial and Preliminary Analysis," November 1996, NGLTF, box 135, folder 8.

118. In 1996, LIFE had the second-largest paid staff of any state LGBTQ lobbying organization in the country (behind only the Empire State Pride Agenda). According to one survey, most state AIDS lobbying groups either had one paid staff member or relied entirely on volunteers. In contrast, LIFE had eight members of staff, and the Empire State Pride Agenda had thirteen. Federation of Statewide Political LGBT Organizations "Creating Change, San Diego," conference program, November 15–16, 1997, NGLTF, box 135, folder 2. A 1996 report commissioned by the National Gay and Lesbian Task Force and written by historian John D'Emilio concluded that "while some statewide organizations seem solidly and permanently established, many more seem to have a pre-

carious, fragile existence. . . . The many state organizations with only volunteers or with only one wildly overworked staff member and budgets below $50,000 per year face the risk of burnout, collapse, or the ebb and flow of volunteer energy." Additionally, Emilio reported that only LIFE and the Empire State Pride Agenda had budgets in excess of $500,000. Emilio, "The State of Statewide Organizing."

119. Thom Cardwell, "Gay Activist John Duran Speaks Out for AB 101," *Bravo! Newsmagazine*, June 20, 1991, 13.

120. Martin, "LIFE 1987 Year End Report."

121. Martin, "LIFE 1987 Year End Report."

122. LIFE Delegate Meeting minutes, October 11, 1990, Dennis Cabaret Papers, ONE National Gay and Lesbian Archives, Los Angeles (hereafter DCP), box 1, folder 15.

123. Deborah Stone, "AIDS and the Moral Economy of Insurance," *American Prospect*, December 5, 2000. Several states, including Colorado, Washington, and Illinois, also instituted some form of mandatory testing. Art Agnos to Arlo Smith, June 14, 1985, AAP, box 13, folder 15.

124. Stone, "AIDS and the Moral Economy of Insurance."

125. Mike Lawrence, "Insurers Get AIDS Bill Break," *Chicago Sun-Times*, June 25, 1987, 7.

126. Lawrence, "Insurers Get AIDS Bill Break."

127. ILGTF, "Report of 1987 ILGTF State Bills Project," n.d., Illinois Gay and Lesbian Task Force records, Gerber/Hart Library and Archives, Chicago (hereafter ILGTF), box 1, folder: 1987 State Legislation Project.

128. Intergovernmental Health Policy Project, "Crimes and Punishments: State Criminal Laws for Individuals with HIV/AIDS who Knowingly Expose or Transmit HIV," December 1991, Henry A. Waxman Papers, UCLA Library Special Collections, Charles E. Young Research Library, University of California, Los Angeles (hereafter HWP), box 248, folder: "1996 Ryan White CARE Act."

129. For an overview of the "victims" rights' movement, see Paul M. Renfro, *Stranger Danger: The Politics of Child Protection from Etan Patz to AMBER Alert* (Oxford University Press, 2020).

130. Hoppe, *Punishing Disease*; René Esparza, "Black Bodies on Lockdown: AIDS Moral Panic and the Criminalization of HIV in Times of White Injury," *Journal of African American History* 104, no. 2 (2019): 250–280.

131. Quoted in Hoppe, *Punishing Disease*, 108.

132. Quoted in Hoppe, 108.

133. "There Ought to Be a Law," *Daily News of Los Angeles*, December 4, 1987, N24.

134. Singer et al., "The Polls—a Report: AIDS," 592.

135. "The Times Poll: 42% Would Limit Civil Rights in AIDS Battle," *Los Angeles Times*, July 31, 1987, 1.

136. General Social Survey, "Require AIDS Victim Wear ID Tags," GSS Data Explorer, accessed September 14, 2021, https://gssdataexplorer.norc.org/variables/5047/vshow.

137. Rand Martin, "LIFE 1988 Year End Report," n.d., BSWP, box 2, folder 34.

138. Richard Paddock, "Legislature Faces Record 105 Bills to Combat AIDS," *Los Angeles Times*, March 13, 1988, 3.

139. Martin, "LIFE 1988 Year End Report."

140. Martin.

141. Scot De Orio, "Punishing Queer Sexuality in the Age of LGBT Rights" (PhD diss., University of Michigan, 2017), 295.

142. Martin, "LIFE 1988 Year End Report."

143. Hoppe, *Punishing Disease*, 112–113.

144. Rand Martin, oral interview with author, Sacramento, December 18, 2018.

145. "Proposition 96 and Related Legislation," n.d., SHP, box 8, folder 18.

146. Martin, oral interview with author.

147. Committee to Protect Crime Victims and Public Safety Officers, "A Victim's Rights to Know," poster, 1988, ACT UP Los Angeles Records, ONE National Gay and Lesbian Archives, University of Southern California Libraries, Los Angeles (hereafter AULA), box 16, folder 18.

148. Victor F. Zonana, "The California Elections: Signal to Washington Seen in Prop. 102's Defeat," *Los Angeles Times*, November 10, 1988, 2.

149. Zonana, "The California Elections: Signal to Washington Seen in Prop. 102's Defeat."

150. Zonana.

151. "LIFE 1990 Delegate Survey," BSWP, box 3, folder 10. Even after the organization attempted to improve its diversity in the early 1990s, most of its members were white, gay men. In 1997, only 6 percent of LIFE's member organizations were Black or Latino AIDS Service Organizations. "Winter 1997 LIFE Membership Roster," Hank M. Tavera Papers, Ethnic Studies Library, University of California, Berkeley (hereafter HTP), box 5, folder 3.

152. One government report noted in 1987 that "the San Francisco Antibody Alternative Test Site serves a primarily white male population." California Office of AIDS, "Evaluation of the California AIDS Antibody Alternate Test Site Program," 1987, AIDS History Project collection, ONE National Gay and Lesbian Archives, Los Angeles (hereafter AHPC), box 22, folder 44.

153. "Prop 96 Struggles for Attention," *San Francisco Sentinel*, September 23, 1988, 1, SHP, box 6, folder 16.

154. "Prop 96 Struggles for Attention."

155. Amira Hasenbush et al., "HIV Criminalization in California: Penal Implications for People Living with HIV/AIDS," Williams Institute, December 2015, http://williamsinstitute.law.ucla.edu/wp-content/uploads/HIV-Criminalization-California-UpdatedJune-2016.pdf.

156. For more on the bipartisan roots of the carceral state, see Elizabeth Hinton, *From the War on Poverty to the War on Crime: The Making of Mass Incarceration in America* (Harvard University Press, 2017); Julilly Kohler-Hausmann, *Getting Tough: Welfare and Imprisonment in 1970s America* (Princeton University Press 2017).

157. Melinda Cooper, *Family Values: Between Neoliberalism and the New Social Conservatism* (Zone Books, 2017), 189.

158. Richard P. Nathan and Fred C. Doolittle, "The Budget Cuts: The Day After," *Challenge* 26, no. 6 (1984): 32.

159. Cristy Jensen and Ruth Ross, "California," in *Reagan and the States*, ed. Richard P. Nathan and Fred C. Doolittle (Princeton University Press, 2014), 332.

160. Martin, "LIFE 1987 Year End Report."

161. Deukmejian vetoed similar antidiscrimination bills each year between 1986 and 1988. "Digest of AB 87," 1988, AAP, box 14, folder 15.

162. "AB 87: Implementing the Surgeon General's Recommendation to Confront the AIDS Epidemic," April 27, 1987, AAP, box 14, folder 15.

163. Stan Hadden to Fourth National AIDS Conference Delegation, April 17, 1986, SHP, box 2, folder 6.

164. Memorandum from Larry Bush to Art Agnos, 1987, AAP, box 14, folder 15.

165. Sponsored by Dannemeyer and Doolittle, Proposition 102 would have made HIV a reportable condition, allowing the state government to quarantine PWAs. The California electorate rejected it in November 1988, by a margin of two to one. Lori Olszewski, "Doctors Vow to Push AIDS-Reporting Lawsuit," *San Francisco Chronicle*, December 2, 1988, A9.

166. Daniel M. Fox, "The Politics of HIV Infection: 1989–1990 as Years of Change," in *AIDS: The Making of a Chronic Disease*, ed. Elizabeth Fee and Daniel M. Fox (University of California Press, 1989), 141.

167. "T-Cell Testing Recommendation Affect Planning Activities," *Intergovernmental AIDS Reports* 2, no. 2 (July-August 1989): 1.

168. Marlene Cimons, "AZT Found to Delay AIDS in Those Free of Symptoms," *Los Angeles Times*, August 18, 1989, 1.

169. Quoted in "T-Cell Testing Recommendation Affect Planning Activities."

170. In New Jersey, for example, the state established a series of "assessment centers" in 1989 to provide regular testing of T-cell levels in those with HIV infection and distribute the drug AZT to delay the onset of symptoms. Fox, "The Politics of HIV Infection," 138.

171. John Vasconcellos, "FY 1988–89 Budget," press release, May 18, 1988, SHP, box 3, folder 11.

172. Vasconcellos, "FY 1988–89 Budget."

173. Vasconcellos.

174. Rand Martin, "Roar of the Tiger, Song of the Loon: A 1988 Debriefing," n.d., SHP, box 7, folder 30.

175. Vasconcellos, "FY 1988–89 Budget."

176. Martin, "Roar of the Tiger, Song of the Loon."

177. Ray O'Loughlin, "Duke Slashes AIDS in State Budget," *Bay Area Reporter*, July 21, 1988, 1.

178. Gerry Braun, "Policy Shift is Seen in Increased Funding for AIDS Programs," *Sacramento Bee*, January 8, 1988, clipping, SHP, box 3, folder 7.

179. Ray O'Loughlin, "Duke Slashes AIDS in State Budget."

180. Ray O'Loughlin.

181. Vasconcellos, "FY 1988–89 Budget."

182. Amy Stevens, "Governor's AIDS Cuts Draw Fire," *Los Angeles Times*, July 15, 1988, 3.

183. David Roberti, "Democrat Legislators Respond to Deukmejian Budget Vetoes," press release, July 8, 1988, SHP, box 3, folder 9.

184. David Roberti to Lyn Colon, December 12, 1989, SHP, box 1, folder 5.

185. LIFE, "Governor Slashes AIDS Budget," press release, July 7, 1989, SHP, box 3, folder 9.

186. LIFE, "Governor Slashes AIDS Budget."

187. LIFE HIV/Healthcare Policy Committee minutes, July 20, 1994, HTP, box 5, folder 3.

188. AIDS Budget Coalition, "California Augments Achieve Victory in FY'95 Budget," press release, July 8, 1994, HTP, box 5, folder 3.

189. Vasconcellos, "FY 1989–90 State AIDS Budget," 6.

190. Laurie McBride, "AB 2810: Bouncing Back from the Veto," *Lifelines: The Official Newsletter of the LIFE AIDS Lobby and the LIFE League*, October–December 1994, 3, Lobby for Individual Freedom and Equality Papers, 1997–19, GLBT Historical Society, San Francisco (hereafter LIFE), box 1, folder 3.

191. LIFE Executive Committee Conference Call minutes, September 23, 1989, BSWP, box 4, folder 7.

192. LIFE, "Governor Wilson Unveils Stable AIDS Budget Despite 26 Percent Growth in Caseload," January 14, 1990, BSWP, box 4, folder 7.

193. LIFE AIDS Lobby, "Recommendation for Financing the HIV Epidemic in California," November 16, 1990, ONE Subject File collection, ONE National Gay and Lesbian Archives, Los Angeles, folder: "Lobby for Individual Freedom and Equality."

Chapter 3: Anti-Feminism, Bisexuality, and the Protean Politics of Child Protection

1. Thomas J. Lee, "Legislator Leaves her Mark on the State: Conservative Penny Pullen Shines," *Daily Herald*, August 2, 1987, 1.

2. David Duschene, "Abortion Foes: No Retreat," *Northwest Herald*, November 25, 1992, 23.

3. David Awbrey, "Penny Pullen Works Way Up the Conservative Ladder," *Herald and Review*, February 25, 1979, 45; "Penny Pullen," *Daily Herald*, October 23, 1976, 59; Mary Gillespie, "She Has Righteous Perspective: Rep. Penny Pullen Listens to Her Heart," *Chicago Sun Times*, August 12, 1987, 3. On the shifting emphasis of conservatism from anti-communism to broader social issues in the 1970s and 1980s, see Lisa McGirr, *Suburban Warriors: The Origins of the New American Right* (Princeton University Press, 2001), 217–261.

4. Jim Thomas, "Three Gay Rights Bills in Illinois," *Gay News-Telegraph*, April 1983, 4; American Legislative Exchange Council, "Homosexuals: Just Another Minority Group?" *State Factor* (May 1985), 8, National Gay and Lesbian Taskforce Records, Division of Rare and Manuscript Collections, Cornell University Library, Ithaca, New York (hereafter NGLTF), box 152, folder 30.

5. "Penny Pullen Oral History Session One," conducted by Mark R. DePue, April 15, 2020, Illinois Statecraft Oral History Project, Abraham Lincoln Presidential Library, Springfield, Illinois (hereafter ALPL).

6. Penny Pullen, "Capitol Comment," April 15, 1987, emphasis in original, NGLTF, box 125, folder 13.

7. Thomas Hardy, "Pullen: A Backer of AIDS Testing," *Chicago Tribune*, July 24, 1987, 3.

8. Quoted in Seth Dowland, *Family Values and the Rise of the Christian Right* (University of Pennsylvania, 2015), 168.

9. Quoted in Gillian Frank, "'The Civil Rights of Parents': Race and Conservative Politics in Anita Bryant's Campaign Against Gay Rights in 1970s Florida." *Journal of the History of Sexuality* 22, no. 1 (2013): 127.

10. For more on the myth that gay men were a threat to children, including work on the Anita Bryant campaign, see Dowland, *Family Values and the Rise of the Christian Right*, 157–180; Gillian Frank, "Save Our Children: The Sexual Politics of Child Protection in the United States, 1965–1990" (PhD diss., Brown University, 2009); Frank, "The Civil Rights of Parents"; Paul M. Renfro, *Stranger Danger: The Politics of Child Protection from Etan Patz to AMBER Alert* (Oxford University Press, 2020), 25–56.

11. On the absence of bisexuals from many histories of sexuality, see Loraine Hutchins, "Bisexual History: Let's Not Bijack Another Century," in *The Routledge History of Queer America*, ed. Don Romesberg (Routledge, 2018), 250–261.

12. Dowland, *Family Values and the Rise of the Christian Right*, 144.

13. Phyllis Schlafly, "What's Wrong with 'Equal Rights' for Women?," *Phyllis Schlafly Report* 5, no.7 (February 1972).

14. On the history of the campaign against the ERA, see Donald T. Critchlow, *Phyllis Schlafly and Grassroots Conservatism: A Woman's Crusade* (Princeton University Press, 2005); Stacie Taranto, "Defending 'Women Who Stand By the Sink': Suburban Homemakers and Anti-ERA Activism in New York State," in *Making Suburbia: New Histories of Everyday America*, ed. John Archer, Paul J. P. Sandul, Katherine Solomonson (University of Minnesota Press, 2015), 36–50; Robert O. Self, *All in the Family: The Realignment of American Democracy Since the 1960s* (Hill & Wang, 2012), 452–496.

15. Donald T. Critchlow and Cynthia L. Stachecki, "The Equal Rights Amendment Reconsidered: Politics, Policy, and Social Mobilization in a Democracy," *Journal of Policy History* 20, no.1 (January 2008): 160.

16. Critchlow, *Phyllis Schlafly and Grassroots Conservatism*, 235–239.

17. Critchlow and Stachecki, "The Equal Rights Amendment Reconsidered," 159. For a comprehensive account of the history of the ERA in Illinois, see Cynthia L. Stachecki, "Why the Equal Rights Amendment Failed in Illinois: The Clash of Politics and Ideology" (PhD diss., Saint Louis University, 2012).

18. David Awbrey, "Penny Pullen Fights Against ERA," *Southern Illinoisan*, February 25, 1979, 17; Rob Karwarth, "Pullen Leads Abortion Foes' Fight," *Chicago Tribune*, September 26, 1; "Penny Pullen Oral History Session One."

19. "CWA Press Conference," *Concerned Women for America Newsletter* 1, no. 6 (June-July 1980): 2; "STOP ERA," *Decatur Daily Review*, April 28, 1980, 9; "Penny Pullen Oral History Session Two," conducted by Mark R. DePue, April 22, 2020, Illinois Statecraft Oral History Project, ALPL; Ill. H. Deb., 80th Cong., Reg. Sess. (1977), https://ilga.gov/House/transcripts/Htrans80/HT060277.pdf.

20. Mary Gillespie, "She Has Righteous Perspective: Rep. Penny Pullen Listens to Her Heart," *Chicago Sun Times*, August 12, 1987, 3.

21. STOP ERA, "ERA Is Not the Way," n.d, Georgia State University Library Exhibits, accessed October 21, 2022, https://exhibits.library.gsu.edu/current/items/show/3213.

22. Quoted in Critchlow, *Phyllis Schlafly and Grassroots Conservatism*, 225.

23. Frank, "The Civil Rights of Parents"; Gillian Frank, "Phyllis Schlafly's Legacy of Anti-Gay Activism," Slate, September 6, 2016, https://slate.com/human-interest/2016/09/phyllis-schlaflys-legacy-of-anti-gay-activism.html; Alison Lefkovitz, *Strange Bedfellows: Marriage in the Age of Women's Liberation* (University of Pennsylvania Press, 2012), 75–101; Chauncey, *Why Marriage?*, 111–112.

24. Phyllis Schlafly, "ERA and Homosexual 'Marriages,'" *Phyllis Schlafly Report* 8, no. 2 (November 1974), Atlanta Lesbian Feminist Alliance Archives, Duke University Library (hereafter ALFAA), box 15, folder 24.

25. "Equal Rights Amendment . . . Effects on Family Life," n.d., Florida Governor's Commission on the Status of Women Files, series 79, Florida State Archives (hereafter FGCSWF), box 5, folder: "ERA Correspondence." For more on how the rhetoric of child endangerment influenced the anti-ERA movement, see Frank, "The Civil Rights of Parents."

26. "Stop ERA," *Daily Republican-Register*, April 28, 1980, 3; Ira Latimer, "A Reply to Editorial CBS 2," March 21, 1974, ERA Central Records, Chicago History Museum (hereafter ECR), box 1, folder 12; Illinois Eagle Forum, "The ERA: (Equal Rights Amendment) Myths vs. Facts," n.d., ERA Illinois Records, Special Collections and University Archives, University of Illinois at Chicago (hereafter EIR), box 1, folder 1.

27. ERA Opposed, "The ERA Springs Some Surprises," n.d., EIR, box 1, folder 2.

28. For an account of Jack Baker's and Michael McConnell's push for marriage equality in the early 1970s, see William N. Eskridge and Christopher R. Riano, *Marriage Equality: From Outlaws to In-Laws* (Yale University Press, 2020), 5–33.

29. ERA Opposed, "The ERA Springs Some Surprises."

30. State Representative Betty J. Hoxsey, "Springfield Report: ERA Returns," *Moral Majority Report of Illinois* 1, no. 1, (June–July, n.d.), ERAmerica Records, Library of Congress, box 117, folder: "Moral Majority."

31. Eagle Forum, "The ERA-Gay-AIDS Connection," n.d., probably late 1983, NGLTF, box 154, Folder 39; Ellen Goodman, "For the Wastebasket," *Washington Post*, January 17, 1984, A15; "Schlafly Links ERA with AIDS," *Network News*, November-December 1983, 5.

32. Justin McCarthy, "Gallup Vault: Fear and Anxiety During the 1980s AIDS Crisis," Gallup Vault, June 18, 2019, https://news.gallup.com/vault/259643/gallup-vault-fear-anxiety-during-1980s-aids-crisis.aspx.

33. "Poll Finds Many Resigned to Huge AIDS Death Toll," *Los Angeles Times*, October 16, 1987, 32.

34. Theresa F. Rogers et al., "AIDS—An Update," *Public Opinion Quarterly* 57, no.1 (Spring 1993): 92.

35. Katie Leishman, "Heterosexuals and AIDS: The Second Stage of the Epidemic," *Atlantic*, February 1987, 39–58; "New Warning on Threat of AIDS to Straights," *San Francisco Chronicle*, December 15, 1987, A10.

36. For a summary of the string of AIDS bills passed by the states in 1987, see Joe Davidson, "States Turn Out a Flood of AIDS-Related Bills as Issues Remains in Talking Stages in Washington," *Wall Street Journal*, August 20, 1987, 1.

37. C. Everett Koop, *Surgeon General's Report on Acquired Immune Deficiency Syndrome* (United States Public Health Service, 1986), 31.

38. Koop, "Surgeon General's Report on Acquired Immune Deficiency Syndrome," 34.

39. "Koop Sticks to AIDS Statements," *Daily Chronicle*, March 13, 1987, 3. For more on conservative critiques of Koop's report, see Anthony Michael Petro, *After the Wrath of God: AIDS, Sexuality, and American Religion* (Oxford University Press, 2015), 53–90.

40. Alessandra Stanley, "AIDS Becomes a Political Issue: The New Right Seeks to Make It a Litmus Test for Republicans," *Time*, March 23, 1987, https://content.time.com/time/subscriber/article/0,33009,963806,00.html.

41. Schlafly's involvement in AIDS politics is almost wholly absent from scholarship on her. In his otherwise comprehensive biography of Schlafly, for example, Donald Critchlow does not mention the disease once, even claiming that Schlafly "shied away from controversies over homosexual rights." Critchlow, *Phyllis Schlafly and Grassroots Conservatism*, 300.

42. Phyllis Schlafly, "AIDS: The Challenge and a Plan of Action," *Phyllis Schlafly Report* 20, no. 12 (July 1987), NGLTF, box 125, folder 14.

43. Schlafly, "AIDS: The Challenge and a Plan of Action"; Phyllis Schlafly to Eagle Forum Members, July 1987, NGLTF, box 125, folder 14; Deborah L. Gertz, "AIDS Bills: Testers and Tracers v. Educators and Researchers," *Illinois Issues* 53 (August and September 1987): 53–56; Timothy Drake, phone interview with the author, August 25, 2019.

44. Schlafly, "AIDS: The Challenge and a Plan of Action"; Phyllis Schlafly to Eagle Forum Members, July 1987; Mike Matulis, "Gay Methods Instruction Banned, Abstinence Training OK'd," *Pantagraph*, May 7, 1987, 5; Carol Knowles, "Tough Political Choices on AIDS Measures," *Daily Republican-Register*, September 16, 1987, 13 Carol Knowles, "Pending Illinois AIDS Bills Range Between Extremes," *Dispatch*, September 14, 1987, 6; Timothy Drake, Phone interview with the author, August 25, 2019.

45. Tracy Baim, "Does the Gay Community Deserve Any Political Respect?" *Windy City Times*, August 13, 1987, ILGTF, box 6, folder: 129.

46. Pullen, "Capitol Comment," emphasis in original.

47. Schlafly, "AIDS: The Challenge and a Plan of Action."

48. Pullen, "Capitol Comment."

49. Jon Nordheimer, "AIDS Specter for Women: The Bisexual Man," *New York Times*, April 3, 1987, A1.

50. Maureen Downey, "Bisexual Men Must Confront AIDS," *Chapel Hill Newspaper*, April 26, 1987, 67; Maureen Downey, "Women, Fearing AIDS, Should Question High-Risk Activities," *Salt Lake Tribune*, May 16, 1987, 11; Maureen Downey, "AIDS Connection with Bisexuality Throws Researcher for a Loop," *Courier-Journal*, June 21, 1987, 112; Maureen Downey, "Dating a Closet Bisexual a Problem for Women Worried About AIDS," *Ledger-Enquirer*, April 23, 1987, 16.

51. Leishman, "Heterosexuals and AIDS." For more media accounts warning of threat posed by bisexuality to women, see Susan Day, "Tragedy of AIDS Hits Home," *Minneapolis Star and Tribune*, April 1, 1987, 15A; Carey Quan Gelernter, "A Sexual Orientation That's Been Out of the Public Eye Is Now Getting More Scrutiny," *Seattle Times*, September 4, 1987, C1.

52. Nordheimer, "AIDS Specter for Women."

53. Randy Shilts, "AIDS Not Spreading Fast Among Straights," *San Francisco Chronicle*, March 24, 1987, 1.

54. Don Thompson, "Suburbs Create Political Power Base That Continues to Grow," *Daily Herald*, October 12, 1997, 4.

55. On the political, economic, and demographic differences between Chicago and downstate Illinois, see James D. Nowlan, Samuel K. Gove, and Richard J. Winkel Jr., *Illinois Politics: A Citizen's Guide* (University of Chicago Press, 2010), 1–23; James D. Nowlan and J. Thomas Johnson, *Fixing Illinois: Politics and Policy in the Prairie State* (University of Chicago Press, 2014), 7–20; Devin Hunter, "Urban/Rural Frictions in the Midwest: The Chicago-Downstate Battle for Legislative Reapportionment in Illinois, 1953–1965," in *The Conservative Heartland: A Political History of the Postwar American Midwest*, ed. Jon K. Lauck and Catherine McNicol Stock (University of Kansas Press, 2020), 95–114.

56. Bob Wiedrich, "A Barrier We Must Leap," *Chicago Tribune*, July 13, 1981, 16.

57. Samuel K. Gove and James D. Nowlan, *Illinois Politics and Government: The Expanding Metropolitan Frontier* (University of Nebraska Press, 1996), 27.

58. Gove and Nowlan, *Illinois Politics and Government*, 22.

59. Michael W. Frank, Peter F. Nardulli, and Paul M. Green, "Representation, Elections, and Geo-Political Cleavages: The Political Manifestations of Regionalism in Twentieth-Century Illinois," in *Diversity, Conflict, and State Politics: Regionalism in Illinois*, ed. Peter F. Nardulli (University of Illinois Press, 1989), 215.

60. Nowlan and Johnson, *Fixing Illinois*, 7–20; Charles J. Orlebeke, "Illinois," in *Reagan and the States*, ed. Richard P. Nathan and Fred C. Doolittle (Princeton University Press, 1987), 303–331.

61. Illinois Department of Public Health and Illinois Interagency Task Force, *The Response to AIDS and HIV Infection* (State of Illinois,1990), 12.

62. Kyle Riismandel, *Neighborhood of Fear: The Suburban Crisis in American Culture, 1975–2001* (John Hopkins University Press, 2020).

63. Diane Dungey, "AIDS: Now Its Hitting Home," *Daily Herald*, August 9, 1987, 1.

64. Amy R. Mack, "Battle vs. AIDS Enlists Nation, County, Cities," *Northwest Herald*, February 20, 1987, 1–2.

65. Mike Lawrence, "Legislators Scrambling to Respond to Electorate's Alarm over the Disease," *Chicago Sun-Times*, May 31, 1987, 13.

66. Lawrence, "Legislators Scrambling to Respond to Electorate's Alarm over the Disease"; John Kass, "AIDS Package Caters to Voters Back Home," *Chicago Tribune*, July 1, 1987, 10.

67. Lawrence, "Legislators Scrambling to Respond to Electorate's Alarm over the Disease."

68. Kass, "AIDS Package Caters to Voters Back Home."

69. Timothy Drake, phone interview with the author, August 25, 2019; ILGTF, "Phone Tree: Guidelines for Effectives Action," n.d., NGLTF, box 55, folder 38; "Political Perspectives: Building a Statewide Organization," *GayLife*, February 12, 1982, 6, ILGTF, box 2, folder: "ILGTF in the News, 1982"; IGLTF, "Report of 1987 IGLTF State Bills Project"; Handwritten notes on IGLTF's 1987 lobbying efforts by unidentified individual, n.d., NGLTF, box 55, folder 38.

70. IGLTF, "Board Member Data Sheets," n.d., probably 1988, IGLTF, box 2, folder 45.

71. John Kass and Steve Daley, "The AIDS Dilemma: Lawmakers and Lobbyists Try

to Please Everyone," *Chicago Tribune*, September 6, 1987, 61; John Kass, "AIDS Package Caters to Voter Back Home," *Chicago Tribune*, July 1, 1987, 10; Daniel Egler and Jean Davidson, "AIDS Bills Focus on Education," *Chicago Tribune*, September 22, 1987, 1; Timothy Drake, phone interview with the author, August 25, 2019.

72. Charles N. Wheeler III, "Thompson Gets Sweeping Set of Anti-AIDS Bills," *Chicago Sun-Times*, June 30, 1987, 4; "Demos Retain Control of Legislature," *Daily Republican-Register*, November 5, 1986, 17; "Legislature Passed All AIDS Bills," *Southern Illinois*, June 26, 1987, 2; IGLTF, "Report of 1987 IGLTF State Bills Project"; Handwritten notes on IGLTF's 1987 lobbying efforts by unidentified individual.

73. Charles N. Wheeler III, "Gov. James R. Thompson, 1977–1991: The Complete Campaigner, the Pragmatic Centrist," *Illinois Issues*, December 16, 1990, 12–16.

74. Tom Brune, "Gays Ask Thompson to OK Bills," *Chicago Sun-Times*, August 11, 1987, 20; "IGLTF Meets with Governor Thompson in Historic First for Illinois," *Illinois Gay and Lesbian Task Force Bulletin* 1, no. 4 (October 1987): 1, Tracy Baim Editorial Files (Alexander Street); Williams Burks, "Governor Meets with Gay Group," *Chicago Outlines*, September 15, 1987, 1; Johanna Stoyva, "Opposition to AIDS Bills Escalates; Veto Campaign Underway," *Chicago Outlines*, July 2, 1987, 3; Grant Thornley, "AIDS Bill Veto Push," *Chicago Outlines*, July 16, 1987, 11.

75. Thornley, "AIDS Bill Veto Push"; Johanna Stoyva, "AIDS Bills: Fighting the Good Fight," *Chicago Outlines*, July 16, 1987, 6; NGLTF State Action Lobby, "The March on Washington and Back to the Statehouses: A Political Action Packet on State-Related Issues," n.d., NGLTF, box 100, folder 68.

76. IGLTF, "Sample Letter to Governor James R. Thompson," July 1, 1987, NGLTF, box 55, folder 38.

77. Tracy Baim, "Rep. Pullen, Gay Man Appointed to Reagan AIDS Commission," *Chicago Outlines*, July 30, 1987, 16.

78. Tracy Baim, "Thompson Vetoes Patient Care, Contact Tracing," *Chicago Outlines*, September 24, 1987, 1, 5; Doug Finke, "Thompson Signs AIDS Legislation," *State-Journal Register*, September 22, 1987, 1.

79. Harold Washington to Members of the Illinois House of Representatives, September 21, 1987, Community Services Sub-Cabinet Series, Mayoral Records, Harold Washington Archives and Collections, Chicago Public Library (hereafter CSSS), series 2: AIDS, 1985–1988, box 28, folder 28; Tracy Baim, "State AIDS Council Looks at HIV Connection," *Chicago Outlines*, September 3, 1987, 3.

80. Paul Cotton, "Premarital HIV Testing Hits Snags: As Two States Implement Testing, Counselling Quality Varies, Costs Are an Issue and Critics Decry Diversion of Resources from Groups at Higher Risk of Infection," *Medical World News* 29, no. 4 (February 22, 1988): 21; Don Colburn, "Illinois, Louisiana Become First States to Require AIDS Test Before Marriage," *Washington Post*, January 1, 1988, A11.

81. Cotton, "Premarital HIV Testing Hits Snags."

82. Mike Hasten, "Capitol Report: All Considered, It Was a Good Session," *Sunday Advertiser*, July 17, 1988, 53.

83. Sandra G. Boodman, "Premarital AIDS Testing Annoying Many in Illinois: Some Couples Head Out of State to Say 'I Do,'" *Washington Post*, July 30, 1988, A1.

84. Michael Closen et al., "Mandatory Premarital HIV Testing: Political Exploitation of the AIDS Epidemic," *Tulane Law Review* 68, no. 1 (1994–95): 98–99.

85. Closen et al., "Mandatory Premarital HIV Testing," 98–99.

86. "AIDS, Marriage and Folly in Illinois," *New York Times*, February 1, 1988, A30.

87. "AIDS Testing Is Repealed," *Daily Chronicle*, September 12, 1989, 1.

88. "Group Against Proposed AIDS Education Programs in Schools," *Montgomery Advertiser*, August 8, 1987, 16; "Schlafly Urges Teachers to Stress Abstinence," *Montgomery Advertiser*, April 5, 1987, 35; "Parents Improve State Curricula: AIDS Education in Alabama," *Education Reporter*, April 1988, 1–2.

89. "Parents Improve State Curricula," 2.

90. David Anderson, "Conflict Stews at U. Over Sexual Health Information," *Daily Utah Chronicle*, March 27, 1996, 4; "'Pro-Family' Woman Builds Record," *Messenger-Inquirer*, November 13, 1988, 20; Courtney Brenn, "Washoe Panel Tackles Sex-Education Proposal," *Reno Gazette-Journal*, February 15, 1988, 1, 10; People for the American Way Foundation, "Teaching Fear: The Religious Right's Campaign Against Sexuality Education," September 1996, https://files.pfaw.org/uploads/2017/01/teaching-fear-1996-report.pdf. For more on campaigns for abstinence-only sex education during the early years of the AIDS epidemic, see Kristy L. Slominski, *Teaching Moral Sex: A History of Religion and Sex Education in the United States* (Oxford University Press, 2021), 209–240.

91. Diane de Mauro, "Sexuality Education 1990: A Review of State Sexuality and AIDS Education Curricula," *SIECUS Report* 18, no. 2 (December 1989): 1–9.

92. "Pullen: Conservative's Influence Grows with GOP," *Daily Herald*, August 2, 1987, 9; Sandra Boodman, "Views of Four U.S. AIDS Panelists Hit," *Washington Post*, August 26, 1987, A1; Gillespie, "She Has Righteous Perspective"; Gary Bauer, "Penny Pullen for AIDS Commission," July 7, 1987, Gary Bauer Files, Ronald Reagan Presidential Library, Simi Valley, California (hereafter GBF), box 5, folder: "AIDS Commission."

93. For more on this wave of legislation, see chapter 2.

94. "Public Health Officials, Do Your Jobs," *New American*, May 23, 1988, 17, Bill Bahlman Papers, Elihu Burrett Library, Central Connecticut State University (hereafter BBP), box 1, folder 96. On the history of ALEC and its influence over state politics, see Alexander Hertel-Fernandez, *State Capture: How Conservative Activists, Big Businesses, and Wealthy Donors Reshaped the American States—and the Nation* (Oxford University Press, 2019).

95. Hoppe, *Punishing Disease*, 123–129; Todd Heywood, "The Crime of Being HIV Positive," *Advocate*, April 1, 2013, https://www.advocate.com/print-issue/current-issue/2013/04/01/crime-being-positive?page=0,0.

96. Hoppe, *Punishing Disease*, 127.

97. P. J. Engelbrecht, "A Decade of IMPACT: Lesbigay PAC Folding as Merger with Illinois Federation Falls Through," *Outlines*, October 8, 1997, 15.

98. IMPACT, "By-Laws," n.d., IMPACT Illinois, Inc. records, 1987–1996 (unprocessed collection), Gerber/Hart Library and Archives, Chicago, Illinois (hereafter IMPACT).

99. McCormack and Associates, "Recruitment Profile: IMPACT," March 24, 1993, IMPACT.

100. "A Summary Report: Lesbian/Gay Voter IMPACT '88," n.d., Carole Powell

Papers, Gerber/Hart Library and Archives, Chicago, Illinois (hereafter CPP), box 1, folder 1.

101. "A Summary Report: Lesbian/Gay Voter IMPACT '88."

102. "IGLTF Hires Lobbyist," *Illinois Gay and Lesbian Task Force Bulletin* 3, no. 1 (January 1988): 1, Tracy Baim Editorial Files (Alexander Street).

103. "IGLTF Board of Directors Meeting Agenda," September 7, 1991, IGLTF, box 5, folder 92; Central Gay and Lesbian Task Force, "Board of Directors Meeting Minutes," October 3, 1991, IGLTF, box 5, folder 89.

104. "IGLTF Launches Statewide Lobbying Program," *Illinois Gay and Lesbian Task Force* 3, no. 5 (September 1989): 2. See the contents of IGLTF, box 4, folder 84 for a sample of these "action alerts."

105. "Quiet Year on AIDS Issues in Legislature," *Illinois Gay and Lesbian Task Force Reports* 1, no. 2 (Autumn 1990): 3, NGLTF, box 20, folder 2; Lana Hostetler, "Legislative Wrap Up, Spring 1990 Session," August 1990, CPP, box 2, folder 41.

106. Rex Wockner, "Illinois Gay/AIDS Legislation Update," *Outlines*, July 1991, 21; "Editorial," *Outlines*, May 1991, 4; Timothy Drake, phone interview with the author, August 25, 2019; "Task Force Final Report," 1991, IGLTF, box 5, folder 92; IGLTF, "List of Priorities in Activities as Specified by Individual Board Members Attending a Strategy Session," 1991, IGLTF, box 5, folder 92.

107. Rex Wockner, "Gays' Arch Foe Pullen Defeated," *Outlines*, April 1992, 23; Rex Wockner, "Rosemary Mulligan: The Gay Interview," *Outlines*, May 1992, 24.

108. Quoted in Wockner, "Gays' Arch Foe Pullen Defeated."

109. Wockner.

110. IMPACT, Meeting of the Board of Directors Minutes, January 4, 1994, IMPACT; IMPACT, Meeting of the Board of Directors Minutes, February 17, 1994, IMPACT.

111. "Evaluation of Lesbian/Gay Voter IMPACT '88," n.d., CPP, box 1, folder 1.

112. Rex Wockner, "IMPACT Dinner Breaks Record," *Outlines*, March 1991, 25; "50 Pols+ Attend IMPACT Dinner, $85,000 Raised," *Outlines*, March 1990, 23.

113. "Skip the Brunch," poster of unknown origins, October 17, 1993, IMPACT.

114. IMPACT, "The 5th Annual Woman of Impact Brunch," 1993, Tracy Baim Editorial Files, Windy City Box G (Alexander Street).

Chapter 4: An Unequal Epidemic

1. "Thousands March Demanding End to Legal Discrimination," *Montrose Voice*, May 5, 1989, 1; "Thousands March on Texas State Capitol," *This Week in Texas*, May 5–11, 1989, 19–20; Rex Wockner, "Gay March Largest Ever Held in Texas," *Gay and Lesbian Times*, May 12, 1989, 3; Clay Robison, "Gay Rights Rally Draws Thousands: AIDS Funds Urged at Austin March," *Houston Chronicle*, May 1, 1989, 1.

2. Glen Maxey, phone interview with author, July 18, 2019; Lesbian/Gay Rights Lobby, "Lobby Day at the Legislature: Schedule of Events," Dennis Vercher Collection, University of North Texas Special Collections (hereafter DVC), box 3, folder 19; Michael Milliken, "Life! Liberty! Justice for All!" *AIDS Update*, June 1989, 10.

3. Glen Maxey, phone interview with author, July 18, 2019; "Monumental AIDS Protest at Capitol," *This Week in Texas*, May 12–18, 17–19; Sherry Jacobson, "Legislators

Avoiding So-Called Gay Issues," *Dallas Morning News*, clipping, Linda Jebavy Mitchell Collection, University of North Texas Special Collections (hereafter LJMC), box 1, folder 6.

4. "Legislature OKs Patched-Together AIDS Omnibus Bill," *Dallas Morning News*, May 30, 1989, clipping, Resource Center LGBT Collection of the University of North Texas Libraries (hereafter RCC), box 51, folder 114.

5. As chapters 2 and 3 demonstrated, California's antibody testing law and Illinois's HIV criminalization statute were copied almost verbatim by several states.

6. Intergovernmental Health Policy Project, "A Synopsis of State AIDS Laws Enacted During the 1983–1987 Legislative Sessions," 1988, National Gay and Lesbian Taskforce Records, Division of Rare and Manuscript Collections, Cornell University Library, Ithaca, New York (hereafter NGLTF), box 131, folder 29.

7. The term *legislative capacity* refers to the ability of legislatures to execute their core functions, which include crafting laws, overseeing the executive branch, and passing budgets. Political scientists have long recognized that factors like lawmaker pay, session lengths, staffing levels, physical facilities, and institutional rules all influence legislative capacity. During the early years of the AIDS epidemic, the time legislatures spent in session was one of the most critical components of legislative capacity, as the disease required a swift and rapid response. For an illuminating recent summary of the political science literature on legislative capacity, see Alexander Bolton and Sharece Thrower, *Checks in the Balance: Legislative Capacity and the Dynamics of Executive Power* (Princeton University Press, 2022), 17–42.

8. Texas Department of Health, *Annual Report of the Texas Department of Health* (Austin, 1989), 32.

9. For a comprehensive introduction to the history of the Texas sodomy statute, see Wesley G. Phelps, *Before* Lawrence V. Texas*: The Making of a Queer Social Movement* (University of Texas Press, 2023).

10. On the institutional weakness of state legislatures in the middle of the twentieth century, see Peverill Squire, *The Evolution of American Legislatures: Colonies, Territories, and States, 1619–2009* (University of Michigan Press, 2012), 286–297. This is not to say that state governments as a whole were institutionally weak. As chapter 1 outlined, state government bureaucracies underwent a rapid process of expansion and modernization during the New Deal period. See Karen M. Tani, *States of Dependency: Welfare, Rights, and American Governance, 1935–1972* (Cambridge University Press, 2016).

11. Squire, *The Evolution of American Legislatures*, 297–301.

12. Squire, 302; John C. Teaford, *The Rise of the States: Evolution of American State Government* (Johns Hopkins University Press, 2003), 198–201.

13. Russell L. Smith and William Lyons, "Legislative Reform in the American States: Some Preliminary Observations," *State & Local Government Review* 9, no. 2 (May 1977): 38.

14. On the varying policymaking capacities of the states in the late twentieth century, see John M. Carey et al., *Term Limits in the State Legislatures* (University of Michigan Press, 2000), 145–149; Peverill Squire, "Legislative Professionalization and Membership Diversity in State Legislatures," *Legislative Studies Quarterly* 17, no. 1 (February 1992): 69–79; Alexander Bolton and Sharece Thrower, *Checks in the Balance: Legislative Capacity and the Dynamics of Executive Power* (Princeton University Press, 2022), 156–186.

The term *citizen legislature* refers to a legislative chamber made up of part-time members who hold other occupations.

15. Council of State Government, *The Book of the States, 1984–1985* (CSG, 1984), 104–107.

16. David L. Sollars, "Institutional Rules and State Legislator Compensation: Success for the Reform Movement?" *Legislative Studies Quarterly* 19, no. 4 (November 1994): 509.

17. As late as 1998, an estimated 89 percent of lawmakers in Texas held other careers while in office. H. W. Jerome Maddox, "Working outside of the State House (And Senate): Outside Careers as an Indicator of Professionalism in American State Legislatures," *State Politics and Policy Quarterly* 4, no. 2 (Summer 2004): 217.

18. Janice C. May, *The Texas Constitution* (Oxford University Press, 2011), 95. Under the Texas Constitution, the governor could call special legislative sessions, which became more frequent during the 1990s.

19. Molly Ivins, "Inside the Austin Fun House," *Atlantic*, March 1975, 49.

20. Citizens Conference on State Legislatures, *The Impact of the Texas Constitution on the Legislature* (CCSL, 1973), 55.

21. For two comprehensive overviews of Texas state politics in the 1970s and 1980s, see Wayne Thorburn, *Red State: An Insider's Story of How the GOP Came to Dominate Texas Politics* (University of Texas Press, 2014), 97–134; Sean P. Cunningham, *Cowboy Conservatism: Texas and the Rise of the Modern Right* (University Press of Kentucky, 2010), 209–236.

22. Glen Maxey, phone interview with author, July 18, 2019; Dennis Vercher, "Sodomy Law Reform: In Texas, It May Be a While," *Dallas Voice*, August 18, 1989, 7.

23. Melinda D. Kane, "Timing Matters: Shifts in the Causal Determinants of Sodomy Law Decriminalization, 1961–1998," *Social Problems* 52, no. 2 (2007): 214. On the history of state sodomy statutes in the 1960s and 1970s, see William N. Eskridge Jr., *Dishonorable Passions: Sodomy Laws in America, 1861–2003* (Viking Press, 2008), 136–228.

24. On the history of Section 21.06 and the broader history of the Texas sodomy statute, see Phelps, *Before* Lawrence v. Texas, 17–54.

25. Don Ritz, "Dallas Attorney Lobbying for Anti-Gay Legislation," *Dallas Fort Worth Gay News*, March 18, 1983, 6; Peter Hecht, "New Right Opposition Tests the Clout of Gays," *Dallas Times Herald*, October 7, 1984, 22A.

26. H. Clem Mueller to "Concerned Texan," undated letter, accessed September 12, 2022, https://texashistory.unt.edu/ark:/67531/metadc177453/?q=%22H.%20Clem%20Mueller%22.

27. Don Ritz, "Entire Fifth Circuit Appeals Court to Hear 21.06," *Dallas Voice*, February 8, 1985, 1.

28. Jackie Calmes, "Legislator Says Homosexuals Pose Health Threat," *Dallas Morning News*, April 20, 1983, 16; H. Clem Mueller to "Concerned Texan."

29. Bill Ceverha, "House Bill 2138," Texas Human Rights Foundation Records, Dolph Briscoe Center for American History, University of Texas at Austin (hereafter THRFR), box 4B38, folder "HB 2138."

30. Texas House of Representatives, Criminal Jurisprudence Committee Transcripts, April 19, 1983, THRFR, box 4B38, folder "HB 2138."

31. "Who Is Paul Cameron," September 25, 1985, DVC, box 1, folder 15.

32. David A. Noebel, Wayne C. Lutton, and Paul Cameron, *Acquired Immune Deficiency Syndrome: Special Report* (Summit Research Institute, 1987), 139.

33. Texas House of Representatives, Criminal Jurisprudence Committee Transcripts, April 19, 1983, THRFR, box 4B38, folder "HB 2138."

34. Texas House of Representatives, Criminal Jurisprudence Committee transcripts.

35. Lesbian/Gay Rights Advocates, untitled press release, July 9, 1983, NGLTF, box 156, folder 8.

36. In addition to supporting Ceverha's bill, the DDAA tried to reinstate the sodomy statute through the courts. The organization provided financial aid and legal assistance to the successful appeal effort in the Fifth Circuit Court that led to Section 21.06's reinstatement in 1985. Phelps, *Before* Lawrence v. Texas, 140–143.

37. In a major blow to the gay movement, the Supreme Court then upheld the constitutionality of a similar sodomy law in Georgia in 1986.

38. Quoted in Texas Human Rights Foundation, "Sodomy Law Shown to Promote Anti-Gay Violence and Hinder Efforts at AIDS Education and Prevention," press release, July 19, 1990, Texas Human Rights Foundation Collection, University of North Texas Special Collections (hereafter THRFC), box 2, folder 54.

39. Eric Celeste, "Gay Inc," *D Magazine*, June 1, 1992, https://www.dmagazine.com/publications/d-magazine/1992/june/gay-inc/.

40. William Waybourn, phone interview with the author, September 2, 2019.

41. Scott De Orio, "The Invention of Bad Gay Sex: Texas and the Creation of a Criminal Underclass of Gay People," *Journal of the History of Sexuality* 26, no. 1 (January 2017): 82; Allan H. Terl, "An Essay on the History of Lesbian and Gay Rights in Florida," *Nova Law Review* 24, no. 3 (2000): 801–803.

42. Meridith Raimondo, "Dataline Atlanta: Place and the Social Construction of AIDS," in *Carryin' on in the Lesbian and Gay South*, ed. John Howard (New York University Press, 1997), 357.

43. Senate Commerce Committee, Reg. Sess. (F.L. 1988), FSA, tape 1; Senate Appropriations Committee, Reg. Sess. (F.L. May 27, 1988), FSA, tape 1; Audio Recording of Senate Floor Debate, Reg. Sess., (F.L. May 31, 1988), FSA, tape 1; Audio Recording of Senate Floor Debate, Reg Sess. (F.L. June 6, 1988), FSA, tape 1; Audio Recording of House Floor Debate, (F.L. May 11, 1988), FSA, tape 1; Audio Recording of House Floor Debate, Reg Sess. (F.L. June 3, 1988), FSA, tape 1.

44. On the epidemiology of AIDS in Florida, see Julio Capó Jr., "It's Not Queer to Be Gay: Miami and the Emergence of the Gay Rights Movement, 1945–1995" (PhD diss., Florida International University, 2011), 201–215.

45. Tex. H.B. 1102, 69th Leg., R.S. (1985).

46. "Maxey Named to Post," *Dallas Voice*, December 19, 1986, 13.

47. Pat Cramer and Rich Bailey to LGRL Board Members, March 3, 1989, Louise Young and Vivienne Armstrong Papers, University of North Texas Special Collections (hereafter LYVA), box 1, folder 2.

48. Glen Maxey, phone interview with author, July 18, 2019; "Gay Lobby Has New Name and New Lobbyist for New Year," *This Week in Texas*, December 19–25, 1986, 17; Dennis Vercher, "LGRA Fights the Good Fight in the Texas Legislature," *Dallas Voice*,

August 22, 1986, 8; Glen Maxey and Pat Chramer, "Our Texas Gay Rights Lobby: A Summer Update Between Legislative Sessions," *This Week in Texas*, May 23–29, 1986, 29–30.

49. Glen Maxey, phone interview with author, July 18, 2019; "Bills to Repeal 21.06 Filed in House and Senate," *Austin Lesbian/Gay Political Caucus Newsletter*, February 1989, 1, LYVA, box 1, folder 6.

50. Glen Maxey, phone interview with author, July 18, 2019; Vercher, "Sodomy Law Reform."

51. "Gay Rights Lobby Sponsors Parcel of Bills," *This Week in Texas*, March 13–19, 1987, 17.

52. Glen Maxey, phone interview with author, July 18, 2019; Intergovernmental Health Policy Project, "A Synopsis of State AIDS Laws Enacted during the 1983–1987 Legislative Sessions."

53. Glen Maxey, "Gay Rights Lobby Fine Tunes Texas AIDS Legislation," *This Week in Texas*, June 12–18, 1987, 29; "LGRL Executive Director's Report," March 13, 1987, NGLTF, box 100, folder 35; "Rights Put in Texas Quarantine Law," *Update*, June 24, 1987, 3.

54. Ronald Bayer, *Private Acts, Social Consequences: AIDS and the Politics of Public Health* (Free Press, 1988), 190–192.

55. On the case of Fabian Bridges and other media accounts of "noncompliant" HIV carriers in the mid-1980s, see René Esparza, "Black Bodies on Lockdown: AIDS Moral Panic and the Criminalization of HIV in Times of White Injury," *Journal of African American History* 104, no. 2 (Spring 2019): 250–280; Karma R. Chávez, *The Borders of AIDS: Race, Quarantine, and Resistance* (University of Washington Press, 2021), 54–57.

56. Chávez, *The Borders of AIDS*, 54.

57. Glen Maxey, phone interview with author, July 18, 2019; Maxey, "Gay Rights Lobby Fine Tunes Texas AIDS Legislation."

58. Maxey, phone interview with author; Maxey, "Gay Rights Lobby Fine Tunes Texas AIDS Legislation."

59. Maxey, phone interview with author; Maxey, "Gay Rights Lobby Fine Tunes Texas AIDS Legislation."

60. Maxey, phone interview with author; Maxey, "Gay Rights Lobby Fine Tunes Texas AIDS Legislation."

61. Maxey, "Gay Rights Lobby Fine Tunes Texas AIDS Legislation."

62. Maxey, phone interview with author, July 18, 2019.

63. On the common trope that homosexuality was dangerous and unhealthy, see Katie Batza, "Sickness and Wellness," in *The Routledge History of Queer America*, ed. Don Romesberg (Routledge, 2018).

64. Maxey, phone interview with author, July 18, 2019.

65. M. J. Rowe and C. C. Ryan, "Comparing State-Only Expenditure for AIDS," *American Journal of Public Health* 78, no. 4 (April 1988): 426, 428.

66. Rowe and Ryan; Rebecca Ashery, "New AIDS Initiatives," *NIDA Notes* 1, no. 4 (December 1986): 3.

67. Rowe and Ryan, "Comparing State-Only Expenditure for AIDS," 426; Centers for Disease Control and Prevention, "HIV/AIDS Surveillance Report," CDC, January 1989,

https://www.cdc.gov/hiv/pdf/library/reports/surveillance/cdc-hiv-surveillance-report-1988-vol-1.pdf.

68. Thomas C. Hayes, "Texas Picks Up the Pieces," *New York Times*, June 19, 1988, C1.

69. Ruth SoRelle, "Cleric Named as Head of AIDS Panel: Calls Disease Texas' Top Health Problems," *Houston Chronicle*, October 29, 1987, 1.

70. Glen Maxey, phone interview with author, July 18, 2019; "Gay Man Appointed to State AIDS Task Force," *Dallas Voice*, October 30, 1987, 3.

71. Maxey, phone interview with author, July 18, 2019; "Gay Man Appointed to State AIDS Task Force."

72. Sherry Jacobson, "Texas' AIDS Efforts Fall Short, Panel Says," *Dallas Morning News*, August 20, 1988, 1.

73. Legislative Task Force on AIDS (Tex. 1988), TSR, tape 1212, side 2.

74. Legislative Task Force on AIDS (Tex. 1988), TSR, tape 1197, side 2.

75. Jacobson, "Texas' AIDS Efforts Fall Short, Panel Says."

76. Legislative Task Force on AIDS, "AIDS in Texas: Facing the Crisis," January 1989, 37.

77. Legislative Task Force on AIDS.

78. Legislative Task Force on AIDS, 89.

79. Legislative Task Force on AIDS, 9–11.

80. Sherry Jacobson, "AIDS Bill Passage Is Urged," *Dallas Morning News*, March 29, 1989, clipping, RCC, box 51, folder 114.

81. Senate Committee on Health and Human Services, Reg. Sess. (Tex. 1989), TSR, tape 0993, side 1; Senate Committee on Health and Human Services, Reg. Sess. (Tex. 1989), TSR, tape 0993, side 2; Senate Committee on Health and Human Services, Reg. Sess., (Tex. 1989), TSR, tape 0995, side 1.

82. Senate Committee on Health and Human Services, Reg. Sess. (Tex. 1989), TSR, tape 0994, side 2.

83. Senate Committee on Health and Human Services, Reg. Sess., (Tex. 1989), TSR, tape 0994, side 1.

84. "LGRL Urges Action," *Austin Lesbian/Gay Political Caucus Newsletter*, February 1989, LYVA, box 1, folder 6.

85. Lesbian/Gay Rights Lobby, "Lobby Day at the Legislature: Schedule of Events."

86. Jacobson, "Legislators Avoiding So-Called Gay Issues"; Maxey, phone interview with author, July 18, 2019.

87. Dales Rice, "Senate Approves Wide-Ranging AIDS Proposal," *Dallas Times Herald*, May 16, 1989, clipping, RCC, box 51, folder 114.

88. "Legislators to Redraft Omnibus AIDS Bill after House Vote is Delayed," *Dallas Morning News*, May 20, 1989, clipping, RCC, box 51, folder 114; Sherry Jacobson, "Two Assail Rights Bill for AIDS Patients," April 18, 1989, clipping, RCC, box 51, folder 114.

89. House Public Health Committee, Reg. Sess. (Tex. 1989), Texas House Recordings, Archives and Information Services Division, Texas State Library and Archives Commission (hereafter THR), tape 1, side B.

90. House Public Health Committee, Reg. Sess. (Tex. 1989), THR, tape 2, side B.

91. Roy Bragg and Ruth SoRelle, "AIDS Measure Gets Panel OK," *Houston Chronicle*,

May 12, 1989, 1; Sherry Jacobson, "House Compromises to Approve AIDS Bill," *Dallas Morning News*, May 24, 1989, clipping, RCC, box 51, folder 114.

92. Quoted in "AIDS Measure Gets Panel OK."

93. Quoted in "AIDS Measure Gets Panel OK."

94. Jacobson, "House Compromises to Approve AIDS Bill."

95. Dennis Vercher, "Lawmakers Struggle for Compromise on AIDS Bill," *Dallas Voice*, May 26, 1989, clipping, RCC, box 51, folder 114; Sherry Jacobson, "House and Senate Narrowly Approve AIDS Compromise," *Dallas Morning News*, May 30, 1989, RCC, box 51, folder 114; Maxey, phone interview with author, July 18, 2019.

96. Ruth SoRelle, "AIDS Bill Beginning of Battle Against Disease: Lawmakers Boost Spending to $18.4 million in Biennium," *Houston Chronicle*, June 4, 1989, 9; "Legislature OKs Patched-Together AIDS Omnibus Bill"; Maxey, phone interview with author, July 18, 2019.

97. Maxey, phone interview with author, July 18, 2019.

98. "Lesbian/Gay Community Moves Ahead in the Legislative Arena," *Lobby Report: The Quarterly Newsletter of the Lesbian/Gay Rights Lobby of Texas*, June 1989, 1.

99. Dick Stanley, "State Denies Funds to AIDS Program under New Law," *Austin American-Statesman*, January 4, 1990, A1.

100. "Mattox Overrules TDH's Anti-Gay/Lesbian Guidelines," *Lobby Report: The Quarterly Newsletter of the Lesbian/Gay Rights Lobby of Texas*, February 1990, 1;3; David Morris, "Gay Group Denied AIDS Funding," *Gay Community News*, January 21–27, 1990, 1.

101. Glen Maxey, "Action Alert," *Dallas Voice*, December 22, 1989, 5.

102. "AIDS Funding Proposals Criticized," *Houston Chronicle*, January 19, 1990, 3; "Mattox Overrules TDH's Anti-Gay/Lesbian Guidelines."

103. Texas Attorney General, Opinion JM-1135, January 11, 1990, 5979.

104. "Austin Gets Minority AIDS Funds Reinstated," *BLK*, May 1990, 25; William Waybourn, phone interview with the author, September 2, 2019; Dennis Vercher, "AIDS Resource Center Is Denied State AIDS Grant," *Dallas Voice*, December 15, 1989, 3.

105. Rowe and Ryan, "Comparing State-Only Expenditure for AIDS," 426; Bennet Roth, "Legislature Passes AIDS Measure," *Dallas Times Herald*, May 30, 1989, clipping, RCC, box 51, folder 114.

106. Texas Department of Health, "Annual Report: HIV Services Program," Bureau of HIV and STD Control HIV Division, January 1991, 21–22.

107. "State Funding, FY 1992: Spending Is Up Nationwide, but Efforts Fail to Keep Pace with Growing Caseload," *Intergovernmental AIDS Reports* 6, no. 4 (May 1993), 6.

108. "State Funding, FY 1992." The early 1990s recession hit the Californian economy especially hard, as the state had a high proportion of defense jobs cut after the end of the Cold War. Between 1990 and 1993, two-thirds of jobs lost in the US economy were in California. Sarah Coleman, *The Walls Within: The Politics of Immigration in Modern America* (Princeton University Press, 2021), 111.

109. Tammye Nash, "Best and Worst from Statehouse," *Dallas Voice*, April 5, 1991, 3; "72nd Legislative Session Ends in Success," *Lobby Report: The Quarterly Newsletter of the Lesbian/Gay Rights Lobby of Texas*, September 1991, 5; Laurie Eiserloh, "Update: An Overview of the Recent Session of the Texas Legislature," *Dimensions*, July 1991, 24–25.

110. "LGRL Restructures in Face of Budget Shortfall," *This Week in Texas*, August

7–13, 1992, 15; Rick Antoine, "Lobbyist Discusses LGRL's Plans for Elections, 1993 Legislative Session," *New Voice*, July 3–9, 1992, 4; Rick Antoine, "LGRL Board Says Staff Position Was Cut to Avoid Future Budget Problems," *New Voice*, August 7–13, 1992, 5.

111. "AIDS Funding, Along with Many Other Crucial Programs, Were Scheduled for Huge Cuts," *Lobby Report: The Quarterly Newsletter of the Lesbian/Gay Rights Lobby of Texas*, October 1993, 2.

Chapter 5: A New Federal Role Is Born

1. Dan Royles, "HIV/AIDS in the United States," in *Global Encyclopedia of Lesbian, Gay, Bisexual, Transgender, and Queer History*, ed. Howard Chiang (Charles Scribner & Sons, 2019), 740.

2. Kaiser Family Foundation, "Trends in U.S. Government Funding for HIV/AIDS: Fiscal Years 1981 to 2004," KFF, March 2004, https://www.kff.org/wp-content/uploads/2013/01/issue-brief-trends-in-u-s-government-funding-for-hiv-aids-fiscal-years-1981-to-2004.pdf.

3. Cong. Rec., 101st Cong., 2nd Sess., S6187 (1990).

4. Jennifer Brier, *Infectious Ideas: U.S. Political Responses to the AIDS Crisis* (University of North Carolina Press, 2009), 78–121; Sarah Schulman, *Let the Record Show: A Political History of ACT UP New York, 1987–1993* (Farrar, Straus & Giroux, 2021); Anthony Michael Petro, *After the Wrath of God: AIDS, Sexuality, and American Religion* (Oxford University Press, 2015), 53–90; Lucas Richert, "Reagan, Regulation, and the FDA: The US Food and Drug Administration's Response to HIV/AIDS, 1980–90," *Canadian Journal of History* 44, no. 3 (Winter 2009): 467–488.

5. For three works that provide a thorough analysis of AIDS policymaking in Congress, see Jennifer Brier, "The Immigrant Infection: Images of Race, Nation and Contagion in Public Debates on AIDS and Immigration," in *Modern American Queer History*, ed. Allida M. Black (University of Pennsylvania Press, 2001), 253–270; Nancy E. Brown, "AIDS and the Politics of Disability in the 1980s" (PhD diss., Purdue University, 2019); Jonathan Bell, "Between Private and Public: AIDS, Health Care Capitalism, and the Politics of Respectability in 80s America," *Journal of American Studies* 54, no. 1 (February 2020): 159–183. However, even these works make no or only passing reference to the Ryan White CARE Act, one of the most significant laws enacted by Congress in response to the epidemic. To their credit, sociologists and political scientists have developed a more dense and insightful body of literature on the CARE Act, with a particular focus on the law's implementation in the 1990s. Much of this work, however, is largely silent on the links between the legislation and the San Francisco model of care. For a sample of this literature, see Patricia D. Siplon, *AIDS and the Policy Struggle in the United States* (Georgetown University Press, 2002), 93–110; Thomas G. Rundall et al., "Impact of the Ryan White CARE Act on the Availability of HIV/AIDS Services," *Policy Studies Journal* 27, no. 4 (July 2005): 826–839; Mark C. Donovan, *Taking Aim: Target Populations and the Wars on AIDS and Drugs* (Georgetown University Press, 2001), 53–68; Celeste Watkins-Hayes, *Remaking a Life: How Women Living with HIV/AIDS Confront Inequality* (University of California Press, 2019), 80–134.

6. Other major pieces of AIDS-related legislation passed by Congress in the late 1980s

and early 1990 included the 1988 Health Omnibus Programs Extension, which provided new resources for prevention education and biomedical research; the 1990 American Disabilities Act, which prohibited employment discrimination against PWAs; and the 1990 AIDS Housing Opportunity Act, which expanded housing assistance for PWAs.

7. Kaiser Family Foundation, "U.S. Federal Funding for HIV/AIDS: Trends Over Time," KFF, March 5, 2019, https://www.kff.org/hivaids/fact-sheet/u-s-federal-funding-for-hivaids-trends-over-time/#:~:text=The%20Ryan%20White%20HIV%2FAIDS%20Program%2C%20the%20largest%20HIV%2D,same%20as%20the%20FY18%20level.

8. On the growing political clout of the local gay rights movement in San Francisco during the 1960s and 1970s, see Jonathan Bell, "'To Strive for Economic and Social Justice': Welfare, Sexuality, and Liberal Politics in San Francisco," *Journal of Policy History* 22, no. 2 (April 2010): 193–225; Martin Meeker, "The Queerly Disadvantaged and the Making of San Francisco's War on Poverty, 1964–1967," *Pacific Historical Review* 81, no. 1 (February 2012): 21–59; Clayton Howard, *The Closet and the Cul-de-Sac: The Politics of Sexual Privacy in Northern California* (University of Pennsylvania Press, 2019). The San Francisco public health department had established a liaison office with the local gay and lesbian community in 1980 and had preexisting contract relationships with a number of local queer voluntary groups. On the connections forged between the city public health department and the gay rights movement in the 1970s and early 1980s, see Jonathan Bell, "Making Sexual Citizens: LGBT Politics, Health Care, and the State in the 1970s," in *Beyond the Politics of the Closet: Gay Rights and the American State Since the 1970s*, ed. Jonathan Bell (University of Pennsylvania Press, 2020), 58–82; Mervyn Silverman, "San Francisco: Coordinated Community Response," research paper, 1987, Donald F. Baker Collection, University of North Texas Special Collections, Denton, Texas (hereafter DBC), box 1, folder 6.

9. California Council in Partnerships, "The California AIDS Partnerships Roundtables," January 1987, Steve Morin Papers, 1992–04, GLBT Historical Society, San Francisco, California (hereafter STP), box 17, folder 7. A full account of San Francisco's early approach to AIDS is beyond the scope of this chapter, which is more concerned with the spread of the city's system of nonprofit–government partnerships to other municipalities and states. For more on San Francisco's initial response to the epidemic, see Brier, *Infectious Ideas*, 45–77; Josh Sides, *Erotic City: Sexual Revolutions and the Making of Modern San Francisco* (Oxford University Press, 2011), 175–204; Dan Royles, *To Make the Wounded Whole: African American Responses to HIV/AIDS* (University of North Carolina Press, 2020), 64–93.

10. The idea of working through private entities to deliver public goods stretches back to the beginning of the American Republic. As a rich and varied body of scholarship has revealed, public–private partnerships have been a central feature of American statecraft for centuries. But the 1960s marked an important turning point in the wider history of these partnerships, as the number of government grants available to nonprofit entities ballooned due to Lyndon B. Johnson's Great Society. Landmark Great Society legislation like the 1964 Economic Opportunity Act, the 1966 Demonstration Cities and Metropolitan Development Act, and the 1967 Social Security Amendments funneled vast amounts of federal revenue to voluntary organizations via new grant programs. For a few samples of the vast literature on public–private partnerships in the history

of American state development, see Gary Gerstle, *Liberty and Coercion: The Paradox of American Government from the Founding to the Present* (Princeton University Press, 2015), 89–124; William B. Novak, "The Myth of the 'Weak' American State," *American Historical Review* 113, no. 3 (June 2018): 752–772; Elisabeth S. Clemens, *Civic Gifts: Voluntarism and the Making of the American Nation-State* (University of Chicago Press, 2020). For more on the rapid expansion of the voluntary sector after the 1960s, see Lestor M. Salamon, *Partners in Public Service: Government-Nonprofit Relations in the Modern Welfare State* (John Hopkins University Press, 1995); Lestor M. Salamon, "The Rise of the Nonprofit Sector," *Foreign Affairs* 73, no. 4 (July-August, 1994): 109–122; Claire Dunning, *Nonprofit Neighborhoods: An Urban History of Inequality and the American State* (University of Chicago Press, 2022); Andrew Morris, "The Voluntary Sector's War on Poverty," *Journal of Policy History* 16, no. 4 (October 2004): 275–305.

11. David C. Hammack, "Introduction: Growth, Transformation, and Quiet Revolution in the Nonprofit Sector over Two Centuries," *Nonprofit and Voluntary Sector Quarterly* 30, no. 2 (June 2001): 167.

12. On the relationship between municipalities, urban governance, and the nonprofit sector after the Great Society, see Christof Brandtner and Claire Dunning, "Nonprofits as Urban Infrastructure," in *The Nonprofit Sector: A Research Handbook*, 3rd ed., ed. Walter W. Powell and Patricia Bromley (Stanford University Press, 2020), 271–291.

13. Elizabeth A. Armstrong, *Forging Gay Identities: Organizing Sexuality in San Francisco, 1950–1994* (University of Chicago Press, 2002), 113–133; Bell, "Making Sexual Citizens," 61–68.

14. Peter S. Arno, "The Nonprofit Sector's Response to the AIDS Epidemic: Community-based Services in San Francisco," *American Journal of Public Health* 76, no. 11 (November 1986), 1325–1330, AIDS Office of the San Francisco Department of Public Health Records, San Francisco History Center, San Francisco Public Library (hereafter AODPH), box 3, folder 23.

15. Silverman, "San Francisco."

16. For more on the early history of the AIDS service industry, see Royles, "HIV/AIDS in the United States," 735.

17. US Conference of Mayors, *Local Responses to Acquired Immune Deficiency Syndrome (AIDS): A Report of 55 Cities* (Government Printing Office, 1984).

18. Coleen Johnson (Director of Psychological Services, APLA), "Testimony before Assembly Health Committee Hearing on Los Angeles County AIDS Budget," 1985, SHP, box 5, folder 35.

19. Peter S. Arno, "The Economic Impact of AIDS," *JAMA: Journal of the American Medical Association* 258, no. 10 (September 1987): 1376–1377; Peter S. Arno, "The Nonprofit Sector's Response to the AIDS Epidemic," *American Journal of Public Health* 76, no.11 (November 1986): 1325–1330.

20. A. A. Scitovsky et al., "Medical Care Costs of Patients with AIDS in San Francisco," *JAMA: Journal of the American Medical Association* 256, no. 22 (December 1986): 3103–3106.

21. Quoted in Jesse Green et al., "The $147,000 Misunderstanding: Repercussions of Overestimating the Cost of AIDS," *Journal of Health Politics, Policy and Law* 19, no. 1 (Spring 1994): 80.

22. Michael L. Millenson, "AIDS Cost Forces New Approach," *Chicago Tribune*, Octo-

ber 11, 1987, 10; "$60,000 or $147,000? A Dispute over Cost of AIDS Hospital Care," *San Francisco Chronicle*, June 9, 1986, 28; Ronald Sullivan, "Cost of AIDS Care Is Half What Was Projected, Economist Reports," *New York Times*, June 8, 1986, 30.

23. Green et al., "The $147,000 Misunderstanding," 69–90.

24. Green et al., 72–73.

25. Green et al., 79; David E. Bloom and Geoffrey Carliner, "The Economic Impact of AIDS in the United States," *Science* 238, no. 4840 (February 1988): 604–610.

26. SyteMetrics/McGraw-Hill, Inc., "Case Study of Miami: AIDS Service Demonstration Project," June 27, 1989, National Commission on Acquired Immune Deficiency Syndrome Records, National Library of Medicine, National Institutes of Health, Bethesda, Maryland (hereafter NCAID), box 5, folder 16.

27. Health Council of South Florida, "AIDS in South Florida: A Plan for Action," March 4, 1986, Institute for Health Policy Studies AIDS Resource Program records, Archives and Special Collections, UCSF Library, San Francisco, California (hereafter: IHPS), box 6, folder 36.

28. Intergovernmental Health Policy Project, "National Survey of State Spending for AIDS," 1989, the Bush Administration and the AIDS Crisis: White House Staff and Office files, OA/ID 06961-018, Gale Archives of Sexuality and Gender.

29. "AIDS Resource Center Is Denied State Funds," *Dallas Morning News*, December 13, 1989, clipping, Linda Jebavy Mitchell Collection, University of North Texas Special Collections (hereafter LJMC), box 1, folder 6.

30. Intergovernmental Health Policy Project, "National Survey of State Spending for AIDS."

31. On the Medicaid waiver program implemented by the Omnibus Budget Reconciliation Act of 1981, see Jonathan Engel, *Poor People's Medicine: Medicaid and American Charity Care Since 1965* (Duke University Press, 2006), 188.

32. "Fact Sheet: AIDS Medi-Cal Waiver," March 19, 1987, IHPS, box 1, folder 29.

33. US House of Representatives Subcommittee on Health and the Environment of the Committee on Energy and Commerce, *Health Budget Reconciliation Amendments* (Government Printing Office, 1986), 45.

34. Phoebe A. Lindsey et al., "Medicaid Home and Community-Based Waiver for Acquired Immunodeficiency Syndrome Patients," special suppl., *Health Care Finance Review* (1990): 109–118.

35. Robert Wood Johnson Foundation, "AIDS Health Services Program," press release, January 1986, National Gay and Lesbian Taskforce Records, Division of Rare and Manuscript Collections, Cornell University Library, Ithaca, New York (hereafter NGLTF), box 115, Folder 18a.

36. Mervyn Silverman, phone Interview with the author, September 3, 2019.

37. In the early 1980s, Morrison oversaw ward 5B in San Francisco General Hospital, which was the world's first dedicated inpatient AIDS ward. For more on the history of this ward, see Andrea Milne, "'A Caring Disease': Nursing and Patient Advocacy on the United States' First AIDS Ward," (PhD diss., University of California, Irvine, 2017).

38. Silverman, phone Interview with the author, September 3, 2019; Drew Altman, phone Interview with the author, September 4, 2019.

39. Robert Wood Johnson Foundation, "AIDS Health Services Program."

40. SyteMetrics/McGraw-Hill, Inc., "Executive Summary."

41. US Department of Health and Human Services, "HRSA AIDS Activities," n.d., NGLTF, box 118, folder 26.

42. Green, et al., "The $147,000 Misunderstanding," 82. On the modelling of HRSA's grants on the San Francisco system of care, see US Department of Health and Human Services, *AIDS Service Demonstration Programs: Three Year Report, 1987–1989* (Government Printing Office, 1991).

43. Vincent Mor et al., "Developing AIDS Community Service Consortia," *Health Affairs* 12, no. 1 (Spring 1993): 189.

44. Rich and varied interdisciplinary literature exists on the professionalization and institutionalization of the AIDS service industry in the 1980s. For a few of the most important works on the topic, see Cindy Patton, *Inventing AIDS* (Routledge, 1990); Urvashi Vaid, *Virtual Equality: The Mainstreaming of Gay and Lesbian Liberation* (Knopf Doubleday, 1995); Charles Perrow and Mauro F. Guillén, *The AIDS Disaster: The Failure of Organizations in New York and the Nation* (Yale University Press, 1990); Susan M. Chambré, *Fighting for Our Lives: New York's AIDS Community and the Politics of Disease* (Rutgers University Press, 2006).

45. US Department of Health and Human Services, "AIDS Service Demonstration Programs."

46. Stephen Joseph, "AIDS: A Tale of Two Cities: A Report to the Mayor, October 19, 1987," Edward I. Koch Collection, La Guardia and Wagner Archives, LaGuardia Community College, New York (hereafter EKC), AIDS Subject Files, series 80049–5.

47. Joseph, "AIDS: A Tale of Two Cities."

48. Joseph.

49. Joseph.

50. "Swamped by Surge in AIDS: GMHC Forced to Curtail Caseload," *Outweek*, October 17, 1990, 16. For more on the financial strains on the AIDS service industry in New York City during the late 1980s, see Chambré, *Fighting for Our Lives*, 92–107.

51. City of Dallas, "Recent AIDS Budget Funding History," 1987, Louise Young and Vivienne Armstrong Papers, University of North Texas Special Collections (hereafter LYVA), box 1, folder 35; "Dallas Last in Providing AIDS Funds," *Dallas Times Herald*, September 5, 1988, clipping, LJMC, box 1, folder 3; Vincent Mor et al., *Networking AIDS Services* (University of Chicago Press, 1994), 32–34.

52. "Project Description: AIDS ARMS Network," Dennis Vercher Collection, University of North Texas Special Collections, box 2, folder 36.

53. "AIDS Agencies Short of Cash," *Houston Chronicle*, September 26, 1991, 17; Dennis Vercher, "AIDS Network Director Announces Resignation," *Dallas Voice*, September 6, 1991, 3;9; "AIDS Funds Mismanaged: Network Failed to Pass Along Grants to Agencies," *Dallas Times Herald*, September 25, 1991, clipping, Resource Center LGBT Collection of the University of North Texas Libraries (hereafter RCC), box 506, folder 22; Dennis Vercher, "AIDS Network Narrows Fund Gap," in unknown newspaper, undated clipping in RCC, box 506, folder 22.

54. Dennis Vercher, "AIDS Network's Role Questioned: Government Agencies, Complaining of Poor Oversight, Issue Warnings," *Dallas Voice*, December 6, 1991, 6.

55. "AIDS Funding Agency Director Apologizes for Mismanagement," *Dallas Morning News*, September 26, 1991, clipping, RCC, box 506, folder 22.

56. Between 1982 and 1990, the federal government allocated only 5 percent of its

AIDS budget towards HIV healthcare, with the majority of funding going toward biomedical research, surveillance, and prevention efforts. National Organizations Responding to AIDS, "Testimony on H.R. 4470: The AIDS Prevention Act of 1990," April 19, 1990, Daniel Patrick Moynihan papers, Library of Congress (DPMP), box 1724, folder 2. On the early congressional response to AIDS and the maneuvering of Waxman and Westmoreland, see Mark Carl Rom, "Gay and AIDS: Democratizing Disease?" in *The Politics of Gay Rights*, ed. Craig A. Rimmerman, Kenneth D. Wald, and Clyde Wilcox (University of Chicago Press, 2000), 217–248.

57. On the Helms amendment, see Royles, *To Make the Wounded Whole*, 91–92.

58. "AIDS Action Council: Fact Sheet," n.d., NGLTF, box 128, folder 12. For the role played by the AAC during debates over AIDS legislation in the late 1980s, see Brown, "AIDS and the Politics of Disability in the 1980s," 266–295.

59. In 1986, the GMHC and the AIDS Project Los Angeles established public policy departments to lobby elected officials at the state and federal levels. The SFAF did the same one year later. "Malkin and Ross: GMHC Advocates in Albany," *Volunteer*, May/June 1990, 7; "AIDS and Legislation," *Issues: A Quarterly Publication of AIDS Project Los Angeles* 1, no. 1 (Spring 1987), 3; San Francisco AIDS Foundation, "1987 Annual Report," NGLTF, box 129, folder 14. The vast majority of the initial funding for the AAC also came from these three organizations. AIDS Action Council, "Annual Meeting of the Board of Directors," October 11, 1986, AIDS Action Foundation records, Special Collections Research Center, Gelman Library, George Washington University (hereafter AAFR), box 29, folder 4.

60. Quoted in John-Manuel Andriote, *Victory Deferred: How AIDS Changed Gay Life in America* (University of Chicago Press, 1999), 226. For more on the "degaying" of AIDS, see Vaid, *Virtual Equality*, 74–76.

61. National Organizations Responding to AIDS, "Membership List," April 6, 1989, AAFR, box 9, folder 9.

62. Of the one hundred and forty organizations under NORA's umbrella in 1990, only four were openly gay. Jonathan Broder, "AIDS Lobby A Reckoning Force," *San Francisco Examiner*, May 20, 1990, 1.

63. Quoted in Dick Thompson, "The AIDS Political Machine," *Time*, January 22, 1990, http://content.time.com/time/subscriber/article/0,33009,969229-2,00.html.

64. "National Organizations Responding to AIDS: Fact Sheet," n.d., AAFR, box 9, folder 9.

65. Mathilde Krim, "Remembering Terry: The Ryan White (Care) Act," *American Foundation for AIDS Research Newsletter* 1, no. 4 (January-March 1990); Senate Committee on Labor and Human Resources, "HIV Emergency Relief Grant Program: A Report to Accompany S.2240," April 18, 1990, NGLTF, box 120, folder 48.

66. Ray O'Loughlin, "Congress Rescues Massive AIDS Bill: Confidentiality Guarantee Cut Out; Research Effort Expedited," *Bay Area Reporter*, October 20, 1988, clipping, STP, box 5, folder 17.

67. Quoted in "Omnibus Health Bill," *CQ Almanac*, 1989, 308.

68. On the effects of drugs like AZT and aerosolized pentamidine on the costs of HIV/AIDS treatment, see chapter 2 of this book.

69. Presidential Commission on the Human Immunodeficiency Virus, *Report of the*

Presidential Commission on the Human Immunodeficiency Virus Epidemic (Government Printing Office, 1988), 17.

70. On the insurance industry's efforts to remove PWAs from their rolls in the mid-1980s, see Bell, "Between Private and Public."

71. National Public Health and Hospital Institute, "AIDS Epidemic Causes Severe Financial Drain on Hospitals; Future Rationing of Care Possible, According to Study," August 10, 1989, NGLTF, box 117, folder 39.

72. On the AIDS epidemic and emergency room crisis of the late 1980s, see Melinda Cooper, *Family Values: Between Neoliberalism and the New Social Conservatism* (Zone Books, 2017), 202–203.

73. On the wide pressures faced by public hospitals and emergency rooms in the late 1980s, see Beatrix Hoffman, *Health Care for Some: Rights and Rationing in the United States Since 1930* (University of Chicago Press, 2012), 169–187; Beatrix Hoffman, "Emergency Rooms: The Reluctant Safety Net," in *History and Health Policy in the United States: Putting the Past Back in*, ed. Rosemary A. Stevens, Charles E. Rosenberg, and Lawton R. Burns (Rutgers University Press, 2006), 250–272.

74. Thomas Killip, "Hospitals in New York City: A System under Stress," in *Public and Professional Attitudes toward AIDS Patients*, ed. David E. Rogers and Eli Ginzburg (Routledge, 1989), 76.

75. Bruce Lambert, "Flaws in Health Care System Emerge as Epidemic Rages," *New York Times*, February 8, 1989, A1.

76. In a survey of the twenty-six cities most severely affected by AIDS in early 1990, the US Conference of Mayors bluntly concluded that "local governments are increasingly unable to respond effectively to the health care needs of their citizenry." US Conference of Mayors, "The Impact of AIDS on America's Cities: A 26 City Report," *AIDS Information Exchange* 7, no. 2 (April 1990), 1, STP, box 10, folder 3.

77. *Financing AIDS Early Intervention and Treatment Services: Hearing before the Subcommittee Health and the Environment*, 103rd Cong., 1st Sess., 231 (1990).

78. Michael T. Isbell, "AIDS and Access to Care: Lessons for Health Care Reformers," *Cornell Journal of Law and Public Policy* 3, no. 1 (1993): 40.

79. "AIDS: An Expanding Emergency," *Washington Post*, May 5, 1990, A20; Bob Moos, "AIDS Epidemic Requires Federal Disaster Assistance," *Dallas Morning News*, March 23, 1990, clipping, DPMP, box 1724, folder 7; "Cities Need 'AIDS Disaster' Relief," *Atlanta Constitution*, March 8, 1990, A22.

80. Lambert, "Flaws in Health Care System Emerge as Epidemic Rages."

81. *The American Health Care Crisis: A View from Four Communities*, 101st Cong., 1st Sess. (1990).

82. Tom Sheridan, phone Interview with the author, August 29, 2019.

83. Senate Committee on Labor and Human Resources, "HIV Emergency Relief Grant Program."

84. Sheridan, phone Interview with the author.

85. Senate Committee on Labor and Human Resources, "HIV Emergency Relief Grant Program."

86. Edward M. Kennedy, letter to Senate Committee on Labor and Human Resources, February 1990, NGLTF, box 120, folder 48.

87. National Organizations Responding to AIDS, letter to Senators, March 6, 1990, NGLTF, box 120, folder 49.

88. One memo outlining the lobbying strategy for the passage of the CARE Act put this point explicitly: "San Francisco needs money not for hospital construction, but for outpatient care that reduces costs and helps patients avoid unwanted hospital stays." Memorandum by Chris Collins to Don Francis, Carlton Goodlet, Lee Smith, and Ahimsa Sumchai, February 26, 1990, AIDS Office of the San Francisco Department of Public Health Records (SFH 4), San Francisco History Center, San Francisco Public Library (hereafter AOSFDPH), box 18, folder 38.

89. For the growing role of state and local governments in the allocation of federal grants to nonprofit organizations after the 1960s, see Dunning, *Nonprofit Neighborhoods*, 113–146; Tracy Neumann, "Privatization, Devolution, and Jimmy Carter's National Urban Policy," *Journal of Urban History* 40, no. 2 (March 2014): 283–300.

90. For more on the history of New Federalism, see chapter 1 of this book.

91. For more on the devolutionary features of the CARE Act, see Patricia D. Siplon, "Washington's Response to the AIDS Epidemic," *Policy Studies Journal* 27, no.4 (November 1999): 796–808.

92. Gerry Hinton to Senator Edward Kennedy, April 12, 1990, NGLTF, box 120, folder 49. For other letters in support of the CARE Act from representatives of state and local governments, see Governor Richard F. Celeste (Chairman of Committee on Human Resources, National Governor's Association) to Senator Edward Kennedy, April 4, 1990, NGLTF, box 120, folder 49; John P. Thomas (Executive Director of the Health Committee, National Association of Counties) to Senator Edward Kennedy, March 1, 1990, NGLTF, box 120, folder 49.

93. Cong. Rec., 101st Cong., 2nd Sess., S6211 (1990).

94. Cong. Rec., 101st Cong., 2nd Sess., H3552 (1990).

95. Cong. Rec., 101st Cong., 2nd Sess., S3545 (1990).

96. Sheridan, phone Interview with the author.

97. "Kennedy and Hatch Unveil $600 Million Anti-AIDS Bill," *Salt Lake Tribune*, March 7, 1990, A4.

98. Sheridan, phone Interview with the author.

99. For a small sample of the myriad of letters received by lawmakers from members of NORA in favor of the CARE Act, see the letters contained in NGLTF, box 120, folder 49; DPMP, box 1725, folder 2; J. Roy Rowland Papers, Richard B. Russell Library for Political Research and Studies, University of Georgia Libraries, Athens, Georgia (hereafter JRRP), box 8, folder 11.

100. American Medical Association, "Statement of the American Medical Association on Financing AIDS Health Care," press release, April 19, 1990, DPMP, box 1725, folder 2; American Hospital Association, "Statement of Paul C. Rettig, Executive Vice President, American Hospital Association, Upon the Introduction of the Comprehensive AIDS Resources Emergency Act," press release, March 6, 1990, NGLTF, box 120, folder 49; "Meeting Schedule in Washington D.C.," March 1, 1990, AODPH, box 18, folder 38. For some of the testimony provided by members of NORA in favor of the CARE Act, see *Financing AIDS Early Intervention and Treatment Services*.

101. Pat Christen, letter to AIDS Service Organizations, March 19, 1990, NGLTF,

box 120, folder 48; Pat Christen, letter to AIDS Service Organizations, March 23, 1990, NGLTF, box 120, folder 48.

102. "Comprehensive AIDS Resources Emergency (CARE) Act of 1990 Fact Sheet," n.d., DPMP, box 1724, folder 9.

103. "San Francisco AIDS Foundation and Local Business Leaders Endorse Impact Aid for AIDS Disaster Areas Across the Country," press release, March 19, 1990, NGLTF, box 120, folder 48.

104. Ronald K. Shelp to Daniel Patrick Moynihan, May 1, 1990, DPMP, box 1724, folder 9.

105. National Leadership Coalition on AIDS, "Directory of Member Organizations and Representatives," February 1990, AODPH, box 18, folder 38.

106. "Business Leaders Call for More U.S. AIDS Funds," *Los Angeles Times*, March 30, 1990, clipping, DPMP, box 1724, folder 7; Robert D. Haas, "CEO Breakfast Attendees," April 12, 1990, AODPH, box 19, folder 1.

107. Robert D. Haas to President George H.W. Bush, May 3, 1990, AODPH, box 19, folder 1.

108. "Bush Reluctantly Signs AIDS Measure," *CQ Almanac*, 1991, 582–589.

109. Donovan, *Taking Aim*, 62.

110. Cong. Rec., 101st Cong., 2nd Sess., S6168–86 (1990).

111. Donovan, *Taking Aim*, 63.

112. "Bush Reluctantly Signs AIDS Measure," 587.

113. Sheridan, phone Interview with the author.

114. Trevor Hoppe, *Punishing Disease: HIV and the Criminalization of Sickness* (University of California Press, 2018), 130–131. In the course of my research into the implementation of the CARE Act, I have found no examples of the federal government threatening to withdraw funding from states because they had no HIV criminalization statute on the books.

115. Lawmakers also rejected an amendment offered by Dannemeyer that would have required states to collect the names and addresses of people who tested positive for HIV. The House ultimately approved a substitute amendment that gave the states discretion over whether to make HIV reportable by name to public health agencies. William Dannemeyer to J. Roy Rowland, May 2, 1990, JRRP, box 11, folder 9.

116. "Bush Reluctantly Signs AIDS Measure," 587.

117. Cong. Rec., 101st Cong., 2nd Sess., H3522 (1990).

118. Cong. Rec., 101st Cong., 2nd Sess., S6195 (1990).

119. Cong. Rec., 101st Cong., 2nd Sess., S6195 (1990). For more on Helms's opposition to the CARE Act, see Robert Hunt Ferguson, "Mothers Against Jesse in Congress: Grassroots Maternalism and the Cultural Politics of the AIDS Crisis in North Carolina," *Journal of Southern History* 83, no. 1 (February 2017): 107–140.

120. Memorandum by Tom Sheridan and Donna Richardson to Susan Campbell, Chai Feldblum, Bill Flannagan, Katherine McCarter, Ginny Schubert, and Curt Decker, April 24, 1990, NGLTF, box 120, folder 48; Memorandum by Chris Collins to Lee Smith, March 9, 1990, AODPH, box 18, folder 38; Andrew E. Manatos to Robert Dole, April 26, 1990, AODPH, box 19, folder 1; Memorandum by Chris Collins to Art Agnos, May 1, 1990, AODPH, box 19, folder 1; Sheridan, phone Interview with the author.

121. This connection between the dedication of the CARE Act to Ryan White and the specific effort to overcome Helms's filibuster threat was outlined to me during an interview with NORA's policy director Tom Sheridan. Sheridan, phone Interview with the author.

122. For more on the rhetoric surrounding Ryan White in the 1980s, see Paul M. Renfro, *The Life and Death of Ryan White: AIDS and Inequality in America* (University of North Carolina Press, 2024); Ruth D. Reichard, *Blood and Steel: Ryan White, the AIDS Crisis, and Deindustrialization in Kokomo, Indiana* (McFarland Press, 2021); Watkins-Hayes, *Remaking a Life*, 115–117.

123. Quoted in Paul M. Renfro, "The Poster Child for AIDS Obscured as Much About the Crisis as He Revealed," *Time*, November 30, 2023, https://time.com/6340507/ryan-white-world-aids-day/.

124. For an example of a news report that argued that Ryan White contracted HIV through "no fault of his own," see Richard K. Shull, "Speaking of Ryan White and Two Kinds of Luck," *Indianapolis News*, April 4, 1990, 8.

125. Cong. Rec., 101st Cong., 2nd Sess., S6122 (1990). A content analysis of the congressional debate over the CARE Act revealed that lawmakers mentioned children 41 percent of the time they discussed the subpopulations affected by AIDS, even though they compromised only 1.7 percent of PWAs at the time. Gay men were four times less likely to be mentioned than children. Donovan, *Taking Aim*, 63–65.

126. Debbie Howlett, "Mother Keeps Up Ryan's Fight," *USA Today*, April 27, 1990; Jeanne White, letter to Senators, April 26, 1990, DPMP, box 1724, folder 8.

127. "Bush Reluctantly Signs AIDS Measure," 588.

128. "Bush Reluctantly Signs AIDS Measure," 588.

129. The differences between the House and Senate versions of the law were minimal, and the conference committee had little difficulty in resolving them. "AIDS Resource Act Provisions," *CQ Almanac*, 1990, 584–89, The Bush Administration and the AIDS Crisis: White House Staff and Office files, OA/ID 06980-001, Gale Archives of Sexuality and Gender.

130. White House, "Statement of Administration Policy: H.R. 4785—AIDS Prevention Act of 1990," June 12, 1990, Bush Administration and the AIDS Crisis: White House Staff and Office files, OA/ID 04807-015.

131. "Bush Reluctantly Signs AIDS Measure," 589.

Chapter 6: Public Health Divided

1. "Non-Medicaid Funds for HIV Patient Care," *Intergovernmental AIDS Reports* 2, no. 4 (October-November 1989), 1–5.

2. Kaiser Family Foundation, "Trends in U.S. Government Funding for HIV/AIDS: Fiscal Years 1981 to 2004," KFF, March 2004, https://www.kff.org/wp-content/uploads/2013/01/issue-brief-trends-in-u-s-government-funding-for-hiv-aids-fiscal-years-1981-to-2004.pdf.

3. Philip R. Lee (Director, U.S. Public Health Services), "Written Testimony: Ryan White CARE Act Reauthorization before the Senate Committee on Labor and Human Resources," February 22, 1995, Vivent Health Records, 1985–2019, University

of Wisconsin-Milwaukee Libraries (hereafter VHR), Subseries: Federal Government: 1990–1999, box 3, folder 7.

4. From a research standpoint, these three localities also left a sizeable paper trail of the various funding disputes over the CARE Act while many other places contained only sparse documentation on the law's implementation. Archival holdings in the University of North Texas special collections, the Harris County Archives, and the George Washington special collections contained reams of useful material: financial records of AIDS service organizations, grant applications, minutes of planning council meetings, newspaper clippings, and correspondence with federal administrators.

5. Julian K. Tolver, "Study Highlights Funding Disparity," *Urban Times*, October 1993, clipping, Jim Graham Papers, Special Collections Research Center, George Washington University (hereafter JGP), series 1, subseries 3, box 6, folder 2.

6. Robert J. Buchanan, "Ryan White CARE Act and Eligible Metropolitan Areas," *Health Care Finance Review* 23, no. 4 (Summer 2002): 150.

7. Robert J. Buchanan, "HIV Consortia Services Funded by Title II of the Ryan White CARE Act: A Survey of the States," *AIDS and Public Policy Journal* 11, no. 3 (Fall 1996): 129.

8. Buchanan, "HIV Consortia Services Funded by Title II of the Ryan White CARE Act," 130–133.

9. Office of Inspector General, *The Ryan White CARE Act: Consortia Activities* (Department of Health and Human Services, 1994).

10. Health Resources and Services Administration, HIV Services Division, "Site Visit Report: State of California Title II Program," June 9–10, 1994, Public Health and Environmental Services Records, Harris County Archives, Houston, Texas (hereafter PHESR), box 2181, folder: "HRSA Andy Kruzich (Correspondence)."

11. The CARE Act permitted state governments to use federal funds for four different kinds of activity: the establishment of HIV consortia for the coordination of outpatient care, the subsidizing of health insurance for HIV-positive people, the purchasing of effective drug therapies, and the direct funding of home-based care services.

12. Office of Inspector General, "The Ryan White CARE Act," B2.

13. On the history of gay rights activism in Dallas and Houston, see Whitney Cox, "Trouble at the 'Crossroads': Divisions over the Use of Religious Symbols as AIDS Memorials in Houston, 1991," *Journal of the History of Sexuality* 29, no. 2 (May 2020): 162–186; John D. Goins, "Confronting Itself: The AIDS Crisis and the LGBT Community in Houston" (PhD diss., University of Houston, 2014); Scott De Orio, "The Invention of Bad Gay Sex: Texas and the Creation of a Criminal Underclass of Gay People," *Journal of the History of Sexuality* 26, no. 1 (January 2017): 53–87.

14. Wesley G. Phelps, "The Politics of Queer Disidentification and the Limits of Neoliberalism in the Struggle for Gay and Lesbian Equality in Houston," *Journal of Southern History* 84, no. 2 (2018): 311–348; Andrew H. Whittemore, "The Dallas Way: Property, Politics, and Assimilation," in *Planning and LGBTQ Communities: The Need for Inclusive Queer Spaces*, ed. Petra L. Doan (Routledge, 2015), 39–55; Joshua Hollands, "Work and Sexuality in the Sunbelt: Homophobic Workplace Discrimination in the US South and Southwest, 1970 to the Present" (PhD diss., University College London, 2019), 73–77.

15. "Dallas Last in Providing AIDS Funds," *Dallas Times Herald*, September 5, 1988,

clipping, Linda Jebavy Mitchell Collection, University of North Texas Special Collections (hereafter LJMC), box 1, folder 3.

16. Gregory S. Thielemann et al., "The Ryan White Act in Dallas," *Policy Studies Journal* 27, no. 4 (November 1999), 818–819.

17. Dallas Gay Political Coalition, "DGPC Election News," November 1986, Louise Young and Vivienne Armstrong Papers, University of North Texas Special Collections (hereafter LYVA), box 1, folder 38; Donald Maison, phone Interview with the author, September 15, 2019.

18. Vivienne Armstrong and Al Calkin, "Election Alert: The Political Action Committee of the Lesbian/Gay Political Coalition of Dallas," 1986, LYVA, box 1, folder 31.

19. Gregory S. Thielemann and Joseph Stewart Jr., "A Demand-Side Perspective on the Importance of Representative Bureaucracy: AIDS, Ethnicity, Gender, and Sexual Orientation," *Public Administration Review* 56, no. 2 (March-April 1996): 170.

20. Catalina Camia, "Board Is Named to Allocate Funds for Fighting AIDS," *Dallas Morning News*, December 21, 1990, clipping, Resource Center LGBT Collection of the University of North Texas Libraries (hereafter RCC), box 49, folder 47; "Member List: HIV Planning Council Composition," n.d., Dennis Vercher Collection, University of North Texas Special Collections (hereafter DVC), box 1, folder 61.

21. Wolfgang Bielefeld and Richard Scotch, "Institutionalizing AIDS: Policy, Institutional Culture, and the Response to the HIV Epidemic in Dallas," *Research in Social Policy* 4 (1996): 49.

22. H.B. 2138 Criminal Jurisprudence Committee transcripts, April 19, 1983, Texas Human Rights Foundation Records, Dolph Briscoe Center for American History, University of Texas at Austin, Box 4B38, folder: "HB 2138."

23. H.B. 2138 Criminal Jurisprudence Committee transcripts; "New Antigay Sex Bill Dead, for Now, in Texas Legislature," *Advocate*, July 21, 1983.

24. Quoted in Camia, "Board Is Named to Allocate Funds for Fighting AIDS."

25. Bruce Monroe to Lee F. Jackson, n.d., letter reprinted in *Dallas Voice*, January 4, 1991, 13.

26. "Hot Tea," *This Week in Texas*, January 4–10, 1991, 49.

27. Michael Milliken, "And the Beat Goes On," *AIDS Update*, July 1991, 1, clipping, LJMC, box 8, folder 2; "County Proceeds with Care Allocations," *Dallas Voice*, July 5, 1991, clipping, RCC, box 49, folder 34; "Allocation of AIDS Funds Assailed," *Dallas Morning News*, June 20, 1991, 34A, clipping, RCC, box 49, folder 34; Kris Mullen, "AIDS Funding Disputed: Two Large Care Groups Call Panel Homophobic," *Dallas Times Herald*, June 20, 1991, RCC, box 49, folder 34.

28. Michael J. Witkowski to Lee F. Jackson, June 26, 1992, DVC, box 1, folder 42; Lee F. Jackson to Don Maison, July 6, 1992, DVC, box 1, folder 42; Thielemann et al., "The Ryan White Act in Dallas."

29. New York City HIV Health and Human Services Planning Council, "HIV Planning Composition," 1991, Gay Men's Health Crisis records, Manuscripts and Archives Division, New York Public Library (hereafter GMHC), box 353, folder 12.

30. New York City Mayor's Press Office, "Ronald Johnson, City Coordinator for AIDS Policy Received Harlem Life Award," NYC.gov, press release, April 11, 1997, http://www.nyc.gov/html/om/html/97/sp185-97.html.

31. Pat Burke, "County Backs More HIV Members for CARE Act Planning Council," *Update*, February 20, 1991, A7; "Title I Planning Council Membership Roster," 1992, AIDS Office of the San Francisco Department of Public Health Records, San Francisco History Center, San Francisco Public Library, box 29, folder 20; "Minutes of the Meeting of the Boston Ryan White CARE Act Title I Planning Council," June 8, 1993, Boston AIDS Consortium Records, Special Collections and University Archives, University of Massachusetts Amherst Libraries (hereafter BACR), box 2, folder 1; G. Stephen Bowen, "First Year of AIDS Service Delivery Under Title I of the Ryan White CARE Act," *Public Health Reports* 107, no.5 (September-October 1992): 491–499.

32. Division of HIV Services, Health Resources and Services Administration, "Supplement to Application Guidance for Title I HIV Emergency Relief Program: Questions and Answers," 1991, GMHC, box 353, folder 14; Memorandum by Helen Fox to Maurice Jones, John Paul Barnich, Euegene Harrington, John Lenore, and Luis Fuentes, January 15, 1993, Charles Henley Papers, Harris County Archives, Houston, Texas (hereafter CHP), folder: "AIDS Alliance, Ryan White Funding—Memos, Faxes, Correspondence"; Burke, "County Backs More HIV Members for CARE Act Planning Council"; National Association of People with AIDS, "Policy Statement on the Reauthorization of the Ryan White CARE Act," July 1994, VHR, subseries: Federal Government: 1990–1999, box 3, folder 4.

33. Health Resources and Services Administration, HIV Services Division, "Participation of People with HIV Disease on Title I HIV Health Services Planning Councils," November 1994, PHESR, box 2181, folder: "HRSA Correspondence, 1994"; Scott Mackey, "Dallas Struggles with Policy Urging Greater HIV-Positive Representation," *Dallas Voice*, December 2, 1994, 7.

34. Lee, "Written Testimony."

35. Thielemann et al., "The Ryan White Act in Dallas," 824.

36. Mackey, "Dallas Struggles with Policy Urging Greater HIV-Positive Representation"; Dallas Eligible Metropolitan Area HIV Health Services Planning Council, "Application for Comprehensive AIDS Resources Emergency Act—Title I Formula and Supplemental Funding," September 30, 1999, https://dallascounty.civicweb.net/document/208806/.

37. Thielemann et al., "The Ryan White Act in Dallas," 824.

38. Thielemann et al.

39. Martha M. McKinney, "Consortium Approaches to the Delivery of HIV Services Under the Ryan White CARE Act," *AIDS and Public Policy Journal* 8, no. 3 (Fall 1993): 115–116.

40. Ruth Sorelle, "New AIDS Alliance Splinters at the Seams: Repercussions Seen as Being Far-Reaching," *Houston Chronicle*, January 24, 1993, clipping, CHP, folder: "AIDS Alliance, Ryan White Funding—Newspaper Clippings."

41. Ruth Sorelle, "Plan Seeks to Coordinate AIDS Actions," *Houston Chronicle*, October 6, 1988, 1; Sorelle, "New AIDS Alliance Splinters at the Seams"; Greater Houston AIDS Alliance, "Board of Directors Membership Roster," PHESR, box 2184, folder: "GHAA General."

42. "AIDS Panel Elects Seven," *Houston Chronicle*, January 17, 1989, 18.

43. "Bylaws of Greater Houston AIDS Alliance, Inc.," July 19, 1991, PHESR, box 2184, folder: "GHAA Minutes."

44. Sorelle, "New AIDS Alliance Splinters at the Seams"; Gene Harrington, "The New Epidemic: Takeover of GHAA Client Files by Harris County Creates an Atmosphere of Intimidation," *This Week in Texas*, October 16–22, 1992, 45; Greater Houston AIDS Alliance, "Annual Board of Directors Meeting," February 6, 1992, PHESR, box 2184, folder: "GHAA Minutes"; Greater Houston AIDS Alliance, "Boards of Director Meeting," December 19, 1991, PHESR, box 2184, folder: "GHAA Minutes."

45. Ruth Sorelle, "AIDS Alliance Ignores Lindsay's Warning to Cut Quarrelling," *Houston Chronicle*, July 10, 1992, 25.

46. Andrea D. Greene, "Add Minorities to AIDS Panel, Critics Say," *Houston Chronicle*, clipping, CHP, folder: "AIDS Alliance, Ryan White Funding—Newspaper Clippings"; Sheri Cohen Darbonne, "County Judge Jon Lindsay Pulls the Plug on Greater Houston AIDS Alliance," *New Voice*, July 24—30, 3.

47. Memorandum by Ronald B. Dear to Maurice Jones, February 10, 1993, PHESR, box 2184, folder: "GHAA General"; Harris County, Texas v. Greater Houston AIDS Alliance, Inc, No. 92-55636, District Court of Harris County, 133rd Judicial District, December 21, 1992, PHESR, box 2184, folder: "GHAA General"; Craig Washington to Jon Lindsay, September 15, 1992, CHP, folder: "AIDS Alliance, Ryan White Funding—Memos, Faxes, Correspondence."

48. Lisa Teachey, "AIDS Activists Decry Files Decision: Group Blasts Lindsay as Traffic Blocked on Westheimer," *Houston Chronicle*, September 28, 1992, 9.

49. "Two Gay Rights Activists Arrested," *Houston Chronicle*, July 25, 1992, 13; "New Clinic, Renewed Protest," *Houston Chronicle*, August 1, 1992, 33; Sheri Cohen Darbonne, "Two Queer Nation Demonstrators Arrested in Separate Incidents in July," *New Voice*, July 31–August 6, 1992, 6; Sheri Cohen Darbonne, "Montrose Clinic Breaks Ground for New Facility; Guest Speaker Protested," *New Voice*, August 7–13, 1992, 1; Memorandum by ACT UP/Gulf Coast to Houston Region HIV Case Managers, January 13, 1993, CHP, folder: "AIDS Alliance, Ryan White Funding—Memos, Faxes, Correspondence."

50. Memorandum by Fox.

51. Andrea Greene, "U.S. Health Department to Review AIDS Dispute: Lock Agencies Bickering over Services," *Houston Chronicle*, March 27, 1993, 26; "Inquiry into AIDS Funding Complete," *Houston Chronicle*, March 31, 1993, 17; Thomas Hyslop to Helen Fox, April 29, 1993, CHP, Folder: "AIDS Alliance, Ryan White Funding—Memos, Faxes, Correspondence."

52. Eric Goosby to Judge Lindsay, April 12, 1993, PHESR, Box 2181, Folder: "HRSA Correspondence"; Health Resources and Services Administration, HIV Services Division, "Houston Metropolitan Area: Title I Visit," March 29–30, 1993, PHESR, Box 2181, Folder: "HRSA Correspondence"; Ruth Sorelle, "Changes Urged in Operations of AIDS Panel," *Houston Chronicle*, April 16, 1993, 25.

53. Sorelle, "Changes Urged in Operations of AIDS Panel."

54. Sue Cooper to Eric Goosby, July 16, 1993, PHESR, Box 2181, Folder: "HRSA Eric Goosby (Correspondence)"; Lane Lewis to Eric Goosby, July 13, 1993, PHESR, Box 2181, Folder: "HRSA Eric Goosby (Correspondence)"; Eda Valero-Figueira to Mary Ann DePoe, May 28, 1993, PHESR, Box 2181, Folder: "HRSA Correspondence"; Health Resources and Services Administration, HIV Services Division, "Site Visit Report: Houston EMA," August 3–5, 1994, PHESR, Box 2181, Folder: "HRSA Andy Kruzich (Correspondence)."

55. Health Resources and Services Administration, HIV Services Division, "Site Visit Report: Houston EMA," April 6–8, PHESR, Box 2181, Folder: "HRSA Site Visit 1994."

56. Greater Houston Ryan White Planning Council, "Roster of the FY Title I Planning Council Members," 1999, Ryan White Planning Council Records, Harris County Archives, Houston [hereafter RWPCR], Folder: "Application for FY 2000 Ryan White Title 1 Formula and Supplemental Funds."

57. Memorandum by Fox; Thielemann et al., "The Ryan White Act in Dallas," 823; Eda Valero-Figueira to Mary Ann DePoe; Health Resources and Services Administration, HIV Services Division, "HIV Services Planning Council," June 25, 1993, PHESR, box 2181, folder: "HRSA Correspondence."

58. Office of Inspector General, "Audit of the Ryan White Comprehensive AIDS Resources Emergency Act of 1990, Title II, Administered by the Health Resources and Services Administration" (Department of Health and Human Services, 1997), 8; Health Resources and Services Administration, "Comments on the OIG Report, 'Audit of the Ryan White Comprehensive AIDS Resources Emergency Act of 1990, Title II, Administered by the Health Resources and Services Administration,'" accessed May 23, 2022, https://oig.hhs.gov/oas/reports/region1/19701500.pdf.

59. Office of Inspector General, "Audit of the Ryan White Comprehensive AIDS Resources Emergency Act of 1990, Title II Administered by the State of Connecticut" (Department of Health and Human Services, 1996), 6–12.

60. On the links between residential segregation, race, and the AIDS service industry, see Dan Royles, *To Make the Wounded Whole: African American Responses to HIV/AIDS* (University of North Carolina Press, 2020), 30–69; Timothy Stewart-Winter, "AIDS and the Urban Crisis: Stigma, Cost and the Persistence of Racism in Chicago, 1981–1996," in *Beyond the Politics of the Closet: Gay Rights and the American State Since the 1970s*, ed. Jonathan Bell (University of Pennsylvania Press, 2020); Jennifer Brier, *Infectious Ideas: U.S. Political Responses to the AIDS Crisis* (University of North Carolina Press, 2009), 45–77; Darius Bost, "At the Club: Locating Early Black Gay AIDS Activism in Washington, D.C.," *Occasion* 8 (August 31, 2015): 1–9.

61. Margaret Engel, "District Boosts AIDS Budget to $889,000," *Washington Post*, November 16, 1985, 6.

62. On the early outreach efforts of Whitman-Walker, see Bost, "At the Club," 5–6.

63. Quoted in Bost, 5.

64. Lisa M. Keen, "First-of-a-Kind AIDS Forum for Black Gays Held at ClubHouse," *Washington Blade*, September 30, 1983, 17; Margaret Engel, "AIDS Cases Multiplying in the Area," *Washington Post*, June 13, 1985, 7.

65. Quoted in Rick Harding, "Black Gay Leaders Search for a Way to Help the Ailing," *Washington Blade*, February 28, 1986, 3.

66. Quoted in Harding, "Black Gay Leaders Search for a Way to Help the Ailing." For more examples of Black AIDS activists critiquing the Whitman-Walker Clinic in the mid- to late 1980s, see Sandra G. Boodman, "AIDS Spreading Faster Among D.C. Blacks," *Washington Post*, August 8, 1988, D1; Lawrence Washington, "Is there Fairness?" *Washington Blade*, October 5, 1984, 27.

67. Amy Goldstein, "Audit Faults D.C. Payments to AIDS Clinic," *Washington Post*, January 20, 1994, https://www.washingtonpost.com/archive/local/1994/01/20/audit-faults-dc-payments-to-aids-clinic/cdbc0cb6-fe2d-4cd7-b8a2-71f458d30632/.

68. Bowen, "First Year of AIDS Service Delivery Under Title I of the Ryan White CARE Act," 494; "Care Grant Given," *Baltimore Gay Newspaper*, July 5, 1991, 27.

69. Goldstein, "Audit Faults D.C. Payments to AIDS Clinic."

70. John Cloud, "Living, for the Moment," *Washington City Paper*, August 16, 1996, https://washingtoncitypaper.com/article/286865/living-for-the-moment/.

71. Bowen, "First Year of AIDS Service Delivery Under Title I of the Ryan White CARE Act," 494; Alonzo Fair, "The Funding Disparity Facing Communities of Color with AIDS," February 17, 1994, testimony before the Washington, DC, Regional Planning Council, JGP, series 1, subseries 3, box 6, folder 2; Matthew Corey, "Some 'Familiar Faces' at Forum," *Washington Blade*, November 19, 1993, 9.

72. Christopher H. Bates to Jim Graham, July 19, 1994, JGP, series 1, subseries 3, box 9, folder 2; Judith Weinraub, "The Politics of AIDS," *Washington Post*, November 29, 1993, https://www.washingtonpost.com/archive/lifestyle/1993/11/29/the-politics-of-aids/0691aec3-d9d6-4d58-8e7e-f16013242bea/.

73. Amy Goldstein, "AIDS Groups Go Head-to-Head With Whitman-Walker," *Washington Post*, August 25, 1993, https://www.washingtonpost.com/archive/local/1993/08/25/aids-groups-go-head-to-head-with-whitman-walker/7ac53dcd-aeb5-4c12-85dd-2a861a7561f0/.

74. Lou Chibbaro Jr., "New Coalition Hopes to Secure Key AIDS Funds," *Washington Blade*, August 27, 1993, 1, 21.

75. Alonzo Fair to Jim Graham, August 27, 1993, JGP, series 1, subseries 3, box 6, folder 2.

76. On residential segregation and the Anacostia River, see Ashanté M. Reese, *Black Food Geographies: Race, Self-Reliance, and Food Access in Washington D.C.* (University of North Carolina Press, 2019), 47–48; Chris Myers Asch and George Derek Musgrove, *Chocolate City: A History of Race and Democracy in the Nation's Capital* (University of North Carolina Press, 2017), 5.

77. Fair, "The Funding Disparity Facing Communities of Color with AIDS"; Tolver, "Study Highlights Funding Disparity."

78. Fair, "The Funding Disparity Facing Communities of Color with AIDS"; Anne Dievler, "The Politics of Public Health Policy in an Urban Bureaucracy: HIV Prevention, Tuberculosis Control, and Immunization Programs in Washington, D.C." (PhD diss., John Hopkins University, 1996), 86–89; Lou Chibbaro Jr., "Activists: AIDS Funding Biased Against Minorities," *Washington Blade*, September 24, 1993, 25.

79. Richard Rosendall, "No Tax Dollars for Bigots: Testimony Before the Committee on Human Services, Council of the District of Columbia," WordPress, November 8, 1993, http://www.glaa.org/archive/1993/notaxdollarsforbigots1108.shtml. See also Richard Rosendall, "Alliances that Can 'Sabotage' the Cause," *Washington Blade*, September 10, 1993, 40.

80. Memorandum by Hank Carde to Jim Graham, n.d., JGP, series 1, subseries 3, box 6, folder 2; Hamil R. Harris, "Clinic Won't Fire Official Who Falsified Resume," *Washington Post*, October 14, 1993, 6; Shaun Sutner, "Whitman-Walker to Open AIDS Outreach Center in Southeast," *Washington Post*, November 26, 1992, 4.

81. Gregory C. Hutchings, "An Alliance to Defy and Conquer AIDS," *Washington Blade*, September 10, 1993, 41; Julian K. Tolver, "Fighting for African Americans' Sur-

vival," in unknown newspaper, n.d., JGP, series 1, subseries 3, box 6, folder 2; Alvin Peabody, "Minority AIDS Group Protest D.C. Contract," in unknown newspaper, March 17, 1994, JGP, series 1, subseries 3, box 6, folder 2; Alonzo Fair to Jim Graham, August 27, 1993, JGP, series 1, subseries 3, box 6, folder 2.

82. Quoted in "Fighting AIDS in the Capital: Clinic Director Accused of Taking Racist Attitude with Black Patients," *Town Talk*, November 29, 1993, 6.

83. Amy Goldstein, "Black Gays in New D.C. AIDS Coalition Wary About Muslim Doctor's Role," *Washington Post*, September 29, 1993, 8.

84. Abdul Alim Muhammad, "A.I.D.S.: Widespread Death—Clearing the Deck for a New World Order," *Final Call*, February 14, 1985, 28. For more on Muhammad's and the Nation of Islam's response to the AIDS epidemic, see Royles, *To Make the Wounded Whole*, 143–183.

85. Lou Chibbaro Jr., "Black Gays Debate Abundant Life Role in AIDS Education," *Washington Blade*, September 3, 1993, 1, 17, 19; Goldstein, "Black Gays in New D.C. AIDS Coalition Wary About Muslim Doctor's Role"; Royles, *To Make the Wounded Whole*, 177.

86. Quoted in Goldstein, "Black Gays in New D.C. AIDS Coalition Wary about Muslim Doctor's Role."

87. Goldstein; Lou Chibbaro Jr., "Coalition Clashes over Support for AIDS Group," *Washington Blade*, October 1, 1993, 1, 10.

88. Lisa Keen, "Clinic Awarded $1 Million City AIDS Contract," *Washington Blade*, June 17, 1994, 1, 27; Amy Goldstein, "City Giving AIDS Clinic $1.2 Million," *Washington Post*, June 16, 1994, https://www.washingtonpost.com/archive/local/1994/06/16/city-giving-aids-clinic-12-million/c5c5dbcd-2f3c-46d5-9398-bb4d7afd8ced/.

89. Whitman Walker continued to expand rapidly until 2005 when financial troubles forced it to lay off a large number of staff members. In the 2010s, the clinic gradually recovered from its fiscal woes, allowing it to open several new locations in the city and serve approximately fifteen thousand patients a year. Anne Hull, "Whitman-Walker, a Longtime Front in AIDS War, Moves Out," *Washington Post*, December 16, 2008, https://www.washingtonpost.com/wp-dyn/content/article/2008/12/15/AR2008121503352.html?wprss=rss_nation.

90. "Whitman-Walker's Woes," *Washington Post*, June 11, 2005, https://www.washingtonpost.com/archive/opinions/2005/06/11/whitman-walkers-woes/e63f1a59-898f-4d05-9b82-aa1c0ff15afc/.

91. Statistics calculated using data from a *Washington Post* investigation of the AIDS service industry in the District of Colombia. "Map: A Closer Look at AIDS Groups," *Washington Post*, December 13, 2009, https://www.washingtonpost.com/wp-srv/special/metro/aids-funding/map.html.

92. "Map: A Closer Look at AIDS Groups." For more on the disparities between the capacity of nonprofit organizations on the east and west sides of the Anacostia, see Eric C. Twombly, Jennifer Claire Auer, and Kanisha Bond, "Community Anchors East of the River: An Analysis of the Charitable Infrastructure in Wards 7 and 8 in Washington, DC," Urban Institute, January 2006, http://webarchive.urban.org/UploadedPDF/411275_community_anchors.pdf.

93. Debbie Cenziper, "D.C. AIDS Funding Shifted from Needy Neighborhoods,"

Washington Post, December 13, 2009, https://www.washingtonpost.com/wp-dyn/content/article/2009/12/12/AR2009121202900.html.

94. Hortensia Amaro and Carol Hardy-Fanta, "Impact of Ryan White CARE Act Title on Capacity Building in Latino Community Based Organizations: Findings from a Study of Two Cities," August 1995, AIDS Action Foundation records, Special Collections Research Center, Gelman Library, George Washington University, box 47, folder 15.

95. Amaro and Hardy-Fanta, "Impact of Ryan White CARE Act Title on Capacity Building in Latino Community Based Organizations."

96. Amaro and Hardy-Fanta; Charles Henley to Eda Valero Figueira, November 25, 1992, PHESR, box 2181, folder: "HRSA Eda/Glenna/Libby."

97. Statistics for Chicago's 2000 census tracts calculated using the "Create a Report" function in Social Explorer, accessed May 17, 2022, https://www.socialexplorer.com/a9676d974c/explore.

98. On the differing administrative capacities of AIDS service organizations located on Chicago's North and South Sides, see the United Conference of Mayors, "Assessing the HIV-Prevention Needs of Gay and Bisexual Men of Color," 1993, Asian/Pacific AIDS Coalition records, GLBT Historical Society, San Francisco, California (hereafter APAC), box 5, folder 9.

99. Stewart-Winter, *Queer Clout*, 205.

100. Curtis R. Winkle and Andréa Carr, with the assistance of Shyamala Parameswaran, "Evaluation of Ryan White CARE Act Title I as Implemented in Chicago, Illinois," August 12, 1994, 46, ACT UP Chicago Records, Hanna Holborn Gray Special Collections Research Center, University of Chicago Library, box 4, folder 4. For more on residential segregation and the AIDS service industry in Chicago, see Stewart-Winter, "AIDS and the Urban Crisis."

101. Government Accountability Office, "Revising Ryan White Funding Formulas" (GAO, 1996), 4. These figures have been adjusted to take into account the varying costs of AIDS healthcare in different states.

102. Campaign for Fairness, "Ryan White CARE Act Reauthorization," n.d., VHR, subseries: Federal Government: 1990–1999, box 3, folder 3; Campaign for Fairness, "Comparison of Programs Funded Through the Ryan White CARE Act in San Francisco, CA and Milwaukee, WI," n.d., VHR, subseries: Federal Government: 1990–1999, box 3, folder 3; Department of Health and Human Services, "Spending Patterns in Ryan White CARE Act Title I EMAs: Fiscal Year 1992," July 1994, PHESR, box 2181, folder: "HRSA Correspondence, 1994."

103. AIDS Resource Center of Wisconsin, "Ryan White CARE Act Reauthorization: A Proposal for Equity in Per Capita AIDS Funding," April 29, 1994, VHR, subseries: Federal Government: 1990–1999, box 3, folder 2. For more on the funding inequities embedded into the CARE Act, see Patricia D. Siplon, *AIDS and the Policy Struggle in the United States* (Georgetown University Press, 2002), 100–101.

104. AIDS Resource Center of Wisconsin, "Ryan White CARE Act Reauthorization."

105. Cities Advocating Emergency AIDS Relief, "Talking Points: Ryan White CARE Act, Title I," May 1994, VHR, subseries: Federal Government: 1990–1999, box 3, folder 4.

106. Policy feedback theory posits that previously enacted public policies reshape politics and political behavior partly by providing incentives for the creation of new in-

terest groups or the reallocation of resources within existing ones. For an introduction to the theory, see Suzanne Mettler and Mallory SoRelle, "Policy Feedback Theory," in *Theories of the Policy Process*, 3rd ed., ed. Christopher M. Weible and Paul A. Sabatier (Routledge, 2014), 151–182.

107. On policy feedback and the CARE Act, see Siplon, *AIDS and the Policy Struggle in the United States*, 100–101.

108. Campaign for Fairness, "Summary of the Campaign for Fairness in Ryan White CARE Act Funding," n.d., VHR, subseries: Federal Government: 1990–1999, box 3, folder 8.

109. Wisconsin AIDS Service Organizations to Senator Russell Feingold, July 9, 1994, VHR, subseries: Federal Government: 1990–1999, box 3, folder 3.

110. Elinor Burkett, *The Gravest Show on Earth: America in the Age of AIDS* (Houghton Mifflin, 1995), 141–143.

111. Peaches Bass (Executive Director, Maine AIDS Alliance) to Mike Gifford (AIDS Resource Center of Wisconsin), April 26, 1994, VHR, subseries: Federal Government: 1990–1999, box 3, folder 2; Erica Garfin (Executive Director, Vermont AIDS Council) to Mike Gifford, April 21, 1994, VHR, subseries: Federal Government: 1990–1999, box 3, folder 2; Lynette L. Werner (President, Wyoming AIDS Project) to Mike Gifford, April 29, 1994, VHR, subseries: Federal Government: 1990–1999, box 3, folder 2.

112. Pat Christen to Mario Cooper, June 13, 1995, VHR, subseries: Federal Government: 1990–1999, box 4, folder 1.

113. Sheridan Group, "Proposal to Cities Advocating Emergency AIDS Relief," n.d., JMP James F. (Jim) Martin Papers, Richard B. Russell Library for Political Research and Studies, University of Georgia Libraries, Athens, Georgia, series 4: Disability and Health Advocacy, 1977–2008, box 3, folder 2; Open Secrets, "Lobbyists Representing Cities Advocating Emergency AIDS Relief," 1999, https://www.opensecrets.org/Lobby/clientlbs.php?id=F219534&year=1999.

114. Burkett, *The Gravest Show on Earth*, 163.

115. On the "Republican Revolution," see Julian E. Zelizer, *Burning Down the House: Newt Gingrich and the Rise of the New Republican Party* (Penguin, 2021).

116. "New Republican Controlled Congress Brings Uncertainty to AIDS Funding: More Equitable Distribution of Funds Gaining Support," in unknown newspaper, January 19, 1995, VHR, subseries: Federal Government: 1990–1999, box 3, folder 6.

117. "New Republican Controlled Congress Brings Uncertainty to AIDS Funding."

118. "CFF Conference Call," December 8, 1994, VHR, subseries: Federal Government: 1990–1999, box 3, folder 6; Campaign for Fairness, "Proposal for Title II Targeted Access to Care Grants," March 14, 1995, VHR, subseries: Federal Government: 1990–1999, box 3, folder 8; Doug Nelson to Senator Nancy Kassebaum, August 7, 1995, VHR, subseries: Federal Government: 1990–1999, box 4, folder 2.

119. Mark Barnes, "Cooperation Needed to Pass Ryan White Bill," *Washington Blade*, April 14, 1995, 45.

120. "The Ryan White Care Reauthorization Act of 1995: Key Components," March 26, 1995, VHR, subseries: Federal Government: 1990–1999, box 3, folder 8.

121. Quoted in David Schimke, "Blood Money," *Twin Cities Reader*, February 8–14, 1995, VHR, subseries: Federal Government: 1990–1999, box 3, folder 7.

122. Memorandum by Mark Barnes and Christine Lubinski to Marty Ross, Jim Wade,

Michael Iskowitz, Melody Harned, and Kay Holcombe, September 6, 1995, VHR, subseries: Federal Government: 1990–1999, box 4, folder 2; Campaign for Fairness, "Washington Update," October 5, 1995, VHR, subseries: Federal Government: 1990–1999, box 4, folder 2. For more on the legislative debate over the reauthorization of the CARE Act in 1995, see Siplon, *AIDS and the Policy Struggle in the United States*, 100–102.

123. Government Accountability Office, "Ryan White CARE Act: Improved Oversight Needed to Ensure AIDS Drug Assistance Programs Obtain Best Prices for Drugs" (GAO, 2006), 13.

124. Government Accountability Office, "Ryan White CARE Act: Opportunities to Enhance Funding Equity" (GAO, 2000), 2.

125. Southern AIDS Coalition, "Southern States Manifesto: Update 2008, HIV/AIDS and Sexually Transmitted Diseases in the South," UC Berkeley Law, 2008, https://www.law.berkeley.edu/files/bccj/SouthernStatesManifesto_2008-1.pdf.

126. Centers for Disease Control and Prevention, "HIV in the Southern United States," CDC, May 2016, https://www.cdc.gov/hiv/pdf/policies/cdc-hiv-in-the-south-issue-brief.pdf, accessed April 24, 2022.

127. Southern AIDS Coalition, "Southern States Manifesto."

128. Shawn Zeller, "Rural Tug-of-War over AIDS Law," *CQ Weekly*, May 8, 2006, 1202.

129. Alex Wayne, "Changing Face of AIDS a Legislative Dilemma," *CQ Weekly*, October 23, 2006, 2799–2800.

130. On the disproportionate impact of HIV/AIDS on Black Americans in the South, see Linda Villarosa, "America's Hidden HIV Epidemic," *New York Times*, June 6, 2017, https://www.nytimes.com/2017/06/06/magazine/americas-hidden-hiv-epidemic.html; Royles, *To Make the Wounded Whole*, 261–296; Stephen J. Inrig, *North Carolina and the Problem of AIDS: Advocacy, Politics, and Race in the South* (University of North Carolina Press, 2011), 58–85.

131. Stephen J. Inrig, "HIV/AIDS," in *The New Encyclopedia of Southern Culture*, vol. 22: *Science and Medicine*, ed. James G. Thomas Jr. and Charles Reagan Wilson (University of North Carolina Press, 2006), 209.

132. Kaiser Family Foundation, "An Overview of HIV/AIDS in Black America," KFF, July 2007, https://www.kff.org/wp-content/uploads/2013/01/7660.pdf.

133. Alyson O'Daniel, *Holding On: African American Women Surviving HIV/AIDS* (University of Nebraska Press, 2016), 32.

134. National Alliance of State and Territorial AIDS Directors, Henry J. Kaiser Family Foundation, and the AIDS Treatment Data Network, "National ADAP Monitoring Report: Annual Report," KFF, May 2004, https://www.kff.org/wp-content/uploads/2013/01/national-adap-monitoring-project-2004-annual-report.pdf.

135. Government Accountability Office, "Ryan White CARE Act," 20–21.

136. Government Accountability Office, 11.

137. Government Accountability Office, 15–16.

138. Government Accountability Office. In this statistic, the South encompasses ten states: Alabama, Arkansas, Florida, Georgia, Louisiana, Mississippi, North Carolina, South Carolina, Tennessee, and Texas. The Northeast includes the following ten states: Maine, New York, New Jersey, Delaware, Vermont, Massachusetts, Rhode Island, Connecticut, New Hampshire, and Pennsylvania.

139. Kim Chandler, "514 AIDS Patients May Lose Drug Aid $3.5 Million Critical, Health Officer Says," *Birmingham News*, January 13, 2005, 1B; Kaiser Family Foundation, "Waiting for AIDS Medications in the United States: An Analysis of ADAP Waiting Lists," KFF, December 2004, https://www.kff.org/wp-content/uploads/2013/01/fact-sheet-waiting-for-aids-medications-in-the-united-states-an-analysis-of-adap-waiting-lists.pdf.

140. Stephen F. Morin et al., "Responding to Racial and Ethnic Disparities in Use of HIV Drugs: Analysis of State Policies," *Public Health Reports* 117, no. 3 (May-June 2002): 270.

141. Kelly A. Gebo et al., "Racial and Gender Disparities in Receipt of Highly Active Antiretroviral Therapy Persist in a Multistate Sample of HIV Patients in 2001," *Journal of Acquired Immune Deficiency Syndromes* 38, no. 1 (January 2005): 96–103; National Alliance of State and Territorial AIDS Directors, Henry J. Kaiser Family Foundation, and the AIDS Treatment Data Network, "National ADAP Monitoring Report."

142. Southern State AIDS/STD Directors Work Group, "Southern States Manifesto: HIV/ AIDS and STDS in the South: A Call to Action," Wayback Machine, March 2, 2003, https://web.archive.org/web/20040725024609/http://www.hivdent.org/Manifesto.pdf. The Southern State AIDS/STD Directors Work Group was an early name of the Southern AIDS Coalition.

143. Southern AIDS Coalition, "2006 Ryan White Policy Statement," Wayback Machine, 2005, https://web.archive.org/web/20050521012545/http://southernaidscoalition.org/SACPolicy1-%20Ryan%20WhiteFINAL2.pdf.

144. Cong. Rec., 109th Cong., 2nd Sess., S10438–10442 (2006); Cong. Rec., 109th Cong., 2nd Sess., S11242 (2006); Senator Richard Burr, "Senators Burr, Sessions, and Coburn Call for More Equitable Ryan White CARE Act HIV/AIDS Funding," press release, September 14, 2006, https://www.burr.senate.gov/2006/9/senators-burr-sessions-and-coburn-call-for-more-equitable-ryan-white-care-act-hiv/aids-funding.

145. Cong. Rec., 109th Cong., 2nd Sess., S10438–10442 (2006); Cong. Rec., 109th Cong., 2nd Sess., S11242 (2006); Burr, "Senators Burr, Sessions, and Coburn Call for More Equitable Ryan White CARE Act HIV/AIDS Funding"; Cong. Rec., 109th Cong., 2nd Sess., H7731 (2006); Iowa Ryan White Coalition, "Iowa Ryan White Coalition Urges Senate Leadership to Introduce Bill that Includes Testing Provisions and More Monies for Rural and Southern Areas," press release, March 2, 2006, in author's possession.

146. Gary A. Puckrein, "NMHMF Op-Ed on Ryan White Inequities (Title II Focus)," *Outvoices Nashville*, May 1, 2006, https://outvoices.us/nmhmf-op-ed-on-ryan-white-inequities-title-ii-focus.

147. Inrig, *North Carolina and the Problem of AIDS*, 122.

148. Office of the Press Secretary, "Fact Sheet: The Ryan White HIV/AIDS Treatment Modernization Act of 2006," White House, December 19, 2006, https://georgewbush-whitehouse.archives.gov/news/releases/2006/12/text/20061219-4.html.

149. Shefali S. Kulkarni, "States Cutting Back on Drug Programs for HIV Patients," Kaiser Health News, May 22, 2011, https://khn.org/news/adap-waiting-lists/.

150. Chris Fitzsimon, "The Life-Threatening Budget Cuts," NC Policy Watch, March 16, 2010, https://ncpolicywatch.com/2010/03/16/the-life-threatening-budget-cuts/.

151. Kaiser Family Foundation, "Fact Sheet: AIDS Drug Assistance Programs,"

KFF, August 16, 2017, https://www.kff.org/hivaids/fact-sheet/aids-drug-assistance-programs/; Villarosa, "America's Hidden HIV Epidemic."

152. For more on the devastating impact of HIV/AIDS on the South in the 2010s, see Villarosa, "America's Hidden HIV Epidemic"; Dan Royles, "When My Brothers Fell," Baffler, March 2021, https://thebaffler.com/salvos/when-my-brothers-fell-royles.

Conclusion

1. For an excellent account of the anthrax attacks in the fall of 2001, see Philip S. Brachman, "The Public Health Response to the Anthrax Epidemic," in *Terrorism and Public Health: A Balanced Approach to Strengthening Systems and Protecting People*, ed. Barry S. Levy and Victor W. Sidel (Oxford University Press, 2007), 101–117.

2. Gallup, "Americans Call Bioterrorism Most Urgent U.S. Health Problem," November 26, 2001, https://news.gallup.com/poll/5074/americans-call-bioterrorism-most-urgent-us-health-problem.aspx. Of those polled by Gallup in November 2001, 21 percent believed that bioterrorism was the most urgent healthcare issue facing the nation while 19 percent thought it was rising insurance costs or cancer, and only 6 percent indicated that it was heart disease. This poll marked the only time bioterrorism had appeared on the list since 1987.

3. On the public health aspects of the PATRIOT Act, see Gwen D'Arcangelis, *Bio-Imperialism: Disease, Terror, and the Construction of National Fragility* (Rutgers University Press, 2021), 64–65.

4. Public Health Security and Bioterrorism Preparedness and Response Act of 2002, Pub. L. No. 107–188, 116 Stat. 594 (2002).

5. Michael Mair et al., "Passage of S. 3678: The Pandemic and All-Hazards Preparedness Act," *Biosecurity and Bioterrorism* 5, no. 1 (2007): 72–74. For more on the public health establishment's support for the law, see Nellie Bristol and David Marcozzi, "Pandemic and All-Hazards Preparedness Act," *Disaster Medicine and Public Health Preparedness* 1, no. 1 (2007): 9–10.

6. Centers for Medicare and Medicaid Services, "National Health Expenditure Data," CMS, accessed September 19, 2024, https://www.cms.hhs.gov/NationalHealth ExpenditureData.

7. Jeffrey Levi et al., "Financing Public Health: Diminished Funding for Core Needs and State-by-State Variation in Support," *Journal of Public Health Management and Practice* 13, no. 2 (March-April 2007): 97–102. The figures were inflation-adjusted to 2006 dollars.

8. In fiscal year 2015, appropriations for these programs stood at less than half of the $2 billion initially budgeted for by the Affordable Care Act. David U. Himmelstein and Steffie Woolhandler, "Public Health's Falling Share of U.S. Health Spending," *American Journal of Public Health* 106, no. 1 (January 2016): 57.

9. Trust for America's Health, "The Impact of Chronic Underfunding of America's Public Health System: Trends, Risks, and Recommendations, 2019," TFAH, April 2019, https://www.tfah.org/wp-content/uploads/2020/03/TFAH_2019_PublicHealthFunding_07.pdf.

10. This figure is derived from Jonathon P. Leider et al., "How Much Do We Spend? Creating Historical Estimates of Public Health Expenditures in the United States at the Federal, State, and Local Levels," *Annual Review of Public Health* 39 (April 2018), 478.

11. Institute of Medicine, *For the Public's Health: Investing in a Healthier Future* (National Academies Press, 2012), 105–106. This figure includes spending on nonhospital healthcare—immunization/vaccination services, epidemiological surveillance, disease prevention programs, and other public health programs—but excludes Medicaid-related expenditure.

12. Donald Trump to Charles E. Schumer, "Letter to Senate Minority Leader Charles E. Schumer on the Federal Coronavirus Response," GovInfo, April 2, 2020, https://www.govinfo.gov/content/pkg/DCPD-202000233/pdf/DCPD-202000233.pdf.

13. Isaac Stanley-Becker, Toluse Olorunnipa, and Seung Min Kim, "Trump Foments Resistance to Democratic-Imposed Shutdowns, but Some Republican Governors are also Wary of Moving too Fast," *Washington Post*, September 17, 2020, https://www.washingtonpost.com/politics/trump-foments-resistance-to-democratic-imposed-shutdowns-but-some-republican-governors-are-also-wary-of-moving-too-fast/2020/04/17/5595e5fa-80c2-11ea-9040-68981f488eed_story.html; Mike DeBonis, Chris Mooney, and Juliet Eilperin, "White House Issues Coronavirus Testing Guidance That Leaves States in Charge," *Washington Post*, April 27, 2020, https://www.washingtonpost.com/politics/white-house-issues-coronavirus-testing-guidance-that-leaves-states-in-charge/2020/04/27/c465cc9c-88a2-11ea-8ac1-bfb250876b7a_story.html; Jeanne Whalen, Tony Romm, Aaron Gregg, and Tom Hamburger, "Scramble for Medical Equipment Descends into Chaos as U.S. States and Hospitals Compete for Rare Supplies," *Washington Post*, March 24, 2020, https://www.washingtonpost.com/business/2020/03/24/scramble-medical-equipment-descends-into-chaos-us-states-hospitals-compete-rare-supplies/.

14. David Willman, "CDC Coronavirus Test Kits Were Likely Contaminated, Federal Review Confirms," *Washington Post*, June 20, 2020, https://www.washingtonpost.com/investigations/cdc-coronavirus-test-kits-were-likely-contaminated-federal-review-confirms/2020/06/20/1ceb4e16-b2ef-11ea-8f56-63f38c990077_story.html.

15. State of California, Exec. Order, N-33-20, March 4, 2020.

16. For a state-by-state breakdown of the stay-at-home orders issued in March and April 2020, see Amanda Moreland et al., "Timing of State and Territorial COVID-19 Stay-at-Home Orders and Changes in Population Movement—United States, March 1–May 31, 2020," *Morbidity and Mortality Weekly Report* (MMWR) 69, no. 35 (September 4, 2020): 1198–1203.

17. A series of detailed statistical studies confirm that the best predictor of when a state implemented social distancing requirements in the spring of 2020 was the partisan affiliation of the governor, even when controlling for other factors like population size, urban density, relative state wealth, the average age of the population, and confirmed case counts. Leonardo Baccini and Abel Brodeur, "Explaining Governors' Response to the COVID-19 Pandemic in the United States," *American Politics Research* 49, no. 2 (2021): 215–220; Michael K. Gusmano et al., "Partisanship in Initial State Responses to the COVID-19 Pandemic," *World Medical and Health Policy* 12, no. 4 (December 2020): 380–389; Christopher Adolph et al., "Pandemic Politics: Timing State-Level Social Distancing Responses to COVID-19," *Journal of Health Politics, Policy, and Law* 46, no. 2 (April 2021): 212–213.

18. These seven states were Arkansas, Iowa, Nebraska, North Dakota, Oklahoma, South Dakota, Utah, and Wyoming.

19. Local health departments also varied significantly in size and complexity. According to a 2010 survey by the National Association of County and City Health Officials, 63 percent served areas with populations of under fifty thousand, 32 percent served populations between fifty thousand and five hundred thousand, and 5 percent served populations larger than five hundred thousand. National Association of County and City Health Officials, "2008 National Profile of Local Health Departments" (NACCHO, 2009), 10.

20. See, for example, Laura Hallas et al., "Variation in US States' Responses to COVID-19 Version 3.0," Coronavirus Government Response Tracker, University of Oxford Blavatnik School of Government, May 2021, Variation in US states' responses to COVID-19 | Blavatnik School of Government (ox.ac.uk).

BIBLIOGRAPHY

Manuscript Collections

Abilene, Kansas
  Dwight D. Eisenhower Presidential Library
    Dwight D. Eisenhower Papers
Athens, Georgia
  Richard B. Russell Library for Political Research and Studies, University of Georgia Libraries
    James F. (Jim) Martin Papers
Austin, Texas
  Austin Public Library, Austin History Center
    Austin Lesbian/Gay Political Caucus Papers
  Briscoe Center for American History, University of Texas at Austin
    Glen Maxey Papers
    Lesbian-Gay Rights Lobby of Texas Records
    Texas Human Rights Foundation Records
Berkeley, California
  University of California, Berkeley, Bancroft Library
    Sara Diamond Collection on the US Right
  University of California, Berkeley, Ethnic Studies Library
    Hank M. Tavera Papers
Boston, Massachusetts
  Special Collections and University Archives, University of Massachusetts Amherst Libraries
    Boston AIDS Consortium Records
Chicago, Illinois
  Chicago Public Library
    Harold Washington Collection
  Gerber Hart Library and Archives
    Carole Powell Papers
    Illinois Gay and Lesbian Task Force Records
    IMPACT Illinois, Inc. Records
    University of Chicago, Special Collections Research
    ACT UP Chicago Records
College Park, Maryland
  National Archives and Records Administration
    Records of the Public Health Service, RG 90

Denton, Texas
University of North Texas, Special Collections
Donald F. Baker Collection
Resource Center LGBT Collection
Digital Collections
Alexander Street LGBT Studies
Tracy Baim Editorial Files
Gale Archives of Gender and Sexuality
The Bush Administration and the AIDS Crisis Records
Houston, Texas
Harris County Archives
Charles Henley Papers
Public Health and Environmental Services Records
Ryan White Planning Council Records
Ithaca, New York
Cornell University Library, Rare and Manuscript Collections
Empire State Pride Agenda Records
Larry Bush Papers
Los Angeles, California
Loyola Marymount University, Department of Archives and Special Collections, William H. Hannon Library
David A. Roberti Papers
ONE National Gay and Lesbian Archives
AIDS History Project Collection
Bill Wuzzy Spaulding Papers
California Human Rights Advocates Records
Concerned Americans for Individual Rights (CAIR) Records
Dennis Cabaret Papers
George Raya Papers
No on 64 Records
ONE Subject File Collection
University of California, Los Angeles, Charles E. Young Research Library
Henry Waxman Papers
Milwaukee, Wisconsin
University of Wisconsin–Milwaukee, Library Special Collection
AIDS Resource Center of Wisconsin Records
New York, New York
New York Public Library
Gay Men's Health Crisis Records
Riverside, California
University of California, Riverside, Special Collections and University Archives
Kay Berryhill Smith and Connie Confer LGBT Activism Collection
San Francisco, California
Gay, Lesbian, Bisexual, Transgender Historical Society
Asian/Pacific AIDS Coalition Records

Bruce Decker Papers
Lobby for Individual Freedom and Equality Records
Stanley Hadden Papers
Steve Morin Papers
San Francisco Public Library
Art Agnos Papers
Milton Mark AIDS Files
San Francisco Department of Public Health AIDS Office Records
San Francisco State University, J. Paul Leonard Library, Special Collections and Archives
Willie L. Brown Jr. Papers
University of California, San Francisco, Archives and Special Collections
Multicultural AIDS Resource Center Records
National Task Force on AIDS Prevention Records
San Francisco AIDS Foundation Records
Washington, DC
George Washington University, Special Collection Research Center
AIDS Action Foundation Records
Library of Congress
Daniel P. Moynihan Papers

Published Primary Sources

American Legislative Exchange Council. "Emergency Power Limitation Act." January 8, 2021. https://alec.org/model-policy/emergency-power-limitation-act/.

Ballotpedia. "States That Did Not Issue Stay-at-Home Orders in Response to the Coronavirus (COVID-19) Pandemic, 2020." Accessed January 27, 2022. https://ballotpedia.org/States_that_did_not_issue_stay-at-home_orders_in_response_to_the_coronavirus_(COVID-19)_pandemic,_2020.

Budget of the United States Government for the Fiscal Year Ending June 30, 1935 (US Government Printing Office, 1934).

Budget of the United States Government for the Fiscal Year Ending June 30, 1951 (US Government Printing Office, 1950).

Budget of the United States Government for the Fiscal Year Ending June 30, 1961 (US Government Printing Office, 1960).

Centers for Disease Control and Prevention. "HIV in the Southern United States." May 2016. https://www.cdc.gov/hiv/pdf/policies/cdc-hiv-in-the-south-issue-brief.pdf.

Coffey, E. R. "Public Health Expands Its Facilities Under Title VI—Federal Social Security Act,. *American Journal of Public Health and the Nation's Health* 31, no. 4 (April 1941): 297–304.

Cole, Jared P. "Federal and State Quarantine and Isolation Authority." Congressional Research Service, 2014.

Collins, Selwyn D., et al. "Mortality from Influenza and Pneumonia in 50 Large Cities of the United States, 1910–1929." *Public Health Reports (1896–1970)* 45, no. 39 (September 26, 1930): 2277–2328.

Department of Health and Human Services. "Audit of the Ryan White Comprehensive AIDS Resources Emergency Act of 1990, Title II, Administered by the Health Resources and Services Administration." Office of Inspector General, 1997.

Department of Health and Human Services. "Audit of the Ryan White Comprehensive AIDS Resources Emergency Act of 1990, Title II Administered by the State of Connecticut." Office of Inspector General, 1996.

Department of Health and Human Services. "The Ryan White CARE Act: Consortia Activities." Office of Inspector General, 1994.

Department of Health and Human Services. "The Ryan White CARE Act: FY 1992 Title I and Title II Expenditures." Office of Inspector General, 1994.

Freckleton, F. Robert. "Progress and Horizons in Immunization." In *Proceedings from the Fifth Annual Immunization Conference*, San Diego, CA, March 12–14, 1968, 2–6.

Government Accountability Office. "Revising Ryan White Funding Formulas." GAO, 1996.

Government Accountability Office. "Ryan White CARE Act: Improved Oversight Needed to Ensure AIDS Drug Assistance Programs Obtain Best Prices for Drugs." GAO, 2006.

Government Accountability Office. "Ryan White CARE Act: Opportunities to Enhance Funding Equity." GAO, 2000.

Health Resources and Services Administration. "Comments on the OIG Report, 'Audit of the Ryan White Comprehensive AIDS Resources Emergency Act of 1990, Title II, Administered by the Health Resources and Services Administration.'" Accessed May 23, 2022. https://oig.hhs.gov/oas/reports/region1/19701500.pdf.

Illinois Department of Public Health and Illinois Interagency Task Force. *The Response to AIDS and HIV Infection*. State of Illinois, 1990.

Institute of Medicine. *For the Public's Health: Investing in a Healthier Future*. National Academies Press, 2012.

Jones, Joseph. *Medical and Surgical Memoirs: Containing Investigations on the Geographical Distribution, Causes, Nature, Relations and Treatment of Various Diseases, 1855–1890*. Clark & Hofeline, 1890.

Kaiser Family Foundation. "An Overview of HIV/AIDS in Black America." KFF, July 2007. https://www.kff.org/wp-content/uploads/2013/01/7660.pdf.

Kaiser Family Foundation. "Trends in U.S. Government Funding for HIV/AIDS: Fiscal Years 1981 to 2004." KFF, March 2004. https://www.kff.org/wp-content/uploads/2013/01/issue-brief-trends-in-u-s-government-funding-for-hiv-aids-fiscal-years-1981-to-2004.pdf.

Kaiser Family Foundation. "U.S. Federal Funding for HIV/AIDS: Trends over Time." KFF, March 5, 2019. https://www.kff.org/hivaids/fact-sheet/u-s-federal-funding-for-hivaids-trends-over-time/#:~:text=The%20Ryan%20White%20HIV%2FAIDS%20Program%2C%20the%20largest%20HIV%2D,same%20as%20the%20FY18%20level.

Kaiser Family Foundation. "Waiting for AIDS Medications in the United States: An Analysis of ADAP Waiting Lists." KFF, December 2004. https://www.kff.org/wp-content/uploads/2013/01/fact-sheet-waiting-for-aids-medications-in-the-united-states-an-analysis-of-adap-waiting-lists.pdf.

Kennedy, John F. "Special Message to the Congress on National Health Needs, February 27, 1962." In *Public Papers of the Presidents of the United States: John F. Kennedy*. Office of the Federal Register, 1963.

Morin, Stephen. "AIDS: Public Policy and Mental Health Issues." In Leon McKusick, *What to Do About AIDS: Physicians and Mental Health Professionals Discuss the Issues*. University of California Press 1986.

National Alliance of State and Territorial AIDS Directors, the Henry J. Kaiser Family Foundation, and the AIDS Treatment Data Network. "National ADAP Monitoring Report: Annual Report." KFF, May 2004. https://www.kff.org/wp-content/uploads/2013/01/national-adap-monitoring-project-2004-annual-report.pdf.

Network for Public Health Law and the National Association of County and City Health Officials. "Proposed Limits on Public Health Authority: Dangerous for Public Health." May 2021, https://www.naccho.org/uploads/downloadable-resources/Proposed-Limits-on-Public-Health-Authority-Dangerous-for-Public-Health-FINAL-5.24.21pm.pdf.

Public Health Service. *Ten Years of Federal Grants-in-Aid for Public Health, 1936–1946*. Superintendent of Documents, 1948.

Southern AIDS Coalition. "2006 Ryan White Policy Statement." Wayback Machine, 2005. https://web.archive.org/web/20050521012545/http://southernaidscoalition.org/SACPolicy1-%20Ryan%20WhiteFINAL2.pdf.

Southern AIDS Coalition. "Southern States Manifesto: Update 2008, HIV/AIDS and Sexually Transmitted Diseases in the South." 2008. https://southernaidscoalition.org/wp-content/uploads/2024/12/2008.Southern-States-Manifesto.pdf.

Southern State AIDS/STD Directors Work Group. "Southern States Manifesto: HIV/AIDS and STDS in the South: A Call to Action." Wayback Machine, March 2, 2023. https://web.archive.org/web/20040725024609/http://www.hivdent.org/Manifesto.pdf.

Twombly, Eric C., Jennifer Claire Auer, and Kanisha Bond. "Community Anchors East of the River: An Analysis of the Charitable Infrastructure in Wards 7 and 8 in Washington, DC." Urban Institute, January 2006. http://webarchive.urban.org/UploadedPDF/411275_community_anchors.pdf.

United Health Foundation. "America's Health Rankings: A Call to Action for People and Their Communities." Wayback Machine, 2006. https://web.archive.org/web/20061223121107/http://www.unitedhealthfoundation.org/ahr2006/media2006/shrmediakit/2006ahr.pdf.

US Conference of Mayors. *Local Responses to Acquired Immune Deficiency Syndrome (AIDS): A Report of 55 Cities*. Government Printing Office, 1984.

Congressional Hearings

The American Health Care Crisis: A View from Four Communities, 101st Cong., 1st Sess. (1990).

Economic Security Act: Hearings, 74th Cong., 1st Sess. (1935).

Financing AIDS Early Intervention and Treatment Services: Hearing before the Subcommittee Health and the Environment, 103d Cong., 1st Sess. (1990).

Intensive Immunization Programs: Hearings, 87th Cong., 2nd Sess. (1962).
Poliomyelitis Vaccine: Hearings, 84th Cong., 1st Sess. (1955).

Newspapers and Periodicals

Advocate
American Prospect
Arizona Republic
Atlantic
Baltimore Gay Newspaper
Bay Area Reporter
Birmingham News
Bravo! Newsmagazine
Chicago Sun-Times
CQ Weekly
Daily News of Los Angeles
Dallas Morning News
Dallas Times Herald
Dallas Voice
Detroit Free Press
Detroit News
Final Call
Foreign Affairs
Houston Chronicle
Kaiser Health News
Lesbian News
Los Angeles Times
Mom Guess What
New York Post
New York Times
New Voice
Outvoices Nashville
Sacramento Bee
San Diego Gayzette
San Francisco Chronicle
San Francisco Examiner
San Francisco Sentinel
Scientific American
This Week in Texas
Town Talk
Update
Washington Blade
Washington City Newspaper
Washington Post

Oral Histories

Anonymous phone interview with the author, December 20, 2018.
Anonymous phone interview with the author, February 3, 2019.
Bosia, Michael. Phone Interview with the author, December 22, 2018.
Bush, Larry. Interview with the author, San Francisco, December 17, 2018.
Drake, Timothy. Phone interview with the author, August 25, 2019.
Keller, Marty. Phone interview with the author, November 11, 2019.
Maison, Donald. Phone Interview with the author, September 15, 2019.
Martin, Rand. Interview with author, Sacramento, December 18, 2018.
Maxey, Glen. Phone interview with the author, July 18, 2019.
Morin, Stephen. Phone interview with the author, October 19, 2018.
Roberti, David. Interview with the author, Los Angeles, December 12, 2018.
Sheridan, Tom. Phone Interview with the author, August 29, 2019.
Topper, Kenneth. Phone interview with the author, November 12, 2018.
Topper, Kenneth. Phone interview with author, December 18, 2018.

Academic Sources

Abercrombie, Thomas Franklin. *A History of Public Health in Georgia, 1733–1950*. N.p., 1950.

Adolph, Christopher, et al., "Pandemic Politics: Timing State-Level Social Distancing Responses to COVID-19." *Journal of Health Politics, Policy, and Law* 46, no. 2 (April 2021): 211–233.

Aimone, Francesco. "The 1918 Influenza Epidemic in New York City: A Review of the Public Health Response." Supplement, *Public Health Reports* 125, no. 3 (April 2010): 71–79.

Alamilla Boyd, Nan. *Wide-Open Town: A Queer History of San Francisco to 1965*. University of California Press, 2003.

Andriote, John-Manuel. *Victory Deferred: How AIDS Changed Gay Life in America*. University of Chicago Press, 1999.

Armstrong, Elizabeth A. *Forging Gay Identities: Organizing Sexuality in San Francisco, 1950–1994*. University of Chicago Press, 2002.

Arno, Peter S. "The Economic Impact of AIDS." *JAMA: Journal of the American Medical Association* 258, no. 10 (September 1987): 1376–1377.

Arno, Peter S. "The Nonprofit Sector's Response to the AIDS Epidemic: Community-Based Services in San Francisco." *American Journal of Public Health* 76, no. 11 (November 1986): 1325–1330.

Asch, Chris Myers, and George Derek Musgrove. *Chocolate City: A History of Race and Democracy in the Nation's Capital*. University of North Carolina Press, 2017.

Atta, Dale Van. *With Honor: Melvin Laird in War, Peace, and Politics*. University of Wisconsin Press, 2008.

Baccini, Leonardo, and Abel Brodeur. "Explaining Governors' Response to the COVID-19 Pandemic in the United States." *American Politics Research* 49, no. 2 (2021): 215–220.

Baldwin, Peter. *Disease and Democracy: The Industrialized World Faces AIDS*. University of California Press, 2007.

Balogh, Brian. *The Associational State: American Governance in the Twentieth Century.* University of Pennsylvania Press, 2015.

Barry, John M. *The Great Influenza: The Story of the Deadliest Plague in History.* Viking, 2005.

Bates, R. M. "Government by Improvisation? Towards a New History of the Nineteenth-Century American State." *Journal of Policy History* 33, no. 3 (July 2021): 287–316.

Batza, Katie. *Before AIDS: Gay Health Politics in the 1970s.* University of Pennsylvania Press, 2018.

Batza, Katie. "Sickness and Wellness." In *The Routledge History of Queer America*, edited by Don Romesberg. Routledge, 2018.

Batza, Katie. "Tactical Deployments of Respectability: Religion, Race, and Rights in the United States Heartland early-AIDS Response." In *Resist, Organize, Build: Feminist and Queer Activism in Britain and the United States During the Long 1980s*, eds. Sarah Crook and Charlie Jeffries. State University of New York Press, 2022.

Bayer, Ronald. "Ethics and Infectious Disease Control: STDs, HIV, TB." In *Ethics and Public Health: Model Curriculum*, eds. Bruce Jennings, Jeffery Kahn, Anna Mastroianni, and Lisa S. Parker. Health Resources and Services Administration, 2003.

Bayer, Ronald. *Private Acts, Social Consequences: AIDS and the Politics of Public Health.* Free Press, 1988.

Bayer, Ronald, and Laurence Dupuis. "Tuberculosis, Public Health, and Civil Liberties." *Annual Review of Public Health* 16 (1995): 307–326.

Beam, Myrl. *Gay, Inc: The Nonprofitization of Queer Politics.* University of Minnesota Press, 2018.

Bell, Jonathan. "Between Private and Public: AIDS, Health Care Capitalism, and the Politics of Respectability in 80s America." *Journal of American Studies* 54, no. 1 (February 2020): 159–183.

Bell, Jonathan. *California Crucible: The Forging of Modern American Liberalism.* University of Pennsylvania Press, 2012.

Bell, Jonathan. "Making Sexual Citizens: LGBT Politics, Health Care, and the State in the 1970s." In *Beyond the Politics of the Closet: Gay Rights and the American State Since the 1970s*, edited by Jonathan Bell. University of Pennsylvania Press, 2020.

Bell, Jonathan. "Rethinking the 'Straight State': Welfare Politics, Health Care, and Public Policy in the Shadow of AIDS." *Journal of American History* 104, no. 4 (March 2018): 931–952.

Bell, Jonathan. "To Strive for Economic and Social Justice": Welfare, Sexuality, and Liberal Politics in San Francisco." *Journal of Policy History* 22, no. 2 (April 2010): 193–225.

Bell, Jonathan, ed. *Beyond the Politics of the Closet: Gay Rights and the American State Since the 1970s.* University of Pennsylvania Press, 2020.

Bielefeld, Wolfgang, and Richard Scotch. "Institutionalizing AIDS: Policy, Institutional Culture, and the Response to the HIV Epidemic in Dallas." *Research in Social Policy* 4 (1996): 39–53.

Bloom, David E., and Geoffrey Carliner. "The Economic Impact of AIDS in the United States." *Science* 238, no. 4840 (February 1988): 604–610.

Bloom, Nicholas Dagen. *How States Shaped Postwar America: State Government and Urban Power*. University of Chicago Press, 2019.

Blue, Rupert. "Epidemic Influenza and the U.S. Public Health Service." *Modern Hospital* 11 (December 1918): 425–426.

Bolton, Alexander, and Sharece Thrower. *Checks in the Balance: Legislative Capacity and the Dynamics of Executive Power*. Princeton University Press, 2022.

Bost, Darius. "At the Club: Locating Early Black Gay AIDS Activism in Washington, D.C." *Occasion* 8 (August 31, 2015): 1–9.

Bost, Darius. *Evidence of Being: The Black Gay Cultural Renaissance and the Politics of Violence*. University of Chicago Press, 2018.

Bowen, Stephen. "First Year of AIDS Service Delivery Under Title I of the Ryan White CARE Act." *Public Health Reports* 107, no. 5 (September–October 1992): 491–499.

Brachman, Philip S. "The Public Health Response to the Anthrax Epidemic." In *Terrorism and Public Health: A Balanced Approach to Strengthening Systems and Protecting People*, edited by Barry S. Levy and Victor W. Sidel. Oxford University Press, 2007.

Brandt, Allan M. *No Magic Bullet: A Social History of Venereal Disease in the United States Since 1880*. Oxford University Press, 1985.

Brandtner, Christof, and Claire Dunning. "Nonprofits as Urban Infrastructure," in *The Nonprofit Sector: A Research Handbook*, 3rd ed., edited by Walter W. Powell and Patricia Bromley (Stanford University Press, 2020), 271–291.

Brier, Jennifer. "The Immigrant Infection: Images of Race, Nation and Contagion in Public Debates on AIDS and Immigration." In *Modern American Queer History*, edited by Allida M. Black. Temple University Press, 2001.

Brier, Jennifer. *Infectious Ideas: U.S. Political Responses to the AIDS Crisis*. University of North Carolina Press, 2009.

Bristol, Nellie, and David Marcozzi. "Pandemic and All-Hazards Preparedness Act." *Disaster Medicine and Public Health Preparedness* 1, no. 1 (2007): 9–10.

Bristow, Nancy K. *American Pandemic: The Lost Worlds of the 1918 Influenza Epidemic*. Oxford University Press, 2012.

Bristow, Nancy K. "'You Can't Do Anything for Influenza': Doctors, Nurses and the Power of Gender during the Influenza Epidemic in the United States." In *The Spanish Influenza Pandemic of 1918–19: New Perspectives*, eds. Howard Phillips and David Killingray. Routledge, 2003.

Buchanan, Robert J. "HIV Consortia Services Funded by Title II of the Ryan White CARE Act: A Survey of the States." *AIDS and Public Policy Journal* 11, no. 3 (Fall 1996): 118–143.

Buchanan, Robert J. "Ryan White CARE Act and Eligible Metropolitan Areas." *Health Care Finance Review* 23, no. 4 (Summer 2002): 149–157.

Burkett, Elinor. *The Gravest Show on Earth: America in the Age of AIDS*. Houghton Mifflin, 1995.

Canaday, Margot. *Queer Career: Sexuality and Work in Modern America*. Princeton University Press, 2023.

Canaday, Margot. *The Straight State: Sexuality and Citizenship in Twentieth Century America*. Princeton University Press, 2009.

Canaday, Margot, Nancy F. Scott, and Robert O. Self. "Introduction." In *Intimate States:*

Gender, Sexuality, and Governance in Modern U.S. History, edited by Margot Canaday, Nancy F. Scott, and Robert O. Self. University of Chicago Press, 2021.

Capó, Julio. *Welcome to Fairyland: Queer Miami Before 1940*. University of North Carolina Press, 2017.

Capozolla, Christopher. *Uncle Sam Wants You: World War I and the Making of the Modern American Citizen*. Oxford University Press, 2010.

Capozolla, Christopher, et al. "Interchange: World War I." *Journal of American History* 102, no. 2 (September 2015): 496–497.

Carey, John M., et al. *Term Limits in the State Legislatures*. University of Michigan Press, 2000.

Carpenter, Nancy Weiland. "AIDS Initiatives in Massachusetts: Building a Continuum of Care." *New England Journal of Public Policy* 1 (1988): 429–439.

Carroll, Tamar W. *Mobilizing New York: AIDS, Antipoverty, and Feminist Activism*. University of North Carolina Press, 2015.

Cebul, Brent, Lily Geismer, and Mason B. Williams, eds. *Shaped by the State: Toward a New Political History of the Twentieth Century*. University of Chicago Press, 2019.

Cebul, Brent, and Mason B. Williams. "'Really and Truly a Partnership': The New Deal's Associational State and the Making of Postwar American Politics." In *Shaped by the State*.

Chambré, Susan M. *Fighting for Our Lives: New York's AIDS Community and the Politics of Disease*. Rutgers University Press, 2006.

Chandra, Siddharth, Julia Christensen, and Shimon Likhtman. "Connectivity and Seasonality: The 1918 Influenza and COVID-19 Pandemics in Global Perspective." *Journal of Global History* 15, no. 3 (November 2020): 408–420.

Chauncey, George. *Gay New York: Gender, Urban Culture, and the Makings of the Gay Male World, 1890–1940*. Hachette, 1994.

Chauncey, George. *Why Marriage? The History Shaping Today's Debate over Gay Equality*. Basic Books, 2004.

Chávez, Karma R. *The Borders of AIDS: Race, Quarantine, and Resistance*. University of Washington Press, 2021.

Citizens Conference on State Legislatures. *The Impact of the Texas Constitution on the Legislature*. CCSL, 1973.

Clemens, Elisabeth S. *Civic Gifts: Voluntarism and the Making of the American Nation-State*. University of Chicago Press, 2020.

Clemens, Elisabeth S. *The People's Lobby: Organizational Innovation and the Rise of Interest Group Politics in the United States, 1890–1925*. University of Chicago Press, 1997.

Closen, Michael, et al. "Mandatory Premarital HIV Testing: Political Exploitation of the AIDS Epidemic." *Tulane Law Review* 68, no. 1 (1994–95): 71–116.

Cogan, John F. *The High Cost of Good Intentions: A History of U.S. Federal Entitlement Programs*. Stanford University Press, 2017.

Coleman, Sarah. *The Walls Within: The Politics of Immigration in Modern America*. Princeton University Press, 2021.

Colgrove, James. *Epidemic City: The Politics of Public Health in New York*. Russell Sage Foundation, 2011.

Colgrove, James. "Reform and Its Discontents: Public Health in New York City During the Great Society." *Journal of Policy History* 19, no. 1 (January 2007): 3–28.

Colgrove, James. *State of Immunity: The Politics of Vaccination in Twentieth-Century America*. University of California Press, 2006.

Conis, Elena. "Measles and the Modern History of Vaccination." *Public Health Reports* 134, no. 2 (March/April 2019): 118–125.

Conis, Elena. *Vaccine Nation: America's Changing Relationship with Immunization*. University of Chicago Press, 2015.

Conlan, Timothy. *From New Federalism to Devolution: Twenty-Five Years of Intergovernmental Reform*. Brookings Institution Press, 1998.

Cooper, Melinda. *Family Values: Between Neoliberalism and the New Social Conservatism*. Zone Books, 2017.

Cotton, Paul. "Premarital HIV Testing Hits Snags: As Two States Implement Testing, Counselling Quality Varies, Costs Are an Issue and Critics Decry Diversion of Resources from Groups at Higher Risk of Infection." *Medical World News* 29, no. 4 (February 22, 1988): 21.

Council of State Government. *The Book of the States, 1984–1985*. CSG, 1984.

Cowie, Jefferson. *The Great Exception: The New Deal and the Limits of American Politics*. Princeton University Press, 2017.

Cox, Whitney. "Trouble at the 'Crossroads': Divisions over the Use of Religious Symbols as AIDS Memorials in Houston, 1991,." *Journal of the History of Sexuality* 29, no. 2 (May 2020): 162–186.

Critchlow, Donald T. *Phyllis Schlafly and Grassroots Conservatism: A Woman's Crusade*. Princeton University Press, 2005.

Critchlow, Donald T., and Cynthia L. Stachecki. "The Equal Rights Amendment Reconsidered: Politics, Policy, and Social Mobilization in a Democracy." *Journal of Policy History* 20, no.1 (January 2008): 157–176.

Cunningham, Sean P. *Cowboy Conservatism: Texas and the Rise of the Modern Right*. University Press of Kentucky, 2010.

D'Arcangelis, Gwen. *Bio-Imperialism: Disease, Terror, and the Construction of National Fragility*. Rutgers University Press, 2021.

de Mauro, Diane. "Sexuality Education 1990: A Review of State Sexuality and AIDS Education Curricula." *SIECUS Report* 18, no. 2 (December 1989): 1–9.

De Orio, Scott. "The Closet." In *Global Encyclopedia of Gay, Lesbian, Bisexual, Transgender, and Queer History*, edited by Howard Chiang. Charles Scribner & Sons, 2019.

De Orio, Scott. "The Invention of Bad Gay Sex: Texas and the Creation of a Criminal Underclass of Gay People." *Journal of the History of Sexuality* 26, no. 1 (January 2017): 53–87.

Derickson, Alan. *Health Security for All: Dreams of Universal Health Care in America*. Johns Hopkins University Press, 2005.

Derthick, Martha. "Compensatory Federalism." In *Greenhouse Governance: Addressing Climate Change in America*, edited by Barry G. Rabe. Brookings Institution Press, 2010.

Donovan, Mark C. *Taking Aim: Target Populations and the Wars on AIDS and Drugs*. Georgetown University Press, 2001.

Dowland, Seth. *Family Values and the Rise of the Christian Right*. University of Pennsylvania, 2015.

Duberman, Martin. *Hold Tight Gently: Michael Callen, Essex Hemphill, and the Battlefield of AIDS*. New Press, 2014.

Dunning, Claire. *Nonprofit Neighborhoods: An Urban History of Inequality and the American State*. University of Chicago Press, 2022.

Earle, Valerie A. "Post-1935 Developments in Southern State Public Health Programs." *American Journal of Public Health* 41, no. 11 (November 1951): 1403–1409.

Engel, Jonathan. *Poor People's Medicine: Medicaid and American Charity Care Since 1965*. Duke University Press, 2006.

Eskridge, William. *Dishonorable Passions: Sodomy Laws in America, 1861–2003*. Viking, 2008.

Eskridge, William N., and Christopher R. Riano. *Marriage Equality: From Outlaws to In*-Laws. Yale University Press, 2020.

Esparza, René. "Black Bodies on Lockdown: AIDS Moral Panic and the Criminalization of HIV in Times of White Injury." *Journal of African American History* 104, no. 2 (Spring 2019): 250–280.

Etheridge, Elizabeth W. *Sentinel for Health: A History of the Centers for Disease Control*. University of California Press, 1992.

Evans, Peter B., Dietrich Rueschemeyer, and Theda Skocpol, eds. *Bringing the State Back In*. Cambridge University Press, 1985.

Faderman, Lillian, and Stuart Timmons. *Gay L.A.: A History of Sexual Outlaws, Power Politics, and Lipstick Lesbians*. Basic Books, 2006.

Ferguson, Robert Hunt. "Mothers Against Jesse in Congress: Grassroots Maternalism and the Cultural Politics of the AIDS Crisis in North Carolina." *Journal of Southern History* 83, no. 1 (2017): 107–140.

Fox, Daniel M. "The Politics of HIV Infection: 1989–1990 as Years of Change." In *AIDS: The Making of a Chronic Disease*, edited by Elizabeth Fee and Daniel M. Fox. University of California Press, 1989.

Fox, Daniel M. "The Politics of Public Health in New York City: Contrasting Styles Since 1920." In *Hives of Sickness: Public Health and Epidemics in New York City*, edited by David Rosner. Rutgers University Press, 1995.

Frank, Gillian. "'The Civil Rights of Parents': Race and Conservative Politics in Anita Bryant's Campaign against Gay Rights in 1970s Florida." *Journal of the History of Sexuality* 22, no. 1 (2013): 126–160.

Frank, Michael W., Peter F. Nardulli, and Paul M. Green. "Representation, Elections, and Geo-Political Cleavages: The Political Manifestations of Regionalism in Twentieth-Century Illinois." In *Diversity, Conflict, and State Politics: Regionalism in Illinois*, edited by Peter F. Nardulli (University of Illinois Press, 1989) 197-221.

Gebo, Kelly A., et al. "Racial and Gender Disparities in Receipt of Highly Active Antiretroviral Therapy Persist in a Multistate Sample of HIV Patients in 2001." *Journal of Acquired Immune Deficiency Syndromes* 38, no. 1 (January 2005): 96–103.

Gerstle, Gary. *Liberty and Coercion: The Paradox of American Government from the Founding to the Present*. Princeton University Press, 2015.

Gerstle, Gary. "The Resilient Power of the States across the Long Nineteenth Century: An Inquiry into a Pattern of American Governance." In *The Unsustainable American State*, edited by Lawrence Jacobs and Desmond King. Oxford University Press, 2009.

Gerstle, Gary. *The Rise and Fall of the Neoliberal Order: America and the World in the Free Market Era*. Oxford University Press, 2022.

Gerstle, Gary. "A State Both Strong and Weak." *American Historical Review* 115, no. 3 (June 2010): 779–785.

Gerstle, Gary, Nelson Lichtenstein, and Alice O' Connor. *Beyond the New Deal Order: US Politics from the Great Depression to the Great Recession* University of Pennsylvania Press, 2019.

Gertz, Deborah L. "AIDS Bills: Testers and Tracers v. Educators and Researchers." *Illinois Issues* 53 (August and September 1987): 53–56.

Gordon, Colin. *Dead on Arrival: The Politics of Health Care in Twentieth-Century America*. Princeton University Press, 2013.

Gordon, Colin. "Why No National Health Insurance in the U.S.? The Limits of Social Provision in War and Peace, 1941–1948." *Journal of Policy History* 9, no. 3 (July 1997): 277–310.

Gostin, Lawrence O., and Lindsay F. Wiley. *Public Health Law: Power, Duty, Restraint*. University of California Press, 2016.

Gould, Deborah. *Moving Politics: Emotion and Shifting Political Horizons in the Fight Against AIDS*. University of Chicago Press, 2009.

Gove, Samuel K., and James D. Nowlan. *Illinois Politics and Government: The Expanding Metropolitan Frontier*. University of Nebraska Press, 1996.

Green, Jesse, et al. "The $147,000 Misunderstanding: Repercussions of Overestimating the Cost of AIDS." *Journal of Health Politics, Policy and Law* 19, no. 1 (Spring 1994): 69–90.

Greenfield, Myrtle. *A History of Public Health in New Mexico*. (University of New Mexico Press, 1962).

Gusmano, Michael K., et al. "Partisanship in Initial State Responses to the COVID-19 Pandemic." *World Medical and Health Policy* 12, no. 4 (December 2020): 380–389.

Gutterman, Lauren Jae. "'Caring for Our Own': The Founding of Senior Action in a Gay Environment, 1977–1985." *Radical History Review* 139 (January 2021): 178–199.

Hacker, Jacob S. *The Divided Welfare State: The Battle over Public and Private Social Benefits in the United States*. Cambridge University Press, 2002.

Halberstam, Jack. *In a Queer Time and Place: Transgender Bodies, Subcultural Lives*. New York University Press, 2005.

Halliwell, Martin. *American Health Crisis: One Hundred Years of Panic, Planning, and Politics*. University of California Press, 2021.

Hammack, David C. "Introduction: Growth, Transformation, and Quiet Revolution in the Nonprofit Sector over Two Centuries." *Nonprofit and Voluntary Sector Quarterly* 30, no. 2 (June 2001): 157–173.

Hanhardt, Christina B. *Safe Space: Gay Neighborhood History and the Politics of Violence*. Duke University Press, 2013.

Hartman, Andrew. *A War for the Soul of America: A History of the Culture Wars*. University of Chicago Press, 2015.

Hawley, Ellis W. *The Great War and the Search for a Modern Order: A History of the American People and Their Institutions, 1917–1933*. Waveland Press, 1979.

Henderson, D. A., et al. "Public Health and Medical Responses to the 1957–58 Influenza Pandemic." *Biosecurity and Bioterrorism: Biodefense Strategy, Practice, and Science* 7, no. 3 (September 2009): 266–267.

Hertel-Fernandez, Alexander. *State Capture: How Conservative Activists, Big Businesses, and Wealthy Donors Reshaped the American States—and the Nation*. Oxford University Press, 2019.

Himmelstein, David U., and Steffie Woolhandler. "Public Health's Falling Share of U.S. Health Spending." *American Journal of Public Health* 106, no. 1 (January 2016): 56–57.

Hinton, Elizabeth. *From the War on Poverty to the War on Crime: The Making of Mass Incarceration in America*. Harvard University Press, 2017.

Hobson, Emily. *Lavender and Red: Liberation and Solidarity in the Gay and Lesbian Left*. University of California Press, 2016.

Hoffman, Beatrix. "Emergency Rooms: The Reluctant Safety Net." In *History and Health Policy in the United States: Putting the Past Back in*, edited by Rosemary A. Stevens, Charles E. Rosenberg, and Lawton R. Burns. Rutgers University Press, 2006.

Hoffman, Beatrix. *Health Care for Some: Rights and Rationing in the United States Since 1930*. University of Chicago Press, 2012.

Hogarth, Rana A. *Medicalizing Blackness: Making Racial Differences in the Atlantic World, 1780–1840*. University of North Carolina Press, 2017.

Hoppe, Trevor. *Punishing Disease: HIV and the Criminalization of Sickness*. University of California Press, 2018.

Howard, Clayton. *The Closet and the Cul-de-Sac: The Politics of Sexual Privacy in Northern California*. University of Pennsylvania Press, 2019.

Howard, Clayton. "Gay and Conservative: An Early History of the Log Cabin Republicans." In *Beyond the Politics of the Closet*.

Howard, John. *Men Like That: A Southern Queer History*. (Chicago, 1999).

Huberfield, Nicole, et al. "Federalism Complicates the Response to the COVID-19 Health and Economic Crisis: What Can Be Done?" *Journal of Health Politics, Policy and Law* 45, no. 6 (December 2020): 951–965.

Humphreys, Margaret. *Yellow Fever and the South*. Johns Hopkins University Press, 1992.

Hunter, Devin. "Urban/Rural Frictions in the Midwest: The Chicago-Downstate Battle for Legislative Reapportionment in Illinois, 1953–1965." In *The Conservative Heartland: A Political History of the Postwar American Midwest*, edited by Jon K. Lauck and Catherine McNicol Stock. University of Kansas Press, 2020.

Hutchins, Loraine. "Bisexual History: Let's Not Bijack Another Century." In *The Routledge History of Queer America*.

"IGLTF Meets with Governor Thompson in Historic First for Illinois." *Illinois Gay and Lesbian Task Force Bulletin* 1, no. 4 (October 1987): 1.

Influenza Encyclopedia: The American Influenza Epidemic of 1918–1919: A Digital Encyclopedia. University of Michigan Center for the History of Medicine and Michigan

Publishing, University of Michigan Library. Accessed July 1, 2025. https://www.influenzaarchive.org/cities/index.html.

Inrig, Stephen J. "HIV/AIDS." In *The New Encyclopedia of Southern Culture*. Vol. 22: *Science and Medicine*, eds. James G. Thomas Jr. and Charles Reagan Wilson. University of North Carolina Press, 2006.

Inrig, Stephen J. *North Carolina and the Problem of AIDS: Advocacy, Politics, and Race in the South*. University of North Carolina Press, 2011.

Institute of Medicine. *For the Public's Health: Investing in a Healthier Future*. National Academies Press, 2012.

Irwin, Julia F. "An Epidemic Without Enmity: Explaining the Missing Ethnic Tensions in New Haven's 1918 Influenza Epidemic." *Urban History Review* 36, no. 2 (Spring 2008): 5–17.

Isbell, Michael T. "AIDS and Access to Care: Lessons for Health Care Reformers." *Cornell Journal of Law and Public Policy* 3, no. 1 (1993): 7–53.

Johnson, Colin R. *Just Queer Folks: Gender and Sexuality in Rural America*. University of Minnesota Press, 2013.

Johnson, David K. *The Lavender Scare: The Cold War Persecution of Gays and Lesbians in the Federal Government*. University of Chicago Press, 2004.

Johnson, Kimberley S. *Governing the American State: Congress and the New Federalism, 1877–1929*. Princeton University Press, 2006.

Kane, Melinda D. "Timing Matters: Shifts in the Causal Determinants of Sodomy Law Decriminalization, 1961–1998." *Social Problems* 52, no. 2 (2007): 211–239.

Katznelson, Ira. *Fear Itself: The New Deal and the Origins of Our Time*. Liveright, 2013.

Kennedy, David M. *Freedom from Fear: The American People in Depression and War, 1929–1945*. Oxford University Press, 1999.

Kettl, Donald F. "States Divided: The Implications of American Federalism for COVID-19." *Public Administration Review* 80, no. 4 (July–August 2020): 595–602.

Killip, Thomas. "Hospitals in New York City: A System under Stress." In *Public and Professional Attitudes toward AIDS Patients*, edited by David E. Rogers and Eli Ginzburg. Routledge, 1989.

Kohler-Hausmann, Julilly. *Getting Tough: Welfare and Imprisonment in 1970s America*. Princeton University Press, 2017.

Koistinen, Paul A. C. *Planning War, Pursuing Peace: The Political Economy of American Warfare, 1920–1939*. University Press of Kansas, 1998.

Koop, C. Everett. *Surgeon General's Report on Acquired Immune Deficiency Syndrome*. United States Public Health Service, 1986.

Kornhauser, Anne M. *Debating the American State: Liberal Anxieties and the New Leviathan, 1930–1970*. University of Pennsylvania Press, 2015.

Ladd-Taylor, Molly. "Federal Help for Mothers: The Rise and Fall of the Sheppard-Towner Act in the 1920s." In *Gendered Domains: Rethinking Public and Private in Women's History: Essays from the Seventh Berkshire Conference on the History of Women*, eds. Dorothy O. Helly and Susan Reverby. Cornell University Press, 1992.

Lapovsky Kennedy, Elizabeth, and Madeline D. Davis. *Boots of Leather, Slippers of Gold: The History of a Lesbian Community*. Routledge, 1993.

Lassiter, Matthew D. "Political History Beyond the Red-Blue Divide." *Journal of American History* 98, no. 3 (December 2011): 760–764.

Lefkovitz, Alison. *Strange Bedfellows: Marriage in the Age of Women's Liberation*. University of Pennsylvania Press, 2012.

Leider, Jonathon P., et al. "How Much Do We Spend? Creating Historical Estimates of Public Health Expenditures in the United States at the Federal, State, and Local Levels." *Annual Review of Public Health* 39 (April 2018): 471–487.

Leveton, Lauren B., et al. *HIV and the Blood Supply: An Analysis of Crisis Decisionmaking*. National Academies Press, 1995.

Levi, Jeffrey, et al. "Financing Public Health: Diminished Funding for Core Needs and State-by-State Variation in Support." *Journal of Public Health Management and Practice* 13, no. 2 (March-April 2007): 97–102.

Lindsey, Phoebe A., et al. "Medicaid Home and Community-Based Waiver for Acquired Immunodeficiency Syndrome Patients." Special supplement, *Health Care Finance Review* (1990): 109–118.

Maddox, H. W. Jerome. "Working outside of the State House (And Senate): Outside Careers as an Indicator of Professionalism in American State Legislatures." *State Politics and Policy Quarterly* 4, no. 2 (Summer 2004): 211–226.

Maggor, Noam. *Brahmin Capitalism: Frontiers of Wealth and Populism in America's First Gilded Age*. Harvard University Press, 2017.

Mair, Michael, et al. "Passage of S. 3678: The Pandemic and All-Hazards Preparedness Act." *Biosecurity and Bioterrorism* 5, no. 1 (2007): 72–74.

Markel, Howard, et al. "Nonpharmaceutical Interventions Implemented by US Cities During the 1918–1919 Influenza Pandemic." *Journal of the American Medical Association* 298, no. 6 (August 8, 2007): 644–654.

Masur, Kate. "State Sovereignty and Migration before Reconstruction." *Journal of the Civil War Era* 9, no. 4 (December 2019): 588–611.

May, Janice C. *The Texas Constitution*. Oxford University Press, 2011.

Mayeux, Sara, and Karen Tani. "Federalism Anew." *American Journal of Legal History* 56, no. 1 (March 2016): 128–138.

McDermott, Peter. "New Budget for AIDS Project Los Angeles." *Issues: An AIDS Forum* 1, no. 2 (Fall 1987): 8.

McGirr, Lisa. *Suburban Warriors: The Origins of the New American Right*. Princeton University Press, 2002.

McKay, Richard A. *Patient Zero and the Making of the AIDS Epidemic*. University of Chicago Press, 2017.

McKinney, Martha M. "Consortium Approaches to the Delivery of HIV Services Under the Ryan White CARE Act." *AIDS and Public Policy Journal* 8, no. 3 (Fall 1993): 115–116.

Meeker, Martin. "The Queerly Disadvantaged and the Making of San Francisco's War on Poverty, 1964–1967." *Pacific Historical Review* 81, no. 1 (February 2012): 21–59.

Mettler, Suzanne, and Mallory SoRelle. "Policy Feedback Theory." In *Theories of the Policy Process*, 3rd ed., eds. Christopher M. Weible and Paul A. Sabatier. Routledge, 2014.

Michael, Jerrold M. "The National Board of Health: 1879–1883." *Public Health Reports* 126, no. 1 (January–February 2011): 123–129.

Millar, J. Donald, and June Osborne. "Precursors of the Scientific Decision-Making Process Leading to the 1976 National Immunization Campaign." In *History, Science, and Politics: Influenza in America, 1918–1976*, edited by June Osborne. Prodist, 1977.

Milov, Sarah. *The Cigarette: A Political History*. Harvard University Press, 2019.

Mitchell, Daniel J. B. "From Jerry-Rigged to Petered Out: Lessons from the Deukmejian Era for Contemporary California State Budgeting." In *California Policy Options 2008*, edited by Daniel J. B. Mitchell. UCLA School of Public Affairs, 2008.

Mor, Vincent, et al. "Developing AIDS Community Service Consortia." *Health Affairs* 12, no. 1 (Spring 1993): 186–199.

Mor, Vincent, et al. *Networking AIDS Services*. University of Chicago Press, 1994.

Moreland, Amanda, et al. "Timing of State and Territorial COVID-19 Stay-at-Home Orders and Changes in Population Movement—United States, March 1–May 31, 2020." *Morbidity and Mortality Weekly Report* (*MMWR*) 69, no. 35 (September 4, 2020): 1198–1203.

Morris, Andrew. "The Voluntary Sector's War on Poverty." *Journal of Policy History* 16, no. 4 (October 2004): 275–305.

Nathan, Richard P., and Fred C. Doolittle. "The Budget Cuts: The Day After." *Challenge* 26, no. 6 (1984): 32.

Nathan, Richard P., and Fred C. Doolittle, eds. *Reagan and the States*. Princeton University Press, 2014.

Neumann, Tracy. "Privatization, Devolution, and Jimmy Carter's National Urban Policy." *Journal of Urban History* 40, no. 2 (March 2014): 283–300.

Nichols, Christopher McKnight, et al. "Reconsidering the 1918–19 Influenza Pandemic in the Age of COVID-19." *Journal of the Gilded Age and Progressive Era* 19, no. 4 (October 2020): 642–672.

Noebel, David A., Wayne C. Lutton, and Paul Cameron. *Acquired Immune Deficiency Syndrome: Special Report*. Summit Research Institute, 1987.

Nowlan, James D., and J. Thomas Johnson. *Fixing Illinois: Politics and Policy in the Prairie State*. University of Chicago Press, 2014.

Nowlan, James D., Samuel K. Gove, and Richard J. Winkel Jr. *Illinois Politics: A Citizen's* Guide. University of Chicago Press, 2010.

Novak, William J. "The Myth of the 'Weak' American State." *American Historical Review* 113, no. 3 (June 2018): 752–772.

Novak, William J. *New Democracy: The Creation of the Modern American State*. Harvard University Press, 2022.

Novak, William J. *The People's Welfare: Law and Regulation in Nineteenth-Century America*. University of North Carolina Press, 1996.

O'Daniel, Alyson. *Holding On: African American Women Surviving HIV/AIDS*. University of Nebraska Press, 2016.

Olivarius, Kathryn. "Immunity, Capital, and Power in Antebellum New Orleans." *American Historical Review* 124, no. 2 (April 2019): 425–455.

Orren, Karen, and Stephen Skowronek. *The Search for American Political Development*. Cambridge University Press, 2004.

Oshinsky, David M. *Polio: An American Story*. Oxford University Press, 2005.

Parmet, Wendy. "AIDS and Quarantine: The Revival of an Archaic Doctrine." *Hofstra Law Review* 14, no. 1 (1985): 53–90.

Parmet, Wendy. "The COVID Cases: A Preliminary Assessment of Judicial Review of Public Health Powers During a Partisan and Polarized Pandemic." *San Diego Law Review*, no. 57 (2020): 999–1048.

Parmet, Wendy. "Rediscovering *Jacobson* in the Era of COVID-19." *Boston University Law Review Online*, no. 100 (2020): 118–133.

Patton, Cindy. *Inventing AIDS*. Routledge, 1990.

Perrow, Charles, and Mauro F. Guillén. *The AIDS Disaster: The Failure of Organizations in New York and the Nation*. Yale University Press, 1990.

Petro, Anthony Michael. *After the Wrath of God: AIDS, Sexuality, and American Religion*. Oxford University Press, 2015.

Phelps, Wesley G. *Before* Lawrence V. Texas: *The Making of a Queer Social Movement*. University of Texas Press, 2023.

Phelps, Wesley G. "The Politics of Queer Disidentification and the Limits of Neoliberalism in the Struggle for Gay and Lesbian Equality in Houston." *Journal of Southern History* 84, no. 2 (2018): 311–348.

Pfister, Harriet S. *Kansas State Board of Health*. Governmental Research Center, University of Kansas, 1955.

Poen, Monte M. *Harry S. Truman Versus the Medical Lobby: The Genesis of Medicare*. University of Missouri, 1979.

Poterba, James M. "State Responses to Fiscal Crises: The Effects of Budgetary Institutions and Politics." *Journal of Political Economy* 102, no. 4 (August 1994): 799–821.

Potter, Claire Bond. "Paths to Political Citizenship: Gay Rights, Feminism, and the Carter Presidency." *Journal of Policy History* 24, no. 1 (2012): 95–114.

Raimondo, Meridith. "Dataline Atlanta: Place and the Social Construction of AIDS." In *Carryin' on in the Lesbian and Gay South*, edited by John Howard. New York University Press, 1997.

Ramos, Nic John. "Poor Influences and Criminal Locations: Los Angeles's Skid Row, Multicultural Identities, and Normal Homosexuality." *American Quarterly* 71, no. 2 (June 2019): 541–567.

Rao, Gautham. "The Early American State 'In Action': The Federal Marine Hospitals, 1789–1860." In *Boundaries of the State in US History*, edited by James T. Sparrow, William J. Novak, and Stephen W. Sawyer. University of Chicago Press, 2015.

Reese, Ashanté M. *Black Food Geographies: Race, Self-Reliance, and Food Access in Washington, D.C.* University of North Carolina Press, 2019.

Reichard, Ruth D. *Blood and Steel: Ryan White, the AIDS Crisis, and Deindustrialization in Kokomo, Indiana*. McFarland Press, 2021.

Renfro, Paul M. *The Life and Death of Ryan White: AIDS and Inequality in America*. University of North Carolina Press, 2024.

Renfro, Paul M. *Stranger Danger: The Politics of Child Protection from Etan Patz to AMBER Alert*. Oxford University Press, 2020.

Richert, Lucas. "Reagan, Regulation, and the FDA: The US Food and Drug Administration's Response to HIV/AIDS, 1980–90." *Canadian Journal of History* 44, no. 3 (Winter 2009): 467–488.

Riismandel, Kyle. *Neighborhood of Fear: The Suburban Crisis in American Culture, 1975–2001*. John Hopkins University Press, 2020.

Rogers, Theresa F., et al. "AIDS—An Update," *Public Opinion Quarterly* 57, no.1 (Spring 1993): 92–114.

Rom, Mark Carl. "Gay and AIDS: Democratizing Disease?" In *The Politics of Gay Rights*, edited by Craig A. Rimmerman, Kenneth D. Wald, and Clyde Wilcox. University of Chicago Press, 2000.

Rosenkrantz, Barbara Gutmann. *Public Health and the State: Changing Views in Massachusetts, 1842–1936*. Harvard University Press, 1972.

Roth, Benita. *The Life and Death of ACT UP/LA: Anti-AIDS Activism in Los Angeles from the 1980s to the 2000s*. Cambridge University Press, 2017.

Rowe, M. J., and C. C. Ryan. "Comparing State-Only Expenditures for AIDS." *American Journal of Public Health* 78, no. 4 (April 1988): 424–429.

Royles, Dan. "HIV/AIDS in the United States." In *Global Encyclopedia of Lesbian, Gay, Bisexual, Transgender, and Queer History*.

Royles, Dan. *To Make the Wounded Whole: African American Responses to HIV/AIDS*. University of North Carolina Press, 2020.

Royles, Dan. "When My Brothers Fell." *Baffler*, March 2021. https://thebaffler.com/salvos/when-my-brothers-fell-royles.

Rundall, Thomas G., et al. "Impact of the Ryan White CARE Act on the Availability of HIV/AIDS Services." *Policy Studies Journal* 27, no. 4 (July 2005): 826–839.

Salamon, Lestor M. *Partners in Public Service: Government-Nonprofit Relations in the Modern Welfare State*. Johns Hopkins University Press, 1995.

Salamon, Lestor M. "The Rise of the Nonprofit Sector," *Foreign Affairs* 73, no. 4 (July-August, 1994): 109–122.

Schlafly, Phyllis. "What's Wrong with 'Equal Rights' for Women?" *Phyllis Schlafly Report* 5, no.7 (February 1972).

Schulman, Sarah. *Let the Record Show: A Political History of ACT UP New York, 1987–1993*. Farrar, Straus & Giroux, 2021.

Scitovsky, A. A., et al. "Medical Care Costs of Patients with AIDS in San Francisco." *JAMA: Journal of the American Medical Association* 256, no. 22 (December 1986): 3103–3106.

Self, Robert. *All in the Family: The Realignment of American Democracy Since the 1960s*. Hill & Wang, 2012.

Shilts, Randy. *And the Band Played On: Politics, People, and the AIDS Epidemic*. St. Martin's Griffin, 1987.

Shonick, William. *Government and Health Services: Government's Role in the Development of U.S. Health Services, 1930–1980*. Oxford University Press, 1995.

Sides, Josh. *Erotic City: Sexual Revolutions and the Making of Modern San Francisco*. Oxford University Press, 2011.

Singer, Eleanor, et al. "The Polls—A Report: AIDS." *Public Opinion Quarterly* 51, no. 4 (Winter 1987): 580–595.

Siplon, Patricia D. *AIDS and the Policy Struggle in the United States*. Georgetown University Press, 2002.

Siplon, Patricia D. "Washington's Response to the AIDS Epidemic." *Policy Studies Journal* 27, no. 4 (November 1999): 796–808.

Skowronek, Stephen. *Building a New American State: The Expansion of National Administrative Capacities, 1877–1920*. Cambridge University Press, 1982.

Sledge, Daniel. *Health Divided: Public Health and Individual Medicine in the Making of the Modern American State*. University Press of Kansas, 2017.

Sledge, Daniel. "War, Tropical Disease, and the Emergence of National Public Health Capacity in the United States." *Studies in American Political Development* 26, no. 2 (October 2012): 125–162.

Slominski, Kristy L. *Teaching Moral Sex: A History of Religion and Sex Education in the United States*. Oxford University Press, 2021.

Smith, Jane. *Patenting the Sun: Polio and the Salk Vaccine*. William Morrow, 1991.

Smith, Russell L., and William Lyons. "Legislative Reform in the American States: Some Preliminary Observations." *State & Local Government Review* 9, no. 2 (May 1977): 35–39.

Smith-Silverman, Sara. "'Gay Teachers Fight Back!': Rank-and-File Gay and Lesbian Teachers' Activism against the Briggs Initiative, 1977–1978." *Journal of the History of Sexuality* 29, no. 1 (January 2020): 79–107.

Snyder, Lynne Page. "Passage and Significance of the 1944 Public Health Service Act." *Public Health Reports* 109, no. 6 (November–December 1994): 721–724.

Sollars, David L. "Institutional Rules and State Legislator Compensation: Success for the Reform Movement?" *Legislative Studies Quarterly* 19, no. 4 (November 1994): 507–520.

Sparrow, James T. *Warfare State: World War II Americans and the Age of Big Government*. Oxford University Press, 2011.

Sparrow, James T., William J. Novak, and Stephen W. Sawyer, eds. *Boundaries of the State in U.S. History*. University of Chicago Press, 2015.

Squire, Peverill. *The Evolution of American Legislatures: Colonies, Territories, and States, 1619–2009*. University of Michigan Press, 2012.

Squire, Peverill. "Legislative Professionalization and Membership Diversity in State Legislatures." *Legislative Studies Quarterly* 17, no. 1 (February 1992): 69–79.

Starr, Paul. "The Health Care Legacy of the Great Society." In *LBJ's Neglected Legacy: How Lyndon B. Johnson Reshaped Domestic Policy and Government*, edited by Robert H. Wilson, Norman J. Glickman, and Laurence E. Lynn. University of Texas Press, 2015.

Starr, Paul. *The Social Transformation of American Medicine*. Basic Books, 1982.

Stein, Marc. *City of Sisterly and Brotherly Loves: Lesbian and Gay Philadelphia, 1945–1972*. University of Minnesota Press, 2000.

Stein, Marc. *Sexual Injustice: Supreme Court Decisions from Griswold to Roe*. University of North Carolina Press, NC, 2010.

Stern, Alexandra Minna, et al. "'Better Off in School': School Medical Inspection as a Public Health Strategy During the 1918–1919 Influenza Pandemic in the United States." Supplement, *Public Health Reports* 125, no. 3 (April 2010): 68.

Stewart-Winter, Timothy. *Queer Clout: Chicago and the Rise of Gay Politics*. University of Pennsylvania Press, 2016.

Sugrue, Thomas J. "All Politics Is Local: The Persistence of Localism in Twentieth-Century America." In *The Democratic Experiment: New Directions in American Political History*, edited by Meg Jacobs, William J. Novak, and Julian E. Zelizer. Princeton University Press, 2003.

Tani, Karen M. *States of Dependency: Welfare, Rights, and American Governance, 1935–1972*. Cambridge University Press, 2016.

Taranto, Stacie. "Defending 'Women Who Stand by the Sink': Suburban Homemakers and Anti-ERA Activism in New York State." In *Making Suburbia: New Histories of Everyday America*, edited by John Archer, Paul J. P. Sandul, Katherine Solomonson. University of Minnesota Press, 2015.

Taubenberger, Jeffery K., and David M. Morens. "1918 Influenza: The Mother of All Pandemics." *Emerging Infectious Diseases* 12, no. 1 (January 2006): 15–22.

"T-Cell Testing Recommendation Affect Planning Activities." *Intergovernmental AIDS Reports* 2, no. 2 (July-August 1989): 1.

Teaford, Jon C. *The Rise of the States: Evolution of American State Government*. Johns Hopkins University Press, 2003.

Terl, Allan H. "An Essay on the History of Lesbian and Gay Rights in Florida." *Nova Law Review* 24, no. 3 (2000): 793–853.

Thacker, S. B., and D. J. Sencer. "Centers for Disease Control." In *International Encyclopedia of Public Health*, edited by Kristian Heggenhougen. Academic Press, 2008.

Thielemann, Gregory S., et al. "The Ryan White Act in Dallas." *Policy Studies Journal* 27, no. 4 (November 1999): 809–825.

Thielemann, Gregory S., and Joseph Stewart Jr. "A Demand-Side Perspective on the Importance of Representative Bureaucracy: AIDS, Ethnicity, Gender, and Sexual Orientation." *Public Administration Review* 56, no. 2 (March–April 1996): 168–173.

Thomas, William H., Jr. *Unsafe for Democracy: World War I and the U.S. Justice Department's Covert Campaign to Suppress Dissent*. University of Wisconsin Press, 2008.

Thorburn, Wayne. *Red State: An Insider's Story of How the GOP Came to Dominate Texas Politics*. University of Texas Press, 2014.

Tiemeyer, Phil. *Plane Queer: Labor, Sexuality, and AIDS in the History of Male Flight Attendants*. University of California Press, 2013.

Tobey, James A. *The National Government and Public Health*. Johns Hopkins University Press, 1926.

Tomes, Nancy. "'Destroyer and Teacher': Managing the Masses During the 1918–1919 Influenza Pandemic." Supplement, *Public Health Reports* 125, no. 3 (April 2010): 48–62.

Treichler, Paula A. *How to Have Theory in an Epidemic: Cultural Chronicles of AIDS*. Duke University Press, 1999.

Turk, Katherine. "'Our Militancy Is in Our Openness': Gay Employment Rights Activism in California and the Question of Sexual Orientation in Sex Equality Law." *Law and History Review* 31, no. 2 (May 2013): 423–469.

Turner, William B. "Lesbian/Gay Rights and Immigration Policy: Lobbying to End the Medical Model." *Journal of Policy History* 7, no. 2 (April 1995): 208–225.

United States AIDS Program. *United States Cases Reported to CDC*. AIDS Surveillance Report, December 29, 1986, 2.

Vaid, Urvashi. *Virtual Equality: The Mainstreaming of Gay and Lesbian Liberation.* Knopf Doubleday, 1995.

Vider, Stephen. *The Queerness of Home: Gender, Sexuality, and the Politics of Domesticity After World War II.* University of Chicago Press, 2021.

Vider, Stephen. "'The Ultimate Extension of Gay Community': Communal Living and Gay Liberation in the 1970s." *Gender & History* 27, no. 3 (November 2015): 865–881.

Waller, C. E. "Progress Under the Operation of Title VI of the Social Security Act." *American Journal of Public Health* 28, no. 11 (November 1938): 1299–1301.

Wang, Jessica. "Dogs and the Making of the American State: Voluntary Association, State Power, and the Politics of Animal Control in New York City, 1850–1920." *Journal of American History* 98, no. 4 (March 2012): 998–1024.

Wang, Jessica. *Mad Dogs and Other New Yorkers: Rabies, Medicine, and Society in an American Metropolis, 1840–1920.* Johns Hopkins University Press, 2019.

Warner, Margaret. "Local Control Versus National Interest: The Debate over Southern Public Health, 1878–1884." *Journal of Southern History* 50, no. 3 (August 1984): 407–428.

Warner, Michael. *The Trouble with Normal: Sex, Politics, and the Ethics of Queer Life.* Harvard University Press, 1999.

Waserman, Manfred. "The Quest for a National Health Department in the Progressive Era." *Bulletin of the History of Medicine* 49, no. 3 (Fall 1975): 353–380.

Waterhouse, Benjamin C. *Lobbying America: The Politics of Business from Nixon to NAFTA.* Princeton University Press, 2013.

Waters, Robert Craig. "Florida's Omnibus AIDS Act of 1988." *Florida State University Law Review* 16, no. 3 (Fall 1988): 441–529.

Watkins-Hayes, Celeste. *Remaking a Life: How Women Living with HIV/AIDS Confront Inequality.* University of California Press, 2019.

Weston, Kath. "Get Thee to a Big City: Sexual Imaginary and the Great Gay Migration." *GLQ: A Journal of Lesbian and Gay Studies* 2, no. 33 (1995): 253–277.

Whittemore, Andrew H. "The Dallas Way: Property, Politics, and Assimilation." In *Planning and LGBTQ Communities: The Need for Inclusive Queer Spaces*, edited by Petra L. Doan. Routledge, 2015.

Williams, Mason B. *City of Ambition: FDR, La Guardia, and the Making of Modern New York.* W. W. Norton, 2013.

Willrich, Michael. *Pox: An American History.* Penguin Press, 2011.

Witt, John Fabian. *American Contagions: Epidemics and the Law from Smallpox to COVID-19.* Yale University Press, 2020.

Wooten, Heather Green. *The Polio Years in Texas: Battling a Terrifying Unknown.* Texas A&M University Press, 2009.

Woubshet, Dagmawi. *The Calendar of Loss: Race Sexuality and Mourning in the Early Era of AIDS.* Johns Hopkins University Press, 2015.

Wright, Amy. *Gay Rights at the Ballot Box.* University of Minnesota Press, 2012.

Zelizer, Julian E. *Burning Down the House: Newt Gingrich and the Rise of the New Republican Party.* Penguin, 2021.

Zelizer, Julian E. *The Politics of National Security—From World War II to the War on Terrorism.* Basic Books, 2009.

Ziegler, Mary. *Beyond Abortion:* Roe v. Wade *and the Battle for Privacy.* Harvard University Press, 2018.

Theses

Brown, Nancy E. "AIDS and the Politics of Disability in the 1980s." PhD dissertation, Purdue University, 2019.

Capó, Julio, Jr. "It's Not Queer to Be Gay: Miami and the Emergence of the Gay Rights Movement, 1945–1995." PhD diss., Florida International University, 2011.

Cebul, Brent. "Developmental State: The Politics of Business, Poverty, and Economic Empowerment from the New Deal to the New Democrats." PhD dissertation, University of Virginia, 2014.

De Orio, Scott. "Punishing Queer Sexuality in the Age of LGBT Rights." PhD dissertation, University of Michigan, 2017.

Dievler, Anne. "The Politics of Public Health Policy in an Urban Bureaucracy: HIV Prevention, Tuberculosis Control, and Immunization Programs in Washington, D.C." PhD dissertation, Johns Hopkins University, 1996.

Frank, Gillian. "Save Our Children: The Sexual Politics of Child Protection in the United States, 1965–1990." PhD dissertation, Brown University, 2009.

Goins, John D. "Confronting itself: The AIDS crisis and the LGBT community in Houston." PhD dissertation, University of Houston, 2014.

Hollands, Joshua. "Work and Sexuality in the Sunbelt: Homophobic Workplace Discrimination in the US South and Southwest, 1970 to the Present." PhD dissertation, University College London, 2019.

Milne, Andrea. "'A Caring Disease': Nursing and Patient Advocacy on the United States' First AIDS Ward, 1983–1995." PhD dissertation, University of California, Irvine, 2017.

Retzloff, Tim. "Suburb, City, and the Changing Bounds of Lesbian and Gay Life in Metropolitan Detroit, 1945–1985." PhD dissertation, Yale University, 2014.

Stachecki, Cynthia L. "Why the Equal Rights Amendment Failed in Illinois: The Clash of Politics and Ideology." PhD dissertation, Saint Louis University, 2012.

Vivier, Patrick M. "National Policies for Childhood Immunization in the United States: An Historical Perspective." PhD dissertation, Johns Hopkins University, 1996.

INDEX

www.ingramcontent.com/pod-product-compliance
Lightning Source LLC
Chambersburg PA
CBHW020512270326
41926CB00008B/838